MW00514384

THE HUNT FOR HMS *DE BRAAK*

THE HUNT FOR HMS *DE BRAAK*
Legend and Legacy

Other Books by the Author

Raid on America: The Dutch Naval Campaign of 1672–1674
(Coauthor)

Pirates on the Chesapeake:
Being a True History of Pirates, Picaroons, and Raiders on Chesapeake Bay,
1610–1807

The Othello *Affair*

Shipwrecks on the Chesapeake:
Maritime Disasters on Chesapeake Bay and Its Tributaries, 1608–1978

Flotilla: Battle for the Patuxent

Londontown: A Brief History

Shipwrecks of the Civil War:
The Encyclopedia of Union and Confederate Naval Losses

THE HUNT FOR HMS *DE BRAAK*

Legend and Legacy

Donald Shomette

Carolina Academic Press
Durham, North Carolina

For my son, Kyle

Full fathom five thy father lies;
Of his bones are coral made:
Those are pearls that were his eyes:
Nothing of him that doth fade,
But doth suffer a sea-change
Into something rich and strange.

William Shakespeare, *The Tempest, I. ii.*

Library of Congress Catalog Number: 93-70709
International Standard Book Number: 0-89089-513-9
Printed and bound in the United States of America

Carolina Academic Press
700 Kent Street
Durham, NC 27701
(919) 489-7486   FAX (919) 493-5668

Contents

Foreword

The story of HMS *De Braak* reads like the tale of a person falsely accused of a crime and then made to suffer for it. *De Braak* committed no crime, but over the 188 years after her foundering in late May 1798 off Cape Henlopen, Delaware, she was hunted as a "pirate." Believed by many to have captured numerous Spanish prizes during her brief visit to American waters, *De Braak*'s remains were repeatedly sought by men who desired the "treasure" reputed by saga to have been lost with her in a heroic age, on a bold forgotten mission. In the end, much like our allegorical defendant, *De Braak* met her final demise innocent of the historical charges against her. No treasure was found, yet the ship and her rich trove of historical artifacts were salvaged in its pursuit.

The history of *De Braak*, so ably told by Donald G. Shomette, comprises two stories—first, the story of her brief and rather undistinguished military career in two navies, Dutch and English; and second, the tale of her shipwreck and subsequently alleged treasure. The author weaves the two facets of *De Braak*'s history into a readable and scholarly whole. The second part of Shomette's history—*De Braak* as a shipwreck—is a fascinating crazy quilt of legend, misinformation, outright lies, bungling, and greed. Sailors, watermen, adventurers, criminals, salvors, bureaucrats, and politicians walk in and out of *De Braak*'s story with disquieting frequency.

Few shipwrecks in American waters have generated the interest that followed in *De Braak*'s wake. "Interest" is probably the wrong term; "seduction," perhaps, better describes the effect that *De Braak*'s legend exerted on generations of individuals who continually searched Delaware Bay for her resting place. The telling of these stories allows us to share their hopes and ultimate frustrations in the quest for *De Braak*. Theirs is a familiar story, common to most men who have pursued the dream of quick and fabulous wealth, only to find it slip from their grasp.

In the end, *De Braak* was found. Her mythical treasure was not. Shomette has sought to present, for the first time, a full and detailed account of the evolution of the *De Braak* legend. He does not, however, simply retell the tale of a small man-of-war's life and death or record the mythology which effectively enshrouded her history. He goes beyond that to give us an account of her legacy. This legacy is a modern one, born out of her dramatic and ill-conceived salvage, and foreseen by few.

De Braak's legacy stems from the influence her salvage exerted on the process of law: specifically, the process of preservation law. *De Braak*'s final discovery and ultimate fate would have amounted to little more than a historical footnote fifty years from now if other events had not unfolded at the same time. For the United States of the 1980s finally came to grips with the controversial question of what to do with historic shipwrecks. At issue was the court-sanctioned short-term financial gain for the few who engaged in treasure salvage versus the loss of a nation's maritime patrimony for the many.

Shomette gives us a thorough historical grounding in the roots of the controversy, which pitted preservationists against a small but vocal treasure-salvor community. The latter were fresh from a series of well-publicized finds—*Whydah, Atocha,* and, of course, *De Braak.* In the judicial and legislative battles that ensued over the fate of historic shipwrecks in American waters, *De Braak* weighed in as the cause célèbre and the one to which Shomette attributes a key role in turning the tide in this conflict. As an example of legally sanctioned destruction of a historic ship for profit, *De Braak* was "exhibit number one" in the indictment of "business as usual." The author follows this controversy to its climax: the passage of the landmark Abandoned Shipwreck Act of 1987.

In Shomette's explanation of *De Braak*'s role in the legislative debate, we are guided through the complex maze of advocacy and compromise that constitutes lawmaking at the national level. But it is in his final chapter that Shomette treats us to a scholarly discourse on the study of *De Braak*'s physical legacy. Here we are presented with a synthesis of the real wealth of *De Braak*—the careful evaluation by numerous dedicated professionals, including the author, of the 26,000 artifacts raised from the bottom of Delaware Bay.

The "treasure" of *De Braak,* a little over 650 coins, yielded a paltry return for the millions of dollars invested in their recovery. *De Braak*'s real treasure is the historical picture gleaned from the study of the commonplace, the familiar, and the long-forgotten objects of everyday life left to us in her wreck. They comprise the ignored and incidental objects for the salvor but the very stuff of history for the rest of us.

For the student of maritime history, *The Hunt for HMS De Braak* is a thoroughly satisfying work. For those who are entranced by news reports of lost treasure ships, it will provide a sobering lesson. But as Shomette demonstrates, this lesson was lost on almost all of those who searched for *De Braak.* No matter what the reader's background may be, this book does what every good history from Herodotus to Wells has done—it gets the facts right, entertains, and instructs.

Ervan G. Garrison, Ph.D.
Chief of Marine Archaeology and History
National Oceanic and Atmospheric Administration

Preface

On a pleasant summer evening in late August 1984, I sat down in my living room to watch the NBC "Evening News." Newsman John Palmer, substituting for the program's regular anchorman, Tom Brokaw, was about to introduce a late-breaking story regarding the discovery of a sunken eighteenth-century ship off the coast of Delaware. As a maritime historian, I had long maintained a professional interest in the seafaring history of the middle Atlantic seaboard, with a special fondness for the traditions and folklore of maritime disasters, and I was more than familiar with the vessel in question. Indeed, only two days before, I had been summoned to the studio of one of the network's local affiliates, in Washington, DC, to comment on the find. I had patiently sat through several hours of interviews, answering questions about the ship that would be presented momentarily to millions of American viewers from coast to coast. I had little idea then that my interest in the vessel, its history, and the legend it had spawned would come to occupy an inordinate proportion of my waking hours for the next seven years.

"Tonight," Palmer began, "a story of sunken treasure."

Barely a mile from the public beach at Cape Henlopen, Delaware, not far from the pristine little town of Lewes, lay the bones of an ancient wooden warship. She was a diminutive vessel, built about the time of the American Revolution and lost through a quirk of weather while in the service of the British Royal Navy. She was not a powerful ship, and, like many workhorses that simply plod faithfully along in silence until they drop, she had achieved little fame or notoriety during her long life. Her commander had been a colorless, mediocre officer and a man of something less than sterling character. Only a short time before her loss, several members of her crew had participated in the greatest mutiny ever experienced by the Royal Navy. Immediately after her loss, she was little mourned and then was readily forgotten—except along the Delaware coast. There, rumors that she had taken a fortune in captured Spanish gold and silver with her to the bottom soon erupted. Fate thus decreed that this nondescript vessel, which had served under at least three flags during a generally lackluster career, was to become the focus of one of the longest and most expensive series of treasure hunts in American history and, finally, the subject of an archaeological disaster of unprecedented proportions.

Her name was *De Braak*.

The story of the hunt for HMS *De Braak* could have been taken from the pages of a Robert Louis Stevenson novel. It is a remarkable blend of myth and fact, sunken ships and treasure maps, danger and derring-do, fortune hunters and mountebanks. It is the tale of Everyman, of doctors and lawyers, mariners and mystics, con artists and their victims, all seduced by the prospect of a treasure that never was.

In 1986, after nearly a century of salvage work and an expenditure by salvors of millions of dollars, *De Braak* was at last wrested from her tomb at the bottom of Delaware Bay. It was an unceremonious—indeed, brutal—undertaking. In the all-but-bungled salvage effort she was savagely mutilated, and everything within her was thrown back onto the seabed from which she had been raised. Soon afterward her grave site itself was torn asunder by clam buckets wielded in a futile hunt for the elusive gold, silver, and jewels allegedly buried beneath the sucking Delaware mud. It was a sad and humiliating event, as untold numbers of artifacts from the great age of Nelson and Napoleon, the very substance of history itself, were mangled and broken by the frantic, fruitless search for treasure. After surviving for nearly two centuries beneath the sea, eluding discovery by innumerable fortune hunters, *De Braak* was a legend no longer. But in her destruction she had left a legacy far more significant than the vast sums of money that had been expended to find her or the value of the 26,000 artifacts that had been recovered from her ruins—a legacy of knowledge and law.

The hunt for *De Braak* is in many ways an American story, one of aggressive Yankee capitalism at its most daring, where pluck, hard work, and a large dose of high-risk capital are invested in a dream. It is also a story of chicanery, speculation, opportunism, and the media manipulations which accompany most modern treasure hunts, when truth is sacrificed for sound bites and heritage can legally be sold to the highest bidder. This is a narrative of one such event. It is an account of the evolution of the *De Braak* legend and of the curious blend of men, ships, and mania that shaped it. And finally, it is a record of the handful of dedicated archaeologists, scientists, scholars, civil servants, and politicians who strove against the currents to wrest order from chaos.

In attempting to document the history of *De Braak*, the evolution of her legend, and the legacy she was left, it has been necessary to seek the advice, criticism, support, and input of many individuals and institutions. I would like to express my deepest thanks to Charles Fithian and Claudia Melson of the Delaware State Museums, and to David V. Beard of the South Carolina Institute of Archaeology and Anthropology, for generously sharing with me the bountiful fruits of their own extensive research and labors and for providing their unstinting assistance in seeing my own project to fruition. Special thanks must also be given to my longtime colleague and friend, Dr. Fred W. Hopkins, Jr., of the University of Baltimore, with whom I have labored for uncounted months researching *De Braak*, and who has graciously shared with me the product of his own formidable labors. A note of gratitude must be extended to Anne G. Giesecke for providing me with her own remarkable collections on federal and state antiquities legislation. I am equally indebted to Dr. Paul F. Johnston, Curator of Maritime History of the National Museum of American History; Dr. Ervan G. Garrison, Chief of Marine Archaeology and History, National Oceanic and Atmospheric Administration; and Dr. Ralph E. Eshelman, for their critical and sympathetic reading of the manuscript. I would like to thank Nicholas Freda and John Brewer for their computer and photographic assistance. Emory Kristof, of *National Geographic* magazine, deserves a special note of appreciation for supporting my efforts to conduct the ultrasonic mapping of the *De Braak* hull. It is also necessary to acknowledge the staffs of the many institutions that have provided me with assistance in my research efforts on *De Braak*, including the Library of Congress, Washington, DC; the Public Record Office, Kew, London; the National Maritime Museum, Greenwich, London; the Zwaanendael Museum, Lewes, Delaware; the William L. Clements Library, University of Michigan, Ann Arbor; and the Rijksmuseum, Amsterdam. I would particularly like to express my deep sense of gratitude to the Delaware State Museums (until June 1991, the Bureau of Museums and Historic Sites) and to its director, James Stewart, for providing me every assistance, without which this work would have been impossible.

I would be remiss if I did not recognize my debt to the late Howard I. Chappelle and to M.E.S. Laws for their pioneering research on *De Braak*, and to Paul Brodeur for his comprehensive overview of her recovery.

A special word of thanks must be extended to my longtime associate and friend, Jennifer Rutland, for her critical reading, editing, and typing of much of the manuscript.

And finally, I would like to thank my wife, Carol, for her assistance in the field, analyzing the *De Braak* collections, and for putting up with the chaotic mass of books, manuscripts, papers, and prints which have effectively buried most of the flat surfaces of her normally pristine home for the three years during which this work has been in progress.

PART ONE

You look out for the bottom, and I'll look out for the spars.

Captain James Drew, May 25, 1798

ONE

A Bull with Three Sheaves

When the bloated body of Captain James Drew, R.N., washed ashore at Cape
Henlopen, Delaware, on May 28, 1798, it was no surprise to the citizens of the
nearby coastal village of Lewes Town, where the corpse was taken. Like the
inhabitants of waterfront communities along the Delaware River as far north
as Philadelphia, they were well aware of the accident which had claimed the
unfortunate officer's life. Of greater concern, however, had been the disastrous
loss off Cape Henlopen Light of Drew's ship, His Britannic Majesty's sixteen-
gun brig *De Braak*, along with thirty-five of her officers, crew, and marines,
and a dozen Spanish prisoners of war. But the stoic villagers of Lewes were
inured to such catastrophes. Some undoubtedly shook their heads and reflected knowingly. After all, the Delaware was noted for its dangerous currents
and shoals, and for the erratic weather conditions which had brought about
the demise of many proud vessels. Indeed, the waters of the Delaware Capes
were already well on their way to earning a reputation as a veritable boneyard
of sunken ships.[1] Over the years, the citizens of Lewes had witnessed many
such tragedies. Their community, ensconced on the southern lip of Delaware
Bay, was a venerable one, well over one and a half centuries old and owing its
survival to the commerce of the sea.[2] On occasions too numerous to recount,
they had rendered succor in their modest homes to shipwreck victims. Many
inhabitants worked as watermen or pilots and were themselves frequently confronted with the hazards of the Capes and the tributes they demanded. Maritime tragedies were simply an inevitable part of life. The *De Braak* disaster,
however, would prove to be a unique and historic exception.

As after previous shipwrecks, the villagers of Lewes had quickly come to the
aid of the few *De Braak* victims who had drifted ashore, some still alive and
some dead. Among the former, tradition said, had been three Spaniards, prisoners of war who had miraculously saved themselves by clinging to Captain
Drew's leather-covered, mahogany-and-oak sea chest, which had somehow
floated free of the wreck. They had been afforded assistance and shelter by a
local Delaware River pilot named Gilbert McCracken, who, it was rumored
about town, had been rewarded for his troubles in gold and silver. Some

claimed that the coins had come from a vast treasure trove which had gone down with the ship. Whether the reward was real or not, however, the Mc-Cracken family had also acquired the battered sea chest and, for more than 150 years afterward, would proudly point to it as their most precious family heirloom, a memento of that tragic day in 1798.[3]

Gilbert McCracken wasn't the only villager either to succor the fortunate survivors or to be repaid for his kindness in gold and silver—or so later generations would claim. A number of English seamen had been given food and lodging by another Lewes resident named Katherine Marshall. To their hostess, it was said, the survivors had loudly recounted their misfortunes, but more interestingly, had also spoken of the loss of "countless [quantities of] treasure in gold and silver and diamonds" which had disappeared with the ship.[4]

Although the story of Marshall's purported encounter was not published until 1887, nearly ninety years after the fact, the rumor concerning the alleged treasure said to have been aboard *De Braak* apparently took hold immediately. Within a decade it had become a theme of local folklore. Indeed, for many years a story was recounted by Marshall's son Jacob, who had been a mere lad at the time of the tragedy, to the effect that the Englishmen who had visited his mother's house swore that the brig had captured two Spanish galleons, laden "with millions of dollars worth of precious metal," bound from Peru and Mexico to Spain. These same seamen, he claimed, had paid their bill in half-doubloons which they said had come from money casks lying in the hold of the ship.[5]

The generosity of the residents of Lewes, however, was not limited only to the living. Those less fortunate than McCracken's and Marshall's guests were afforded all of the proper Christian rites. Captain Drew's corpse, which had been discovered awash on the beach by a black employee of the Cape Henlopen Lighthouse, was carried to the home of the town's most distinguished citizen and later governor of Delaware, Daniel Rodney, where it lay in state for two days. Then, with all due solemnity, it was interred in a vault beneath the chancel of tiny St. Peter's Episcopal Church in the heart of the village. Other corpses, it was said, were buried in a sailors' cemetery nearby.[6] And, with the burials, the awful tragedy was put to rest, that is, until rumors of the supposed treasure, said to be the greatest in American history, began to spread like weeds in fertile soil. The seeds of legend had been planted.

On April 19, 1751, James Drew was born in the parish of St. Stephens, hard by the little village of Saltash, on the steep banks of the Tamar River border of Cornwall, England. He had the misfortune to be the youngest of seven children brought into the world over an eleven-year period by James and Rebecca Edwards Drew. His family, with roots once planted in the fields of Devonshire and Hertfordshire, was apparently of moderate means and few connections.

The family crest, a bull with three sheaves of wheat in its mouth, reflected their modest agrarian heritage and their Irish lineage.[7]

Although little has been discovered concerning James Drew's youth, it was probable that both he and his closest brother, John, born less than a year before his own birth, had enjoyed minimal latitude in directing their futures generally or in choosing their specific careers. Although they were of a genteel family, with two older brothers, Stephen and William, and three older sisters, they were last in the line of family succession and inheritance. In eighteenth-century English society, theirs was an unenviable position, for, as the historian N. A. M. Rodger observes, "The eldest sons of any families of property had a career automatically, managing the family estates and interests."[8] But the younger sons had to earn a living, since it was quite unheard of for an estate to be divided.

A young man in such circumstances had few choices. There were always careers in the church, the law, or the military that a gentleman might pursue, but these professions were entered with some difficulty and required either money or influence, or both, to gain admission. For a lad of middling means and no inheritance, however, the brightest prospects for a respectable career which offered advancement were to be found in the Royal Navy. Unlike the army, the church, or the legal profession, the navy required neither a bankroll nor family connections and influence. It recruited its future officers early in youth and provided at no cost disciplined, rigorous career training during which a candidate could acquire "education and business together and without expense."[9] For parents eager to provide their youngest sons with opportunities for advancement and a future as cheaply and as early in life as possible, the navy seemed the perfect answer. The service was equally attractive to many young aspirants, most of whom were enrolled between the ages of eleven and fourteen. Many lads, in fact, who possessed "a strong passion for the sea" were frequently inspired to enlist by the promise of adventure, which eased their parents' task considerably. The navy provided not only opportunities for excitement, but also for wealth through the capture of prizes, as well as the possibilities arising from "the grand tour" of remote, exotic places of the world and its peoples that might never otherwise occur. Indeed, the navy, for all of its risks, was rarely short of younger sons of large families ready to join— sons such as James and John Drew.[10]

The environment in which the Drews had been reared may also have provided a strong incentive for the two boys to join the navy, for Saltash lay on the nearly vertical west bank of the Tamar River, opposite the outskirts of one of England's most formidable maritime centers, the Port of Plymouth. First fortified in the fourteenth century and officially chartered in 1439, Plymouth was a naval and maritime hub of the first order. Ensconced in Plymouth Sound, an arm of the English Channel at the confluence of the Plym and Tamar rivers, it was one of the three most strategically situated of England's Channel ports. For the Georgian navy of the mid-eighteenth century, Plymouth served as the home base of the Western Squadron, and by the end of the century it had become a key Royal Navy victualing and outfitting center. The city itself was well fortified with a great citadel dominating both town and harbor, which had been erected by Charles II as a precaution against possible Roundhead insurrection in the seventeenth century.

Plymouth owed much of its ascendancy in earlier days to such powerful patrons as the Hawkins family and Sir Francis Drake, who had helped make it a great center for privateering, mercantile trade, and oceanic enterprise. As one historian described it, Plymouth was "the great arsenal of the west . . . the rendezvous of some of the boldest spirits of the age, the base from which voyage after voyage was made to trade, explore, to colonize, and to wage war."[11] Indeed, it was from Plymouth that Drake had departed in 1577 and to which he had returned, in September 1580, after his historic circumnavigation of the globe. It was also from there that Sir Humphrey Gilbert had sailed forth to found St. John's, Newfoundland, three years later. And it was from there that Drake, after playing at a game of bowls while patiently awaiting word of the approach of the dreaded Spanish Armada, then embarked to help defeat it. From Plymouth the Pilgrims had sailed to found the Plymouth Colony in Massachusetts in 1620, and from Plymouth Captain Cook would venture forth on his remarkable odysseys to the Pacific and the Antarctic that were to change man's view of the world thereafter. And, not surprisingly, it was to Plymouth, with its lusty seafaring hurly-burly, that the strings of James Drew's life and career had been bound.

But it was on the Delaware that they were destined to dramatically unravel. At the age of thirteen, in 1764, soon after the conclusion of England's epic Seven Years' War with France, Austria, and Russia, James Drew saw sea duty for the first time, enrolled as a captain's servant aboard the third-rate, seventy-gun man-of-war *Burford*.[12] The course on which he had set out (or on which his family had thrust him) was, in fact, the surest route in the eighteenth century to a substantial career as a Royal Navy officer. The mode by which he would climb the ladder of command was already well-defined and dictated every step of the way by decades of traditions, rules, and regulations. It was also one which would provide the novitiate with the maximum degree of field experience—and the navy with the best possible officers.

Drew, like most young gentlemen who entered the navy, would begin his career in the ratings. Yet in the eighteenth century it was also common for officers to be promoted from social classes lower than the gentry. To become an officer, one was required to have served at least six years at sea, two of them in the Royal Navy, to have reached the rating of midshipman or master's mate, and then to have passed an oral examination in seamanship. A candidate had to be at least twenty-two years of age. Qualification for warrant rank, although less specific, was equally rigorous and also required extensive sea duty. Yet every prospective officer was required to begin his career on the lower deck, proceeding along one of several well-defined avenues of advancement thereafter. The one taken by James Drew was perhaps the path most commonly open to young gentlemen of his status.

When Drew enrolled as a captain's servant, he may have done so with the classic objective of securing the officer's patronage, or that of other friends or connections, to secure sea experience and to build up qualifying time. Over the next six years, he would occupy a variety of ratings on many different ships. It was a demanding term of apprenticeship, but one which the navy had found more than adequate to mold its young officer candidates into men fully capable of command.[13]

From *Burford* Drew was transferred to HMS *Edgar*, of sixty guns, again as a captain's servant, and then to HM Sloop-of-War *Hound*, of fourteen guns, as a clerk and later as able seaman. He eventually returned to *Edgar* as an able seaman and from there was transferred to another sloop-of-war, *Tamar*, of sixteen guns, as a midshipman. The last of his required years as a midshipman and able seaman were served once again aboard *Edgar*.[14]

Although it might seem to the modern observer that these variations in ratings were erratic at best, such movements were in fact quite normal. Most young candidates began their careers as lowly servants and eventually served as mates or midshipmen for at least two years. The remainder of their time was spent in any ratings available in a ship's complement, sometimes as an ordinary seaman or able seaman, and occasionally as a landsman. Such positions were determined by chance rather than choice. It mattered little if a young gentleman moved from servant to able seaman, then to midshipman and back to servant. In practice, none of these titles had much to do with the actual duties performed. They were, however, fertile grounds for acquiring the widest possible experience and knowledge, with progressively greater responsibilities designated as the candidate advanced. The young officer-to-be would go aloft with grizzled topmen and learn from hands-on experience the mechanics and technology of sailing. He would be taught to hand, reef, steer, splice, knot, sail, fight, and, finally, to command.[15]

Drew had been doubly fortunate in having served aboard a variety of vessels, from the great ships-of-the-line to the speedy little sloops-of-war. Indeed, many career professionals were of the opinion that a great flagship was a less than adequate place for young gentlemen such as Drew to begin their training, for there they were but minnows in a large school of fish, often overlooked and undertrained because of the sheer size of the crew. It was in the smaller vessels—the cutters, sloops, and frigates—that one could gain the most experience in all aspects of seamanship. Being hardened early on by the rough-and-tumble environment of life at sea, however, allowed young candidates such as Drew an opportunity to develop a high level of professional skill and capability, whether gained on great ships or small ones. After profiting more from practical exposure and circumstance than from study, they acquired a comprehensive knowledge of the seamanship needed in every emergency and situation imaginable. For most candidates, the lessons would leave a lifelong imprint.[16]

On June 18, 1771, at the age of 20, James Drew applied for and received his lieutenant's certificate, although he still had several years to go before he would legally be able to accept a commission.[17] Worse, England was not at war, nor were there any prospects for one, and the number of vacancies to be filled was small. Not until 1775, while attached to the flagship of Vice Admiral Samuel Graves, aboard HMS *Preston*, of seventy-four guns, would Drew finally be granted the opening he had long trained for—even as smoldering events in the American colonies threatened to flare into open insurrection against the king and Parliament.

Drew's assignment to *Preston* was perhaps one of the more fortuitous events in his career (despite the less than likely chance for advancement under such circumstances). Admiral Graves was Commander-in-Chief of the North American Station, and serving under an officer of such stature—assuming one could catch his eye—proved to be one of the most direct routes to promotion a young officer could have taken. Although the record is silent about the justification for such promotion, it seems likely that Drew was able to garner enough patronage in the tumultuous days immediately preceding the outbreak of the American Revolution to recommend him. For with war afoot and Boston under American siege, he was undoubtedly provided with frequent opportunities to give a good account of himself.

Whatever his superiors might have thought of him, it would seem that James Drew was among a cadre of young officers roundly despised by the American rebels, to whom he was destined to reveal his darker side. Indeed, his earliest fame would come not from having performed some act of selfless gallantry or heroism but, rather, from having charges of committing military atrocities leveled against him.

American accounts of Drew's war crimes, allegedly committed on the battlefield of Bunker Hill immediately after that most epic of battles, on June 17, 1775, certainly suggest a less than admirable side to the future commander of HM Sloop-of-War Brig *De Braak*. The principal record of his purported actions resulted from American investigations of British brutalities committed at Boston battle sites during the spring and summer of 1775. On December 10 of that year, an American committee led by John Adams was informed in vivid detail of an instance of remarkable savagery supposedly carried out by Drew and a soldier named Bruce shortly after the battle. "Drew," it was reported,

> after walking for some time over the bodies of the dead, with great fortitude, went up to one of our wounded Men, and very Deliberately Shot him through the Head. Bruce advanced further over the Hill, & meeting with a forlorn wretch, begging *Mercy for Gods Sake*! he advanced & with a "damn you, you Bugger you! are you not dead yet?" instantly demolished him—in a day or two after, Drew went upon the Hill again opened the dirt that was thrown over Doctr [Joseph] Warren, spit in his face, jumped on his Stomach & cut off his Head & committed every act of violence upon his Body.[18]

Considering that Warren, a guiding light of the Revolution in Massachusetts and one of America's first patriot-martyrs, was as highly esteemed to some as the illustrious revolutionaries Samuel Adams and John Hancock, the deed was doubly disquieting. Yet the account must be viewed through the lens of history—and with a jaundiced eye—for it had been told to an American, one Benjamin Highborn, by "two Gentlemen belonging to the *Preston*," who had allegedly witnessed the acts. Both of the witnesses reportedly despised Drew for his conduct, although neither lifted a finger to protest his actions.[19] Given that the charges were leveled in a climate rife with rumors, innuendos, and lies that were readily accepted as fact, Drew's purported atrocities could well have been little more than propaganda generated for the masses.

Whether the charges were spurious or not, James Drew's probable patronage and his activities on behalf of the Crown had finally produced results. That he was at last deemed suitable for rank was soon evinced by his formal commission as Second Lieutenant on July 29, 1775. On August 14 he was assigned to the little eight-gun sloop-of-war *Scorpion*, commanded by Captain John Tollemache.[20] For the next five years, *Scorpion* would serve as Drew's home. From the confines of her tiny deck, he would see service in the American theater of war, from New England to the southern colonies, in a revolution destined to change the course of history. Yet, unlike many of his comrades in the Royal Navy, he would serve without notice, much less distinction.

In 1780 Drew was again transferred, this time to the galley *Philadelphia*, on which he would serve for the next two years, and then to the new fourteen-gun brig-sloop *Otter*, always as Second Lieutenant. Service aboard *Otter*, a new class of gunship with which the navy was experimenting, varied slightly from Drew's previous assignments, not only because the vessel was rigged and sailed somewhat differently from the standard sloop-of-war, but also because of the dramatic innovation in naval ordnance with which she was partially armed, the carronade.[21]

For the next decade Drew's career advanced fitfully and then, dramatically, suffered a setback, with little note or comment. From 1782 until 1786 he served with minimal distinction aboard *Otter*. "Don't break the rules or make waves" might well have been his motto, for he knew that tenure, if not ability, was working in his favor. He was, like most of his colleagues, only an average officer in a very great navy. In 1786 he was transferred again, this time to HMS *Powerful*, a new third-rate, seventy-four-gun ship-of-the-line.[22] It was to be the largest warship upon which James Drew would ever serve as a general officer. It would also be the greatest vessel he would ever have the privilege to command, for on December 1, 1787, he was promoted to the post of ship's commander, a position he would retain for two years. Then, suddenly, without apparent cause, he was transferred to an inferior vessel, the little sixteen-gun sloop *Echo*.[23] The effect was much like the captain of a modern nuclear-powered aircraft carrier's being transferred at the apex of his career to a diesel-powered patrol boat.

Drew's reaction to the demotion went unrecorded, but he persevered, apparently with little public rancor. Between February 1789 and May 1790, he made several successful cruises in *Echo* to the coast of Newfoundland and Labrador, and then to Portugal.[24] On May 29, 1790, eight days after *Echo* was finally paid off, he was given command of another small vessel, a weather-worn, fifteen-year-old, fourteen-gun sloop-of-war named *Fly*.[25] Nearly a month after assuming command of *Fly*, Drew took her out on a preliminary cruise to the Isle of Guernsey and back. Then, on July 27, he set sail for Canadian waters and, on October 14, took up patrol near St. Johns, Newfoundland, in company with HMS *Salisbury* and *Pegasus*. Two weeks later, he was en route to Lisbon, Portugal, escorting the valuable Newfoundland fishing fleet to markets there. Throughout his tenure as commander of the old sloop, Drew found her to be in constant need of attention, for she was worn out and cranky. By November 23, he had brought her back to England for much-needed repairs, dropping anchor in Plymouth Harbor where she would be taken into drydock.[26]

For the next three months, as *Fly* was being repaired, James Drew attended to matters of a more personal nature. Like many officers, he was a bachelor who might well have sought female companionship, temporarily, whenever and wherever opportunity permitted. Apparently, while on shore leave, probably in January 1791, he entered into a brief amorous relationship with a woman named Sarah. Some Drew genealogists and descendants believe that, when she first began her liaison with the captain, Sarah was possibly a servant in the household of his older brother William and his wife, Betty. The problem, however, was not the domestic situation as such, but that Sarah either already was or soon would be the wife of one John Paine.[27]

Drew, like many mariners whose days ashore were usually few and merry, apparently viewed the liaison as nothing more than a casual fling. Indeed, open relationships between officers and other men's wives were not uncommon, even among members of the high command. Vice Admiral Thomas Pye, in one such well-publicized incident, had openly taken up with the wife of a customs officer, a woman who was bonded to him by the debts of both her father and her husband.[28] And, as one observer of the times so aptly commented, "There is nothing permanent in these attachments; the exigencies of the Service comes to his rescue and he is free to hunt in new pastures."[29] And so it was with James Drew and Sarah Paine, for soon afterward, duty issued its clarion call. *Fly*, having been repaired and refitted, was ready to put to sea again. On March 11, the captain set sail from Plymouth for Portsmouth, then for Labrador and Newfoundland, leaving his erstwhile love and any possible complications resulting from their liaison behind. Drew would remain on the American Station until November 1, 1791. Two weeks later he returned to Plymouth, and, on December 3, *Fly* was paid off.[30]

When the little sloop was decommissioned, it probably aroused mixed emotions in the captain and his crew. The system of "paying off" was an ancient one which had remained largely unaltered for centuries. Indeed, the procedure was the same one followed since the times when ships had put to sea only in the summer and their crews were paid upon their return in the fall. Such a ceremony officially ended a vessel's commission, as well as those of her officers, when the commissioner of the yard and his coterie of clerks came aboard with cash to pay the vessel's company.[31] For Drew, this meant that his commission would be at an end until another assignment was authorized by the Navy Board. For most of his men, however, there would be a few days of well-earned frolic ashore and then a return to service aboard the same or another ship—willingly or by the rough conscription of the press gangs.

Drew's return to Plymouth, however, was confounded by what must certainly have been an upsetting discovery. Sarah Paine, the wife of another man, had borne him a daughter, baptized on October 16, 1791, at St. Mary's Church, Portsea, as Maria Paine. Fortunately for Drew, as genealogist Frank Cresswell has suggested, Maria, although the product of an illicit union, had been lawfully acknowledged by Sarah and her husband as their own, in accordance with the custom of the era. Indeed, the couple might even have received a cash settlement for doing so, in order to avoid besmirching the Drew family name and embarrassing the child's natural father.[32]

The birth of an illegitimate daughter was apparently viewed by James Drew as little more than the unfortunate, if slightly troublesome, product of a merry shore leave, for he never acknowledged paternity. Indeed, the only evidence that Maria Paine was his daughter appeared many years later, in 1812, when Drew's sister-in-law Betty left a gold watch to the child in her will, wherein Maria was described as the "daughter of the late Captn. James Drew."[33] Yet, by merely ignoring the existence of his offspring, Drew was also violating an unwritten but strict code among naval officers, most aptly described by one

Captain Edward Wheeler, an officer of similar ilk, who declared that "the *children of love* are more naturally and properly the heirs of your inheritance than those of the modern Southfield or New Market matches, or the unwished for consequences of dull conjugal duty."[34]

Whether the birth of an illegitimate child had any influence upon Drew's subsequent actions or naval career is uncertain. That he chose this particular time, however, to abandon naval service temporarily and to emigrate to the United States would suggest some link. But there were other possible contributing factors as well, such as the Royal Navy's stand down from the continued wartime footing of the past several decades and the related economic necessity of reducing the general officer corps. Beginning in 1789, the French Revolution had brought new masters to England's archrival, who, in their zeal to destroy anything smacking of the aristocracy, had demolished the French Navy, including its officer corps of noble aristocrats.[35] There was simply no immediate threat or major enemy on the seas with which to contend. It is also possible that other romantic interests influenced Drew's decision. Whatever his reasons might have been, one thing is certain: James Drew left the navy and sailed for America very soon after *Fly* had been paid off. Within four months of his arrival in New York City, he had married the daughter of a prominent New York businessman.

Lydia Watkins was born about 1760 on the British West Indian island of St. Christopher (St. Kitts) to a successful Welsh trader named John Watkins and his wife, Lydia Stillwell Watkins. Baby Lydia's mother had been the youngest of "the six beautiful sisters," daughters of one Richard Stillwell, a successful trader, a leader in the Presbyterian church of New York, and a landowner in Shrewsbury, New Jersey, who made his residence near Dock Street in lower Manhattan. The résumé of Lydia's father, John Watkins, would undoubtedly have included trading in tobacco, rum, sugar, and perhaps even slaves, at least before he settled his family in New York. Upon his arrival he had purchased a farm from one Jan Dykman in Harlem Heights (near the modern 152d Street and St. Nicholas Avenue) and had reestablished himself as a merchant trader.[36]

Exactly when and how James Drew first met Lydia Watkins is unknown. One of Lydia's descendents, Elizabeth Maunsell Bates Carrick, has speculated that they might have been introduced in 1791, while James was serving in American waters, by Lydia's uncle, Lieutenant General John Maunsell. The general had once held an active commission in the British army, but had withdrawn from service during the American Revolution to live in Ireland. In 1782 he had returned to America to make his home in New York. Others have speculated that it was an ancestral relationship between the Drews and Maunsells in old England which had prompted the couple's meeting.[37]

The match between Drew and Watkins apparently developed rapidly. As they were on a relatively equal social footing—he being a naval officer of forty and she a moderately well-to-do lady of thirty-two—the association would probably not have been unacceptable to either family. Whatever his motives might have been, within a few months of his arrival in America, James Drew had married Lydia Watkins. The ceremony was held in New York's Trinity Church on April 10, 1792, nine days before James' 41st birthday, and was performed by the Reverend Benjamin Moore, assistant minister of the church, who was the husband of Lydia's cousin, Charity Moore, and a future bishop of New York.[38]

The newlyweds soon took up residence in Harlem Heights, then referred to as the "out ward" of New York City. Domestic life, however, rapidly lost its appeal for the veteran officer, who kept a watchful eye (as did the entire Western world) on the deteriorating situation in Europe. By the spring of 1792 England's archrival, France, had again embarked upon a war of conquest. Her foes on the continent, Austria, Prussia, and Holland, suffered the onslaught of the French army, even as England desperately sought to revitalize her stoutest line of defense, the Royal Navy. Whether motivated by patriotism, the opportunity to resume his naval career, or sheer boredom with married life (or a combination of all three), by mid-April 1793 James Drew had resolved to return to England and seek a new commission in the navy. Perhaps at Lydia's request, he drew up his last will and testament.

> I Captain James Drew of the British Navy and at present a resident of the (out)ward of the City of New York do make this my last Will and Testament as follows to wit I so give and regulate and devise unto my true and lawful wife Lydia give all and every part of my Estate Real and Personal and I do appoint my wife Lydia Drew with her Brothers Charles Watkins and Samuel Watkins Executors of this my last Will and Testament sealed and dated this eighteenth day of April 1793 James Drew. Signed and delivered in the presence of Mr. John Maunsell Major General His Britannic Majestys Service, Elizabeth Maunsell.[39]

Drew wasted little time. By June he had returned to Saltash and immediately begun a letter-writing campaign to the Navy Board in hopes of securing a commission. On one occasion he wrote "to Inform their Lordships that I shall feel myself extremely happy in any appointment they may be pleased to give me." On another, in October 1793, he unsuccessfully sought a reappointment to his old command aboard the *Fly*. Yet every effort met with failure. More than a year later, he was still at it, writing to "inform their Lordships and I am ready to serve wherever they may think proper."[40] The Navy Board, however, remained unmoved, although affairs on the continent continued to deteriorate.

In France the situation was chaotic. The Reign of Terror, beginning in 1793, had resulted in the execution or exile of three-quarters of the French navy's officer corps by 1794, even as a twenty-eight-year-old army officer of Corsican birth named Napoleon Bonaparte was emerging as a commander marked by destiny. Word of Bonaparte's remarkable victories over the Austrians in north-ern Italy spread rapidly across Europe, arousing the Western world as few events in the recent past had done. But for James Drew, the prospects for a commission and action in the great war seemed increasingly remote. By March 1795, after nearly three years of inaction on half-pay, Drew was undoubtedly despondent over the Navy Board's apparent lack of interest in his offers to serve, "not having been employ'd since the 2nd of Dec. 1791 when I was paid off in the command of the Fly Sloop of War."[41]

For Europe the war against France continued to go from bad to worse. By the spring of 1797, England hovered on the brink of disaster. The apparently invincible armies of the French Revolution, led by young Bonaparte, had swept victoriously across vast portions of the continent. Great Britain, with a pop-ulation of barely eight million people and riddled with political and social dis-content, was now standing almost alone against a foe fifty-million strong. On the European mainland a tremendous invasion force massed along the Chan-nel coast, preparing for a decisive thrust against the almost bankrupt island nation. Then, at the very height of the worst crisis in English history since the threat of the Spanish Armada, 50,000 Englishmen in 113 ships of the British fleet mutinied.

The insurrection began on Easter morning, when the crews of sixteen great ships-of-the-line anchored at Spithead, outside of Portsmouth, deposed sixty-five of their most hated officers. The mutiny quickly spread to the Nore, at the mouth of the River Thames, to another dozen ships-of-the-line and then to England's other outports and vessels of every rate. The mutineers rose almost as one to protest impossible living conditions, short pay, inedible rations, poor care for the sick, impressment, and brutalities of every kind condoned and committed by the officer corps. They sought the right to occasional leave to see their families and, as the mutiny progressed, a royal pardon for their ac-tions. But the foremost of their demands was a promise from the Admiralty that the worst officers under whom they had served would not be returned to command. The navy agreed and negotiated an end to the insurrection, then hung its leaders. But the message had been received.[42] It was then, during the waning days of the greatest naval insurrection in British history, that James Drew, at forty-six years of age a career "plodder" with an undistinguished re-cord and perhaps less than a sterling moral character, was summoned to his last command.

T W O

The Dutch Flag Down

By late spring the Great Mutiny had been largely suppressed, but Plymouth, England remained a powderkeg. The average navy tar, after years of suffering brutalities and ill-treatment, was still disaffected with the officer corps, a factor which had undoubtedly been instrumental in Drew's call-up at this particular time. After many years out of service, he had finally been assigned to take command of a ship at Plymouth, where distrust of the officers currently in place was particularly strong. The situation in the port was explosive, even anarchistic. As recently as June 10, a plan for blowing up the naval powder magazine at Keyham Point, near the victualing yard, another plan to set French prisoners of war free, and a third to "overthrow government" had only been narrowly averted by naval authorities. When Drew began to draw wages as commander of a Royal Navy warship on June 13, and then arrived to take command of her three days later, Plymouth was still in a state of upheaval.[1] It was imperative that as many ships of the fleet still in port be put to sea as soon as possible to prevent a resurgence of the mutiny as much as to stem an impending French amphibious invasion of the nation.

It is uncertain if Drew, as he surveyed his new charge, a weathered-looking craft called *De Braak*, was aware of her history. She was a brig-rigged vessel, officially classed as a sloop-of-war for commission and payroll purposes, new to the Royal Navy.[2] She was, however, anything but a novice to sea duty. *De Braak* had, in fact, served under two and possibly three national flags during her long career, yet her documentary origins are still clouded in mystery. That she was built prior to 1781 and the onset of the Fourth Anglo-Dutch War, when she first appears on Dutch navy lists as having been purchased by the Admiralty of the Maas, is certain. Some authorities have suggested that she was specifically built for the Dutch naval service. The noted naval historian Howard I. Chapelle, of the Smithsonian Institution, accepted her origins as Dutch, basing his conclusion entirely upon later Royal Navy drafts of her hull configuration and rig.[3] A few have posed the theory that she was even American built, constructed well before her service in the Netherlands navy, perhaps during the closing days of the American Revolution, or that she had seen

French service before being sold to the Dutch. Still others believed her to have been an English-built vessel, originally intended as a privateer, then captured by the French and later sold to the Dutch in 1781, when the Anglo-French conflict occurred during the American Revolution.[4]

While in Dutch naval service, *De Braak* was documented as a vessel of 255 tons, mounting a single mast, and fore-and-aft rigged. With a deck of eighty-four feet, a keel length for tonnage of fifty-seven feet, four-and-three-fourths inches, an extreme beam of twenty-eight feet, eleven inches, and a depth of hold of eleven feet, two inches, she was typical of a class of very large, fast cutters constructed during the late eighteenth century and employed by the Dutch as revenue cutters, privateers, or naval dispatch boats. Most Dutch vessels in her class were planked with oak and pine from the Baltic. However, *De Braak*'s keel was constructed of elm, suggesting possible British or American origins. Her frames, stem, and stern posts were of white oak, possibly of British origin, or procured from such Baltic timber outlets as Memel, Danzig, or Stettin. Her interior component, such as partitions, bulkheads, and shot lockers were of red pine, possibly from the Baltic port of Riga.[5] Ships of her specific class employed in regular Dutch naval service, observing a tradition established in the seventeenth century, were usually given canine names. Her own name meant "beagle," a fast dog highly prized as a hunting animal and often depicted in paintings by the Dutch masters.[6]

At the onset of the Fourth Anglo-Dutch War, *De Braak* was rated to carry twenty guns but perhaps mounted somewhat fewer, owing to her diminutive size. Her initial service was under the command of a certain Lieutenant Bach, who presided (on paper, at least) over a crew of 100 men. Her record while in the service of The Netherlands, however, is still a gray area, owing to the destruction of a substantial portion of the Dutch archives in a fire in the nineteenth century and during the two World Wars of the twentieth. The remaining archives provide only the sketchiest of backgrounds.

Between August 2 and 10, 1784, while under the command of Captain Alexander Gijsbert de Virieux, *De Braak* is known to have sailed out of Texel Roads for Malaga, Spain, to rendezvous with the fleet of Rear Admiral Jan van Kinsbergen. Soon afterward, Gijsbert de Virieux was ordered to assume command of the thirty-six-gun frigate *Jason*, and *De Braak* was placed under Captain Cornelis de Jong. On December 6, 1784, she joined the squadron commanded by Captain Pieter Melvill at Toulon, France. Melvill's squadron, presumably including De Jong and his cutter, would not return to The Netherlands until 1787. The career of *De Braak* over the next six years is virtually unknown.[7] Indeed, not until February 25, 1793, when she was placed under the command of one Lieutenant Johann Von Grootinwray, are the threads of her career again woven into the fabric of history.[8]

Lieutenant Grootinwray's first assignment aboard *De Braak* was to be anything but uneventful. On February 1, slightly over three weeks before the lieutenant took command, France declared war on England and Holland. Fifteen days later, a French army division under the command of General Charles-François du Périer Dumouriez invaded The Netherlands. *De Braak* was immediately ordered to assist two other warships in defending the fortress city of Willemstad against invading forces. Then, on March 1, Dumouriez was routed by an allied force of Dutch and Englishmen at the Roer River and withdrew from the Low Countries.[9]

Later, on December 19, 1794, having been promoted to the rank of captain, Grootinwray was directed to escort a convoy bound for the Dutch South American colony of Surinam. The infectious bacterium of revolution, however, had succeeded in spreading from France to The Netherlands, and in January Willem V, Prince of Orange, was forced to flee and establish a government in exile. Not surprisingly, *De Braak*'s orders were changed. She was now instructed to sail from the Texel and join a small Dutch squadron in the North Sea led by Captain Gerard Corthuys, commander of the frigate *Medemblik*, to escort a convoy of merchantmen to the East Indies. Obliged to traverse the English Channel on the initial leg of the voyage, Grootinwray first visited the port of Plymouth, arriving there on January 10, 1795, and then proceeded on to Falmouth, on the coast of Cornwall. Here, he again stopped, undoubtedly for the purpose of topping off his provisions of wood and water before attempting the long voyage ahead.[10]

The decision to put into Falmouth was, unhappily for Grootinwray and his crew, to prove their undoing. The swirl of events and the shifting alliances during the dynamic ascendancy of Napoleonic France moved far too rapidly for anyone to predict. It was not uncommon for one day's allies to be the next day's foes. While the diminutive warship lay at anchor in Falmouth Harbor, war was declared between the new Dutch Batavian Republic, a satellite of the French revolutionary government, and England. Although Grootinwray could not have known it, his ship's fate was all but sealed.[11]

Moored adjacent to a big Dutch East Indiaman which had put in with her, and in immediate danger of internment, *De Braak* was not alone in her predicament. Indeed, nearly half a dozen other Dutch warships and twenty-four merchantmen, presumably the convoy bound for the East Indies, had been trapped by events. All faced an uncertain future. Grootinwray, like the other naval commanders, must have pondered his position with some pessimism. Fighting his way to the open sea was out of the question. His ship was lightly armed with only twelve guns, four-pounder long guns and half-pounder swivels, and was manned by less than two-thirds of her 1785 complement. She stood little chance of forcing her way past the British men-of-war and forts guarding the harbor. There was, in fact, no alternative but to await notification of the intentions of his country's former ally.[12]

The British Admiralty's reaction to the declaration of war, of course, was immediate. On January 20, 1795, His Majesty's warships were instructed to prevent all Dutch vessels in English ports from sailing, and to employ force of arms if necessary. In the days that followed, *De Braak* lay idle at anchor as negotiations were carried on between the British government and the Prince of Orange, who had fled to England, to determine her disposition and that of the other Dutch vessels in port. Their numbers and force were not taken lightly by the English, who saw them as a ready-made addition to the nation's hard-pressed navy. The Dutch naval flotilla was of substantial force, including the big, sixty-four-gun man-of-war *Zeeland*; the fifty-four-gun *Braakel*; the *Tholen*, of thirty-six guns; the *Pyl*, of sixteen guns; and the cutter *Miermin*, of fourteen guns. And, of course, there was *De Braak*.[13]

Despite ongoing negotiations, the disposition of the six warships remained undetermined for more than a year. Finally, on Friday, March 4, 1796, a decision was made, and dispatch sent from Plymouth to London announcing the navy's intentions. "All the Dutch ships of war in this harbour," it stated,

> consisting of one ship of 64, one of 50 guns, a frigate, and two sloops of war [*sic*], were yesterday taken possession of by the commanding officer of this port; the Dutch flag was taken down, and the British hoisted in its stead, and their crews were put on board the prison [ship] and some other ships of war in the harbour.[14]

The wrangling had ended. At Falmouth, Captain Wooldridge, commander of the British brig-sloop *Fortune*,[15] which was armed with a battery of fourteen four-pounders, was instructed to take *De Braak*, the lone Dutch warship at that port, under his charge. On June 13, 1796, the Admiralty officially ordered Wooldridge to take command of the little cutter and to notify her captain that he was to surrender his vessel. Grootinwray and his men were informed that they could either remain with their ship under the authority of the Prince of Orange, or return to their homeland as paroled prisoners of war. Sixty chose to return to The Netherlands, while five elected to remain.[16]

Having been instructed to bring the cutter around to Plymouth for refitting, Wooldridge noted that he would be obliged to strip his own crew of twenty-five men (no small demand in a period of serious manpower shortages in England) to carry out the order because the Dutchman was "very heavily rigged." The captain was also, no doubt, affected by the quite commonly held English aversion to the class of Dutch cutter he was charged with manning. Indeed, the cutter rig on craft greater than sixty-five feet in length was quite unpopular with the Royal Navy, no matter what the nationality of the vessel. They simply took too many men to work the sails. And *De Braak* was a full eighty-four feet in length. Nevertheless, when sternly instructed "to proceed to Plymouth," Wooldridge followed his orders dutifully.[17]

Five days later, the cutter was shifted from Falmouth Harbor to a new anchorage in Carrick Roads, preparatory to departure, and placed under the command of one Lieutenant King, a petty officer, and four men.[18] On June 27 an additional seventeen hands were taken on board. The remaining Dutch crew members still held aboard, nearly a score of men, were removed. Then, in company with *Fortune* and the fifth-rate forty-four-gun frigate *Expedition, De Braak* sailed for Plymouth Sound. Although the frigate and the cutter soon parted company in heavy seas caused by a strong gale, *De Braak* and her escort reached their destination safely the same day.[19]

On August 26 it was officially determined that all of the Dutch warships which had been assembled at Plymouth were to be surveyed to ascertain their condition, usefulness, and suitability for induction into the Royal Navy. The chief surveyor of the Plymouth Dockyard informed the Admiralty on September 1 that the required survey could not be completed unless the vessels were entirely unrigged and all of their guns removed. Only then could they be heeled, thoroughly inspected, and have their lines taken.[20] Accordingly, the request was approved, and the work quickly completed. A week later all of the vessels were reported to be in good condition. All had been found suitable for commissioning and were to be put into fighting trim within six weeks. On September 15, it was publicly announced that the vessels were "ordered to be got ready for commission immediately."[21] *De Braak* would prove to be the lone exception.

Following her survey, *De Braak*'s sails and cables were reported as having been cut (possibly by Grootinwray in a last gesture of defiance during his internment aboard), and anchors and other stores as having been carried away. One might conjecture that the latter items were lost in transit from Falmouth to Plymouth or possibly to dockyard scavengers from other ships being outfitted.[22] But the British bias against the Dutch cutter rig was simply too great for the Admiralty to withstand, even though the Navy Board had been informed that the vessel could be readied for sea in only three weeks, owing to her superior condition. On September 10 the Navy Board changed its collective mind and directed that *De Braak* be converted into a brig. She would then be reclassified and commissioned as a sloop-of-war. Nine days later the order was officially issued. The warship, for the record, would henceforth be known as *Braak*, although most would continue to refer to her throughout the remainder of her career by her old name, *De Braak*.[23]

The surgery necessary to convert a single-masted cutter to a brig would prove to be more than superficial. Once stripped of guns, stores, and furnishings, most of her rigging, including her mast, were removed. In dry dock, her lines were taken by John Marshall, Surveyor of the Navy, who drew a set of plans showing her decks and hull configuration, noting them to be "as when taken." Another set of plans, labeled "as fitted," were then produced to show the required alterations.[24]

Before addressing the major alterations and additions, the dockyard shipwrights employed in the refitting were first obliged to replace or repair injured or deteriorated timbers. Working fast and efficiently, they afforded only enough time and attention to replace the worst dry-rotted timbers before moving on to more significant alterations. They then set to work, raising the gunwales two feet and building port cabins for the captain's party, starboard cabins to serve as the clerk's office and toilet in the stern. The cabins were roofed over and skylights added. An aft ladderway was taken out and replaced with a hatch leading down to the breadroom. A glass "companion" was opened forward of the hatch to permit natural light into the lower deck. *De Braak*'s original pumps were removed and a ladderway cut through the deck to the officers' quarters. A hood with hinged side and top was erected over it.[25]

While operating as a cutter, *De Braak* had employed a windlass in her bow, rather than a capstan, to raise anchor. The Plymouth shipwrights used an existing companion to install a new capstan much more suitable for her new brig rig. Wooden tubes for the suction pumps were installed, and holes were pierced through the decks for installation of the mainmast and foremast. The lower deck was completely rearranged, with several cabins torn out and replaced by new ones to accommodate the ship's new lieutenant, master, captain's clerk, purser, surgeon, and gunner. Two more cabins were constructed forward for the carpenter and boatswain. A new shot locker was built, and a lead-lined fire-hearth pit constructed to receive a cast-iron "Brodie Patent" stove for cooking. And so it went, with shipwrights working diligently to meet navy specifications and to field *De Braak* as quickly as possible.[26]

Finally, the hull had to be sheathed in copper. This was a necessary, if expensive, expedient employed to prevent the disastrous effects of boring shipworms common to temperate and tropical environments. The sheathing had the added benefit of discouraging fouling barnacle growth and that of other marine life which might otherwise affect the ship's sailing and maneuvering efficiency.[27]

In addition to the new substantial alterations underway, on September 30 the Admiralty requested that *De Braak* be armed with carronades in lieu of the traditional long guns which had for years provided the deadly kick in a British broadside. The Navy Board readily approved the request and directed that she be thus armed.[28] In so doing, they were providing the little warship with the very latest technology in naval ordnance. It was, in fact, nothing less than an early application of one of the most important technological advancements in firepower of the Napoleonic Age—an innovation which would in fact influence the evolution of naval tactics during the remaining years of fighting ships under sail.

That carronades had been ordered for *De Braak* is not surprising. Manufactured by the Carron gun works in Scotland, this terrifyingly destructive ordnance was uniquely suited for small vessels of less than twenty guns and, by the early 1790s, was finding widespread employment on such craft throughout

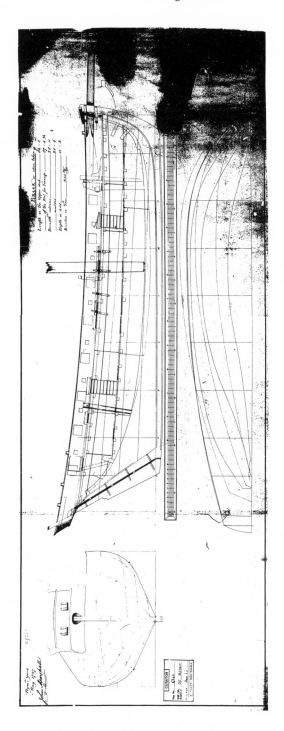

Admiralty draft of *De Braak* "as when taken." (*Delaware State Museums*)

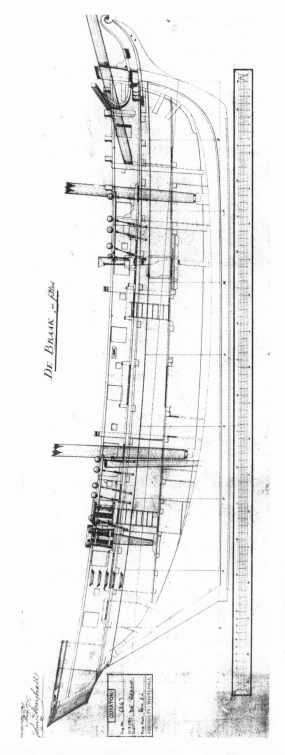

Admiralty draft of *De Braak* "as fitted," that is, after her conversion from cutter to brig. (*National Maritime Museum, London*)

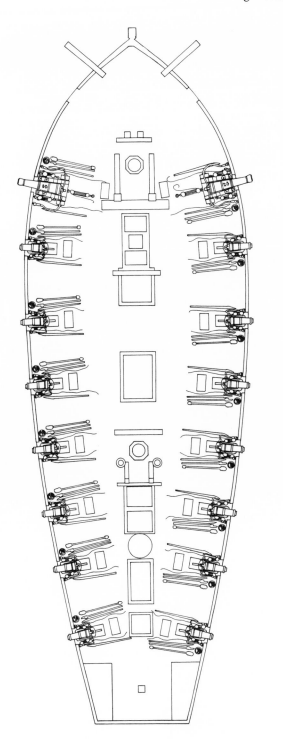

Gun deck plan of HMS *De Braak*. (*Delaware State Museums*)

the Royal Navy. The improvement in killing-and-mutilating firepower was heralded by some as the ultimate sea gun. Normally mounted on a slide rather than a truck carriage, the carronade was in fact preferable for small vessels such as *De Braak* because it was shorter and lighter, being approximately a quarter of the weight of long guns of the same caliber. Carronades could be swiftly loaded and were capable of firing more rapidly than the average long guns of the day. Although lacking in long-range accuracy, in close combat (which the Royal Navy favored) they were deadly. Their superior hull-crushing capabilities were favored by British and American naval tacticians alike, for they believed that an enemy's hull, guns, and manpower, rather than his sails and rigging, should be the targets in battle.[29]

The carronade had quickly earned the sobriquets of "smasher" from the British and "devil gun" from the French. *De Braak*'s new short-barreled weapons were 1,200 weight each (i.e., 1,456 pounds), a standard weight in the eighteenth century. Stubby in appearance and firing a twenty-four-pound ball, each gun featured a muzzle extension to prevent the rigging at the ship's sides from being ignited by the blast of the firing gun. Each had disbark sites at the first reinforce ring and at the muzzle, permitting the gunner far more accurate sighting than the commonly used line-of-metal.[30]

Once fully refitted, armed, and manned, HM Sloop-of-War *De Braak* would prove to be, it was hoped, a welcome addition to the hard-pressed Royal Navy in one of its bleakest hours. On June 16, Captain James Drew boarded his new command for the first time, only three days after she had been declared ready for service and her crew had begun to draw wages. Her complement of eight-five officers and men had already been entered into her muster and pay books. All that was necessary thereafter was for the brig to be provisioned and readied for service in the English Channel.[31]

T H R E E

A Sudden Flaw of Wind

Captain James Drew launched into his new command with unconditional zeal. The exigencies of the war, he knew, demanded it. There was precious little time to whip both ship and crew into order or to fill the few remaining billets still vacant. On July 7 he was issued instructions to commence convoy duty on the English coast as soon as his vessel was in fighting trim. There were, indeed, innumerable reasons for haste, not the least of which was the Admiralty's desire to remove as many disaffected seamen as possible from the mutinous atmosphere of Plymouth.[1]

On July 15 Drew ordered two gunports cut in *De Braak*'s bow. The following day he wrote to the Admiralty, requesting that two bow-chasers be sent in place of two of the carronades slated for his battery. Four days later, a pair of six-foot, six-pounder long guns mounted on truck carriages were brought aboard and rolled into position at the newly cut gunports. Drew intended to put the guns to good use. Although he had been assigned to what many officers considered the most tedious duty in the navy, he saw it as an opportunity to take a few prizes. Chase guns were an absolute necessity for such work, for they offered, if not accuracy, range, which was a valuable asset in any pursuit. And as the war continued to expand, there were prizes aplenty to be had— even in home waters—including the rich Spanish merchantmen sailing from the Americas with sugar, cocoa, copper, and, on rare occasions, gold and silver as well. Indeed, with Napoleon's flirtation with Spain, and the latter's hostility toward England, Spanish shipping had become fair game for every ambitious captain in the Royal Navy. As early as September 27, 1796, all British commanders had been instructed "to detain and bring in all Spanish ships that they might fall in with." It was an order that James Drew, who had never taken a prize in his life, fully intended to obey.[2] His primary mission, however, was another matter.

The protection of seaborne trade, upon which the prosperity and, indeed, the very survival of the British Empire depended, was of paramount importance in the war against Napoleon. Owing to the heavy demands on the main British battle fleets, there was a chronic shortage of ships and men suitable for the defense of the trade and supply routes which kept Britain afloat, in both home waters and overseas. In England's own backyard, British shipping was frequently subjected to the depredations of swarms of French privateers working the English Channel and ports along the Bay of Biscay. Others harried the American trade by lurking about the periphery of major U.S. outports. And now, with America's impending turn against France, Yankee shipping had also begun to suffer even more from the assaults of French raiders.

There was, of course, a defense. Experience had shown that vessels which sailed in convoys, escorted by even such small ships of war as *De Braak*, had a far greater chance of survival than those that did not. In 1793, the British government instituted the Convoy Act (later modified and strengthened as the Compulsory Convoy Act of 1798), which vastly improved the English convoy system. Indeed, by 1798 it was legally required and economically obligatory for all British merchantmen to travel under armed escort. Insurers, such as Lloyds of London, required that all underwritten vessels be sent out in convoys. Most masters of ships were obliged to sign agreements stipulating that they would not sail independently, and ship owners were frequently called upon to help defray the navy's expenses incurred while providing for the common defense.[3] The wear and tear upon the men and ships of the Royal Navy charged with maintaining that system were grueling, to say the least, and *De Braak* would suffer her share of stress.

By late summer James Drew had finally completed preparations for sea duty and was soon actively engaged in convoy service in the Channel and the Irish Sea. On September 13, 1797, he reported to Admiralty Secretary Evan Nepean on *De Braak*'s safe arrival at Milford Haven with the Plymouth trade. Duty had extracted its toll, however. On September 27, the captain reported that one Lieutenant Percy Dove had been hospitalized and would be unfit for duty for the foreseeable future. He therefore requested that his own nephew, young Lieutenant John Drew, son of his brother Stephen, currently serving aboard HMS *Cerberus* under the command of another brother, Captain John Drew, be appointed in Dove's place. The request was approved.[4]

De Braak remained almost continually at sea, despite the onset of winter weather of the worst sort. In December the British Isles were ravaged by gales. The damage to both the military and the merchant marine was substantial. On December 11, HMS *Marlborough*, of seventy-four guns, was driven ashore at Plymouth at the same time that a gunboat, incongruously named *Love and Friendship*, was bilged and sunk.[5] A sloop called the *Four Sisters* was destroyed on the Ramshead, to the west of Plymouth. As the tempest continued, the Channel ports soon became crowded with ships seeking refuge. Prognostications for the immediate future were dour. "The very high gales of winds from the Southward," reported the *Times* of London, "will occasion, we fear, ruinous losses and accidents at sea. We never recollect to have witnessed a more tempestuous gale than throughout yesterday."[6]

Disasters continued to occur at a dizzying rate. Two colliers were lost with their crews on the Brambles, between Cowes Harbor and Calshot Castle.[7] On December 18, the transport *Eagle* was stove against Ramsgate Pier. The *Prince of Piedmont*, en route from Barbados to London, was driven ashore and lost at Chichester, and the *Marquis of Worcester* was sunk off Weymouth. HMS *Impeteux*, a seventy-four-gunner, made a signal of distress and was promptly driven onto the Spit at Portsmouth, fouling a number of other ships in the process.[8] On the following day, the litany of disasters continued unabated. Reports of casualties flowed into London. "We had this morning," one such report stated,

> a most tremendous hurricane of wind from South West. Several ships have left their anchors, and three ships are driven on shore in Stokes Bay, one of which is the Cadiz packet of Hull; she is driven up to high-water mark, but has yet received no material damage, she makes no water. The *Britannia*, of Minehead for Oporto, was enabled to get into the harbor [of Portsmouth] with the loss of one anchor. One other vessel on shore, we hear, is a yellow-sided brig belonging to Weymouth.[9]

Ultimately, all of the vessels driven ashore in Stokes Bay became total losses.[10]

The continuing storm did not overlook *De Braak*. On December 11, James Drew reported that his ship had lost her mast and that she would have to put into port to make repairs. On December 21, reports out of Portsmouth included the following:

> Arrived the *De Braak* sloop of war, of 18 guns, Capt. J. Drew, from a cruise, with loss of main-mast, which appears to have gone by the board; but whether it was occasioned by a gale of wind or in an action, is not ascertained; there is a probability however, that it was by the latter, as a number of shot holes appear in several of her sails.[11]

That *De Braak* had engaged in a skirmish or firefight is possible. That the damage inflicted upon her mast resulted from the weather, however, is certain. Drew noted, somewhat ruefully, that his ship's mainmast had been lost because she was simply overmasted in the first place, but it was only at the explicit direction of the Admiralty that he had come into Plymouth to refit.[12]

On December 24, while still in port, Drew was instructed to make good any and all defects of his ship and then to take on provisions for three months of Channel duty.[13] An attack by Napoleon's armies was still uppermost in the minds of many Englishmen, and the protection of the Channel and its trade was central to the British defense strategy. "The Invasion of England," noted the *Times* of London, "is at present, in France, the order of the day."[14] It was also the single greatest concern of the British Admiralty. Despite her initial orders, however, *De Braak* was not destined to remain in home waters for long, or to participate in the defense of the British Isles. On February 8, 1798, Drew's instructions were changed: he was directed to take on provisions for a six-month voyage. The brig, it was undoubtedly rumored, would be heading for the western hemisphere![15]

While Drew saw to *De Braak*'s repairs, he would probably have taken the opportunity to visit his home and family in nearby Saltash. He most certainly would have paid a visit to his elder brother, the Reverend Stephen Drew, who also served as the town's mayor and, from time to time, as a prize agent. Family gatherings, however, must have been small. James's wife was still in New York, and several of his relatives were at sea, serving aboard HMS *Cerberus*, under the command of his brother John.

Captain John Drew had been born a year before James and was frequently mistaken for his twin. But, unlike James, he had achieved an enviable reputation as an aggressive commander "of exemplary character." He had risen steadily in the service since receiving his lieutenant's rating in September 1777. Within six years of his commission, he had been appointed post captain. In 1795, after a series of important commands, he was given HMS *Cerberus*, a fast, thirty-two-gun frigate attached to the Western Squadron and home-ported (conveniently) at Plymouth. Drew's influence was substantial enough to get several family members who had chosen a naval career assigned to his ship, including Stephen's sons, Acting Lieutenant James William Drew and Lieutenant John Drew.[16]

In 1796 *Cerberus* had been ordered to patrol on the Cork Station and, under Captain John Drew's able command, experienced repeated successes against enemy shipping. In July she captured a four-gun French privateer cutter. In September, while in company with HMS *Diane* and *Seahorse*, she took the rich Brazilian ship *Santa Cruz*. In May 1797, she captured the French privateer *Dunkerque*. The following autumn, the ten-gun privateer brig *L'Indemnité*, the Spanish schooner *San Noberta*, of four guns, the twelve-gun French privateer *Franklin*, and the ten-gun French cutter *L'Hirondelle* were taken in rapid succession. She also made three recaptures: the Danish ship *Graff*, the schooner *Friendship*, and the *Jackson James*. In November 1797, she took her most important prizes, the sixteen-gun privateer *L'Épervier* and two days later, the twenty-gun sloop *Le Renard (Reynard)*, both coppered and termed "very fine ships." The Reverend Stephen Drew would later serve as Saltash prize agent for the sale of the two privateers. Both ships would eventually be purchased for and commissioned by the Royal Navy. From all the evidence, it would seem that the Saltash Drews and the Royal Navy had become something of a corporate family.[17]

The morning of January 11, 1798, was raw and blustery at Plymouth. A hard wind, attended by heavy seas and rain, had been blowing throughout the night, "with great violence," from the south. Although work may well have continued ashore on outfitting *De Braak*, conditions in the harbor were becoming increasingly dangerous for incoming and outgoing vessels. Indeed, negotiating the entrance to the sheltered confines of the Hamoaze, the great anchorage basin in which many of the navy's ships were moored, was on such days a hazardous undertaking at best. When HMS *Cerberus* sailed into Cawsand Bay from Cork with her most recent prizes, *L'Épervier* and *Le Renard*, the storm was at its height. Within a short time after arriving, *Le Renard*, manned only by a prize crew, was in danger of being driven onto the rocks in Firestone Bay and barely managed to negotiate her way into the sanctuary of the Hamoaze. It was not so with *Cerberus*.[18]

By 1:30 P.M. the gale had abated somewhat, and the wind had veered a little to the southwest. *Cerberus* had been obliged to ride out the storm in Cawsand Bay. But after months of hard duty on station patrol, Captain John Drew was anxious to get ashore—for many reasons. First and foremost, important dispatches had to be delivered from Rear Admiral Robert Kingsmill at Cork to the Port Admiral at Plymouth. There was also the immediate business of the two prizes to be addressed. Finally, there was the need to deliver a certain Captain Pulling, former commander of HMS *Penguin*, of eighteen guns, who had recently been promoted to post captain and had come to Plymouth to take on his new command. Drew may have been somewhat amused by Pulling's appointment, for it was well known that he had only recently married Admiral Kingsmill's daughter, a move which no doubt had a positive impact on his career. He was then returning to Plymouth aboard *Cerberus* from the Cork Station to join his bride and to take command of his new charge, HMS *Hindustan*, of fifty-four guns, lying in the harbor. But, unlike Pulling, Captain John Drew was married only to the navy. The sole family he looked forward to seeing was living in Saltash.[19]

Accordingly, at the earliest moment possible, Captain John Drew ordered *Cerberus*'s barge manned and lowered. Taking with him his teenaged nephew, Acting Lieutenant James William Drew, as well as Captain Pulling, two midshipmen, the coxswain, a black servant, and six seamen to pull the oars, Drew set out from Cawsand Bay for the Hamoaze. Although the sea "ran very hollow," the boat at first encountered little difficulty until she came abreast of Redding Point, at the entrance to the Hamoaze. At about 2:00 P.M., as the little craft crawled across a narrow channel called the Bridge, situated between St. Nicholas Island and Mount Edgecombe, sea turbulence began to increase. By then the chilly winds had abated even more, but "the swell of the sea was there very heavy; occasioned by the strong ebb tide from the harbour running counter to the Southerly wind and sea, the ground being very rocky, and the water shoal."[20]

As the barge pulled abreast of St. Nicholas, a heavy swell suddenly broke over the boat, nearly swamping her and instantly rendering the situation perilous. Captain Drew, alarmed, tore off his coat and prepared for the worst. He advised everyone aboard "to consider of the best means of saving their lives" if another swell should strike the water-filled boat. Almost immediately, his worst fears were realized as two giant waves struck in fatal succession and the barge foundered. Two sailors, not knowing how to swim, clung desperately to the only things remaining afloat, a pair of oars, and were driven ashore and saved. Captain Drew, struggling hopelessly against the waves, sank within sight of the two seamen. Everyone else aboard, including young Lieutenant James William Drew and Captain Pulling, perished in the frigid waters of the bay. Little was salvaged from the calamity save Captain Drew's coat, in the pocket of which were found the dispatches for the Port Admiral of Plymouth.[21]

The tragic loss of one of the Royal Navy's most promising officers was soon reported by the London press in a long postmortem befitting a hero. The blow, for both the navy and the Drew family, was a heavy one. For the navy, however, the gap left by Captain John Drew's death would eventually be filled by the promotion of Stephen Drew's other son, Lieutenant John Drew, to commander of *Cerberus*. For Captain James Drew, "that very able officer" and commander of HM Sloop-of-War *De Braak*, however, the loss of his beloved brother left a wound that never had time to heal before his own death occurred 134 days later. Ironically, the memory of John Drew's tragic demise would be resurrected nearly two centuries later as a means for continuing one of the longest treasure hunts in history.[22]

De Braak's refitting proved more extensive than had been anticipated. As late as February 17, 1798, the little brig was still in port, even though Drew had already received orders to proceed to Cork and to report to Admiral Kingsmill, under whose direction he was to "collect such Trade bound to North America" as might be ready to sail. Similar instructions had been issued to Captain Francis Pender, commander of the sixty-four-gun ship-of-the-line *St. Albans*, then outfitting at Spithead. On February 24, additional orders pertaining to the joint convoy were drafted and dispatched to Admiral George Vandeput, commander of the North American Station at Halifax, informing him that he was to take both *De Braak* and *St. Albans* under his command upon their arrival there.[23]

It was the Admiralty's intention that *St. Albans* sail from Spithead on March 1 to convoy the American trade, mostly American-owned merchantmen, to American ports. She was first to rendezvous, however, off Cork with *De Braak*, which would be escorting the Irish trade. Drew was specifically ordered, upon his meeting with *St. Albans*, to "put himself and the Trade assembled" under Pender's command and protection. The whole fleet of nearly fifty vessels would then proceed to Delaware. From Delaware Bay, *De Braak* would turn south with those vessels bound for southern ports. *St. Albans* would sail

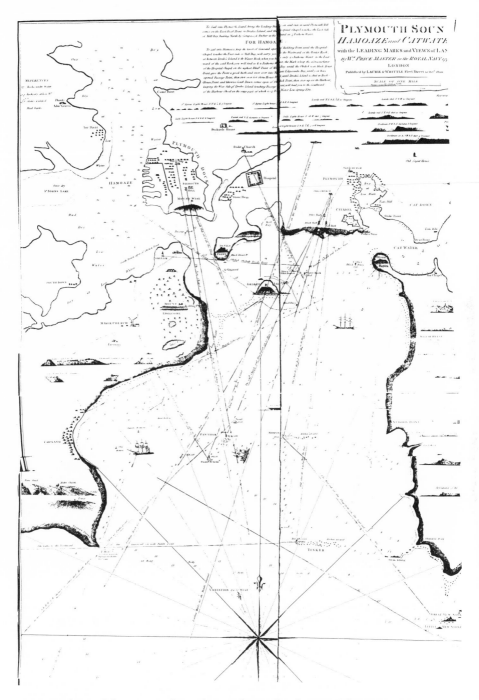

Nautical chart of the approach to Plymouth, England, 1798. The great Hamoaze anchorage off the Royal Navy dockyards is at upper left. (*Library of Congress*)

north, escorting her own convoy of ships to Philadelphia, New York, Boston, and Halifax.[24]

British protection of the American trade had, in recent months, become a political, economic, and military imperative. As a neutral nation at the outset of England's war with France, the United States at first had been able to reap enormous profits by exporting goods to both belligerents. Both sides vied for American support. In 1795, however, a significant shift in the balance of Yankee sympathies emerged with the ratification of Jay's Treaty between the United States and Great Britain. The treaty had been designed to resolve long-standing disputes over territory and compensation for damages resulting from the American Revolution. The following year, when the House of Representatives voted appropriations to put the treaty into effect, diplomatic efforts by France notwithstanding, a schism between the United States and the French Republic seemed inevitable. Finally, in January 1798, France decreed that all vessels of any nationality carrying British goods would be subject to seizure. Almost immediately, French privateers and regular naval vessels began to prey upon American shipping. Although the Royal Navy followed suit, frequently stopping and seizing Yankee ships carrying French goods, conflict between the United States and France seemed imminent. By early 1798, protection of the Anglo-American trade had, for England, become a diplomatic necessity if Yankee support against France were to become a reality. Convoys, such as those assigned to *St. Albans* and *De Braak*, were crucial to England's garnering American support in the war against Napoleon.

James Drew's instructions cautioned that extreme care be taken not to part company with his charges. Owing to a dangerous infestation of the U.S. middle Atlantic seaboard by French privateers, which had been preying upon both British and American merchantmen, vessels bound for the Chesapeake Bay were to be escorted by *De Braak* directly into the bay before the remainder of the fleet could be released to sail south. Vessels bound for Georgia and South Carolina were then on their own, although Drew was specifically instructed to "use his best endeavors to see [the merchant ships] in safety off their respective ports." After having shepherded his flock to their destinations, he was then to turn north and make directly for Halifax, where he was to place himself under Admiral Vandeput.[25]

Orders notwithstanding, *De Braak*'s long tenure in port may not have been entirely due to her extensive refitting. On February 18, Drew informed the Secretary of the Admiralty, Evan Nepean, that his nephew, Lieutenant John Drew, was at sick quarters. It seems quite possible that the lieutenant may have suffered from some melancholia induced by the deaths of his brother and uncle, as well as the generally unhealthy conditions of duty at sea in the eighteenth century. It is also quite possible that with the command of *Cerberus* open, any excuse to remain in port to lobby for that posting would do. And as the tightly knit Drew clan looked out first and foremost for their own kin, such a scheme would not seem out of the question. If that was, indeed, the intent, it succeeded beyond expectation, for Lieutenant John Drew was soon given command of his late uncle's ship. Unwittingly, by requesting his nephew's replacement, James Drew had also saved the young officer's life.

But there were other, more serious problems to attend to which had hindered sailing. Drew complained of having trouble with "three of the most seditious and mutinous men in the Kings Service." Two of the men had been transferred to his ship from HMS *Saturn* and one from *Ramilles*, both of seventy-four guns.[26] The crew of each vessel had, only the year before, been among the first to join the Great Mutiny, and both ships had continued to offer resistance well after the revolt had been put down.[27] Drew was fearful, therefore, that the three miscreants might "be capable of corrupting the minds of the Briggs company however well disposed at present, and which nothing but the energy of the Officers can counteract." Without the assistance of a lieutenant, the situation was serious. Drew promptly requested that a new lieutenant be appointed to fill his nephew's position and attend to the problem. One Thomas Hickson, an Irishman, was assigned to the post.[28]

Drew's problems with the few rebellious seamen and his own illness were soon overshadowed by the mission at hand—one which could no longer be postponed. By the end of February, ten ships which were to sail under *De Braak*'s protection had gathered at Plymouth for the first leg of their voyage to America. *De Braak*'s final complement of seventy-three officers and men and twelve able Royal Marines was assembled, comprising an international lot, if ever there was one. Although at least thirty-five of the men were west-country men from the counties of Devon, Wiltshire, and Cornwall, ten were from Ireland. There were also one each from New York, Hamburg, Sweden, and Portugal, and three from Greenock, Scotland. Six were from Gloucestershire and five from Warwickshire. The remainder were from various unidentified places throughout England.[29]

There could be no further delay. The maintenance of trade was imperative to the war effort, and every convoy counted. Thus, on March 1, with the east wind at her back, the little brig *De Braak* and her covey of merchantmen, briefly accompanied by the cutter *Cygnet*, sailed from Plymouth. Soon afterward, while stopping at Falmouth, undoubtedly to pick up any additional vessels wishing to join, the convoy was temporarily brought to anchor by strong southwesterlies. Drew dutifully took a count of the fleet and reported the delay. Five days later, on March 7, the convoy was still anchored in Carrick Road, detained by westerly winds. Drew chafed under the delay. He had been informed that his immediate arrival at Cork was of "the utmost importance," and he fumed at the lethargy of the "heavy Convoy" he was charged with protecting. Unburdened by his charges, he quipped in exasperation, "I alone could get there shortly." His belated arrival at Cork, however, was not without some benefit, for an even larger fleet of merchantmen, more than twice the size of the one he had escorted out of the Channel, had used the additional time to assemble and prepare for the long Atlantic voyage.[30]

Drew's belated departure was not an uncommon event during the age of sail, when men, materials, ships, and, most importantly, the weather all had to be in alignment before a convoy could leave port. Indeed, it was not until March 14 that *De Braak*'s co-escort, HMS *St. Albans*, and her own contingent of a dozen merchantmen were finally ready to sail. Then, in order to ensure that no vessel had been overlooked, *St. Albans*'s commander, Captain Pender, dispatched his Channel escort, HM Cutter *Nimble*, into Falmouth to collect any vessels which had arrived after Drew's departure.[31]

Once the *St. Albans* convoy had swept beyond the Lizard and Land's End, the southwesternmost tip of the Cornwall Peninsula, the voyage to the rendezvous point to meet *De Braak* and the Irish fleet off Cape Clear proved uneventful. Finally, on March 26, off Galley Head, Pender's little armada of merchantmen fell in with Drew and his own convoy, swollen now to thirty American and four British merchantmen, most of which had been picked up at Cork. Both Pender's and Drew's orders directed them to proceed under joint convoy "towards their places of destination (keeping during [their] course to the southward as circumstances point)." The combined fleet, numbering forty-four merchantmen and two warships, therefore, turned their prows southwestward.[32]

On April 1, off the Azores, Pender sighted two strange sails and signaled Drew to give chase. Within a short time, the suspect vessels were discovered to be HMS *Magnamine* and the privateer *Victory*, a French prize late of Boston. Soon afterward, the weather began to deteriorate. By the following day, the convoy was being buffeted about by increasingly turbulent winds. Although Pender could count all of the convoy ships, *De Braak*, bringing up the rear, began to fall ever further astern. By late April 2, *De Braak* was "almost out of sight . . . on a stern bearing NE by N45." Pender fired a signal gun to call the brig up in an effort to keep the convoy together. But the next two days of stormy weather aborted every effort to maintain order. By April 4, the flotilla had become so dispersed that only seven merchantmen were within sight of the big man-of-war. *De Braak* had disappeared.[33]

For the following seven weeks, the whereabouts and activities of Captain James Drew and his ship were still unknown. Legend has filled this historic vacuum in time by attributing to one of the Royal Navy's least illustrious "plodders," an adequate but undistinguished officer, the saga of a brilliant raid on a Spanish treasure fleet and the single-handed capture of between three and ten heavily laden treasure ships. Some wags would even claim that Drew was sailing under "secret orders" to harass the Spanish in the Caribbean. Oth-

ers would say that *De Braak* had made for Kingston, Jamaica, to take aboard
the payroll for His Majesty's garrison at Halifax and a cargo of gold for the
Dutch West India Company. It mattered little to the wonderful yarn-spinners
of later ages that the last great Spanish treasure flotas had sailed in 1778, a full
twenty years before the final voyage of Captain James Drew. And it mattered
even less that only rarely did ships bearing the treasures of a not-so-new world
depart from the Americas. The Halifax garrison was paid in local currency.
And the Dutch West India Company had long ceased to exist. All that counted
for the storytellers was *De Braak*'s having literally vanished for seven weeks—
seven weeks in which innumerable adventures and marvelous exploits were
alleged to have been carried out by the suddenly bold sailor from Saltash.[34]

But meanwhile, what of *St. Albans*? In mid-April, the convoy had encountered another gale, and at least two more vessels, the *Dispatch* of New York
and the *Eleven Sons* of New London, had parted company with the fleet.[35] On
June 2, in latitude 40°23', longitude 70°, the big warship fell in with the snow
William (J. Hall, master), en route from Bordeaux to Philadelphia. Pender saw
fit to detain and examine the vessel, as she had just sailed from an enemy port,
possibly with French cargo in her hold. The British behaved in a less than
friendly manner. "Captain Pender," it was reported in the American press two
weeks later,

> broke open six letters, that he returned with the [mail] bag, and kept 48 letters
> that belonged to the bag. The first lieutenant, behaved with much insolence,
> broke open the letters in the possession of the passengers, in their presence, and
> kept them. Captain Hall demonstrated against this conduct, and Capt. Pender
> informed him, if he did not approve of his doing with the papers as he thought
> proper, he might appeal to the court of admiralty at Halifax, where he would
> find him; but on examining the papers, a certificate of restitution was found
> among them, with six hundred pounds damages granted to the captured, the
> vessel having lately detained in Plymouth, in England, which induced Capt. Pen-
> der to alter his resolution of sending the vessel to Halifax.[36]

With *De Braak* gone, Pender had little choice but to carry on with his mission and escort the southern trade, hitherto assigned to Drew, as far south as
the Chesapeake before heading north. By Thursday, May 24, he had sighted
the Virginia Capes, "Cape Henry Lighthouse W by N" three or four leagues,
and "Smith's Island WSW5 leagues." Despite the breakup of the convoy on
several occasions, and the failure of many to rejoin, Pender's voyage had been
moderately fruitful. When the *Norfolk Herald* reported the sighting of the *St.
Albans* convoy off the capes, where "the Chesapeake trade and the Norfolk
vessels left them and came in," it was noted that the big warship had two
prizes with her. One of the vessels was the American brig *Betsey*, from New
England, bound for Wiscasset with bale goods when she was captured by a
French corvette off the Azores. Retaken by Pender, she had become a lawful

prize. The second vessel was an armed schooner which had been flying British colors, ostensibly bound from Gonaives in the West Indies to Philadelphia, "but whose conduct and maneuvers round the fleet, as well as the irregularity of her papers," made Pender suspect that she was a French privateer in disguise. Although she had "Philadelphia" lettered on her stern and had hoisted an American flag when she first ran into the fleet, the British warship had kept her guard up. When the schooner fired on the brig *Helen*, one of the convoy ships, her true intentions seemed clear to Pender. Not one to stop and ask questions, he seized her off the Virginia Capes. She proved to be the American privateer schooner *Triton*, commanded by John Thornton, belonging to Philadelphia and owned by one P. Bail. As the intruder was laden with a rich cargo of coffee from a French colonial port, Pender decided to retain her as a prize.[37]

Then, after arriving off the Chesapeake Capes and having seen at least seven ships safely into the bay, Pender proceeded north to the Delaware. Reaching the Delaware Capes on May 25, he dutifully saw three more members of his convoy, *Manchester, Clothier,* and *Nancy*, bound for Philadelphia, into the river. Two days later, off Sandy Hook, he parted with his remaining charges and by June 9, accompanied only by his two prizes, had come to safe anchor at Halifax.[38]

But where was *De Braak*?

The first recorded encounter with the long-lost brig occurred in the early hours of Friday, May 25, when the American sloop *President*, Captain Skidmore commanding, bound from Philadelphia, sighted and fell in with an unidentified armed vessel twenty miles south of Cape Henlopen. Skidmore, who had been informed the day before by a captain going into the Delaware that he had been chased off the capes by a privateer, was himself hailed by an unidentified brig, "which as he could not distinguish her colours, he took to be a French privateer." In a classic case of mistaken identity, Skidmore "immediately put about and stood in for the Delaware, in consequence of which seven shots were fired at him, but to no effect."[39]

The vessel from which the sloop *President* had barely escaped during the night, it would later be learned, had been *De Braak*.[40]

James Drew had arrived off the Delaware Capes only hours after Pender's departure. He had made, given the circumstances, the best time possible in reaching the appointed rendezvous point—but to no avail. His orders had been quite explicit: he was not to become separated from the convoy. And, as one astute observer later noted, "As he was an officer with nearly thirty years service in the Royal Navy and had tried desperately to get appointed to a command, it is not likely that he went prowling for prizes."[41] Nevertheless, his ship was not alone. According to accounts which were conveyed to New York several days later by one Vincent Low, *De Braak* had parted company with *St.*

Albans somewhere off the Western Islands (the Azores) while in pursuit of a strange sail and had been unable to rejoin the convoy. Then, on or about April 30, she fell in with and captured a Spanish prize, sixty days out of Río de la Plata in South America, bound for Cadiz. The prize, identified by Drew as *St. Francis dehaveren*, alias *Commerce de Londros*, and by Low and the media as *Don Francisco Xavier*, was laden with a substantial cargo of 200 tons of copper bars, a quantity of cocoa, and other goods valued at £160,000 sterling.[42] A prize crew, consisting of a prize master, Lieutenant Thomas Griffith, and approximately eleven sailors, was immediately placed aboard. Griffith was issued instructions to take "all possible care not to part company." In the event that the prize was unavoidably separated from *De Braak*, he was directed "to repair to Cape Henry in the Chesapeak" and await Drew's arrival. At least fifteen Spanish seamen were taken prisoner, and most were transferred to the brig to reduce the possibility of an uprising.[43] It was a significant moment in the long naval career of James Drew, for the Spanish ship was to be his first and last prize.

By the afternoon of May 25, the brig and her captive were prepared to enter the Delaware to take on water. A pilot named Andrew Allen, master of the Lewes pilot boat *Friendship*, had soon come up and was taken aboard. Another pilot boat hovered nearby. Onboard *De Braak*, Drew was eager to get on with the business at hand, although his concerns were no longer with conducting a convoy but with securing a single rich prize. Better yet, there was the distinct possibility that he might soon have a reunion with his wife, Lydia, who was faithfully awaiting him in New York. Certainly, the tragic sequence of events which would not only deny Lydia her long-awaited reunion, but would also influence the traditions of Delaware for generations to come, was anything but expected.[44]

For nearly a century after the catastrophe which claimed the life of James Drew and many of his men, a single American eyewitness account of the final moments preceding the loss of *De Braak* would be handed down from generation to generation. It would be retold countless times and become part of the oral history of Delaware. Although marred by editorial embellishments before finally appearing in print in 1887, at least part of pilot Andrew Allen's purported tale is worth recounting.

When Allen was taken aboard the little British warship, he was immediately informed by Captain Drew that he was "constrained" to go into Lewes for water. "The captain," it was recorded,

> was in a hilarious mood. He had had good luck, he said, and the pilot must drink to his health. But a storm was brewing in the southwest. Ominous clouds were looming behind Rehoboth; and so, while the captain had gone down into the cabin for another bumper, Pilot Allen ordered the light sails screwed up. When the captain returned to the deck and noted what had been done he ordered the

sails sheeted home again, and turning to Allen, with an oath, said, "You look out for the bottom, and I'll look out for the spars."[45]

At about 4:00 P.M., *De Braak* entered Old Kiln Road, off Lewes, under mainsail and reefed topsail. There was an air of excitement as her officers and crew made ready to drop anchor about a mile from Cape Henlopen Light. The brig's six-oared cutter had already been deployed and lay alongside, waiting to carry the captain ashore to Lewes Town to secure fresh water. Nearby, the Spanish prize, by now with only a nine-man prize crew aboard (still under the command of Thomas Griffith), prepared to do likewise. Drew's servant busied himself tying his master's scarf.[46]

Whatever freak weather condition it was that struck *De Braak* on that fatal day in May 1798—variously described as a "thunder gust," a "violent squall," or a "sudden flaw of wind" by those closest to the scene—its impact was unexpected and devastating. The brig heeled over on her beam ends so quickly that within seconds she was filling up with seawater through her open hatches. Those unfortunate souls who were below decks had absolutely no warning or hope of escape. The scene was one of pandemonium and terror as the Delaware's waters poured through the hatchways, tossing goods, ballast, and bodies about indiscriminately. Topside, the heavy guns broke free and caromed across the deck, cutting down screaming men in their paths.[47]

Quarter gunner Samuel Mitchell, among the more fortunate crewmen on deck, later testified that he and thirty-two other men, including the boatswain, managed to scramble aboard the cutter lying alongside and reached safety aboard the Spanish prize even as *De Braak* slipped beneath the sea. The captain, his lieutenant, purser, surgeon, gunner, carpenter, four midshipmen, clerk, cook, armorer, three men from the carpenter's crew, a steward, three ship's boys, eleven seamen, four marine privates, and twelve Spanish prisoners—forty-seven men in all—were lost in only an instant.[48]

When Samuel Mitchell and the other survivors boarded *Xavier* and looked back to the spot where their ship had been just moments before, all that could be seen was her topgallant masthead standing proud above the water. A headcount on board the prize revealed that the prizemaster, boatswain, quartermaster, and thirty-one crewmen, as well as one sergeant, one corporal, and nine marine privates, were all that remained of *De Braak*'s original complement. Of the captured crew of the Spanish prize, only three survived.[49] Captain James Drew, of the Saltash Drews, was nowhere to be seen.

F O U R

Sailors, They Get All the Money

At the fatal moment when *De Braak* heeled over, filled, and sank, Andrew Allen had literally thrown himself into the little cutter lying alongside in a desperate effort to save his life, breaking his leg in the process.[1] But he survived to tell the tale, as did others who made their way to safety aboard the Spanish prize. Despite the traumatic events, however, there could be no immediate period of mourning. A war was on, and the Delaware was a rich hunting ground for French privateers eager to pounce upon any undefended vessel that fell their way, such as the prize ship *Don Francisco Xavier*. Indeed, with the United States soon to become actively engaged in its own "quasi-war" with France, enemy privateers had grown extremely bold on the Delaware coast, brazenly taking both British and American prizes within sight of the Capes. Barely an hour after *De Braak*'s sinking, in fact, the American schooner *Liberty*, bound from Philadelphia, was chased a "full four miles within the Capes of the Delaware" before escaping from one such raider. Fortunately for the stunned Englishmen aboard *Xavier*, they had been entirely overlooked by the menacing enemy warship.[2]

In the hours directly following the disaster, a decision had to be made about the immediate course of action. Not surprisingly, it was concluded that several members of the crew should board one of the pilot boats in the vicinity, perhaps Allen's, and proceed up the Delaware River to inform the British consul at Philadelphia of the catastrophe.

On Saturday, soon after the pilot boat's departure, Captain Skidmore, in *President*, fell in with *Xavier* and was informed by the still skittish crew of *De Braak*'s loss and of the fact that about "sixty of the crew (officers included) were unfortunately drowned." Immediately afterward, he encountered the pilot boat with several of the survivors aboard and was informed that the *Xavier* was a prize which had been taken only days before the disaster and was calculated to be worth £160,000.[3]

The British consul at Philadelphia, Phineas Bond, was undoubtedly shocked to hear the survivors' tales of the accident. The first accounts reported that Drew, his lieutenant, and thirty-eight officers, seamen, and marines had been lost. The consul reacted by immediately setting out for Lewes to conduct a firsthand investigation. Later, of course, there would have to be an official naval court of inquiry and, possibly, courts martial back home, but it was his duty to obtain expeditiously as much information as was then available. If there were even the slightest chance of salvaging the ship, it was his business to find that out.

At Lewes, Bond discovered the worst reports to be true: Captain Drew, most of his officers, a substantial portion of the crew, and most of the Spanish prisoners of war had perished. A black employee of the Cape Henlopen Lighthouse named Jacob Bailey had, in fact, just found the captain's body washed up on the shore, not far from the lighthouse itself. Bond's only consolation was that the prize and her rich cargo of strategically valuable copper were, for the moment, safe.[4]

The consul moved quickly to counter any unanticipated events, such as the arrival of an enemy privateer on the scene. He arranged for *Xavier* to be brought up the Delaware and moored under the shelter of a defense works below the city, probably Fort Mifflin. Then, on May 28, he penned a report to the British secretary of state for foreign affairs, Lord Grenville, informing him of the ship's loss, "within a short distance of Cape Henlopen," as well as the deaths of *De Braak*'s captain, officers, crew, and prisoners.[5]

By June 2, *Xavier*, alias *Commerce de Londros* or *Commerce of London*, had arrived safely at Philadelphia, after which Bond was able to prepare complete lists of both the survivors and the known dead. Two men could not be accounted for and might have been among those who reached shore. The two lists, enclosed with the consul's still unposted letter of May 28 to Lord Grenville, were then dispatched to Vice Admiral Vandeput in Halifax by the next boat. The lists sent by Bond had been compiled "to the best of his knowledge by the Boatswain, Jas. Williams," the most reliable eyewitness to the event with whom the consul could consult.[6]

Bond also sent communiqués informing the British consuls at Norfolk and Boston of the accident and outlining the steps which he felt should be taken in the navy's best interests. The prize, he recommended, should be sent to Halifax as soon as possible. The few Spanish prisoners who had survived and were still in British custody were to be transported to Philadelphia, where they would be "given up to the agents of Spain."[7]

Within a week, news of the disaster had spread as far south as Norfolk and as far north as New York. For some, the tragedy was particularly personal. "The accident," reported one sympathetic newspaper, "is a melancholy one, but it is greatly heightened by the circumstance of the captain's lady being so near as New York, where she was every hour in anxious expectation of the happiness of meeting him."[8]

On June 23, Vice Admiral George Vandeput, having received the consul's communiqués, formally reported the loss of *De Braak* to the British Admiralty and informed them that he was planning a salvage attempt. It was just possible that the brig, said to lie in shallow water, might be raised. He could, he said, afford to dispatch HMS *Assistance*, of fifty guns, under the command of Captain Jonathan Oakes Hardy, to the Delaware to study the situation. A second vessel, the new sloop-of-war *Rover*, although on patrol duty off Cape Breton, would be sent down as soon as she returned from her cruise to convoy *Xavier* to Halifax. But fate ruled otherwise, for *Rover* was wrecked on the island of Porto Nova in the Gulf of St. Lawrence on June 23, the same day Vandeput's letter to the Admiralty was being written. *Assistance*, the admiral soon realized, would be obliged not only to investigate the situation at Cape Henlopen, but also to convoy the prize home.[9]

On August 12, Vandeput informed the Admiralty of the loss of *Rover*, the second Royal Navy casualty in North American waters in as many months. With his report, he included a brief clipping from the *New York Gazette* detailing the sinking of *De Braak*. By that time, however, *Assistance* had already arrived on the Delaware.[10] Captain Hardy had sailed on July 4 with vague instructions to determine whether it would be possible to salvage the sunken brig from her grave, but his principal mission became convoying *Xavier* to Halifax. On July 21, Hardy arrived off the Delaware Capes and bespoke the ship *Hero*, from New York, in want of a pilot. The following day he reported to Bond, in Philadelphia, that *De Braak* was

> driven in 13 fatm water and must have been so violently shook [as to] be full of Sand and Mud so as to render my Exertions to sweep under her Bottom very uncertain in the Effect and also very equivocal whether the Expense would not be very great of the undertaking, so much to outweigh the Returns to Government.[11]

Salvage operations, he suggested, if undertaken, should be contracted out, with remuneration to the contractors based on whatever was recovered from the wreck.[12]

Hardy had discovered, much to his dismay, that several of *De Braak*'s crew members, upon arriving in Philadelphia, had deserted and then "been received into [a] Ship of War of the [United] States."[13] The remaining crew was less than orderly. In fact, Griffith was in such a "state of mind as to require confinement."[14] Undoubtedly, many others were equally traumatized by the experience. The situation was soon stabilized, however, when a lieutenant, a midshipman, and two loyal seamen were dispatched from another British warship, the *Topaze*, patrolling off Sandy Hook, New Jersey, to take command of the *Xavier*.[15]

Bond pressed forward on the issue of salvage. He requested Hardy to provide him with the specific numbers of vessels, personnel, and various types of equipment that would be necessary to raise and recover the sunken warship.

On July 27, Hardy replied that "four Vessels of about 80 Tons Burden each . . . well found with Cables & anchors & good windlasses" would do nicely. The necessary tackle for weighing, he said, "would be two Cables of 13 Inch— Four Hausers of 7 Inch Four Setts of heaving down Blocks that will serve the said Hausers." All four vessels would also have to "be well found with Greased Tackle." He advised Bond that he would need to secure as many pumps as he could locate to facilitate operations.[16]

On July 30, Bond informed Hardy that he had attempted to locate and contract with the necessary ship owners, but had met with objections. The ship contractors, he complained, were unhappy with the stipulation that they would only receive an "Allowance of Salvage." Nevertheless, two days later, he managed to secure four vessels at a charge of $50 per day each. But the craft were poorly manned, with barely enough crewmen aboard to sail them, much less to carry out a major salvage operation. The consul expressed "a Confidence that Seamen will be supplied from Assistance to make up the difference." As for directing the operation, the owners of the four vessels had secured the services of a certain Captain Franklin to manage their ships and to supervise the outfitting of the expedition.[17]

In the meantime, Bond queried Hardy as to whether, upon his return to Halifax, he might not also "convoy Trade from the Delaware."[18] Hardy was indignant not only at the consul's so casually suggesting a requisition of Royal Navy personnel from his ship, but that he had also had the effrontery to request the captain to expand his assigned mission. His main directive was simply to escort *Xavier* to Halifax. Nevertheless, he replied that if any vessels were ready for sea as soon as *Xavier* was, they might join the convoy, but there could be no delay.[19]

Hardy moved expeditiously and dispatched Mr. Seargill, master of *Assistance*, to assume command of the prize and ready her for the voyage. Seargill was also instructed to examine the hired salvage vessels for fitness and readiness. He launched into his mission with vigor and was soon "Zealously engaged" in both undertakings.[20] Despite Hardy's determination to depart as soon as possible, a point which had been clearly made in his correspondence with Bond, the consul continued to assume that the captain would remain on the Delaware to assist in the recovery of *De Braak*. On August 5, he wrote the captain, expressing his wish that Hardy consider the salvage work and the convoy of *Xavier* a "combined" mission and that he do everything he could to facilitate the salvage operation before *Assistance* sailed. The prize, Bond pointed out, had been outfitted with new cables, and thus "could lay securely in the Road [Whorekill Roads at Lewes] while [the] Attempt was [being made] to weigh the Sloop of War."[21] Hardy refused.

Delays in pressing forward with the salvage effort ensued. On August 6, Bond informed Hardy that, owing to problems in obtaining the necessary cordage for the hired vessels, the recovery attempt would have to be postponed until at least August 18. He was quick to note, however, that once the salvage had been completed, all pumps, blocks, cordage, and other materials which had either been purchased or hired by the crown would be immediately returned. If the operation were a success, and *De Braak* recovered, he added, "she was not to be sent to Philadelphia where a contagion had already showed itself." This "contagion" proved to be an outbreak of yellow fever, which had been reported in the press only the day before but had made its appearance a week earlier. Owing to the epidemic, Bond felt that it would be wiser to bring *De Braak* to either Wilmington or Marcus Hook, where she could be safely reoutfitted and prepared for sea duty. He requested that Hardy take precautions during the salvage effort because "many Valuables were on Board" the wreck, although he failed to elucidate just what these were. By his unfortunate choice of the term "Valuables," undoubtedly meaning the ship's equipage, guns, stores, and other gear, all of which were of critical importance to the navy, the consul planted one of the "clues" that would be interpreted to mean "treasure" by fortune hunters in years to come.[22]

Despite the lack of cordage and Bond's pessimism about a starting date, the fitting out of the four salvage vessels moved forward far more expeditiously than expected. On August 7, accompanied by *Xavier*, the little squadron of salvage boats sailed from Philadelphia for Whorekill, arriving at their destination the following day. Upon reaching the roads, Captain Franklin immediately offered to place himself under Hardy's command. Unfortunately, Hardy, whose orders were to put to sea for Halifax as soon as the prize had come down, had no intention of supervising the operation.[23] He sent the salvage boats back to Philadelphia on August 11 with a curt note to Bond expressing his regrets that the consul "could possibly misconceive" the captain's intentions regarding the salvage operation. Indeed, Hardy stated, he had already expressed "in the most expedient manner" the fact that his departure schedule depended entirely upon the arrival of *Xavier* and nothing else. Admiral Vandeput had never intended to employ *Assistance* in any major salvage work to begin with. Furthermore, he was "certain that the Admiral would highly disapprove of the great daily expense of 200 [dollars] for *Vessels* only without men." Indeed, for that amount, he quipped, the salvors "ought to find as many [men] as necessary." But the question was moot. With *Xavier* in sight, Hardy could afford to remain in the Delaware no longer.[24]

On August 12, Sailing Master Seargill and *Xavier*, alias *Commerce of London*, joined *Assistance*. On the following morning, with the ebb tide, the two ships sailed for Halifax, where they arrived on August 27. En route, Hardy took the opportunity of filling the many vacancies aboard his ship. *De Braak*'s boatswain, master's mate, and the handful of surviving Royal Marines were entered into his ship's muster book.[25]

Two days after Hardy's return, Vice Admiral Vandeput informed the Admiralty of his safe arrival. With the captain's intelligence and related information from Philadelphia, not to mention the firsthand data provided by *De Braak*'s survivors, which suggested that the brig's main topgallant mast was out of the water at ebb tide, the admiral was still confident that her recovery was possible. But it had to be a navy job, with ships specifically outfitted for the mission. Therefore, he ordered two ships, HMS *Hind*, a sixth-rate, 592-ton, twenty-eight-gun frigate commanded by Lieutenant Joseph Larcom, and the salvage brig *Vixen* to the Delaware to attempt to raise the late Captain Drew's ship.[26]

Vixen was a small vessel of only 140 tons burden, normally assigned to the Halifax Dockyard. She had, however, all of the necessary gear on board, having been specifically fitted out for salvage work of the kind deemed necessary on the Delaware. She was undoubtedly the most appropriate craft for the job. Vandeput promptly requisitioned her for duty and ordered a certain Captain Dunbar, commander of the small brig-sloop *Spencer* (a vessel of the same rate as *De Braak*), and forty-five of his men to take charge of her. Dunbar was instructed to sail for the Delaware in *Vixen* accompanied by—and under the protection of—*Hind*.[27] Although the two Royal Navy ships, which had sailed on September 3, may have aroused local interest upon their arrival off the Delaware twelve days later, Captain Dunbar and his men, in any event, were apparently not interested in local concerns. They set to work immediately after having taken a pilot on board to see their ship safely into the bay. On the day following their arrival, the salvors prepared to run sweeps with a thirteen-inch cable slung between their two ships, in hopes of thus snagging *De Braak* and pulling the cable beneath her hull. Then, using wind and tide to their advantage, they would loosen the wreck from the sucking muds of the bottom and drag her into shoal water to be pumped out. The effort was rewarded with immediate results: the brig was quickly snared, no small feat for vessels dragging under sail. On September 17, one of *De Braak*'s anchors, with cable and buoy, was salvaged. The occasion undoubtedly spurred hopes of further success in recovering the ship itself—that is, until one thirteen-inch cable was lost "while endeavoring to raise the Braak."[28]

On the 18th, Lieutenant Larcom recorded the fact that the small bower anchor recovered on the 17th was cut in half and used to weigh down sweep lines for another try. Although a studding-sail boom was next to be recovered, the effort to get a firm grip again on the brig ended in failure. Another attempt was ordered. The two ends of the severed cable were clinched in preparation for yet another sweep. If the salvagers could winch down on *De Braak* after snagging her at low water, it might still be possible to utilize the force of the rising tide to help pry her loose from the mud.

On September 19, the third and final attempt was made to recover the wreck. Again, the weight of the hull and the terrific restraining force imposed on it by the muds defeated the effort. The strain was simply too great. This time the cable and the small bower sweep were carried away entirely. Frustrated after four back-breaking days of work, the British finally surrendered *De Braak* to the Delaware. That night Lieutenant Larcom recorded the following note in his log: "At 11 gave it over, finding we could not lift here [*sic*] and our spare cables being broke. Lost kedge anchor & 6. Saild, Vixon [*sic*] in company."[29] At 11:30 P.M., September 19, *Hind* and *Vixen* departed for Halifax under a somber cloud of defeat. Upon arriving there on October 1, they were met by a small boat, dispatched from the navy yard to offload the blocks, cables, and other salvage gear requisitioned for the job, even as the would-be salvors reported immediately to Admiral Vandeput.[30]

Despite the abortive expedition, the admiral considered the salvage attempt to have been carried out as thoroughly as possible. He later wrote that he was completely satisfied that Dunbar had used every practicable means to recover His Majesty's property, and he recommended that no further efforts be expended. The Admiralty board was in complete agreement. *De Braak*, already an old vessel by navy standards, was written off as not worth any further expenses.[31] For Vandeput, perhaps, approval of the failed effort, whatever its shortcomings, was a sensible move with respect to the *De Braak* tragedy and the cloud such accidents tended to generate over officialdom. There was, after all, a war on and the disposition of a rich prize to be dealt with. HMS *Assistance* and *Hind* were again free for patrol duty, perhaps even to capture more French and Spanish prizes. And Admiral George Vandeput, as commander of the station to which *De Braak* had officially been assigned, would be one of the principal beneficiaries of the sale of *Xavier* and her cargo.

The goods and materials aboard *Xavier* were of immense value to the British, especially in the midst of a war with France and Spain. The 200 tons of copper would be readily used in England; much of it would undoubtedly become sheathing for the bottoms of His Majesty's fleet or would be employed in other war-related products. The cocoa, hitherto a luxury item but more recently a staple on the English market, would find eager buyers in both Halifax and England. Indeed, *Xavier*'s cargo, as well as the profits derived from the sale of the ship itself, *would* prove to be a veritable treasure.

Later folktales notwithstanding, *Don Francisco Xavier*, with her valuable copper and cocoa, was undoubtedly the only treasure ship HM Sloop-of-War *De Braak* had ever taken. As the late Howard I. Chapelle and his British research associate, M. E. S. Laws, would point out in their study of the two vessels, published by the Smithsonian Institution in 1963, *Xavier* had last sailed from Río de la Plata in South America, a place which was anything but a transshipment center for treasure. Had there been large amounts of gold, silver bullion, or specie (which, in the glory days of the great Spanish treasure fleets of the sixteenth and seventeenth centuries, might well have been carried aboard merchant galleons), in 1798 it would have been found only on armed frigates sailing in convoys of three or more ships of war. And if, by some freak incident, treasure had been placed on board *Xavier*, it would undoubtedly have been transferred to her captor for better protection after the capture. Yet such an exchange could not have taken place without the knowledge and participation of the crew, whose prize claims would certainly have survived in the official record.[32] But there were never any official statements about treasure made by the survivors in Admiralty court or during the prize proceedings, nor by the British consul in Philadelphia, Admiral Vandeput, the Royal Navy, or any representatives of the British government.

Ironically, the rational desire of the Royal Navy to recover its own valuable property, a warship sunk in moderately shallow waters whose mast would mark her gravesite for several months afterward, would soon find a peculiar niche in the *De Braak* legend. It would eventually be interpreted by some to mean that *Hind* and *Vixen* had only sought the ship's recovery because of a vast treasure that purportedly went down with her. Gradually, the notion would become accepted as fact, even by reputable historians.

In October 1799, the first announcement of payment of prize monies resulting from the sale of *Xavier* and her cargo was published at Halifax. For the survivors of the *De Braak* disaster, this was long-awaited news; like most sailors in the Royal Navy, they had gone to sea for prize money. Indeed, at overseas stations such as Halifax, where ships could not be paid off, prize money was frequently the only source of income for seamen, while in home ports it was the stuff upon which local economies were based. The chance to acquire prize money was a principal factor in the development of competent fighting crews for the Royal Navy. "You can't think how keen our men are," wrote one admiral. "The hope of prize money makes them happy [and] a signal for a sail brings them all on deck." The abiding prospect of a reward for their services over and above their meager wages, and all that such temporary riches promised, was perhaps best illustrated by a popular ballad of 1781, first sung after the French had suffered a major naval defeat. It had been chanted by a crowd of women at Gosport beach when the French prisoners were brought ashore by the victorious English seamen.

> Don't you see the ships a-coming?
>   Don't you see them in full sail?
> Don't you see the ships a-coming
>   With the prizes at their tail?
> Oh! my little rolling sailor,
>   Oh! my little rolling he;
> I do love a jolly sailor,
>   Blithe and merry might he be.
> Sailors, they get all the money,
>   Soldiers, they get none but brass;

I do love a jolly sailor,
   Soldiers, they may kiss my arse.
Oh! my little rolling sailor,
   Oh! my little rolling he;
I do love a jolly sailor,
   Soldiers may be damned for me.[33]

Prize money was important to the officers as well, all the way up to the commander in chief. Many senior-level officers, such as Admiral Vandeput, became wealthy men without having to lift a finger. The common seaman might make a few pounds, perhaps enough to keep him in liquor and women for a week or two. The junior commissioned officers might make a few score pounds. The captain's share might be in the hundreds, but the admiral could make thousands since, as Rodger points out, "he shared in all the prizes taken on his station" whether he was present at the captures or not. For flag officers, to secure and retain command of a rich station, "and to keep it free from the intrusions of a superior, was the ideal of luck."[34] For those serving in the Royal Navy, from the lowliest ship's boy to the commander in chief, prize money was everything.

At Halifax, payment of the prize money derived from the sale of *Xavier* and her cargo was carried out at the establishment of Messrs. W. Goodall and J. Turner, on behalf of the prize agents Grassie and Company. Recalls for those unable to collect their shares would be held at the same place on the first Monday of each month from October 1799 onward. However, owing to the probability that many of *De Braak*'s surviving crew members had by that time shipped out aboard other vessels, an announcement was published in the British press that the unclaimed shares of prize money due to second, fourth, and fifth classes of officers and seamen, or their legal representatives, would be paid off at the Crown and Sugar Loaf on Garlick Hill, London, on March 13, 1800.[35]

Although the prize money was paid out, most of the *De Braak* survivors were unable to collect their back wages. On December 1, 1799, the commander of HM Sloop-of-War *Dasher*, of eighteen guns, Captain George Tobin, reported to the Admiralty that among his crew were ten seamen from *De Braak* who had been informed by the Navy Board that they would be unable to collect back pay until after a formal court martial had been held.[36] On December 22, Admiralty Secretary Evan Nepean dispatched a communiqué to Admiral Vandeput, asking if he had ordered a court martial to inquire into the loss of *De Braak* and, if not, ordering him to do so at his first opportunity and to forward the court's verdict to him.[37] In the meantime, certain steps were taken to rectify the back pay owed to Tobin's men. On January 9, 1801, the *De Braak* pay book maintained by the Admiralty noted that at least eight of the ten *De Braak* seamen aboard *Dasher* had been paid the wages in arrears.[38]

Not until February 23, 1801, well over two and a half years after the loss of
De Braak, was a formal inquiry (but not a court martial) conducted by the
Navy Board. The proceedings were anything but intensive (which would not
have been the case had the brig been carrying gold or silver). Only one statement, that of quarter gunner Samuel Mitchell, was secured. Mitchell, in fact,
would be the only eyewitness crew member to tender an official report. In his
short deposition he provided details concerning the loss, as well as an outline
of general information about the ship and her crew, but he made no mention
at all of treasure. Nor were there to be any official recriminations. The entire
event was deemed an unavoidable accident.[39]

On August 7, 1802, execution of Drew's will was granted to his brother Stephen, a "creditor" of the deceased, who sought probate from Lydia and from
Charles and Samuel Watkins, executors of James Drew's estate. On June 27,
1803, after the necessary trans-Atlantic legalities had been resolved, the will
was finally proved, with Stephen Drew assuming control of James's estate and
share of the prize money.[40]

The loss of three Drews—James, John, and young James William—within
the space of one year would not go unmemorialized by their families either in
England or the United States. In Saltash, the Reverend Stephen Drew and
other members of the family erected an elegant marble plaque in St. Nicholas
Church, a venerable twelfth-century place of worship overlooking the Tamar
River. The six-foot memorial was mounted on the church wall adjacent to the
elevated pulpit where all of the parishioners could see it. The raised marble
portraits of the three Drews, carved in the classic Romanesque style so popular throughout Europe, were at the apex of the plaque, with the artist's
impressions of the two disasters which had taken their lives carved below. The
memorial's inscription, apparently carved by a stonecutter who had never
heard of (or could not spell the name of) the remote bay half a world away in
which James Drew had died, read:

> Sacred to the Memory of
> JOHN & JAMES DREW, Captains in his *Majestys Navy*,
> Also JAMES W.M DREW, *Acting Lieutenant*,
> The First & Third were Unfortunately drowned in cruising
> Cawsand Bay Jan.Y 11.
> 1798 the Second was also Unfortunately Shipwrecked & Drowned
> in Sailing up the Debaware
> 25th. *May Following.*
> *This Memorial is Erected by the Surviving Afflicted Relatives.*[41]

Grief-stricken Lydia Drew did not fail to honor her husband, even after re-
marrying two years later. In 1832, she erected a memorial, a rectangular mon-

ument set in the graveyard of St. Peter's Episcopal Church, on the west corner of Second and Market streets in Lewes. Again a stonecutter erred, recording the date of Drew's death as June 10 instead of May 25.

Here Rest
the Remains of
CAPTAIN JAMES DREW
who commanded
HIS BRITANNIC MAJESTY'S
sloop of war *De Braak*
in which he lost his life
when she foundered at the
Capes of Delaware
the 10th June 1798
He was beloved for his virtues
and admired for his bravery
His affectionate Relic
has erected this Monument
to perpetuate his
MEMORY[42]

For the Drew family, the *De Braak* tragedy was over. For the Royal Navy, the books had been closed ten years earlier, on May 14, 1822. On that date, Sarah Williams, widow of *De Braak*'s boatswain, finally received payment, long overdue, for services rendered by her husband while a crew member aboard the doomed warship.[43]

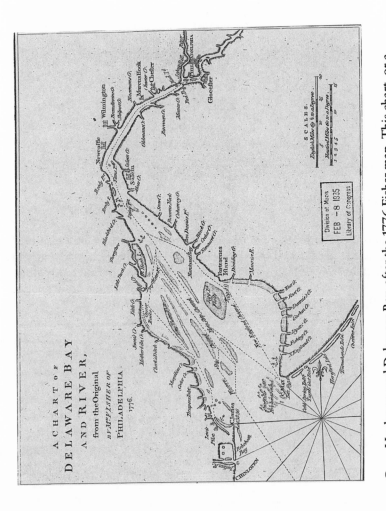

Cape Henlopen and Delaware Bay, after the 1776 Fisher map. This chart, or a facsimile, was employed by the first treasure hunting expeditions to search for *De Braak. (Library of Congress)*

PART TWO

I propose to land the treasure in Philadelphia.

Dr. Seth Pancoast, July 1888

Children's Dreams and Old Men's Fantasies

Gilbert McCracken shielded his eyes from the sun as he gazed northward across the silver dunes of Cape Henlopen. Not far ahead he could discern the great whitewashed, hexagonal lighthouse which had served for years as his beacon and, on occasion, his salvation. As a veteran bay and river pilot, he had depended on the structure by day as a landmark and reference; at night, he had been guided by its light through the ever-shifting channels and shoals lacing the mouth of Delaware Bay. His was an honorable profession, which he hoped would be taken up by his then fourteen-year-old son, Henry, who had come along with him. Perhaps someday the lighthouse that had guided him so well would also serve as his son's beacon. It was, after all, more than just a light: it was a symbol of continuity, a stable benchmark on the banks of an ever-changing world. At that moment, however, there was pressing business to attend to—business which had been put off for far too long.

As McCracken and his son trudged across the sands, the old pilot might well have repeated for young Henry the oft-told tale of the tragedy which had occurred nearly seven years earlier, when His Britannic Majesty's man-of-war *De Braak* had gone to the bottom a mile or so from the lighthouse. The youth, who had been only seven years old at the time, although quite familiar with the story, was always eager to hear again the tale of the ragged Spaniards who had saved themselves by clinging to a battered old sea chest. He particularly enjoyed the part where his father told of saving the poor fellows, of taking them into his own home and offering them succor. His father, he knew, for some unknown reason had kept the old chest, perhaps as a memento of the event. It had belonged, as Henry would one day tell his own son, to none other than the commander of *De Braak*, Captain James Drew himself.

Henry had undoubtedly heard the village old-timers speculating endlessly over the possibility of sunken treasure resting in the hold of the hapless man-of-war. After all, she *had* taken a Spanish vessel—maybe even several—laden with a cargo of reputedly great value. The tales they told were, indeed, the stuff of children's dreams and old men's fantasies, and most took the treasure stories with a grain of salt. Young Henry was not so sure. Now that his father suddenly seemed intent on documenting the approximate position of the site, albeit seven years after the wreck, the youth's curiosity was piqued. Could there actually be treasure in the hold of the old ship, as the stories claimed? Had his father been merely biding his time until local interest had waned enough to permit him to take bearings on the wreck's location without raising suspicion?

Despite young Henry's speculations and the tales of the townfolk, the location of the wreck site was, in fact, well known to many mariners in the area, almost from the day the ship had gone down. For months the wreck's masts had stood above the water, clearly marking her final resting place for anyone and everyone to see. Indeed, her bones had made their own distinct impressions on the environment. "For many years after the catastrophe," it was reported, "the water was seen to eddy around the spot where De Braak went down, going about in 'sucksation,' as the sailors used to say."[1] After the disaster there had been plenty of time for pilot Allen, the survivors aboard *Don Francisco Xavier*, or anyone else who might have happened upon the scene to have taken the wreck's bearings. The British salvage teams had experienced little difficulty in relocating the site when they had descended upon the Delaware in late 1798. Thus, the actual motivation for McCracken's return to record the location seven years after the tragedy, subsequent speculations notwithstanding, remains obscure. In later years, his objective would seem entirely clear to his descendants. They would state unequivocally that he had hiked out to the Cape Henlopen Lighthouse to "set the bearings of the wreck for the purpose of aiding some future efforts, as he told his son, to raise the hulk and its uncounted treasures."[2] And, as any competent pilot (or surveyor) would have done, he used as his datum the loftiest permanent landmark available.

In the years to come, no one bothered to ask, for the record, why a seasoned mariner who knew the Delaware perhaps as well as any man alive had waited so long before attempting to record the location of *De Braak*'s final resting place. Nor did anyone bother to question why he had not attempted to recover the treasure for himself—if a treasure existed at all.

The Cape Henlopen Lighthouse, the third permanent light station to be erected in British America, was a simple but sturdy affair.[3] Its conception was first made public in an advertisement in the *New York Mercury* on January 4, 1762, when "a Scheme of a Lottery for Raising 3,000 pounds to be applied to [the] erection of a lighthouse on Cape Henlopen" was announced. The station was intended to be the permanent replacement for a crude wooden lighthouse built about 1725. On November 27, 1762, the Pennsylvania government ordered two hundred acres of land on top of the cape to be surveyed for the benefit of the lighthouse project by one John Penn. Commissioners were appointed to raise additional funds, by means of both subscription and lottery, with which to maintain the light and navigational buoys at the mouth of the Delaware. In 1764 Henry Fisher, an acknowledged leader of the brotherhood of Delaware River pilots and a resident of Lewes, was asked to select the site for the new facility. Soon stone, brick, and other building materials were being unloaded in Lewes for the largest construction project ever mounted on the cape to that time.[4]

Tradition has it that the massive granite blocks intended for the tower were carried down from the Brandywine Hills, while the bricks for the keeper's cottage were brought in from England by ship. The stones and bricks were unloaded at an ancient wharf on Lewes Creek and from there transported by boat up the little waterway (whose course at that time was much further to the east than in later years) to within a mile of the proposed site. They were then conveyed across the Great Dune, probably by oxen, to the construction site, situated well inland amid a sparse pine forest. When the lighthouse was finally completed in 1765, and its lamp lit for the first time, the base of the 115-foot tower stood sixty-five feet above sea level. It was the loftiest man-made structure on the Atlantic Coast between Sandy Hook, New Jersey, and the Virginia Capes.[5]

Until the American Revolution, the Cape Henlopen Light served as a reliable beacon to thousands of ships plying the hazardous maw of Delaware Bay. With the onset of hostilities, its strategic importance to navigation was underscored when it became a prime target for marauding British raiders bent on disrupting American commerce and shipping. The lighthouse was attacked. The wooden steps leading up to the tower were burned, along with the keeper's lodgings. Operations were discontinued for more than a decade. Then, in 1789, the United States government assumed control of such services by creating the Lighthouse Establishment, which immediately asserted authority over the dozen standing light stations on the Atlantic Coast, including the fire-scarred pharos at the mouth of the Delaware. After finally being repaired in 1792, the Cape Henlopen Light became once again the most important navigational landmark at the entrance to the busiest waterway in America. Its massive lantern, almost eight feet square and lit by no fewer than eight lamps, could be seen at night from ten leagues out to sea.[6]

Thirteen years later, as Gilbert McCracken and his son prepared to take bearings on the position of a sunken ship whose actual mission had been all but forgotten, even by those who had fielded her, the Cape Henlopen Lighthouse would become their datum and the key to one of the greatest treasure hunts ever mounted in American history—for a treasure that didn't exist.

Gilbert McCracken was a third-generation American, poured in the rugged mold of his seafaring grandfather and founder of the clan, Captain David

McCracken. Gilbert undoubtedly looked upon the Cape Henlopen Light with something akin to affection, for, like the lighthouse, he too had been born in 1765. Both had served well the mariners plying Delaware waters, and both were destined to claim a small piece of Delaware history as their own.

The tradition of piloting on the Delaware, which McCracken had chosen as his life's work, was a well-established one. The earliest bay and river pilots had been Nanticoke Indians of the Leni-Lenape tribe, who had guided Dutch and British explorers past the shifting shoals of the bay's entrance. The Indians had continued in such employment for more than a century. As late as 1765, the year in which the Cape Henlopen Light had been lit, a minister of the Friends' Society, visiting the region for the first time, could write: "We made Cape Henlopen and a pilot came on board who proved to be a native Indian." The Indians, however, were by then being supplanted by whites, many of whom took up residence in the village of Lewes Town. This new breed of pilot was typified by hardworking, industrious men with such solid, simple names as Bailey Art, David Johnson, and Henry Fisher. They not only labored on the waters, but also engaged in other occupations ashore to supplement their meager incomes. Many became prominent citizens of the community as well as members of a tight, if competitive, fraternity. Most of those residing in Lewes lived close together in a row of houses referred to locally as Pilot Town, which bordered on the southwest bank of Lewes Creek. From this convenient location they could scurry to their vessels, make sail, and set off with minimal delay in spirited races to be the first to meet incoming ships. A few pilots were less than qualified.[7] "Vessels off the Delaware," noted one cautionary navigational guide, "upon hoisting a jack at the foremast-head, will be immediately furnished with a pilot.... None are to be depended on, unless they have branches and a certificate from the Board of Wardens of Philadelphia."[8]

Gilbert McCracken had come to the Delaware to lay down roots and had methodically done so. He had built a home in Lewes, had earned his pilot's certificate, and had set up practice. In September 1790, he had married a Philadelphia girl named Mary Webster and nine months later found himself the proud father of a son and heir, Henry F. McCracken.[9] Like most men who made their living from the sea, he paid strict attention to every nuance of tide, wind, and weather, as well as the comings and goings of ships and the men who sailed them. In his line of work, he had undoubtedly witnessed many maritime catastrophes. But none had been quite so noteworthy as the loss of *De Braak*.

Gilbert McCracken's descendants liked to tell and retell the story of his intimate involvement in the legendary vessel's story. Their tales would not be diminished by time. Whether McCracken actually believed the rumors of treasure running rampant or even whether he had actually offered assistance to the Spanish survivors has never been proved. That his descendants and a multitude of others believed he did, however, is a fact beyond question. And it was a wonderful yarn.

The reliability of McCracken's effort to document the location of *De Braak*'s final resting place, regardless of his motive for doing so, was never doubted. Perhaps he had been consumed by a belated passion concerning the site's potential as a treasure trove. Perhaps, with local rumors increasing in an apparently geometric progression, he merely wished to play it safe, intending to try his own hand at salvage some time later. More than likely, he was simply concerned to document the location of the wreck as evidence of its position began to fade, as any good pilot would have done with any potential hazard to navigation. For whatever reason, in or about the year 1805, Gilbert Mc-Cracken and his son plotted the bearings of the wreck in fourteen fathoms of water. From Cape Henlopen Lighthouse: East northeast by north one half east, a mile and a half to sea. With a lead pencil he prudently transcribed the data on a sheet of paper, which was later slipped between the pages of the safest—or, possibly, handiest—book available, the McCracken family Bible.[10]

Unwittingly, by scribbling down the bearings (which were, in fact, something less than accurate), Gilbert McCracken had planted a seed which, bequeathed to several successive generations of his own progeny and to innumerable others, flowered as a legacy of unfruitful hopes and dreams based upon a myth. For some, ready to commit their personal fortunes and those of many others in pursuit of a treasure trove whose existence was inferred from this dubious map, the treasure hunt would become an obsession, fed by an insatiable passion for gold and silver. For most, their zeal and greed would not be grounded in fact but in folklore and, later, spurred on by outright fictions and pseudo-historical concoctions created for the purpose of sustaining the lust for treasure. But always there would be blind faith, rooted in Gilbert McCracken's bearings and unquestioned belief in the legend of *De Braak*. For all who sought her elusive remains, however, McCracken's legacy would net only years of hard and dangerous work, bitter acrimony, unending legal nightmares, and, in the end, financial ruin.

S I X

Every Contrivance for Wrecking

For nearly seven decades the *De Braak* legend smoldered and spread, filling the voids of casual meetings and backyard gossip along the Delaware waterfront. It was a superb subject for the local habit of "yarning," a community ritual practiced in every rural area and small town of the state. Most communities had their favorite yarns, and shipwreck-and-treasure tales were usually prominent among them. A particularly distinctive feature of Delaware yarn-telling was that the teller never duplicated another man's tale, even though the plot line was the same.[1] The result was much the same as in the age-old game of "whispers," where a circle of children would pass a story around, each child whispering it into the next one's ear. By the time the story had come full circle, it bore little resemblance to the original.

And so it was with the tale of the loss of *De Braak*. Fact became subtly and inextricably interwoven with fiction. Rumors and folklore became accepted truths as the memory of events and dates grew foggy in the minds of aging men. Old-timers, for instance, recalled events surrounding the British salvage efforts which, over the passage of years, became more twisted and distorted with each telling. By the 1880s, several of Lewes's hoarier citizens were certain that the salvage effort, which had been carried out in 1798, had actually occurred just before the War of 1812. "An English frigate," the story went, "accompanied by a sloop, came to the mouth of the bay to raise the wreck. They bridled it with the stoutest hawsers, but they never budged her."[2] As time passed, the account of the pre-War of 1812 salvage effort became even more garbled and acquired a patina of truth all its own, complete with fictional names for the vessels and even a second salvage attempt.[3]

Gilbert McCracken's documentation of the wreck's approximate position remained an open family "secret" for years, a story which became an integral part of the *De Braak* legend. In later years, Gilbert's grandson, Samuel Storer McCracken, also a Lewes pilot and sailor, inherited the family Bible from his father, Henry. But no one considered the possibility of actually recovering the wreck and its reported riches until after the Civil War and the advent of modern diving technology.[4]

In 1867, Captain Charles Sanborn, "a noted submarine diver," learned of *De Braak*'s alleged treasure and began to contemplate securing a concession from the United States government, which then legally claimed title to all abandoned shipwrecks, to raise it. Sanborn began to conduct his own research into the loss of the ship. He traveled to Halifax, Nova Scotia, specifically "for the purpose of getting information." His investigation soon bore fruit when he apparently discovered a newspaper account published in 1798 which more than titillated his interest. The brief article had reported:

> H.B.M. sloop-of-war Braak, we are informed, was capsized off the capes of Delaware, returning from a successful cruise of the Spanish Main. She had on board 70 tons of copper and an immense amount of treasure, consisting of gold and silver bars and precious stones.[5]

Captain Sanborn, undoubtedly elated by his discovery, traveled back to the United States soon afterward, it was said, with the fullest intention "of returning the following spring to begin [salvage] operations." But before he could pursue his objective, he fell ill and died.[6] Word of his discovery, however, did not pass away with him, but added even greater plausibility to the legend.

A decade later, in 1877, a British frigate was said to have appeared off Lewes and "hovered for days over the spot where the De Braak went down." Whatever her actual intentions might have been (the site was, after all, a common anchorage), the simple villagers of Lewes paid the visitor little attention, until, that is, the frigate's steward, having apparently jumped ship and settled in Lewes, reported "that [the British] left a dumb buoy over a mound about a mile from the [Delaware] Breakwater, and nearly two miles northeast from Cape Henlopen." With some elderly residents recalling that the location was in the vicinity of *De Braak*'s purported resting place, the immediate assumption made was that the British had marked the spot for a later, surreptitious recovery effort. Again the old legends of treasure were dusted off, told, and retold, with each retelling taking on its own peculiar twist. Treasure fever swept through Lewes like an epidemic. And among those most severely infected was Sam McCracken, owner of the McCracken family Bible and its page of cryptic navigational data.[7]

In the spring of 1879, the epidemic gained national attention when it was reported in the *New York Times* that three men, "uncommunicative as to who they are," appeared in Lewes and began inquiring about the wreck. It was evident to the locals that their objective was "to ascertain the probability of recovering the riches from the wrecked ship." One of the men revealed that during a visit to nearby Rehoboth Beach in the summer of 1878, he had received positive information that a great amount of treasure had gone down with several ill-fated ships along the coast between Cape Henlopen and Rehoboth. This report of treasure, along "with evidence that much of it may be hard to access," led him to conduct further inquiries. All three men were said to possess the various skills needed to effect a salvage. One had some knowledge of civil engineering, while another was a professional diver who, two years earlier, had been employed by the United States government. The third was reputed to be the brains of the group. The information they were able to elicit, however, was little more than folklore.[8]

When the *New York Times* picked up the story and published it under the provocative headline "Seeking Sunken Money. Hunting for Gold Buried in the Atlantic," it did so with great panache. "It has been a great many years since the wrecks in question occurred," read the *Time*'s report,

> and no doubt by this time the sunken vessels are covered by the constantly changing channels, with nothing visible to mark their resting places. It has been said that the Delaware seacoast undergoes more changes than any other ocean shore. South of Cape Henlopen the waves of the Atlantic now roll over spots where once large islands, covered with woods, were to be seen, and where ships once could easily sail there are now shoals, rapidly becoming islands. These freaks on the part of nature make it doubtful if the adventurers will ever set eyes on the sunken riches. But while it may be true, and it very likely is, that the money is beyond human reach, the fact that it lies there cannot be gainsaid. Its existence is proved by history and recent events.[9]

The "history," as reported by the *Times*, was a heady blend of fact and fiction. According to the newspaper, the most prominent of the Delaware treasure wrecks was a French ship called *De Brock*, an armed vessel which had been commanded by a young American named James Drew and manned by a French crew. *De Brock* had reportedly done excellent service during the early part of the American Revolution and had made several captures. In about the third or fourth year of the war, she had conveyed a "large quantity of gold coins and arms from France to America, the arms belonging to the colonial forces and the money secretly loaned to the colonies."[10] Although she had been chased by several British frigates, she had managed to reach the safety of Sinepuxent Bay, near the site of modern Ocean City, Maryland. There the money and munitions were landed and conveyed in wagons up the Delmarva peninsula to Wilmington under an armed escort of Delaware militia commanded by Colonel David Hall, accompanied by a cohort of French soldiers who had come over aboard *De Brock*. When the caravan arrived at Wilmington, the arms were disposed of according to orders and the money was stored in the cellar of a house occupied by French officers. Both the Frenchmen and the money remained comfortably ensconced in the house throughout the winter. In the spring, however, as the troops began to mobilize for the coming season's campaigns, robbers entered the house in the dead of night and absconded with the entire hoard. The thieves left no clues, and no arrests were made, although suspects aplenty were to be had.

One suspect was named Cheney Clow, a noted Tory guerrilla, who was said to be "a bold and heartless ruffian" and a man whose "reckless doings and hair breadth escapes still live in tradition." Clow, however, had been hanged for murder at the close of the war, and his possible possession of the treasure remained a mystery.[11] In the meantime, *De Brock* had experienced her own problems. Drew had remained in Sinepuxent Bay, patiently awaiting the departure of his pursuers. Soon after they left, he had put out from the bay, promptly captured two British prizes laden with valuable cargo, including a large number of coins, and then had sailed for Lewes to take on supplies. When nearing the mouth of Delaware Bay, Captain Drew had committed his ship to the care of Andrew Allen, "one of the best pilots about Lewes." With a stiff wind coming on, Allen had immediately ordered *De Brock*'s topsails furled and clew lines hauled.[12] Over Allen's protests, "Drew, full of vanity and, it is said, also full of liquor," ordered all sails reset and prepared to round the cape. The warship promptly "capsized, filled, and went down, taking with her the two prizes and the gold they carried in their holds." The story in the *Times* grew more lurid with every line.

> Some of the crew succeeded in getting into one of the boats, and many of the drowning men swam to it, only to have their fingers or hands cut off with knives and swords, as they caught hold of the gunwales of the boat and endeavored to clamber in, and thus were left to the mercy of the waves. Very few reached the shore alive. Drew was washed in lifeless, and buried in the old Episcopal church-yard with a monument above him, the inscription upon which relates how he died. Allen survived, and from him the story of the untold wealth that went to the bottom with the De Brock has been handed down from generation to generation, and is often related to the Summer tourist by the rough old wreckers with a gusto that is quite amazing. From this wreck much gold has, from time to time been washed ashore, and it is said that a few days after the wreck the father of William Marshall, the Lieutenant-Commander of the post at Lewes during the War of 1812, and several others, secured enough of the precious metal to make them rich for the time being. This came ashore on fragments of the ship, and was picked up on the most seaward point of Cape Henlopen.[13]

The litany of treasure-ship disasters, according to the *New York Times*, did not end with *De Brock*. "Some time between the Revolution and the War of 1812," it was reported,

> an American brig, bound from Liverpool to Baltimore, with specie on board, was wrecked upon a shoal lying out from Synepuxette Beach, and was beaten to pieces by the heavy surf. A gold laden Spanish vessel was also wrecked upon the Hen and Chicken Shoals, just off the beach south of the capes. This is one of the most treacherous and fatal beaches upon the whole Atlantic coast. More wrecks have occurred here than upon any similar extent of shore with which the United States Life-Saving Service have anything to do. Upon this beach, where so often

have been found the corpses of unfortunate mariners, gold and silver coin has been washed up by the waves. No later than last Fall, after the terrific storm in October, two pieces of gold coin and a Spanish dollar were found near the edge of the surf. This, more than anything else, has led the party already alluded to, to think that there is some likelihood of the recovery of a quantity of the lost treasure.[14]

Finally stirred to action by the interest of outsiders, McCracken "set about to put his heirloom to use." For the next year he would spend much of his time attempting to launch an effort to recover the alleged booty. Finally, he secured the interest of the International Submarine Company, a New Haven, Connecticut, salvage firm backed by a consortium of Philadelphia and New York investors. He persuaded the corporate financiers to underwrite the venture by promising to disclose the wreck's location if the ISC provided money, men, and equipment.[15]

Convinced of the validity of McCracken's information, in 1880 the ISC moved with resolution to secure a salvage "concession" from the Federal government under Section 3755 of the Revised Statutes of the U.S. Code. In return for granting the concession, the government would receive ten percent of the earnings, to be paid into the United States Treasury. More than $30,000 was then spent in a fruitless effort to locate the wreck. The failure proved nearly fatal to the corporation, whose stock plummeted from a high of twenty-five dollars to a low of seven cents per share. By 1886, the ISC, the first corporation to face the specter of defeat in pursuit of *De Braak*'s mythical treasure, was in desperate straits. As the company teetered on the verge of collapse, with its directors on the point of "throwing up the job," a most unexpected Philadelphia investor came to the rescue. His name was Dr. Seth Pancoast.[16]

A well-known physician, anatomist, and cabalist, Pancoast was born on July 28, 1823, in Darby, Pennsylvania. The son of Stephen Pancoast, a paper manufacturer, and Anna Stroud Pancoast, and a direct descendant of one of the settlers who had come to America with William Penn, Seth had spent his early years in business. At the age of 27, however, in October 1850, he began the study of medicine at the University of Pennsylvania, from which he earned an M.D. degree in 1852. The following year he was made a professor of anatomy at Pennsylvania Female Medical College (later to become the Women's Medical College of Pennsylvania). In 1854, he accepted a chair of anatomy at the Pennsylvania Medical College, a position which he held until 1859 when he retired and became an emeritus professor. Private practice and writing then consumed much of the doctor's time. Pancoast was a prolific author. In 1855, he wrote *An Original Treatise on the Curability of Consumption by Medical Inhalation and Adjunct Remedies*; three years later he published *Onanism-Spermatorrhoea* and *Porneio-Kalogynomia-Pathology*, which were followed in

1859 by the *Ladies's Medical Guide and Marriage Friend* and, in 1873, *The Cholera: Its History, Cause, Symptoms and Treatment*. His interests were not limited to medicine, but extended to theosophy and particularly the study of the occult. His personal library on the subject was considered the largest and most complete in the United States.

For more than a decade, Pancoast devoted himself to studying the Cabala, an occult theosophy of rabbinical origin, widely transmitted in medieval Europe and based on esoteric interpretations of the Hebrew Scriptures. The ideas and concepts gleaned from his cabalistic readings, curiously enough, had soon become synthesized with his medical and scientific interests, leading to the production of a series of extraordinary works. In 1877, the first of his published treatises on this subject appeared: *The Kabbala; or the True Science of Light; an Introduction to the Philosophy and Theosophy of the Ancient Sages.* Pancoast's work was said to be the first book written in English which attempted to explain the "Ten Sephiroth," providing the mystical interpretation of the Holy Scriptures contained therein. This work was followed soon afterward by another inauspiciously titled study, *Blue and Red Light: or, Light and Its Rays as Medicine; Showing that Light is the Original and Sole Source of Life, as It Is the Source of All the Physical and Vital Forces of Nature, and that Light is Nature's Own and Only Remedy for Disease, and Explaining How to Apply the Red and Blue Rays in Curing the Sick and Feeble.* Although seeming to suggest a new and powerful therapeutic idea, the book was actually a cabalistic work in which mystery, science, religion, and medicine were incomprehensibly interwoven.

While working as a teacher, doctor, and author, Pancoast had also found time for three marriages: the first, to Sarah Saunders Osborn; the second, to Susan George Osborn; and the third, to Carrie Almena Fernald. Each of his wives provided him with numerous children. Not surprisingly, the doctor's studies and his family dominated his life—until, that is, the hunt for *De Braak* became his all-consuming obsession.[17]

Seth Pancoast was not only a scholar, but also an entrepreneur, with connections and financial resources of his own. Yet the means by which he was induced to consider involving himself in the search for sunken treasure off Cape Henlopen can only be speculated upon. Perhaps he had learned of it at a stockholders meeting or had simply read about it in the *New York Times*. In 1887, it was reported that a mysterious "man named Teissweis assisted the doctor in his exploration and gave information which led to its discovery."[18] When convinced to lend a hand to the International Submarine Company's faltering efforts, however, Pancoast not only took an interest, he nearly took over! To prepare the way, he purchased 70,000 of the company's 400,000 shares of stock and agreed to furnish whatever capital would be necessary to conduct future searches, in return for which he expected to receive half of the treasure.[19]

In the fall of 1886, Dr. Seth Pancoast set out upon his first quest for HM Sloop-of-War *De Braak*. Like McCracken's coordinates and the embellished local tales of the disaster, however, other information available to the doctor was also woefully inadequate. According to his questionable sources, the warship he sought was believed to have been a privateer, 200 feet in length, and mounting twenty-two guns. That Pancoast's numbers were off by a mere 116 feet and by six guns mattered little, for there were distinct indications that the wreck still existed. It was not, he reported, buried beneath the silts of the Delaware, but resting upon them![20]

Only a few years before, while sweeping for lost anchors in the area, an oyster dredger had snagged and recovered an iron cannon weighing 1,200 pounds. When brought to the surface, its skin was quite soft from years of immersion, but, it was said, "exposure to the atmosphere . . . restored its normal condition." What intrigued Pancoast was not that the gun had somehow been miraculously restored, but that it had been located and raised by sweep lines. The implication was that the clay bottom of the bay was too dense to allow the cannon's burial, even though it had the specific gravity of iron. If a cannon of such weight could rest on the hard surface of the bay floor, he reasoned, why not an entire ship?[21]

Pancoast's information sounded authoritative to the press and to his fellow investors. In reality, however, he knew little about the nature of the treasure for which he searched. Once, when queried about how much booty the "privateer" had carried, he vaguely replied, "I don't know accurately. Probably about nine million dollars. I imagine it is in Spanish doubloons, as that was the form [in] which gold was generally sent to Spain."[22]

The 1886 Pancoast Expedition was conducted in strict secrecy. But the environment in which it was carried out was well known to every Lewes waterman. The bottom of Delaware Bay, in the regions where the doctor's explorations were initially conducted, was covered with a semisoft clay and not with the hardpan that he first assumed. The clay was "largely impregnated with the ooze of the ocean." There was, however, the salvor later pointed out, one glaring exception, an area where a ten-foot mound of sand had collected. "This mound," he reported to the press, "covers an area of about 120 by 35 feet, lying lengthwise across the mouth of the bay," at a depth of nearly sixty feet.[23]

When Pancoast began search operations to locate the mound with grapple irons, he discovered the suspect site approximately two and a half miles from Lewes, in nearly ten fathoms of water. The mound seemed provocative enough, but when a dumb buoy was discovered on the site, not even the stoical doctor could have remained entirely unruffled. The buoy was recovered by divers and found to be constructed from an ordinary nail keg attached to a galvanized wire, which was held in place on the site by a piece of pig iron. The keg floated ten feet beneath the surface of the water. But was it the same buoy allegedly placed there by the British frigate a decade before? And did the mound actually contain the last remains of *De Braak*?

"If anything had been needed to convince Dr. Pancoast," one newspaper article later noted, "that under the mound lay buried the wreck of the veritable *De Braak* and all her reputed wealth, the keg would have supplied it."[24] Pancoast was further enticed by the observations of hard-hat divers sent down to examine the site. "The bottom of the bay in this vicinity," he reported,

> is a hard clayish mud, very tenacious and hard to penetrate. By the action of the waves around are formed at the bottom of the sea, and in cases where there are no constructions mounds are always oval on top. At the place where the wreck is located, however, the mound is hollow on top, indicating conclusively . . . the presence of a wreck. A further proof was afforded when a diver thrust a sharp-pointed iron rod into the top of the mound. The presence of sand was shown by the fact that the rod could be driven in for its length, whereas on the hard clay soil nearby it would penetrate only a few inches. That the wreck of the ship was imbedded in the soil was regarded as certain. It was proved beyond doubt that a vessel had sunk there, because several pieces of wood were dug out and hoisted onboard.[25]

Located in the center of the channel, where it received the brunt of the tide's ebb and flow, the configuration of the mound itself was even more intriguing to Pancoast than the timbers. On its north side, his divers had discovered a series of hillocks, which he believed marked the places where *De Braak*'s cannons had fallen after careening to one side of the vessel as she capsized, thus making "nuclei for deposits."[26] The recovered timbers had iron bolts attached to them. Pieces of the wood were sent to experts, who, Pancoast later reported, identified them as teak. The bolts, according to a promotional prospectus published in 1889, proved to be handmade ones, "such as were used one hundred years ago in the construction of ships, and not in the present day."[27] A new chapter in the *De Braak* legend—that of the teak-built ship—had been opened.[27]

Before any further explorations could be carried out, Pancoast, hindered by rough seas and sour weather, as well as lacking the "proper appliances" for actually excavating the mound, was obliged to terminate operations. Excited by his discoveries, however, he reported his success to the syndicate in glowing terms and immediately prepared for a second season on the site.[28] Quietly, he chartered the little Philadelphia tug *Startle*, a boat employed frequently by the Quarantine Service to inspect vessels arriving from foreign ports, and the *William P. Orr*, a "trim little two-masted schooner" from Lewes, under the command of Captain W. H. Chase.[29] The two vessels were outfitted "with every contrivance for wrecking," including a powerful sand pump, hoisting machines, and steam-driven air pumps for the divers.[30]

By early summer of 1887, Pancoast had hired two new hard-hat divers, Charles F. Pedrick of New Castle, Delaware, and Henry Dwyer, and their assistants, as well as five engineers under the direction of salvage expert Charles

F. Pike, and "a good sized crew" numbering ten men. Provisions for sixty days were procured and carried aboard the two vessels. For some undisclosed reason, the doctor believed the treasure to have been locked up in heavy, three-foot-square wooden boxes. Thus, he outfitted *Orr* with a powerful engine and a derrick to assist in raising the heavy containers. *Startle* was designated as tender and supply boat to the salvage schooner and outfitted accordingly. The dumb buoy, the doctor's "sacred treasure" which had been retrieved from the site in 1886, was permanently mounted as a good-luck charm over the cabin doorway of the machine-laden schooner.[31]

Pancoast was obsessed with security, as would be many expedition launchers who sailed in his wake. He secured an agreement from his men that under no condition would they leave the vessels while engaged in the project, a rule from which only the doctor and his superintendent, Mr. Pike, were considered exempt. And finally, the most elaborate precautions were taken to insure that no one could approach the project area undetected—measures which apparently included purchasing nearby beachfront property to prevent surprise visits by small boats launched from there.[32]

On Saturday, July 2, 1887, the second Pancoast Expedition set sail from the Christian Street Wharf, Philadelphia, bound for Lewes, Delaware. Despite the doctor's efforts to maintain secrecy, the event was noted, with appropriate fanfare, in the local media, which also provided its own distorted accounts of the *De Braak* disaster. One Delaware newspaper reported, prior to the departure, that the "privateer," having put into Lewes for water, had been sunk while departing by an American vessel. Her loss was well known, the skewed account read, because Samuel McCracken had been aboard just before she sank![33]

Within days of his arrival at Lewes, Pancoast was actively engaged in relocating the mound from bearings taken the previous year. Pedrick and Dwyer were ready to begin their work, which was as dangerous as any job could be. Yet the technology they employed had been much improved over that of earlier times. According to one contemporary account, the diver of the 1880s was "not the same man who went down twenty years before." Improvements in his diving paraphernalia enabled him to remain in the water for hours. The use of nonconducting felts for diving clothes and the swift circulation of warm air through the air tubes and helmet permitted dives to be made in relative warmth, with minimal loss of body heat.

> His armour [suit] is lighter, stronger and more comfortable. The air pump which supplies him with air is run by machinery, and not by hand. In place of the signal rope, he can now have a telephone inserted in his helmet, and can talk freely beneath the water as on dry land. He still uses the life line, but it is no longer a necessity. In twenty years, not an accident has happened to him in his submarine life, and even the possibility of a mischance seems far removed. One evil he can-

not overcome. The air which he breathes below the water is compressed, and exerts a peculiar and unhealthy influence upon the lungs and nerves. After many years, the injury becomes so great that he is compelled to leave his business forever. In some instances, he becomes the prey of consumption; in others, of paralysis; and, in still others, of a complete shattering of all physical forces.[34]

Despite such inherent dangers, Pancoast's divers were eager to begin the hunt. *William P. Orr* was brought to a three-point anchor over the site on Wednesday, July 6. At "the first trial," one of the divers reported that he had located the mound, which had been secretly marked the previous season by another dumb buoy. Within hours, a pump was activated, and by the following day, "sand covering the vessel was being removed at a rapid rate."[35]

The excavation soon settled into a routine, with divers descending each day at slack water and working for two to three hours to fix the metes and bounds of the site and then to remove the sands overlaying a part of the purported wreck with a hydraulic pump. Although his divers were operating in an environment of nearly zero visibility, Pancoast announced on July 8, that "nothing but the ribs of the pirate ship remain. The deck has fallen in, worms have long since eaten the timbers, and the only parts remaining are those covered with copper or with copper paint."[36] Ignoring the evidence (copper paint was not used on ship hulls in 1798, nor was *De Braak* a pirate ship), Pancoast was ebulliently optimistic in his predictions for success.

> I expect to clear up everything in sixty days. We will not be interrupted at all, as we own the land adjacent to the place where the wreck lies. No one can come near us without our permission. We are working hard, and will push through as fast as possible.[37]

Despite his advanced age, Pancoast labored tirelessly, personally superintending all operations. He could be seen going in and out of his hotel in Lewes two or three times a day. Local residents wondered out loud about his stamina, as the 64-year-old man strode across the hot, sandy waste that skirted Lewes's waterfront for over a mile to the Old Dominion Company's pier, where the tug *Startle* awaited his orders. Observers noted that he was as "quick and skillful" in moving about the vessel as any sailor of less than half his age, unperturbed by the blistering sun, the occasional storm, or the sailor's fare of tasteless hardtack biscuits.[38] As the days progressed, and the much-heralded treasure failed to appear, many in Lewes began to shake their heads at the unflappable doctor's enterprise. He would simply smile wryly and remind them that the town's most famous son, Governor Rodney, from whose house Captain Drew's body had been taken for burial, used to walk the Henlopen beach and point to the spot where *De Braak* went down, saying that enough wealth was buried there to make every man, woman, and child in the town independent for life. The doctor could afford to be tolerant of nonbelievers, for he was quietly content in the conviction that the lion's share of the great treasure trove would soon be his.[39]

By July 25, the parameters of the site had been explored, and handfuls of decayed wood had been recovered from exposed areas cleared by hydraulic washing. Next, a clam bucket, affectionately dubbed "the masher," was "industriously" employed to remove five to six feet of sand covering the site preparatory to finally clearing the hull. The last stage would be the deployment of a hydraulic suction pump, powerful enough to remove the remaining sands and sediments. These would be pumped upon the deck of the *Orr*, where, "by the aid of a seine, [they would] be carefully scrutinized."[40]

Pancoast, by now estimating that the project would take another six or seven weeks to complete, expected the total cost to reach $20,000. His personal expenses had already surpassed seventy-five dollars per day, but, it was noted, "he is paying it out cheerfully, for he confidently expects to find from five to seven million dollars' worth of precious metal," depending upon how many Spanish galleons *De Braak* had taken. A galleon, the doctor was now quick to point out, usually carried about $3,000,000. He estimated that during the last years of the eighteenth century, Spanish America had sent not less than $30,000,000 annually to the mother country. Much of it had been captured by British privateers, such as *De Braak*.[41]

Despite Pancoast's optimism, zeal, and leadership, and the national attention which had come to focus on him, his efforts were bearing bitter fruit. Money was tight. One of the divers, Henry Dwyer, brought suit against both Pancoast and the owners of the *Orr* for nonpayment of wages. Then, as the salvors worked on the site, one of the expensive sea anchors and a buoy, employed to mark the wreck, were lost and could not be relocated. By mid-September, with foul weather setting in, the site had failed to yield up any treasure and Pancoast was obliged to give up the search. The *Orr* returned to Philadelphia, and the *Startle* to her work as a quarantine inspection boat. The pumps and other machinery were put into storage for the winter in anticipation that operations would be resumed in the spring. Throughout it all, the doctor remained outwardly confident that "he [had] found the place where De Braak [had] sunk."[42] The 1887 Pancoast Expedition, however, had failed to achieve its goals. The doctor's personal financial loss thus far totalled $12,000, and he had wasted two full seasons of his life in a fruitless search. Nevertheless, Seth Pancoast was anything but a quitter. He was well aware that if he removed himself from the picture, there would be many others, especially among the membership of the syndicate which he had helped sustain, who would be only too willing to assume command. The search, he knew, must go on.

The Pancoast Mound

By the spring of 1888, Dr. Seth Pancoast was well into preparations for yet another season on the Delaware. The International Submarine Company, backed by the syndicate of Philadelphia financiers, had once again entered into "a huge contract," or salvage agreement, with the United States government.[1] Having undergone two nonproductive seasons, however, the syndicate had been forced into financial restructuring. One hundred shares of new stock were offered at $300 a share, the first twenty of which were purchased by the Second National Bank of Hoboken. Each stock certificate declared the following:

> It is estimated that the "Braak" contained treasures valued at from $10,000,000 to $20,000,000. In case $10,000,000 are recovered this certificate will entitle — $10,000 and a pro rata upon any greater or lesser amount received by said third party.[2]

This time, the ambitious old salvor would not rely upon a sail-powered vessel and a tug. By June the services of a 185-foot, 537-ton, stern-wheel steamer called the *City of Long Branch* had been leased to Pancoast by one R. P. Dobbins. She was a spacious vessel, 35 feet abeam, with a six-foot depth in hold and a draft of four and a half feet. Both of her Pittsburgh-built simple reciprocating Rees engines had seven-foot strokes. Her twin Ward boilers, carrying a pressure of 180 pounds each, had been manufactured at Charleston, West Virginia. She was capable of a maximum speed of thirteen knots. A relatively new vessel, constructed only five years earlier to serve as a passenger and freight hauler between Long Branch, New Jersey, and New York City, the *Long Branch* was considered by Pancoast and the ISC to be far superior to the *Orr*.[3] Principal among the ship's many attributes were two great entrances on her port and starboard sides, barely a few feet above the surface of the water. Pancoast believed that the portals could be readily adapted to facilitate the deployment and recovery of his divers.[4]

The commander of the *City of Long Branch* was to be Captain Charles A. Adams, an officer and a twenty-five-year veteran of the U.S. Navy. Adams's chosen mate was to be Lieutenant George P. Blow, also of the navy. Both had been given special permission by the Navy Department to participate in the expedition. It was publicly announced that the two officers would "receive their expenses only, and have no interest of any kind in the stock of the company found by Dr. Pancoast."[5] Privately, however, the agreement between Pancoast, the ISC, and Adams was another matter. On July 30, the doctor signed the following agreement with the captain:

> This is to certify that in case ten million of dollars is secured from the sloop of war Braak sunk in Del. Bay in 1798: I will give Charles Adams fifty-thousand dollars as a pro rata upon any greater or lesser amount secured from said vessel as per agreement dated: July 30th 1888.
>
> Seth Pancoast[6]

Neither Adams nor Blow was to receive a salary for his labors, but the former had agreed to accept one percent of the profits for his services, while the latter would receive a half percent. Unlike Adams, however, Blow was never able to negotiate a specific pro rata agreement with Pancoast or the syndicate.[7]

Pancoast again took on Charles Pike to manage all underwater operations, without salary, but promised him one-twelfth of a percent of the profits as his reward. And he again secured the services of diver Charles Pedrick at a salary of $150 for three months, plus a bonus of $10,000 if the treasure was recovered. A crew of fifteen, including engineers, deckhands, firemen, cooks, mates, waiter, steward, and a general utility man, was hired. Pancoast himself would serve as the ship's doctor at no salary. The weekly payroll alone would total $535, not including food and bedding. And there would be, from time to time, additional guests to feed, such as Mrs. Pancoast and her son Edward, Mrs. Adams, and Mrs. Pike, all of whom would spend much time aboard.[8]

For undisclosed reasons, the United States government provided Adams with an impressive collection of charts of Delaware Bay and the vicinity of Delaware Breakwater in which he would be working, as well as fifty drawings of the coast. Included in the collection was a facsimile of a chart printed by Joshua Fisher of Wilmington, which had been produced shortly after the signing of the Declaration of Independence, as well as a map drawn by Captain Sir Andrew Snape Hammond of the Royal Navy in 1779. Adams and Blow studied the maps with interest. The lieutenant eventually concluded that, "by comparison of the charts, it is learned that Cape May has added five miles to its length during the last 100 years, and Cape Henlopen two miles."[9]

The *City of Long Branch* arrived at Coopers Point, in Camden, New Jersey, on June 13 for outfitting at the yard of Charles Hollingsworth. There was much to be done: her boilers had to be hydraulically tested; a new, eight-foot-long section of her shaft had to be forged at Bordentown, New Jersey; her hull required a new coat of paint; a steam winch with a derrick boom attachment capable of raising several tons at a time had to be brought aboard and mounted. Then there was the "search pipe," or hose, which, when connected to a powerful water pump through any one of eight outlets spread around the ship, would provide a high-velocity jet of water to penetrate bottom sediments. A Blake-patented centrifugal suction pump was also brought aboard. This device, when connected to a six-inch diameter pipe, would allow the salvors to draw up the mud and debris which supposedly concealed the wreck.[10]

The work progressed on schedule, and by mid-July, it had been announced that the ship would be ready to sail on Friday, July 20.[11] "The arrangements for dredging and examining the sea bottom," reported one Wilmington, Delaware, paper,

> are said to be as complete as naval science can make them. Instruments seldom met with in the mercantile service have been loaned the expedition by the navy department. Among them is a "station pointer," used almost exclusively in the coast survey for plotting positions of vessels, by which an angle can be had by means of the Vernier attachment as far as 15 seconds.[12]

Pancoast was sanguine about his prospects. "Before two months shall have passed," he informed the New York press, "I propose to land the treasure in Philadelphia." When asked why no earlier major efforts had succeeded in securing the *De Braak* hoard, he explained "that the failure had been due to the variation of the meridian" and that modern equipment and instrumentation would lead the project to success. The doctor was confident that he would no longer suffer from "fisherman's luck."[13]

As the expedition prepared to set off, media interest increased daily. Many wished the salvors well, while others merely chortled. In a *New York Tribune* editorial, Pancoast was derided in a good-natured fashion which would have made Jules Verne smile. "Of course," stated the editorial,

> everybody trusts that the Doctor may be successful. At the same time, everybody remembers that a man gets rich searching for gold and silver "in the deep bosom of the ocean buried" about as often as he is struck by lightning. The Doctor believes he knows just where the bars are lying. But they sank beneath the waves nearly a century ago, and a good deal can happen in a century. Who knows what some submarine cyclone has blown the bars thousands of miles away from the place where they originally came to anchor? Who knows but what some leviathan attracted by their glitter long ago appropriated them for ornaments for his own imposing persons and the persons of his sisters and his cousins and aunts? Who knows but what they have been so grown around and upon by colossal aquatic plants that the attempt to recover them will resemble for hopelessness the attempt to recover one of the cities that have been visited by a lava deluge? The Doctor has our best wishes, but we cannot help feeling that a good plumbing business in hand is worth a dozen of such enterprises in the bush.[14]

Despite the progress being made aboard the *City of Long Branch*, the project was plagued with complications from the outset. On July 18, when a head of steam was worked up in the boilers, a sudden explosion blew the starboard smoke stack completely off the ship. The port stack was only saved by several mangle irons placed around it beforehand. It was clear that the steamer would require a completely new outfit, and a thorough inspection was ordered for July 23. Hollingsworth began making immediate repairs to the damaged machinery, while additional work on the hull was undertaken by Samuel Tilton at Coopers Point. Expenses for repairs and outfitting were soon approaching $5,000, and the expedition had yet to leave the dock.[15] Despite these setbacks, the ship's officers and crew continued to take on board the stores, grappling tackle, and equipage necessary for a full season's operations on the Delaware.[16]

News of the preparations spread across the nation. Not only was the general public interested in the proceedings, but the attention also caused many would-be treasure hunters of every stripe to surface. One such individual was S. H. Coppage of Shelby City, Boyle County, Kentucky. Coppage had read about the project in the Philadelphia *Globe Democrat* and had immediately dispatched a letter to James J. Kane, head of the syndicate sponsoring the project. The Kentuckian informed Kane that he possessed an instrument called "the American Fanomina" with which he could "locate lost gold and silver that has been buried for hundreds of years." Indeed, the machine was capable of finding buried wealth of all kinds. He admitted that he had never employed the instrument over open water, but he was confident of its ability to work there as well. "I am sure," he stated unequivocally, "that I Could Locate it in a Very Short Time."[17] Coppage's offer was discreetly ignored.

By the morning of July 31, all was finally in readiness at Coopers Point. At 3:17 A.M. the *City of Long Branch* backed off into the Delaware River. It was dead low water and the big steamer promptly went aground on a mudbank. After freeing herself, she proceeded to take on a load of coal, and by 6:30 P.M., with pilot J. F. Gray at the wheel, commenced steaming downriver. By the following afternoon, she had come to a secure anchor at Delaware Breakwater.[18]

On August 2, the third Pancoast Expedition began. A boat was dispatched to Lewes to locate and transport Samuel Storer McCracken, whose bearings were considered the key to locating the long-lost treasure. The old pilot must have savored the moment, even though his presence aboard the *Long Branch* was now little more than symbolic. Indeed, through the ISC Pancoast had long before secured his diagram, which purported to show the wreck's location, and had computed the parameters within which he felt the hulk must lie.[19] To ensure that the site could be pinpointed this time, the bearings had been plotted on a large chart by means of sextant angles, using various landmarks and objects ashore which also appeared on U.S. Hydrographic Office charts, principally the Henlopen Lighthouse and the Delaware Breakwater. Pancoast and Pike had then proceeded to relocate points from the previous year's effort where strong indications had suggested the ship lay.[20] Once a point over the proposed wreck site had been established by means of the "Station Pointer," or three-armed protractor, and preliminary dragging had been completed, a square could be laid out with buoys attached to heavy anchors. The enclosed space could then be thoroughly dragged. When the wreck was located, diving could begin. At least, that was the plan.[21]

By midafternoon, grappling operations were ready to commence. Two spars, each thirty-five feet long, were extended from both sides of the stern of the *Long Branch*, allowing a hoop of galvanized wire, 115 feet wide to be dragged. The weighted wire, it was believed, would easily slice through the mud and snag any object resting beneath it or on the surface. Two seventy-five-pound grappling irons would also be run out from the stern to supplement the wire-drag operation. Soon everything was in readiness, and the search began.[22] Within twenty minutes an obstruction was encountered, followed by a full hour of frantic activity. Adams immediately stopped the ship, but held his position while crewmen attempted to haul in the grapnels. The port grapnel came up, but the starboard one remained firmly lodged, despite the onset of a strong flood tide. Bearings were taken and the grapnel freed. Quickly, a buoy attached to a 250-pound anchor was deposited on the site and its position recorded before operations broke off for the day.[23] The excitement aboard the *City of Long Branch* as she returned to her anchorage must have been almost palpable.

The following day the sea was smooth, and the atmosphere hazy, hot, and sultry. With the *City of Long Branch* anchored on the previous day's bearings, adjacent to the marker buoy, at 10:35 A.M. diver Charles Pedrick donned his gear and plunged into the sea from the port aft cargo portal, descending quickly to a depth of nine fathoms. For an hour and a half the crew watched and listened, fascinated, as the diver's bubbles charted his path along the bottom and Engineer Pike carried on a rolling conversation with him through the speaking hose. Pedrick was the epitome of composure, even when he discovered and began to explore a giant mound composed of sticky blue mud covered by a surface sprinkle of small shells. Treasure fever gripped all aboard the steamer.[24]

By noon, the flood tide had begun, and further diving during that day proved impossible. But the results of the morning's work had everyone elated. The "mound," believed to be the same one that Pancoast had been working the year before, had been easily relocated. Pedrick's personal assessment, that the site bore "very favorable indications," was reinforced by several small pieces of decayed wood retrieved from the area.[25]

Adams wasted little time in celebration, preferring to put the nonworking hours of his ship to good use. After all, a steamboat was one of the most sophisticated and complex machines of the age and required special attention in order to function efficiently. First and foremost, she needed a steady diet of coal and water for power, but just as important was the continual pampering by her engineers that kept her intricate machinery running smoothly. Soon after Pedrick had surfaced, the captain decided to put in at the Fish House Pier in Lewes for water. Finding none there, he had turned for the Government Pier (known locally as Iron Pier) and secured 1,500 gallons.[26]

On August 4, the *City of Long Branch* steamed out again from her anchorage off Long Pier at Lewes for the "working grounds" and immediately began dragging operations to determine the perimeter of the mound. Another buoy was deployed. Then, after numerous difficulties, including fouling the grapnel lines and accidentally dragging the buoy markers off mark, the grapnel struck home. Pedrick was again sent to examine the area. To everyone's chagrin, he discovered a "perfectly smooth bottom." The grapnel had dragged. Then, upon closer inspection, it was found to be covered with verdigris, a crust of copper chloride normally formed on copper exposed to air or sea water for long periods of time.[27] The discovery was tantalizing, for the immediate supposition was that the grapnel had been dragged across copper.

Adams decided to call it a day and steamed into Lewes to take aboard a new fish boom, apparently to complement the derrick boom already on board. Expectations and tensions had been running high during these few initial days of the search, and Sunday offered a respite welcomed by all.[28] Adams granted the crew a holiday and permitted the steam in the ship's boilers to run down. For once, there was little to attend to but a few social matters. There was a brief visit by the quarantine tug *Startle*, and the *Long Branch's* decks had to be cleaned, but it was still, after all, a Sunday. At first the weather was clear and sultry. By 4:00 P.M., however, the barometer had plummeted as heavy black clouds, slashed by lightning, began scudding in from the northwest. Soon, the ships anchored under the lee of the Delaware Breakwater were being subjected to heavy squalls, with winds smashing in from all directions. Adams ordered the starboard anchor let go to stabilize the *Long Branch*, an act which resulted in the carrying away of a hawse pipe. Fearing that he might have to make a run for the open sea or risk being stranded or colliding with nearby ships, he ordered the fires started to raise a head of steam. Then, almost as suddenly as it had begun, the storm abated.[29] There was no damage, although everyone aboard had developed a healthy appreciation for the fickle Delaware weather.

After making some necessary repairs on Monday, August 6, the treasure hunters returned to the working grounds and began dragging with two seventy-pound grapnels, attempting to relocate the mound but without success. The next day was worse. While dragging operations were under way, the port boiler sprung a leak and put out the fires, forcing the ship to run at half power. It was a condition which Adams deemed "not very satisfactory and [the] ship not to be depended upon under one boiler in strong headway or with strong breezes." But the search continued. Again, when the grapnels were hauled in, they revealed signs of verdigris. Greatly encouraged, Adams ordered the port anchor dropped, even as Pike helped Pedrick rig his gear for the next dive.[30]

As the diver was suiting up, Dr. Orr, the Quarantine Station physician, accompanied by a party of ladies, came aboard to observe the proceedings. Orr's visit was the last thing the harried commander of the *Long Branch* needed, for problems were suddenly proliferating by the minute. Diving operations had begun later than desired. Then, when Pedrick was finally able to get in the water, he was obliged to come up immediately "on account of the air being too strong," that is, the pressure in his suit being too great. On his second descent, the flood tide began, swinging the ship off its mark. Again Pedrick came up, this time with damage to his diving apparatus. A small hole had been blown in the suit. Still, he was able to report "good indications," and his feet were covered with verdigris and "phospherous" [*sic*].[31]

Upon returning to shore, the ship was boarded by one of the project's principal backers, A. J. Kane, a businessman and member of the Philadelphia syndicate's board of directors.[32] Kane was eager to learn of Adams's progress and was apparently impressed with the captain's abilities now that the site seemed to have been all but located. Adams and Charles Pike informed the company executive that they were quite confident of being in the correct area. They were convinced, however, that the wreck itself could be located only by a diver since management of the cumbersome stern-wheeled steamboat was proving to be a difficult undertaking at best. The ship held poorly against the flood tide and seemed cantankerous in answering the helm. The plan to lay out a ring of buoys around the suspected site was quietly abandoned.

Each new day brought fresh hope. On August 8, the *Long Branch* was moved into a position approximately 300 feet off the No. 1 Buoy in ten fathoms of water. By 9:30 A.M., as soon as the flood had begun to slacken, Pedrick was in the water. Again, the crew monitored his bubbles as they rose to the surface fifty feet off the starboard beam. George Warrington, Pedrick's tender, carefully played out the airhose: 130 feet, 140 feet, 150 feet.[33] As he cautiously picked his way along the seabed, the diver gingerly probed the "soft and slushy black mud" with an iron rod. At 10:45 A.M., he discovered a chunk of wood buried about six inches beneath the sediments. Quickly, he signaled for a rope to be lowered and for his position to be recorded, then hunkered down to await the arrival of the line. As he patiently sat on the bottom, fingering the mud floor beneath him, he discovered a second, larger clump of wood. The piece was three feet, six inches long with one side showing "the square of the lumber." It was entirely detached from the sea bed, although he had at first mistaken the wood for a rock. While Pedrick tried to examine his new find in the murky light, Adams sent out a small boat to take sextant readings on the diver's bubbles and to drop a line down to him. Within a short time, Pedrick signaled for the rope to be raised, dispatching a prize that excited the entire crew.[34]

Now in three pieces the worm-eaten, fused wood was nothing to look at. The pieces had broken off the single wood clump when it hit the side of the boat during recovery. The important thing was that they were fitted with iron bolts, spikes, and locust wood treenails of the kind employed in shipbuilding a century earlier. Closer examination revealed the wood to be stout English oak, and the spikes and treenails to have been handmade.[35] "The wood," Adams recorded in his log, "was fairly riddled in the junction of its groin by worms, with the exception of a long sandworm, evidently a newcomer. No live worms were found nor other living thing."[36] Half an hour later, Pedrick again signaled for a rope. Again the bearings on his bubbles were taken. More than 225 feet of airhose had been played out. And, again, more rotten wood came up. At 11:30 A.M., he signaled a third time for rope. This time he sent up a modern ship's anchor which, from its condition, was thought to have been lost only a few months before. Five minutes later, Pedrick himself came up, carrying yet another small piece of sodden, worm-eaten wood and a small chunk of coral, showing signs of iron oxidization.[37]

Pancoast was elated with the discovery. He was now certain that he had at last pinpointed the locale of *De Braak*'s bones. Upon the *Long Branch*'s return to shore that afternoon, he immediately entrained for Philadelphia. Paying but a short visit to his home—staying only long enough to write three or four telegrams—he then hurried off to the Broad Street station to catch another train for New York.[38] The doctor's excitement was infectious, and the press now followed his every move. "Dr. Pancoast went to New York," stated one Delaware newspaper the day after the discovery, "to get four or five of the best divers that money can hire. He will hurry back to this city and, if possible, will leave the Broad Street station for Lewes on the 3:01 train this afternoon over the Delaware Division of the Philadelphia, Wilmington & Baltimore road."[39]

Pancoast was not entirely truthful with the press. The English oak which Pedrick had recovered was transformed in the telling, undoubtedly to corroborate the doctor's report of two years earlier, to "a petrified piece of teak wood, of which the Braak was built." The fact that it had been found simply lying loose on the bottom was ignored. Other details of the find were also inaccurately reported, possibly in a deliberate effort to throw off others who might also seek the treasure. The grappling irons were said to have been lowered in twelve fathoms of water, three quarters of a mile from shore, when the work was actually being carried out in nine to ten fathoms, a mile from shore.[40]

Meanwhile, back on the Delaware, Captain Adams and his crew continued the exploration, making repairs to the ship whenever possible. The boiler was patched up and a starboard hawse pipe, scavenged from a wrecked schooner, was installed. In their spare time, the crew put in a new "Cucumber Pump" at the well. Success, however, still seemed imminent. On August 9, Pedrick relocated the mound and, while exploring it, promptly sank to his knees in mud. He estimated the plateau to stand a full four feet off the bottom. Several more pieces of decayed wood were recovered. The diver soon began to probe the mound with a four-foot, steel-pointed rod. He found the bottom to be so loose that he could stick the probe plus his whole arm into it without encountering resistance.[41]

Later that evening, much against the better judgment of Captain Adams and Lieutenant Blow, who "deprecate[d] the publicity the expedition [had] gained," two reporters were permitted aboard to record the proceedings. The journalists, an Englishman named Chenold and a Mr. Morrow from the *Philadelphia Ledger*, had undoubtedly been invited by Pancoast as a tactical move to bolster the flagging confidence of some among the group of investors. If the treasure were to be found while they were aboard, then all the better. The move was one that Adams and Blow believed premature; they thought it better to make such an announcement only at the conclusion of the project.[42] This disagreement would prove to be the first of several between the captain and the old mystic.

Despite the nascent schism in the expedition's leadership, spirits aboard the *City of Long Branch* remained high. Pedrick was eager to dive now, even under the most adverse conditions. On August 10, when the wind picked up from the northeast and the ship rolled deeply in the troughs, the diver had willingly prepared to descend until his tender advised caution and the dive was promptly cancelled. Even when Pancoast arrived from New York, bringing with him another diver (and a potential rival to Pedrick), morale remained good.[43]

The new diver was Edward Hickman, who had gained a bit of fame only two years earlier while conducting salvage work on the sunken Cunard steamer *Oregon*. The steamer had been en route from Liverpool when she foundered after a collision off Center Moriches, Long Island, New York, on March 14, 1886. At 2,373 gross tons, she had been the largest vessel ever given up as a total loss off the south shore of Long Island. Within days of the disaster a team of divers, including Hickman, had begun salvaging her cargo and mail, working at depths of up to 120 feet.[44] Pancoast, impressed by such bravado, had hired Hickman for $210 a month, far more than the reliable Pedrick was getting, and had promised him a $10,000 share in the treasure if the expedition proved successful.[45]

Initially, there was surprisingly little animosity, and the project proceeded without any letup. On August 11, while exploring the bottom, Pedrick discovered what at first was believed to be a second mound, close by and similar to the first. It stood four feet high and was thirty feet wide and 100 feet long. While conducting his investigation of the site, Pedrick came upon an anchor weighing between eighty and 100 pounds, attached by a rope to a water-soaked log buoy. Excitedly, he relayed his impression that the anchor and buoy strongly resembled those which had been lost on the spot in 1887. More importantly, the two mounds, he felt, were probably the fore and aft parts of a silt-covered vessel.[46]

Excitement ran high as the usual bearings were taken, and the anchor site marked by a float buoy. Pancoast and Pike, certain that the anchor and buoy discovered by the diver were the same ones they had left on the mound a year ago, were elated. When Hickman made two dives later in the day and retrieved the weighted buoy, which was worm-eaten, saturated, and swollen, it was nevertheless readily identified by Pancoast as his own—and then dumped over the side.[47] There seemed little question that they had relocated the shipwreck. The next step was to begin the excavations that would prove it, and then to find the gold. All visitors were barred from the site, even as word of the proceedings spread quickly along the coast and became front-page news in the daily tabloids.

On Monday, August 13, Adams got the *Long Branch* under way at 6:00 A.M. in order to make the most of the tides. Flood tide would be running at 8:00 A.M., and everyone was eager to get a diver back down on the site as soon as it had passed. Unfortunately, the ship's coal bunkers were almost depleted, and it would soon become necessary to make a run for Delaware City, the nearest port where coal could be procured. The boilers, of course, were still less than reliable; barely 110 to 120 pounds of steam pressure could be worked up in them. The steam winch also needed repairs. Only one dive would be possible that day. Pedrick, however, could not relocate the mound and succeeded only in bringing up several small pieces of decayed wood before the tide shifted. The information derived from these few, pitiful "artifacts" was of little use.[48]

Adams was now obliged to turn the prow of the *Long Branch* upriver for Delaware City, to take on coal, ice, and stores, and to make the necessary repairs. The sixty-mile voyage took seven hours, during which time the relationship between Pancoast and the captain became strained over the subject of expenditures. Primarily at issue was the cost of fuel. There was space in the bunker for 100 tons of coal, but Pancoast refused to purchase more than thirty tons, the amount which had been aboard when he first took over the ship. His reason given was that "he did not wish to return the ship to her owners with any quantity of coal on board." But the real issue was money. The following morning, as provisions and eighty tons of "clear cool and pleasant" canal ice was being loaded, Pancoast and Pike suddenly departed for Philadelphia without explanation.[49]

Soon afterward—and perhaps, not coincidentally—Adams received on board one Joseph Townsend, an officer of the Merritt Wrecking Company of

New York, and a personal guest of Lieutenant Blow. Townsend's presence aboard, particularly in light of later developments, suggests that a conspiracy intended to circumvent or even oust Dr. Pancoast from the directorship of the project may have been quietly brewing. Townsend was a veteran salvor, and it is possible that he was merely invited aboard as an observer or even an advisor, although his name does not appear on the company payroll. Whatever his role, he would remain aboard for several days, quietly observing the operation, as well as making notations on the area being investigated. Townsend's activities occurred without comment by Adams and, apparently the knowledge of Pancoast.[50]

Exploration of the mounds resumed on August 15, but under a new handicap. The marker had again disappeared, probably cut away in the night by a passing steamer. There was no choice but to start over. More explorations were carried out. More worm-eaten wood and a piece from a sail were recovered. Then the mounds were relocated, marked, lost again, rediscovered, and lost once more. They seemed to tease the divers, who would run out of airhose right at their edges, able to reach but never to climb their waist-high plateaus. As always, the searchers were tantalized by the ever-present signs of verdigris.[51]

As the days passed without any significant discovery, Adams began to feel dismay, not only over the hunt's lack of progress, but also over the *Long Branch's* inability to perform as required. "Wind and tide too strong to maneuver to position sought," he recorded in his log after one disappointing day.

> Ship unhandy and unwieldy will not mind helm, nor anything else but wind and sometimes when least expected the tide. Will not come around inside one mile. Backs stern to wind and against tiller. Forward houses and smoke stack act as a foil to keep head from coming into wind.[52]

Then, on August 17, hopes were elevated when Pedrick buoyed a site and proceeded to bring up small fragments of an old deadeye and pieces of rotten wood. He recommended putting down the dredge hose. The dig, it seemed, was imminent. But on the following day, neither Pedrick nor Hickman could relocate the site.[53]

The daily cycle of operations was onerous, and living conditions aboard ship were frequently less than comfortable. On at least one occasion, while the *City of Long Branch* lay at anchor for the evening at Iron Pier, infestations of "millions and millions" of "dog black mosquitoes" made sleep impossible. Netting was of little use, and the mosquitoes eventually became so bad that Adams was obliged to take the ship out and anchor her under Delaware Breakwater for relief. It did little good. "Mosquitoes all night," he complained glumly in his logbook. "Nobody able to sleep."[54]

Weather was another factor which frequently slowed operations. Squalls would blow in from time to time, usually out of the northwest, often with little warning. On August 18, one typical blow arrived while Pedrick was on the bottom. He was immediately brought up, and the *City of Long Branch* made a dash for safety. The ship reached the east end of Delaware Breakwater just as a "heavy thundering rain squall struck us completely hiding [the] Breakwater from view." The storm continued for the better part of the next three days, and fieldwork suffered accordingly. On the 21st, with heavy, black cloud banks rolling in from the sea and the barometer falling, Adams started for Delaware City with his ship, "taking advantage of the bad weather." As the atmospheric conditions further degenerated, he ordered the first fire and abandon-ship drills of the expedition, even as "heavy angry squalls" obliged him to anchor in midstream off the town." Soon the squalls had turned to gale-force winds. At 6:00 P.M., a devastating cyclone passed over the Delaware. On the river, a pilothouse was ripped from a tugboat, a schooner was dismasted, and other vessels were driven ashore. Barns and houses were levelled, and a number of people were killed or seriously injured. Fortunately, thanks to Adams's precautions, the *City of Long Branch* emerged unscathed from the tempest.[56]

On August 24, the expedition returned to the working grounds, prepared to relocate and excavate the mound from which Pancoast's 1887 buoy and anchor had been recovered. Adams decided to give the site a name. He dubbed it, appropriately enough, the Pancoast Mound.[57]

EIGHT

Ultimatum

The morning air of August 24 was cool and pleasant as the crew of the *City of Long Branch* labored to rig up the excavation equipment and take on board provisions from the Lewes pier. By 10:30 A.M. the ship was again actively engaged in dragging for the Pancoast Mound. By late afternoon, the site had been relocated. The centrifugal pump was prepared, the diving gear laid out, and the ship brought to a steady anchor. Then came a three-hour wait for slack water. Finally, at 6:00 P.M., the pump was started and Charles Pedrick dropped down to begin excavation. The effort proved anticlimactic, as twenty minutes later he was driven off by exceptionally strong and unexpected tides.[1]

The following day was little better. As the *Long Branch* was starting for the working grounds, she was overtaken by the tug *Startle*, "with a party of visitors . . . in [the] charge of Mr. A. J. Kane." Adams welcomed them aboard to view the day's proceedings, which unhappily proved less than gratifying for all concerned. Shortly after noon, following some difficulty in maneuvering the ship into position, the test excavation commenced anew. The results proved disappointing. On the bottom, Hickman wielded the suction hose for less than an hour, managing to dig barely two feet into the mound before striking hard bottom. It was apparent that the sediments in which he was working did not hide any portion of the wreck, as first believed. Another section of the mound would have to be staked out and tested.[2]

Captain Adams was doubly disheartened when he learned that his trusted first officer, George Blow, whose working relationship with Pancoast and the syndicate was less than amicable, had decided to withdraw from the project. Soon after the steamer had returned to Lewes on the evening of the 25th, Blow "left the ship, his leave of absence from [the] Navy Department being about to expire and up to this time he not having been able to get a sentiment nor agreement signed with Dr. Pancoast and the Syndicate furnishing the money for the expedition."[3]

Adams had little alternative but to press on. On August 27 it was decided that a new sector of the mound should be explored. Diving operations began at 7:30 A.M., approximately 180 feet southeast of the earlier excavation site.

Investigations by Hickman proved negative. A second dive by Pedrick at yet a third location appeared more positive when a five-foot mound of soft sediment, covered with sand and shell, was discovered. Happily, he also discovered a twelve-foot piece of pipe as well as asounding hose lost by Hickman several days earlier. Not only had Pedrick rediscovered the precise area in which they had been working prior to the loss of their marker buoy, but the pipe provided some intriguing data as well. The lower portion of the piece was covered by verdigris, and between the threads of one end "small pieces of bright metal" could be discerned. The position was quickly marked with a buoy attached to a small anchor and iron grate bars by 300 feet of line.[4]

Again morale soared, only to be squelched by the weather. On Tuesday, August 28, the seas proved too rough to permit any work to be carried out. Then, when operations resumed the following day, Adams was obliged to entertain yet another party of "capitalists" from Philadelphia and Baltimore who had invested in the project and wanted to see some action for their money. They were undoubtedly excited as Hickman donned his diving suit and descended to the bottom, where he proceeded to excavate a trench five feet deep and ten feet long at the edge of the mound. Fully expecting to see barrels of gold and doubloons, however, the visitors soon became bored with the tediousness of operations and demanded to be landed at Lewes. Adams, having little choice, lost the next working period of slack water while returning his guests to shore.[5]

Nevertheless, trenching along several different sectors of the mound continued unhindered for the next few days. Sea conditions were excellent, and work progressed quickly, with excavations penetrating to depths of up to eight feet through the mound. But the results of each new test trench proved less than gratifying. The pump hose seemed to spout little more than sand, mud, shells, and rotten wood onto the decks of the *Long Branch*. Bottom conditions were persistently difficult, and, experienced as they were, the divers could not help but stir up the silts as they walked and worked, forcing them to labor in total darkness. Marker buoys dragged during the nights, and the irascible *Long Branch* was managed only with the greatest of difficulty in irregular currents and running tides during the days. Lines were stretched by the powerful flood tides, and more than a few arguments flared up over misread signals.[6]

The divers began to improvise and refine their exploration techniques in order to work more efficiently in the zero-visibility environment. Using an anchor line planted on the mound as a down line, they could descend to the desired position with ease. Their location on the bottom could be ascertained, monitored, and plotted by their bubbles. Positions were taken on the bubbles relative to the cabin house of the ship. Bearings on standing shore points could then be taken and the positions of the cabin and ship triangulated and plotted on the map. In order to explore along the bottom in the dark without losing their original positions on the mound, the divers attached a line of yarn to an anchor cable. The line was knotted at equal lengths, and each knot was assigned a letter of the alphabet, beginning with "a" at the position closest to the anchor hub. As the diver moved away from the datum, he called out over the communications line each knot's designation as he reached it, then described the terrain and his findings (as determined by touch). "At points a, b, c, and d," one such report sent up by Hickman went, "[I]was off the mound. A very soft spot was at 'a.' [I] was off the mound and on regular bottom at 'g.' "[7]

On September 4 Pancoast again left the ship to attend to business in Philadelphia. Although the search was progressing systematically, the high spirits enjoyed during the first days of the hunt had long since evaporated. Adams plodded on, but may have begun to experience misgivings when he received a telegram informing him that yet another visitor, a certain Mr. Demarest of the famous Merritt Wrecking Company of New York, was en route to meet with the doctor on board the *Long Branch*. The following morning, the captain dispatched a small boat to Lewes to await the visitor's arrival. That evening, Demarest boarded the salvage steamer, his avowed intention being only "to witness some of the work."[8] His stay would not be uneventful.

The treasure hunters were frequently obliged to work under great stress, much of it induced by the quirky weather. On one occasion, thick fog set in so fast that it almost shut the *Long Branch* in while a diver was still on the bottom.[9] And conditions below were always the same—terrible. The divers labored with considerable difficulty to wield the cumbersome and frequently inadequate suction hose against erratic currents in total darkness. The strain was beginning to show. Tensions arose between Adams, the perfectionist, and Hickman, for whom the captain had little affection. Adams found fault with every action the diver took. One one occasion, after Hickman had complained that he could barely get enough suction to dig, even in the softest sediments, the captain recorded in his log that the diver "came up a number of times but could not get suction enough to suit him and could do nothing with the lower end of the suction himself. [He] claimed flood tide was running too strong for him on the bottom."[10] Adams, obviously miffed, went on to note somewhat sarcastically that it was slack water on the surface. How could it be flood on the bottom and slack topside? He felt that Hickman was not doing his job and simply would have to go.

The tedium and frustrations of day-to-day work on the mound were interrupted by a near disaster in early September. At the end of one particularly unproductive day, the barometric pressure rose dramatically. The winds began to pick up and deep troughs formed in the seas. The *Long Branch* raced for the shelter of the Delaware Breakwater. Soon, forty other vessels had also come to anchor under the lee of the breakwater as a terrible "nor' easter" hit the Capes. For Adams and his men, and probably Demarest as well, the evening was merely "disagreeable." For others, it was catastrophic. The gale continued throughout the night. At the height of the storm, someone aboard the *Long Branch* spied rockets piercing the black sky over Cape Henlopen. At daylight, the source of the distress signals was discovered to be a big two-masted schooner that had been driven ashore amid the pounding surf. Relief provided by crews from the Cape Henlopen Life-Saving Station notwithstanding, her situation appeared hopeless. The foul weather continued unabated for nearly twenty-four hours. For several days thereafter, heavy seas prevented the salvors from returning to the working grounds, and their attention remained focused on the doomed vessel. By the morning of Saturday, September 8, the stranded schooner, constantly battered by waves, had begun to go to pieces. At 7:30 A.M., her masts crashed into the sea.[11]

Soon after observing the destruction of the schooner, Adams brought the *Long Branch* down to Lewes to pick up Dr. Pancoast, who had just returned from Philadelphia. The ship's cook, John F. Pedrick, and his young mate, Jim Bartlett, both of whom had been stranded ashore when the storm struck three days earlier, also returned aboard. There was plenty of business to attend to. Fresh water had to be taken on, repairs made, and myriad logistical considerations addressed, not the least of which was the matter of another anchor. Adams had come to the conclusion that, to hold the ship fast in the ever-shifting flood of the Delaware, he needed to secure a 1,300-pound anchor to replace one lost earlier on the working grounds. On September 5 he had made arrangements to rent one, which, three days later, still had not been delivered. He was therefore obliged to borrow a 900-pound anchor from the man who managed the Iron Pier.[12]

Finally, there was the business of Hickman to be settled. The "clouds were hanging heavily and threatening" when Adams made his move. With Pancoast aboard, and apparently with his concurrence, the once highly touted diver was paid one month's wages and summarily discharged, "his services being no longer needed." That his work was unsatisfactory to Adams, Charles Pike, and even Pancoast was probable. Not surprisingly, Hickman, who had put his life on the line with every dive, was deeply incensed at his firing. "He was," noted Adams, "insulting and threatening in his remarks and manner before leaving the ship" to take the 4:45 P.M. train for New York.[13] Once again, the expedition's hopes rested solely upon Charles Pedrick.

On Monday, September 10, when the *Long Branch* returned to the working grounds, the salvors discovered, much to their dismay, that all of their site-marker buoys had sunk. Adams immediately ordered the small boats out, to begin sweeping for the anchor and buoy which had originally marked the mound. The anchor was soon snagged, but before a second sweep could be carried out to secure it, the oncoming ebb snapped the sweep line. The frustrated salvors could do nothing but replace the recovered waterlogged buoys with new ones before heading in. With the expedition delayed by heavy rains the following day, morale plummeted.[14]

On September 12, sea conditions improved. Again, the *Long Branch* put out to the working grounds, only to discover that the swift currents resulting from runoff after several days of hard rain were towing all of the site-marker buoys under. One buoy had disappeared entirely; two more were raised and replaced. A sweep was carried out to recover the fourth, but without success. Adams decided to halt operations for the day, but when he ordered the anchor raised, the steam winch failed. The anchor had to be recovered by block and tackle.[15]

That evening, the salvors, now more dejected than ever, put into Lewes. No sooner had the *Long Branch* tied up at the dock than the cook, John Pedrick, and the mess boy, Jim Bartlett, left the ship without permission. The boy failed to return in time to attend to his duties, and when the cook reappeared, he was too intoxicated to be of any use. Angered by their actions, Adams paid the two men off and fired them, "their services being no longer wanted."[16]

Despite such setbacks and problems, Adams addressed each difficulty as it arose. The broken winch was carefully examined, for without it there could be no anchoring of the ship at will. That evening, work to dismantle the machine began. The cause of the problem was soon discovered: a set key in the wheel cog had not been socketed when assembled, so it had shifted position while under pressure and cracked the hub of the cog. Repairs would be difficult, if not impossible. There was no machine shop in Lewes. The salvors were compelled "to do all our machine work with our own resources which are very limited." By the following day, Adams had succeeded in removing the winch head and the cog. Now it would be a matter of "make-do" by having the town blacksmith shrink on the iron clamp. By 4:30 P.M., work on the winch had been completed.[17]

On September 14, after nine days of wasted energy and expense, the expedition resumed diving operations. New buoys were deployed, the mound was relocated, and Pedrick again began excavation. For once, everything seemed to be on track. The following morning, Adams landed Pancoast and Demarest at Lewes, the latter having been aboard for ten days, "taking in all the points."[18]

Back on site, however, problems appeared again at every turn. Adams was still short of anchors. He needed four to remark the corners of the survey area with buoys, a fifth to mark the excavation site on the mound, and two more on board the ship to provide a stable anchorage in case of bad weather. Unfortunately, there were only six anchors to be had. He was thus obliged to weigh one of the site anchors each night in order to keep two for the ship's evening anchorage. Further, even the act of maneuvering the ship into a working stance to begin operations had become an ordeal. An excerpt from Captain Adam's log best describes the travails of the *Long Branch* and her increasingly frustrated team of treasure salvors.

> Made four attempts to get ship into position, but failed owing to her being unmanageable within reasonable limits—with wind and tide—At 11 tide having made flood, steamed into position and let go stbd anchor—got out both quarter and port bow lines—Waited for slack water—Clouding over and wind increasing from S of Ed. Barom 30.23. Considerable swell getting up. At 5:30 put down pump and Diver Pedrick went down. . . . Pump brought up sand, shells, coal. . . . Diver up at 5.50. Indications not good on the mound. Could not find iron gas pipe prod—Seas too heavy to use pump. Unmoored—weighed stbd and S.E. anchors. Wind increasing heavy sea menacing—ship rolling heavily in trough in sea—Anchored inside Breakwater—Wind increasing from S.E. Heavy swell setting into harbor.[19]

Seth Pancoast was irate over the lack of progress. The expedition was running out of both time and money, and the effort to investigate systematically was yielding little reward. The syndicate was becoming less than supportive, and Adams sometimes seemed to be an enemy in Pancoast's own camp. The doctor resolved, therefore, to resort to an approach which had earlier been entirely ignored by the syndicate. While in Philadelphia, he hired a certain Mr. Cline, a "Divining Rod" man, to locate the precise location of the treasure. Cline's expertise lay in his purportedly mystical ability to locate various minerals by employing a forked branch or stick which would point downward when held over a source. On the evening of September 16, in the midst of a driving rainstorm, Pancoast and the diviner arrived at Delaware Breakwater and boarded the *Long Branch*. For "Old Pan," as he was referred to behind his back, it would be a last ditch effort to achieve success after three years of failure.[20]

By early the following morning the rain had stopped, but the seas were still rough. On the working grounds, the treasure hunters soon discovered that their marker buoys had again been carried off. With slack tide slipping away, they wasted little time in searching for them. Pedrick would have to do the hunting on the bottom. Not unexpectedly, he failed to relocate the mound, the buoys, or any evidence of the wreck through test excavations.[21]

It was now Cline's turn. At 9:15 A.M., Pike, Pedrick, and the diviner set off in a small sailboat to test the divining rod. The seas were still turbulent and the small boat bobbed about almost uncontrollably. The work of divining was carried out with some difficulty. Within an hour and a half, however, the diviner thought he could discern "copper indications" off the *Long Branch's* port quarter, running all the way through to the starboard quarter, as well as "slight gold indications" about four ship lengths ahead of the steamboat. Even

Adams was impressed, and everyone was eager for Pedrick to examine the designated locations.[22]

The problem was that Pedrick, having performed most of the diving, even during Hickman's employment, had grown averse to making two dives a day without compensation. He was bitter, perhaps understandably, about the New York diver's having been paid far more than himself for less diving. Neither Adams nor the crew felt unsympathetic. "There seems to be," the captain noted, "a feeling of suspicion encircling the services of the New York diver." Pedrick chose this strategic moment to make his grievance known, refusing to undertake a second dive without assurances of compensation. As Pancoast had already left for Philadelphia, Adams was forced to promise additional payment from his own pocket in order to satisfy the diver.[23]

Pedrick agreed to continue work. His second dive, however, was impeded by the rough weather and failed to produce the hoped-for discovery "indicated" by Cline's divining rod. Indeed, Pedrick could not even find the usual "indications" of the mound, and the missing buoys were lost for good. The diver made a complete circuit of the ship, as far out as his hose would permit, but the results were still negative. In desperation, as Pedrick worked below, Cline and Pike set out again to divine the area, but returned disappointed to the ship hours later.[24]

The following day was "dark and gloomy all around with indications of settling in thick." Adams was obliged to bring the *Long Branch* up to Iron Pier for water and to take on a rented 1,300-pound anchor capable of holding her steady in the erratic currents of the working grounds. While at the dock, the diviner hastily left the ship, claiming that, with bad weather setting in, "he had not the time to pursue the subject sufficiently at this late stage of the season."[25] The end of the expedition was on everyone's mind, but diving and digging continued as before, albeit with the same frustrating results.

On the evening of September 19, Pancoast returned from Philadelphia. Adams immediately acquainted him with the depressing facts. Winter gales and high seas might be expected at almost any time. Worse, less than ten tons of coal remained in the ship's bunker. It was barely enough to get the *Long Branch* to Delaware City, where it would be necessary to go because there was no coal available anywhere closer to Lewes. Supplies "had been at low ebb for sometime [and were] now entirely exhausted."[26]

Pancoast's response surprised no one. He informed the captain that the "Syndicate was busted," and all of the money raised for the expedition had been spent. He had just returned from a most disagreeable meeting with the syndicate officers and others holding or having an interest in the company certificates. He had left them with an ultimatum: if they refused to raise the $2,500 he needed to purchase coal and other stores and materials, he would bring the *Long Branch* back to Philadelphia, pay off the men, and lay up the steamer. The despondent old doctor, who had spent most of the last three years of his life chasing a dream, was not sanguine about the chances of the money's being raised.[27] There was no longer any choice but to pay off all outstanding debts at Lewes and to take the ship back to Philadelphia. The following day, the *Long Branch* returned to the working grounds for the last time to recover the buoys and anchors that had been left at the site. She then turned about for a final visit to Lewes, where Adams and Pancoast settled their bills and paid off several deckhands, took on water, and returned all their rented gear. Soon afterward, the big steamer departed from Iron Pier for Delaware City. Late that same evening, she arrived amidst a driving rain, nearly out of coal, and with those few individuals remaining aboard in a deep state of gloom.[28]

By the evening of Monday, September 24, the *City of Long Branch* had been brought to a berth just above Oxon Ferry Slip at Camden. Her fires had been hauled, her boilers were blown down, her cocks opened, bilges pumped out, fire hoses coupled, fire room chained up, ports put in, hawsers and fasts properly secured, diving apparatus and portable items removed, and the ship secured. The remaining crew members were paid off, after which the vessel was formally turned over to the care of a permanent watchman named R. T. Pugsley.[29] The third Pancoast Expedition, it would seem, had come to a dismal end.

A Vast Beam of Light

Not long after the *City of Long Branch* had been towed to her berth on Oxon Ferry Slip, Seth Pancoast disembarked to attend a pivotal meeting of the syndicate's board of directors. Among those present were James J. Kane, U.S.N., chairman of the board and a close associate of Captain Adams and Lieutenant Blow, as well as A. J. Kane and J. H. Shreiner. The meeting, which was held in Shreiner's office at Fifth and Chestnut streets in Philadelphia, promised to be anything but pleasant. On the agenda were the controversy over funding and the prospects for the project's survival. The real issue, of course, was Pancoast's continued leadership of and control over the salvage program. With three years of failure behind him, the doctor no longer had the confidence of the board. James J. Kane, who had been maneuvering for control by tightly regulating the flow of money to the operation while placing the onus of the miserly apportionments on Pancoast, saw the doctor's failures as a golden opportunity. He quietly reveled in the old man's imminent downfall and seemed to enjoy watching his destruction.

Despite Pancoast's having already shut down operations, the "tone of the meeting was by no means in favor of abandoning the project." A resolution was adopted in favor of "issuing a card stating that any reasonable amount of money could be furnished" by the syndicate to execute the search. Fifteen hundred dollars could be raised and handed over to Captain Adams immediately if necessary, someone leaked to the press. Under favorable circumstances, $50,000 could be raised in a few days, but only if the last $5,000 which had been supplied to the doctor could be fully accounted for. Until that time, however, no further funds would be made available. Incensed by the implied charge of misuse of funds, Pancoast reminded the board that the syndicate had promised to pay him $10,000 in return "for certain concessions." Despite that promise, the organization had provided him with only a little more than half that amount. While under contract with the ISC, Pancoast reminded the board, he had entered into three subcontracts for the furtherance of the project: one with James J. Kane, representing the syndicate of investors; another with the owners of the *City of Long Branch*; and a third with the officers and crew of the ship, "to obtain such help as was needed, the use of the boat and services of the men." In return, he had promised to provide a quarter of the profits from the treasure.[1] But the board had played the game differently.

Pancoast contended that the syndicate had failed to fulfill its contractual obligations and that, until it did, further work was impossible. The *Long Branch*, which was inadequate in many ways, could not be properly outfitted without additional funds. And, apparently elaborating upon the brief abandonment of the ship by the cook and his young assistant, Pancoast implied that a lack of funds had caused desertions. Next, he tried threats: since the syndicate had refused to live up to its commitment, Pancoast declared (undoubtedly to James Kane's great delight) that he simply could not stay on as project director. No longer intimidated by such posturing, the board ignored the proclamation. Instead they asked why all of the money already given to him had not been used.

Unable to evade the issue any longer, Pancoast admitted that the advance monies had not, in fact, been entirely spent and defended his actions by saying that he was "not to account for what he was legally entitled to." An additional advance of $2,500 would have sufficed to keep the expedition afloat, he said, "but if it [were] with held [*sic*] and the expedition [failed] in consequence, no blame [could] be attached" to him.[2] Pancoast refused either to budge or to account for the money which he claimed belonged to him. With no additional funds being voted, the project was effectively stalled. Stung by the board's unwillingness to provide him with further support and unwilling himself to cover future expenses out of his own pocket, the old mystic surrendered. On Monday, September 24, he boarded the *Long Branch* for the last time and presented Captain Adams with a release, "as master of the vessel and Commander of the Expedition providing $2,500 was not raised," to continue the explorations.[3]

James J. Kane, of course, had never intended to give up the search, but only to eliminate Pancoast as the middleman between the International Submarine Company and his own people. With the doctor's having been refused more funds to continue the search, there was no longer anything to prevent the investor group from launching its own expedition, with the expectation of each member's getting a larger share of the treasure once the site had been found. All that would be necessary was restructuring, raising additional funds, and securing a concession from the ISC, which held the Treasury Department salvage rights to the site.

The board met again, without Pancoast, and, backed by three hundred stockholders, voted to proceed on their own. Under Kane's direction (and probable authorship), the board proposed incorporation under the laws of the state of Pennsylvania as the Ocean Wrecking Company, Limited. To raise the new capital, it would be necessary to enter into a legally binding agreement with the ISC to sublet their contract with the U.S. Treasury Department for

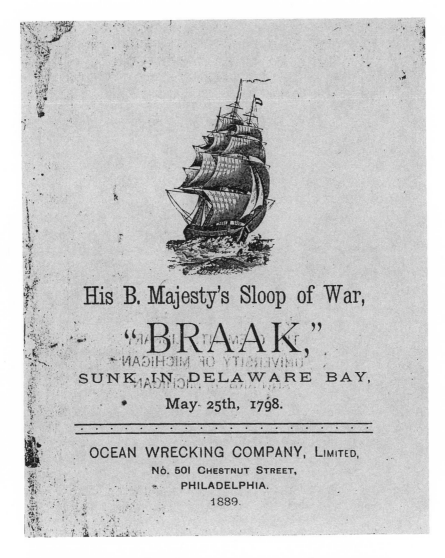

His B. Majesty's Sloop of War,

"BRAAK,"

SUNK IN DELAWARE BAY,

May 25th, 1798.

OCEAN WRECKING COMPANY, Limited,
No. 501 Chestnut Street,
PHILADELPHIA.
1889.

The 1889 Ocean Wrecking Company prospectus used to attract venture capital to support a fourth consecutive season in search of *De Braak*. (*William L. Clements Library*)

the right to salvage *De Braak*. With Pancoast's three years of failure and his subsequent abandonment by the syndicate, there would be little difficulty in securing the ISC's agreement to support a better-organized venture. On Monday, October 1, 1888, after considerable behind-the-scenes negotiation, the ISC and Ocean Wrecking signed a contract which permitted the latter the right to conduct work for three years, with a one-year extension if necessary.[4]

Elated over his coup, James J. Kane informed Captain Adams of the prospects for resuming the expedition. On October 3, he wrote:

> My Dear Adams.
>
> I sent you a telegram Monday night, as I promised, informing you that old "Pan" was checkmated. The contract was signed by the full board of Directors, backed up by three hundred of the stockholders, or I should say by those who hold three hundred thousand shares. Old "Pan" has not found it out as yet, when he does, there will be exhibited some pure and unadulterated cussedness. I am assured of all the money that will be needed for the work next year. I now offer you the command of the expedition to start not later than the 15th of May. Mr. Pike will go with you, and a suitable steamer will be procured with a full outfit, and Capt. Elbridge has volunteered to go with you as Chief Officer, and you can choose your Chief Engineer.[5]

Kane was quick to capitalize on the change of affairs—and command. The Ocean Wrecking Company, Limited, was formally organized as a Philadelphia-based partnership association on January 9, 1889, under an Act of the General Assembly of the Commonwealth of Pennsylvania. A lengthy prospectus for potential investors, apparently written by Kane in late 1888,[6] was then published, which presented the following information: the purported "official history" of *De Braak*, "proof" of the existence of her treasure, a review of previous searches for the treasure, indications of the treasure revealed by the failed 1888 expedition, the causes of the failure, a reprint from *Harper's Weekly* describing current salvage technology employed in the recovery of the sunken steamer *Iberia*, and Ocean Wrecking's proposed plan to recover the *De Braak* treasure. The work was a masterpiece of promotional hype which adroitly combined fact and misinformation in a tantalizing stew. It was a feast which would inadvertently confound and mislead innumerable *De Braak* hunters for the next century.

The history of *De Braak*, as presented in the prospectus, was muddled and only semi-factual, but it was certainly swashbuckling. And in the best capitalist traditions of fund-raising for high-risk ventures, it was skillfully designed to tickle the greed of even the most obdurate investor.

De Braak, it was claimed, had been built in about 1787 by the Dutch navy from oak and teak. The teak had come from

> the Dutch possessions in India, and was used at that period (and in fact up to the introduction of iron) mostly for ships of war. Nearly all the present old

wooden ships of Great Britain are built of teak. This is an important factor to be borne in mind, when we shall refer later on to the undisputed discovery of this particular wood on the mound located as the lost treasure ship.[7]

The ship had first been captured and then commissioned by the French, only later coming into the possession of the British, who armed her with sixteen brass carronades. Under Captain Drew's command, she had been ordered to join the British West India Squadron. Off the Western Isles, Drew had captured "a large Spanish ship from La Plata" laden with gold, silver bars, and precious stones, all of which was promptly transferred to *De Braak*. Off Cape Henlopen she had taken a second ship, the *St. Francis Xavier*, which was stripped of her own valuable treasures and then dispatched to Halifax. When *De Braak* was brought to anchor off Cape Henlopen on May 15, 1798, she had 213 Spanish prisoners aboard and was accompanied by a third Spanish vessel called the *Snow*, "whose valuable treasures were secure in Captain Drew's cabin."[8]

While anchored off the Cape, *De Braak* was boarded by Captain Andrew Allen, who had been brought out by his partner, Captain McCracken, for the purpose of piloting the vessel in. McCracken, however, had withdrawn his boat into Old Kiln Road and remained there, waiting to take Allen off once *De Braak* had come in. Aboard the warship, Allen had entered the cabin to see the captain, who invited him to partake of refreshments, after which he was shown the contents of the locker.

"This is my last voyage at sea," Drew announced. "It has been a remarkably successful one, and when I return home, I am going to buy a title and live like a lord." Later, after reaching shore, Allen reported that he had seen "an immense amount of gold and silver bars, a large number of doubloons, and iron chests containing precious stones, which was private property."[9] Indeed, following the disaster, English and Spanish survivors alike had stated that *De Braak* had taken no less than five prizes while cruising the Spanish Main and had taken aboard all the treasures from them—or so the prospectus reported.

After *De Braak* capsized and sank in ten fathoms of water, the survivors and remaining prisoners had made their way to Philadelphia aboard the *Snow*, which had been serving as a tender to the warship. In August, the British frigate *Assistance*, under the command of one Captain Robert Hall, arrived to take possession of the prize, which was to be condemned and sold at Halifax. Later, Drew's brother applied, on behalf of Mrs. Drew, "for Letters of Administration, hoping to obtain something for his prizes, but the amount was small, as the record states in all the prizes Captain Drew took he removed the treasures to his own vessel.[10]

To add further luster to an already golden fable, the prospectus went on to quote verbatim the account reportedly discovered in 1867 by Captain Sanborn in Halifax, which stated that *De Braak* had gone down with seventy tons of copper and an "immense amount of treasures," consisting of gold, silver bars, and precious stones. The author of the prospectus was inclined to avoid hard, documented evidence, as well as the historic record, relying instead upon word-of-mouth traditions of the Delaware Coast.

> We hardly think it worth while to quote from the official reports in regards to the loss of the "Braak." We have men living today who have conversed with the pilot and others who saw the ship go down, and could testify that for several months her masts were standing; also the members of families who sheltered and provided for the survivors.[11]

Indeed, the reliance upon the "universal belief of the oldest inhabitants of Lewes," based on information handed down from their ancestors who had witnessed the disaster, that there were immense treasures aboard *De Braak*, seemed to outweigh any reliance upon the written record at all.[12]

Two early efforts, the prospectus noted, had been made to raise the ship. The first had been made by *Assistance* in 1798. The second had been made by an unidentified "English frigate and a 74 Gun Ship" which had worked for two months on the project.

> They would heave down on the low water, and when the tide rose their hawsers would snap, or else the bitts to which they were made fast would be broken. Their object was not to raise the vessel to the top of the water, but to lift her a few feet at a time and go on shore, until she could be worked in shallow water. They were unable to start her from the bottom and had to give up.[13]

Abandoned by the British, but lying within a marine league of the coast, *De Braak* had legally become an abandoned vessel and the "absolute property" of the United States Government.[14]

The masts of *De Braak* had remained out of the water for months after she sank—long enough for bearings to be taken from them to points of land and also from the land to the spot "where she lay upright on the hard, blue clay." The ISC, currently in possession of the bearings, had, of course, conducted a careful search of the area. Although the Pancoast expeditions were never mentioned by name, the findings of the doctor's three-year-long effort became the main data base for all future work. At precisely the correct location, the prospectus stated, divers had discovered a six-foot mound, 150 feet long and forty feet wide. As they dragged over it, they had brought up several pieces of timber with iron bolts attached. "Pieces of this wood were sent to experts," who reportedly testified that it was teak. The iron bolts were handmade and were of the kind produced a century earlier. The six-inch Blake suction pump which had been deployed on the mound had brought up great quantities of small pieces of wood and shells, many of them "being thickly coated with copper." Indeed, the points of the grapnels were "coated with copper, and sometimes verdigris," which had come from brass metals "long submerged." The prospectus noted that *De Braak* had sixteen brass guns, which would account for the verdigris. She also carried seventy tons of copper ingots, and chemical action would have caused this copper to be diffused onto the shells and wood in the vicinity. This was proven beyond a doubt when an iron sounding rod, left in the mound in 1887, was found, when taken up, to be "coated with copper."[15]

The mound was covered by soft mud; as it was in the center of the channel, it received the deposits left by the ebb and flow of the tide. When divers examined the mysterious mound, they discovered that a sounding iron, twelve feet long, could easily be forced into it to its full length without encountering any obstructions. On other parts of the bay floor, however, it was impossible to sink the iron more than a few inches, as the clay bottom was solid. An iron cannon of 1,200 pounds had been found near this spot by an oyster dredger looking for anchors some years earlier. The fact that it had been discovered and recovered by a sweep line "proves that the hard body of clay composing the bottom was too dense to allow it to become buried."[16]

The factors cited above, the promoters stated confidently, show "that the prospect of raising the long buried bullion is based on something more than mere speculative surmise." With Ocean Wrecking being in possession of "an authentic copy of the ancient chart" of the channel and roadsteads, success was all but guaranteed—or so it was implied. The 1888 Pancoast Expedition, they wrote, had failed for only three reasons: (1) the expedition began too late in the season; (2) the *City of Long Branch*, a light draft stern-wheeler with two upper decks built in the style of Mississippi River steamers, was unable to hold her position over the wreck when there was any sea or wind turbulence and was therefore unsuitable for ocean wrecking; and (3) the expedition had not been fitted "with electrical appliances, which not only faciliate, but are absolutely necessary in the search of the ocean bed."[17] Despite the failure of the 1888 expedition, however, the effort had provided many strong "indications" that proved the existence of the wreck, which, the promoters assured potential investors, "will have great weight" when reviewed by experts.[18]

The Ocean Wrecking Company's proposal for the 1889 season was ambitious. To fit out a "suitable" expedition, under the command of Captain Charles A. Adams, the company proposed to raise $40,000. Certificates of investment would be issued, and a portion of the recovered treasure would be assigned to the Land Title and Trust Company, located at 608 Chestnut Street, Philadelphia, to pay dividends on the certificates. In the event that ten million dollars worth of treasure was recovered, $100 certificates would pay a dividend of $3,000 each; $300 certificates would pay $10,000 each; and any greater or lesser sum would be paid pro rata.[19]

The company proposed to purchase a steamer "suited in every way for ocean wrecking service." The vessel would be fitted out with a full diving operation, wrecking pumps, submarine search lights, "and all the paraphernalia for the successful prosecution of the search for the lost treasure."[20] The ideal vessel suggested by the company was a powerful, swift, seagoing tug. Differing somewhat from the typical harbor tug, it was higher in the bow and stern and generally broader abeam. Forward, it carried a strong derrick or crane, equipped with pulleys and ropes and powered by a steam hoisting system. Aside from the usual accommodations, it had "a cheerful cabin, in which the divers and laborers can sleep and live." It would be furnished with diving suits, jacks, dynamite cartridges, air pumps, a "dynamo" generator for electricity, electric and magnesium lamps, a submarine glass, grappling irons, and scores of other implements.[21]

With the general location of the site already known, it would be necessary to conduct only a limited sea search before pinpointing the wreck by means of a grappling operation. The most basic form of grappling search was carried out as follows: "It [the tug] reaches the place about where its object lies, throws overboard its tools, and moves rapidly to and fro upon the surface, traveling as far as possible in lines parallel and close together."[22] The grappling equipment available for such work varied widely. The simplest form was the grappling iron, a modified compound hook fastened to the end of a strong rope. Another tool favored by salvors was the modified grapple, so constructed that when it clutched a heavy sunken object it rang a bell on board the tug. Occasionally, two tugs might be employed to tow a long rope capable of sweeping a full quarter of a mile of the bottom at one time. Sometimes, when vessels containing a large amount of ferrous metals were being hunted, the searchers might employ a magnetic drag. This instrument was nothing more than a magnetic or electric needle encased in a waterproof box. When brought near a large mass of iron, "it is detected, and induces a current in an adjacent coil which gives an alarm upon the wrecking tug."[23]

Once the wreck was located and marked by a colored buoy, it could then be examined. In those rare moments when the water was clear, a preliminary survey might be conducted through the use of a "submarine glass." This device was described as "a double tube, of which one half is a simple pipe, closed at the lower end with a piece of fine glass, and the other half is a pipe at whose top is arranged a magnesium light or electric lamp."[24] After the apparatus was lowered into the water from the side of the tug, the magnesium would then be ignited. One pipe would send a powerful beam of light down into the water, "illuminating everything for at least a hundred feet." Through the other pipe, the observer on board the tug could examine everything upon which the light fell. It had been estimated that such an apparatus would permit observation in the waters of Lakes Champlain and George, in New York, to a depth of nearly 100 feet below the surface. In the ocean, off the coast, the range was seventy feet, while in such rivers as the Hudson no more than a twenty-foot range was possible, owing to the large amount of silt in the water.[25]

Once the initial inspection of the site was completed, diving and salvage work could begin in earnest. Although the divers on the three Pancoast expeditions had had to labor well below the five-fathom mark in utter "submarine gloom and darkness, by groping and feeling," since then "electrical science" had improved the situation enormously, and divers could now be provided with light. "The New Expedition this coming summer," therefore, would be

> fitted out with all the approved new appliances of submarine mining, and it [needed] no argument to prove that with electrical lights . . . brought to bear on all objects on the ocean bed, the long sought for treasure [would] have a better chance of being found and raised to the surface.[26]

It had also become possible for the diver to fasten incandescent lamps to his body or his helmet, to carry an electric lantern in his hand or to guide one which had been suspended from the tug above. The latest French technology even allowed a "vast beam of light" to be thrown from the wrecking vessel, making the submerged wreck "as light and bright as if it were upon the shore."[27]

For the 1889 season, Ocean Wrecking had made arrangements with an electric light company

> to furnish a powerful Dynamo, and engine to run it, capable of giving sixteen incandescent lights of one hundred candle power each, making a total of 1,600 candle power, which, when concentrated on the wreck of the "Braak," in the ten fathoms of water where she is located, will make even the minutest object clearly visible.[28]

Properly accoutred, divers could then begin the survey and salvage of the site in detail. The company did not, however, propose to raise the wreck "bodily" from the water. They planned merely "to pump out the mud and debris that has gathered in the hold since the day she went down." This would be accomplished with the aid of powerful wrecking pumps, capable of bringing to the surface twenty-five tons of debris per hour. "Most of the treasure, being in the form of gold and silver bullion, will be easily handled, and sent to the surface in iron baskets."[29]

Raising the cargo would be similar to unloading any ordinary cargo from a ship on the surface. From the derrick on the wrecking tug, a chain would be dropped to the site and attached to an iron basket. If some large object were to be recovered, the chain could be attached directly to it by the diver. When the basket was filled, or the object fastened securely, the diver would give a signal and the article would be hoisted aboard the tug. The only concern during the whole operation would be to prevent the air tube, signal cord, and lifeline of the diver from becoming entangled in the hoisting tackle. "Beyond this, the work is slow, dreary and monotonous."[30]

The expedition, it was proposed, would sail about May 15, 1889, and would "continue work until success crowns their efforts."[31]

By the spring of 1889, the Ocean Wrecking Company syndicate had apparently arranged for the Merritt Wrecking Company of New York to subcontract the search operations off Cape Henlopen. Whether Captain Adams was employed as commander of the operation, or even whether he was involved at all, is unclear. What is certain is that two officers of the Merritt Wrecking Company who had visited aboard the *City of Long Branch* during the 1888 expedition, and who had considerable knowledge of the site, were involved.

Captain Joseph Townsend, master of the salvage steamer *Tamesi*, of Somers Point, New Jersey, was the first to put to sea in the 1889 season.[32] Townsend, who had visited the Pancoast operations in August 1888, was an experienced salvor and a member of a particular breed of Delaware mariners known as "anchor sweepers," who operated with considerable success in and about the Delaware Capes during the latter half of the nineteenth century. The "sweepers" conducted their profitable, if occasionally dangerous, business amid the shoally reaches of Delaware Bay, in areas poorly marked by navigational aids. Each spring they would snag and recover anchors, ranging from 200 to 5,000 pounds, which had been lost during the previous year. Their prizes were frequently dropped off at the Queen Anne Pier in Lewes and then freighted to Philadelphia, where they were sold off as scrap iron.[33]

Townsend's search off Cape Henlopen was only partially successful. On April 25, 1889, after conducting what must have been a preliminary dragging operation, he wrote of encountering a giant chain, later said to be ninety feet long. Inspection of the chain by divers revealed that it led deep into the sand, possibly into a buried wreck. When the salvor attempted to recover this chain with his steam derrick, he was unable to free it. It mattered little to Townsend that *De Braak*'s cables had been rope, not chain, or that the salvage lines employed by *Hind* and *Vixen* had been thirteen-inch rope, not chain. The storytellers of a later day would say that Captain Townsend had enjoyed his own brief encounter with the elusive warship or had snagged the cable lost by *Hind* during the 1798 salvage effort.[34] A new chapter in the *De Braak* legend had been written.

By July the Merritt Wrecking Company of New York had placed Captain Demarest in charge of operations. Although his investigations were not publicized, the record indicates that his efforts were well under way by mid-summer. The Merritt company salvors "were sanguine of success upon their arrival at Delaware Breakwater" in late July.[35] Employing the services of the steam tug *Tuckahoe* as their principal operations platform,[36] they had set to work with a zeal matched only by that exhibited at the outset of the last Pancoast Expedition. By July 26 they had already announced that they had "succeeded in locating the sunken treasure ship *De Braak*." In Philadelphia, of course, a keen interest was again stirred up among the city's prominent financiers and businessmen, especially among those who had invested heavily in the enterprise. But the boastful claims of discovery, like those of Seth Pancoast before them, proved entirely premature. The Merritt Wrecking Company, even when aided by the latest in undersea technology, was forced in the end to admit defeat.[37]

James J. Kane's bubble had burst. His syndicate, however, which had raised tens of thousands of dollars in high-risk investment money to fund the project had emerged unscathed. After all, the small print on their certificates of offering clearly stated "that no liability shall be incurred herein by the Ocean Wrecking Co., Limited, unless the Treasures of the said 'Braak' shall be recovered."[38]

By this time, the search for *De Braak* had ushered the shipwreck into a new era of notoriety. In 1888, the noted American historian John Thomas Scharf had published his monumental, two-volume *History of Delaware*, which was critically acclaimed and destined to become and remain the standard reference work on Delaware history in every library and school system of the state for the next century. Scharf's *History* dedicated a substantial amount of space to *De Braak*. Like most Americans, he too had been seduced by the glamor and adventure of the underwater search for her purported treasure. Notwithstanding his reputable record for historical accuracy, he too had relied upon legend, hearsay, and the hyperbolic propaganda of the Philadelphia financiers. As a consequence, this first major work on the *De Braak* treasure story by a recognized historian was anything but accurate.

De Braak, according to Scharf, had been lost on "May 2, 1798, with nearly all its crew and a large amount of specie on board." Her captain had been "a bold Irish seaman" who had set sail in January 1798 with Letters of Marque against Napoleon and his allies. The ship had been outfitted with a dozen brass cannon and was manned by thirty-eight officers and crew. "After cruising in southern waters several months," he wrote, "the 'De Braak' approached the American shore laden with the fruits of its victories over the enemy and having in tow the Spanish galleon, 'La Platte.' " The prize's treasures were "said to have been (for those times) fabulous, consisting of gold, silver, and diamonds, in coins and metals, amounting to millions of dollars."[39]

Scharf readily conceded that "the stories of this unknown wealth have become a part of the traditions of this coast and their recital has encouraged many efforts to raise the wreck which have not yet been successful." The McCracken data, which he accepted as factual, indicated that the wreck site lay "about a mile from the breakwater, where a mound in the water at a depth of twenty-seven feet, is described. This is supposed to contain the treasure trove" and was the site which Seth Pancoast had systematically begun to uncover in the summer of 1887, "with favorable progress."[40]

Unfortunately, Scharf's *History of Delaware*, with its erroneous account of the loss of *De Braak* and her purported cargo of riches, would form the backbone of a myth, hitherto only a tradition, that would be accepted as fact for nearly a century. It would, indeed, be enlarged upon, twisted, and altered in much the same manner that the folktales from which it sprang had been. *De Braak*, which had been brought to national attention through the tireless efforts of a hardworking but naive Philadelphia doctor in his twilight years, had become a legend, first in lore and then in literature. For Pancoast, however, its legacy was one of conflict, bitterness, and financial ruin. On the morning of December 16, 1889, perhaps broken by the failure of his life's greatest endeavor, Seth Pancoast died at his residence in Philadelphia.[41]

The search which he had initiated would not be resumed seriously for more than four decades. The nation's attentions had turned elsewhere. Economic depression in the 1890s made further capital investment in such high-risk ventures as treasure hunting highly unattractive. America's emergence as a world power during the Spanish-American and the First World Wars focused the entrepreneurial spirit of would-be salvors elsewhere. Although a few, such as the submarine pioneer Simon Lake,[42] would wistfully consider picking up where Pancoast, Townsend, and Demarest had left off, *De Braak* would continue to rest undisturbed on the bottom of Delaware Bay, her legend becoming enshrined as history. And the *De Braak* treasure would continue to grow richer in the hearts and minds of daydreamers.

T E N

Buried in the Sand

In June 1931, treasure fever once again swept the nation. Although America had become deeply mired in the malaise of economic depression, many Americans welcomed the diversions offered by a handful of treasure hunters hell-bent on instant wealth. The craze had been set off partly by the news that nearly $1,000,000 in gold bullion would soon be recovered by a daring deep-water salvage operation on the remains of the ill-fated ocean liner *Egypt*. According to reports in the world press, the liner had gone down nine years earlier while en route from London to Bombay with a cargo of £1,054,000 in gold and silver destined for Indian banks. Owing to the 400-foot depths in which the vessel lay, however, salvage had long been considered all but impossible. Then the world watched with rapt attention as an Italian expedition led by Giovanni Quaglia, utilizing the latest in deep-sea technology, successfully recovered a fortune from the ship's hull.[1] Quaglia was feted with parades and lionized as a hero in Europe and America. His stunning accomplishment became a benchmark in the annals of marine salvage—and a tantalizing example of what enterprise and technology together could achieve for the dedicated treasure hunter. It was heady stuff indeed for a nation in the economic abyss of the Great Depression.

Thus it was hardly surprising that within months of the first incredible efforts to recover the *Egypt*'s gold numerous treasure-hunting expeditions were being launched around the globe. All that was believed necessary to get rich quick was a little ingenuity, a bit of technology, a dash of luck, and a worthy target. Among the many plans hatched during that fateful summer, despite the Depression, was an American syndicate's scheme to locate and recover the legendary booty of *De Braak*. Ralph E. Chapman, the first major entrepreneur who would try his luck on the site in forty-two years, was a well-to-do resident of New York City and, more importantly, a salvor with family ties to the world-famous Merritt, Chapman and Scott Salvage Company, the oldest firm of its kind in the United States—tracing its roots, in fact, to the Merritt Wrecking Company of 1889.[2] Like many, Chapman had long been aware of the *De Braak* tale, by now an old chestnut of a sea story along the middle Atlantic seaboard. But it was not until the euphoric days following the Quaglia success that the man-of-war actually began to reassert its magnetic appeal to members of the professional American salvage industry. Ralph E. Chapman would be among the very first to fall victim to its allure, but he would not be the last.

Chapman's desire to take up the hunt for *De Braak* was undoubtedly fostered by myriad influences. There were, of course, the many well-known and oft-told folktales about the vessel, handed down from generation to generation, which had been altered ever so slightly with each telling to the point where fact and fiction had become indistinguishable. And then there were the less common stories of some kind of actual contact with the site by local watermen or the occasional passing mariner. One such account which might well have inspired Chapman to action was a much-publicized story related by one Benjamin S. Albertson. Although somewhat different from most *De Braak*-contact accounts, Albertson's tale was intriguing and, for some, just enough out of the ordinary to have a ring of truth about it. According to Albertson, the incident occurred during the opening days of America's entry into World War I, when he had served aboard a U.S. Navy minesweeper dragging for German mines near the Delaware Capes. On one particular occasion in 1917 he had been watching the discharge of depth charges during an anti-mine exercise when he was stunned to see "several pieces of wreckage . . . blown into the air, one of which was a small cannon of the type carried by the *De Braak*."[3] Somehow, he managed to secure a small fragment of the wreckage, which proved to be made of teak. Although it is quite doubtful that he even knew what types of ordnance the old warship had carried or of the fact that few, in any, European warships were ever built of teak, Albertson found many listeners who were willing to accept his story at face value. The gun, he swore, had been sent to Philadelphia, but then had mysteriously disappeared. Yet the mere proximity of the supposed incident to Cape Henlopen, together with the piece of teak, served only to whet some appetites for treasure. Soon, the account became one more component of the ever-expanding folklore which had grown up about the wreck. It even reintroduced an older element, that of the teak-built ship, which would continue to find adherents for the next forty years.[4]

Whatever it was that had hooked Chapman, in any case, would remain with him until his premature death. The well-heeled New Yorker attacked the project with a single-minded passion. Through his network of information sources, he soon learned about the existence of the McCracken Bible coordinates and quickly reached an agreement with Gilbert McCracken's great-grandson, Randolph. It had not been difficult to strike a deal, for Randolph McCracken, a fifty-year-old Lewes butcher, had long cherished his own dreams of one day recovering the sunken warship's fabled treasure. Hoping to see his lifelong fantasy finally realized, he eagerly cast his lot with the slick

New York salvor. McCracken turned over his information for a share of what he believed to be a fortune worth between $15 and $40 million lying in the holds of the wreck, waiting for a salvor like Chapman to dig it up.

Unfortunately for Chapman, the McCracken data would prove to be of limited value, for the focus of the bearings, the venerable 165-foot lighthouse erected in 1765 with such fanfare had succumbed to the sea. Abandoned in October 1924, as the nearby shoreline was steadily eroding away, it had finally collapsed into the surf on April 13, 1926. The great stones and blocks of granite that had been hauled across the dunes with such effort were salvaged and sold off for eight dollars a load, some to be used for various building projects in Lewes, Rehoboth, and the surrounding areas, some simply carried off by souvenir hunters for building fireplaces and chimneys in their homes.[5] McCracken's grand datum point had disappeared.

Nevertheless, Chapman proceeded with vigor to prepare for the first twentieth-century expedition to find *De Braak*. Forming a new company, dubbed the Braak Corporation, he procured the expertise and equipment of the Baltimore Derrick and Salvage Company (BD & SC) and the London Salvage Company. A local mariner named Charles Johnston was taken on as a consultant.[6] By midsummer of 1932 Chapman had fielded two boats, the seventeen-ton *Katie Durm*, of Baltimore, and the work launch *Cap*, to begin dragging operations.[7] The BD & SC, which provided the boats, had also contracted to supply a team of experienced industrial salvors under the direction of a veteran deep-sea diver named Charles E. Jackson. As the manager of BD & SC, Jackson had extensive experience, ranging from construction work on Hong Kong's great breakwater to ship salvage. Like most members of the expedition, both Jackson and Johnston were familiar with the *De Braak* legend and were eager to search for the treasure beneath the sea.[8]

The hunt officially began in midsummer. By late July, the operation had been slowed down considerably, as a veritable graveyard of shipwrecks lying scattered about the bottom had to be carefully negotiated by the drag boats. On a single day, for instance, eight hangs had been encountered, all of them requiring time-consuming inspection by divers. Although each proved to be a false lead, together they served as a superb prognostication of what a drag search for the old warship entailed.[9]

On September 24, Jackson, who had been superintending field operations, was heartened when yet another snag was made in the area approximating the ranges provided by McCracken's data. The location also roughly corresponded to the site where the 1917 depth-charging had dislodged fragments of a teak-built wreck. Diver inspection of the site produced promising data, and a 100-ton marine derrick named *Continental*, one of the largest in the world and "equipped with modern salvage devices," including "a 1,000 foot articulated sweep" wire, was summoned from Philadelphia. Chapman himself soon arrived on the scene to take charge of field operations. Five days later, intensive diver investigations of the wreck began in earnest—only to be halted by a disaster.[10]

It probably mattered little to Charles Jackson whether he dived during the day or evening, for the bottom of the sea near Cape Henlopen was always dark. At 8:15 P.M. on September 29, he prepared to make yet another exploratory descent. He was just starting over the side of the *Katie Durm* "when a sudden heavy sea caused the launch to heel over sharply and upset the lamp in the engine room." In an instant, a flash fire caused by the overturned lamp swept through the room, inflicting second-degree burns on assistant engineer James McDowell before rapidly spreading topside. Somehow, McDowell managed to escape and sound the alarm. Chapman, who had just boarded the boat, immediately raced into the chart house to save his precious maps and other data, even as Jackson was being hauled topside and freed of his cumbersome diving suit. Fortunately, *Cap* came alongside within minutes and rescued the entire crew. *Katie Durm*, however, was a total loss. [11]

Although hindered in his quest, Ralph Chapman was not yet ready to give up. By the beginning of November, he had returned to the site with *Cap* and a replacement for *Katie Durm* called *Corsair*.[12] Stubbornly resolved to continue work until the operation would be forced to close down by winter weather, Chapman was roundly supported by his men. One of Jackson's divers, George Tyzack of Philadelphia, typified the team's attitude. During the most chaotic moments of the recent fire, he had lost his diamond engagement ring and became resolved not only to recover the treasure of *De Braak* for his boss, but his ring as well. All of the expeditionaries were equally confident of finding the treasure, as one said half in jest, "to do their bit toward ending the depression."[13]

Operations continued without letup throughout the month, with divers working at depths of up to 100 feet, in two-hour shifts, on a site that Chapman steadfastly believed to be his own *Egypt*. Stormy weather frequently interrupted the work for days on end, but everyone was kept busy repairing equipment and attending to the myriad tasks of keeping a salvage operation afloat. After each lull, work on the site was immediately resumed despite the atrocious bottom conditions and treacherous currents which followed every storm. Jackson and Tyzack spent many hours exploring the wreck in the murky atmosphere of the bottom and eventually developed a rough, working familiarity with the site, not unlike a blind man's knowledge of his own bedroom. But Chapman needed verification that the hulk was indeed *De Braak*, not simply one of the innumerable wrecks encountered in the ships' graveyard.

"About half the ship is buried in sand and everything above the main deck has been battered by the undertow," the salvor noted in frustration.[14] The recovery of diagnostic evidence was imperative to justify the enormous expense of the operation. Chapman's diver team had already begun to recover a variety of artifacts in a concerted effort to confirm the ship's identity. They brought up timbers of various sizes and shapes, framing members, large and small handwrought copper nails, unidentified pieces of iron, and an old iron chain plate, which they had cut off with a hacksaw where it protruded above the bottom, thirty-five feet from the bow.[15] One piece of wood was certified by the Smithsonian Institution as teak, the material with which Chapman fervently believed De Braak to have been built—or so it was reported to the press.[16]

Whether Chapman was actually convinced by the evidence in hand—which was admittedly thin—or was merely attempting to put the best face on the questionable findings is unknown. That he had located a wooden sailing ship, however, was certain. Indeed, he had found numerous wrecks during his search. But since the waters off Cape Henlopen constituted a cemetery of sunken ships, verifying one of them as De Braak would require far more solid evidence than he had thus far produced. Then his salvor's luck really seemed to have run out when his divers reported that they had located signs of four other wrecks in the same area. All were built of teak, and all were of the same contour, length, and construction as De Braak! Suddenly, as if to further confound matters, the calm seas gave way to sharp winds and nasty weather.[17]

By November 29, an early, stormy winter had set in. Having expended $10,000 on the project without recovering a single doubloon, Chapman was finally obliged to terminate work. Yet he remained convinced, at least publicly, that he had found De Braak and, promising to return the following season to finish the job, announced his "success" in a glowing report to the media. Marine surveyors from both New York and Baltimore, he stated, had examined the wood and were "satisfied that the treenail fastenings and hand wrought copper spikes date back to the shipbuilding of 1780." He pointed to two pieces of cast iron, believed to be belaying pins or fittings from the ship's fife rail, as further evidence. They had, he claimed, "been in salt water so long that the metal has changed so that it can be whittled away with a pen knife." Given the materials recovered, as well as the contour of the hull, which he believed corresponded to that of De Braak, there could be no question of her identity. Teasingly, Chapman let it be known that he had authenticated the presence of gold in the wreck, but refused to comment further on the find, titillating the press and the general public even more. The treasure's rumored value skyrocketed from $10,000,000 to $80,000,000. Chapman then boldly informed the New York Times (which had been given exclusive story rights) that he had already developed plans for outfitting an elaborate floating plant with which to move the tons of silt covering the hull, "then to string the wreck preparatory to lifting and carrying it to a marine railway."[18]

Ralph Chapman, however, never had the opportunity to make good on his plans, for that winter he was killed in an automobile accident.[19] Yet the Braak

Corporation, even with its driving force gone, did not immediately collapse. There were others who were more than eager to take up where the ambitious New York salvor had left off.

Within days of the termination of Chapman's 1932 campaign, the Braak Corporation, sponsored in part by a syndicate of New York shipping magnates led by Alan C. Robertson, of Rockville Center, and Alfred E. Jordan, a Manhattan consulting engineer and Mayor of Great Neck Estates, Long Island, had announced new plans to recover the treasure. Robertson and Jordan claimed to have unearthed dramatic new historical and geographical data, including letters from Captain James Drew and Admiralty prize records, which indicated that the little warship had gone down with not only gold and silver bullion taken from no less than three Spanish galleons, but also with a rich cargo of copper ingots.[20]

In December, soon after Chapman's suspension of operations, the splinter group had secretly set out, despite the weather, to drag the entire mouth of the Delaware River. In the course of their survey, they struck a wreck which they fervently believed to be *De Braak*. A small piece of the vessel was recovered and, upon examination by a wood specialist, proved to be lignum vitae, which the two treasure hunters claimed was commonly used in ship construction of the eighteenth century. They also recovered specimens of greenheart and camphor, leading them to state publicly that not only had *De Braak* been a Dutch vessel, but that she was of Javanese construction.[21] Secure in the belief that, unlike Chapman, they had actually discovered the fabled ship, they purchased the old Fire Island Lightship (*No. 68*), rechristened her *Captain Drew*, and began fitting her out at the Tebo Yacht Basin in Brooklyn, New York, for heavy salvage operations. Captain J. A. Winkstrom, of Baltimore, was hired to serve as her master.[22]

Despite Robertson and Jordan's dramatic reports of their alleged success in locating *De Braak*, national events were conspiring to foil the plans of the new leaders of the Braak Corporation. On March 4, 1933, the banking system of the United States collapsed and practically every bank in America closed. On March 26, still hoping to launch their venture and trying to alleviate investor anxieties, despite the nation's mushrooming economic disaster, Alfred Jordan made a desperate attempt to present the pursuit of *De Braak*'s supposed treasure as a lucrative business venture. "We're not just romanticists," he declared, "we're business men. It is our belief that the survey we have made of the coast, as a result of new data discovered, will enable us to recover the cargo of the old warship. If we fail, well, others have sought and failed, and we will be no worse than they were."[23]

But like others before it, the Braak Corporation was doomed to collapse. Because of the bank "holiday," the *New York Times* noted in a brief postmortem on the venture, "people became afraid to risk any sizable capital, and so the lightship never steamed into Delaware Breakwater."[24] But the lure of *De Braak* continued to be a fatal attraction.

E L E V E N

Weather Witch

During the summer of 1935, a group of "sportsmen and socialites" led by
Charles N. Colstad, an engineer from Attleboro, Massachusetts, and a
twenty-one-year-old youth just out of college named Richard T. Wilson, of
Providence, Rhode Island, became the next to cast their hats into the ever-
widening ring of *De Braak* treasure seekers.[1]

Like their predecessors, the Colstad organization had conducted a preliminary survey off Cape Henlopen. Like Chapman, they had also acquired the
McCracken bearings by promising the ever-hopeful Randolph McCracken a
seven-and-a-half percent share of the booty. Colstad drew his datum lines on
a 1933 geodetic survey map as a blue ring running from Delaware Bay to a
point on the Cape Henlopen coast, which he marked as the site of the old lighthouse.[2] And like those who had searched in vain before him, he also under-
took the expensive venture armed with inaccurate or distorted historical data.
Building upon the mistakes of their predecessors, both Colstad and Wilson
believed *De Braak* to have been built of teak, based on "old records in the
possession of the Colstad Corporation."[3]

Colstad's delusions were on a grand scale. He asserted to the press that the
warship was 125 feet in length, thirty feet abeam, and had been armed with
eighteen deck cannon when she went down. He noted that sixteen of the guns
were the same as those aboard when she had been taken from the Dutch, with
two guns later added by Drew. By 1936, the seventy tons of copper said to have
been aboard had grown to 200 tons. The copper bars, Colstad stated (without
divulging his source of information), had been taken from two Spanish galleons bound from La Plata to Spain. Adding further embellishments to an already muddled piece of history, he noted authoritatively that this copper had
been stored "on her deck, and thus, making the vessel top-heavy," had caused
De Braak to capsize. Like his predecessors, Colstad too was certain that he
had located her remains when the preliminary survey ended with the recovery
of a piece of teak from a wreck site.[4] It would seem that the floor of Delaware
Bay was indeed littered with the wrecks of ships constructed of teak!

Convinced that fabulous riches lay in store for them, Colstad and Wilson
chartered a former Boston pilot schooner, the 113-foot *Liberty*, to be used as

a survey and salvage platform. After hiring a diver named Harry Morgan, they began their search in earnest. But like Chapman, who had also begun with the McCracken bearings, the expeditionaries were obliged to estimate the former position of the Cape Henlopen Light in order to compute the wreck's approximate location.[5] As a consequence, Colstad would search more than 1,700 feet to the east of *De Braak*'s actual resting place. Not surprisingly, the dragging operations carried out during that summer and early fall were unsuccessful.[6]

By November 8, with the onset of unseasonably blustery weather that caused numerous delays (attributed by some superstitious members of the *Liberty*'s crew to the influences of a "Weather Witch"), the team had begun to consider suspending their expensive grappling efforts for the winter. "Our daily cost of operation is enormous," Colstad explained in one press interview. Not a word was said, however, about the site from which the teak had been recovered. Yet, undoubtedly with an eye to forestalling potential desertion by investors, he quickly sought to reassure the public that he was hot on the scent. "We have been encouraged in what we have accomplished and believe we are on the right trail."[7]

To the superstitious sailors aboard the *Liberty*, however, their failure to locate *De Braak* was unquestionably the result of a jinx. In order to counteract the jinx that protected the wreck and its treasures and to defeat the wreck's guardian demon, appropriate measures had to be taken. These included drawing pictures of the demon on cardboard and then proceeding to riddle them with gunfire or any missile available, but to no avail.[8] The *Philadelphia Inquirer*, it was later said, had paid considerable attention to the efforts of the *Liberty*'s Gloucester-born skipper, Captain Clayton Morrissey, and his crew when they again attempted to exorcise the "Weather Witch" with votive offerings. The witch was described by one observer as a screaming beldame, a veritable sea hag, who rode the tempests to protect the sanctity of the treasure entrusted to her care. The measures employed by the superstitious mariners to temper her wrath were extraordinary.

"First of all, they constructed a huge Weather Witch," it was reported, "with broomstick, peaked cap and cape, her long gray hair streaming from under her headgear. The witch was given the position of honor in the cabin, offered drink and food, and then was burned, with many incantations, in the galley stove."[9] Captain Morrissey was charged with performing the ceremony and chanting the incantations. The witch's ashes were collected from the stove and placed in a bottle. At sunset, Morrissey scattered them on the sea. Votive offerings notwithstanding, the winds increased soon afterward, growing more violent by the hour. The next morning, when the *Liberty* sailed from Lewes to resume the hunt, the pilot inadvertently turned the ship "against the sun," a grave error in the minds of the seamen. Morrissey immediately brought her about, returned to the pier, and then set out again, to "dispel the ill omen" of sailing against the sun.[10] Despite the crew's acts of obedience to the spirit world, ten days later, after marking the most likely target, the project had to be shut down. Both Colstad and Wilson, however, stated adamantly that they would be back.[11]

Throughout the spring and early summer of 1936, Randolph McCracken fretted over the Colstad Corporation's failure to return. Each day he would walk down to the Lewes waterfront to converse with his friends about the likelihood of the treasure hunters' returning and to scan the horizon anxiously for signs of the *Liberty*. Then, on July 12, it was announced that the Braak Corporation, which had lingered on in name, if not in substance, had finally been allowed "to die a natural death." McCracken became disconsolate. His belief that he would one day inherit the undersea legacy bequeathed to him by his ancestors had never wavered until then, for both the Braak and the Colstad corporations, each of which had promised him a share of the booty in exchange for his priceless data, had apparently called it quits.[12]

McCracken's despondency was short-lived. On August 1, Colstad publicly announced that he was returning for another try. Oddly enough, however, the salvor had scaled down his estimate of the *De Braak* treasure to less than $8 million, a substantial reduction from the original $10 million figure bandied about the previous year. Whatever motivated the downplay is unknown. It did not, however, cool the salvor's ardor for the hunt.[13] Colstad's initial plan for his 1936 campaign called for the deployment of two small boats, a pair of divers, and the most modern undersea excavation equipment available, including "a high pressure pump for scouring sand and gravel away from a wreck thought to be *De Braak*." On August 11, the converted fishing trawler *Nellie L. Parmenter* began to take on salvage and diving gear at Providence, Rhode Island, for what was hoped to be the final push. Not until August 21, however, would *Parmenter*, accompanied by the launch *Doubloon*, finally sail, with a crew of seven under the command of Captain W. A. Twombley of Maynard, Rhode Island.[14] Colstad was determined to succeed where he had failed the year before. At least two full months of operations were scheduled, with work to continue until early November, or "until winter weather makes continuation of their salvage operations impossible." The team was soon joined by Richard Wilson's older brother Ford, who had taken up lodgings aboard the *Nellie L. Parmenter*.[15]

Soon after their arrival on the Delaware, *Parmenter* and the twenty-two-foot motor launch *Doubloon* were in full operation, dragging "a plowing grapnel on the ocean floor for a mile off Cape Henlopen." Once the site had been located, the salvors hoped to employ a "high-powered jetting pump" to excavate the wreck, which Colstad believed to be totally buried and preserved beneath the silts. His divers' work, if and when they found the site, would be fully illuminated by a 250-watt underwater lamp.[16]

The search had come to focus on the region around the Cam Buoy at the entrance to Delaware Breakwater. Within days, the treasure hunters had become unwilling attractions for waterborne sightseeing expeditions, as gaggles of onlookers in chartered fishing boats hovered nearby, hoping for that first glimpse of gold.[17] Once again, however, despite the work of chief diver Jack Talley, whose adventures with a five-foot hammerhead shark and a three-foot-long sea turtle, "with a head the size of a grown man," had attracted the attention of the media, the search was proving less than rewarding.[18] Then, in mid-September, the "Weather Witch" returned, in all her fury, adding her own whammy.

The hurricane which struck the Delaware coast on September 18 was not, as storms go, the most brutal one ever to batter the region. By the time it had careened about Cape Henlopen, on its way from Florida to New England, its winds were reportedly down to eighty-five miles per hour. Tides at Delaware Breakwater were barely four feet above normal. But its impact was destructive nevertheless.[19]

Off the Breakwater, the 500-ton fishing schooner *Long Island*, Captain William N. Bertrand commanding, which had just put out from Lewes, went down south of the Overlook Lightship and within sight of shore. Then the 3,800-ton collier *Ida Hay Atwater*, with forty men aboard, was driven onto Cape Henlopen. Further south along the coast, no fewer than seventy-five wrecks were counted, ranging from skiffs and cabin cruisers to seagoing schooners. At least thirty vessels had sought shelter in the Delaware, and eighteen had found security behind the Breakwater. The damage onshore was also considerable. At Ocean City, Maryland, a half-mile-long stretch of boardwalk was swept away in minutes, and nearby Sinepuxent Bridge, joining the resort town to the island of Assateague, disappeared. Bethany Beach was evacuated, while Lewes and Rehoboth battened down for the worst, as all highways leading to the Delmarva coast became impassable. With power lost, communications were severely crippled. The Delaware National Guard was put on alert. At Lewes, the *Nellie L. Parmenter* and the *Doubloon* remained snugly lashed to their moorings at the Queen Anne Dock and managed to ride out the gale.[20]

Although the storm had sunk or blown off all of Colstad's range markers, the salvor's vessels had suffered little actual damage. The time loss however, was another matter, for expenses continued to mount up, in fair weather or foul, for the lease of vessels, materials, and manpower. For days after the hurricane, weather conditions at Cape Henlopen remained blustery, allowing little or no work to be done. On September 25 another gale, with gusts of thirty miles per hour out of the northwest, struck Lewes. This time, the treasure hunters were not so lucky. The *Doubloon* was ripped from her moorings during the height of the blow and was tossed upon the beach 300 yards away as if she were already a piece of flotsam. Considerable damage was inflicted upon her bow decking. Assisted by members of the Lewes Coast Guard Station, the salvors were obliged to literally manhandle their injured craft onto a marine railway for repairs.[21]

Colstad appeared to be philosophical about the whole thing. In an address to the Lewes Rotary Club that same week, he related tales of his own travails, those of *De Braak* nearly a century and a half earlier, and accounts of other marine disasters that had plagued the Henlopen shores over the years, including the fairly recent loss of *Katie Durm* during the Chapman expedition. Colstad delighted his audience by disclosing details of the sophisticated search-and-recover technology that he was employing, and he suggested that *De Braak* had hitherto eluded discovery because everyone had been looking for a vessel sitting on the bottom. He himself, however, was looking for her *beneath* the bottom![22]

Despite Colstad's optimism, the onset of winter obliged the salvor to give up the hunt again. Although a fortune had already been spent, Colstad and Wilson, like their predecessor Chapman, bravely announced that they would return for a third try in the spring of 1937. Money, however, was in short supply. The following year, Colstad met with Alan Robertson, the venture capitalist who had once made his own attempt to find *De Braak*, in an effort to form a joint-venture syndicate of their two organizations. The principals, however, were unable to come to an agreement, and the deal collapsed aborning. The Colstad-Wilson effort to find *De Braak* became the fifth failure in as many decades.

By the spring of 1937, *De Braak* had become something of a cottage industry at Lewes, thanks to the national media attention. One chronicler of regional history noted that "the legendary worth" of the ship was then calculated to range between one and forty million dollars. A WPA-sponsored writer's project to document the history of Delaware, the results of which were published that year, recorded for the first time the claim that the treasure was indeed so great that two major efforts had been made by the British to raise the ship, in 1798 and 1799. The misinformation, adapted from nineteenth-century folktales, would soon gain a new flock of believers in the ever-expanding lore of *De Braak*.[23]

Like moths to a flame, small-time treasure hunters, curiosity seekers, and the press continued to be drawn to the tiny village of Lewes. Not a few of the local inhabitants were infected by the plague of gold fever, and each told his own version of the *De Braak* story to the media, which treated each tale as if it were gospel, straight from the mouth of Captain Drew himself. One of the more colorful yarners of that time was Jim Bartlett, by then aged sixty-seven, but who had participated in the third Pancoast Expedition as a mess boy.

For half a century Bartlett had nourished his own dream of finding the legendary ship, and he had developed his own peculiar idea of where her bones had come to rest. Excited to action by the recent parade of treasure hunters passing through Lewes, his passions soon got the better of him. Captain Bartlett, who had long borne the nickname "Cheery" because of his happy disposition, was well known in Lewes and enjoyed a certain popularity. His theory about *De Braak*'s wreck site, however, considering all of the recent deep-sea efforts to locate the ship, was unique: Bartlett believed she would be found beneath land rather than water. Pointing to coastal changes at Cape Henlopen during the previous sixty years, he reasoned that the ship lay under forty-five feet of sand along a section of the windswept beach. "Her nose is head in," he stated knowingly, "carried there by the strong rip tides around Cape Henlopen." His calculations of her location, he told one reporter, were based on a seaman's knowledge of wind velocity, direction, tide, and the amount of sail the sloop had carried.[24]

What had really stirred his imagination, however, was an event which had occurred about thirty years earlier as he was working near the shore. Around the year 1907, Bartlett had observed a black preacher named Davis pick up a gold brick on the beach. The brick had been worn thin in the center and was nicked around the edges, but its value was obvious. Quickly befriending the preacher, Bartlett had journeyed with him to Philadelphia, where they had had the gold assayed at the United States Mint and then sold it for $140.[25] Without apparent access to, or knowledge of, the actual records, Bartlett had constructed a wonderful tale, which found its own niche in the ever-growing *De Braak* mythology. "The gold," he informed a reporter from the *New York Times*,

> was a sample bar looted from Spanish galleons, raided by the British sloop, and placed in her cabin by her skipper, Captain James F. Drew, who went down with his ship. There are thirteen more bars somewhere in Drew's cabin . . . as two were taken from each of the seven vessels captured.[26]

In addition to the alleged treasure aboard, Bartlett also stated that there were a number of strong boxes, said to have been buried for safety by British soldiers "who refused to leave money aboard ship when they landed here in 1758." Bartlett was, indeed, a man of many rich and varied tales.

The gregarious captain had first begun to take his imaginings seriously during the Chapman Expedition, later elaborating on them during the Colstad project. He had talked with both Chapman and Colstad, but had found neither to be the least bit interested in his theories or information. But "Cheery" had already worked up a head of steam on his own, and, undismayed, he resolved to dig for the alleged treasure. His method of locating the site was somewhat unconventional. Utilizing a gadget invented by a New Jersey resident that relied upon a property called "spiritual magnetism," which, it was claimed, could locate buried metals "by vibrations much in the manner of a radio wave device," Bartlett was confident that the long-lost shipwreck would become his by default. He was so optimistic, in fact, that he confidently predicted to the national press that he could pinpoint the site to within 150 feet of its location.[27] Once the site had been located, he planned to employ a well-driving machine to drill four test holes in the area. Bartlett was granted a three-year lease for prospecting along the municipally owned beach front by Mayor David W. Burbage and the Lewes Board of Commissioners, who were promised five percent of the recovered treasure for the town coffers. An additional forty percent, Bartlett noted with a groan, would have to go to the government. "All I want," declared the old waterman, "is a couple of gold bricks to hang on my gate post. I know the folks here are so honest, they'll not bother 'em."[28] It was a pleasant thought, but he need not have worried, for his costly, ill-founded efforts amounted to nothing more than a well-publicized chimera.

Photographs

The author has presented in words the history of *HMS De Braak* and offers here a visual account of the great vessel. The author expresses appreciation to those who gave permission to reproduce photographs in this volume, many of them unpublished until their inclusion in this book.

A raised detail in marble on the Drew Memorial in St. Nicholas Church, Saltash, portrays the foundering of a vessel and two sailors clinging to a rock. The picture is an inaccurate rendition of the drowning of Captain John Drew at Plymouth on January 11, 1789 as HMS *Cerberus*, Captain Drew's ship, did not sink with him as the relief suggests. (*Donald G. Shomette*)

Captain James Drew (*top*), Captain John Drew (*middle*), and Acting Lieutenant James William Drew (*bottom*) as they appear on the memorial in St. Nicholas Church, Saltash, England. (*Donald G. Shomette*)

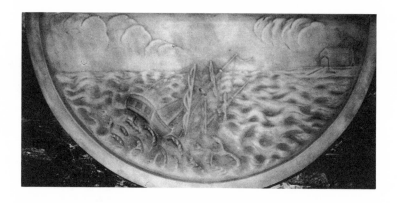

A raised detail in marble on the Drew Memorial in St. Nicholas Church is the only known contemporary portrayal of the loss of *DeBraak*. (*Donald G. Shomette*)

The James Drew Memorial in the churchyard of St. Peter's Episcopal Church, Lewes, Delaware. The memorial, with an inaccurate date of the sinking *DeBraak*, was erected by Drew's widow in 1832, and has been incorrectly assumed by most treasure hunters to be James Drew's gravesite. The captain's remains are interred beneath the chancel of the church. (*Donald G. Shomette*)

The Cape Henlopen Lighthouse, on the Great Dune, shortly before it collapsed into the sea on April 13, 1926. (*Delaware State Museums*)

The McCracken family's Bible in which the location of the wrecksite was kept. (*Delaware State Museums*)

The cryptic page of notations in the McCracken family Bible, recording the location of the wreck of *De Braak*. Two inscriptions appear on the fragile paper, one almost illegible and attributed to Lewes pilot William McCracken, ca. 1805. The second, a transcription of the first, is unattributable, but was written after the collapse of the Cape Henlopen Lighthouse, for the notation refers to the "Hen Light Foundations." (*Delaware State Museums*)

Side-scan sonar signature of *De Braak* wrecksite. Note the horizontal line above the wreck mass. The line is the signature of the mysterious U.S. Lighthouse Service spar bouy. During the 1984 season, the spar was incorrectly believed to be a mast from the ship. (*John Fish*)

Remote sensing expert Alan Bieber and the side-scan sonar (*far right*) accomplished what a century of treasure hunters had failed to do—pinpoint *De Braak*'s resting place. (*The Whale*)

A Sub-Sal diver prepares for a descent on the *De Braak*. (*Claudia Melson*)

The bell recovered from *De Braak*, with the words, "La Patrocle 1781" clearly cast into it, suggests the probable identity and date of commissioning of the vessel during her French incarnation. Patrocles, a Macedonian general (ca. 312–216 B.C.) commanded the fleet of Seleucus I and conducted an exploratory voyage into the Caspian Sea. (*The Whale*)

Sub-Sal Vice President Joseph Wise, President Harvey Harrington, diver Joe Amaral, Alan Bieber, and John Fish (*left to right*) present the second carronade recovered from *De Braak* to the press. The first carronade, recovered without state permission, had been quietly hidden in a creek near Lewes. (*The Whale*)

Sub-Sal's contract historian John Fish, standing in front of a fish tank filled with water and *De Braak* artifacts, examines an X-ray of a flintlock pistol trigger guard for the press. (*The Whale*)

Mariner served as Sub-Sal's principal operations platform for the 1984 salvage season. Note the decompression chamber and lift on the stern. *(The Whale)*

Sub-Sal president and *De Braak* discoverer Harvey Harrington monitors diver conversations aboard *Mariner* during the 1984 season. *(The Whale)*

State agent and marine archaeologist Rob Reedy examines a cannonball and gun tackle encased in concretion. Reedy was later employed by Sub-Sal, Inc., as a contract consultant. *(The Whale)*

The sifting box aboard *Mariner* was employed to sift artifacts brought up in the airlift. (*Claudia Melson*)

Copper Chain recovered during the 1984 operations. (*Claudia Melson*)

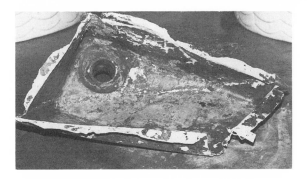

The wrecksite produced a large collection of artifacts, including this lead "kitchen sink," possibly a bath or even a "seat of ease." (*Claudia Melson*)

The famous James Drew mourning ring, inscribed in memory of his brother John, drowned on January 11, 1798. Although the authenticity of the expandable band ring was questioned by many, it was declared genuine by experts from Christie's Auction House of New York. (*Delaware State Museums*)

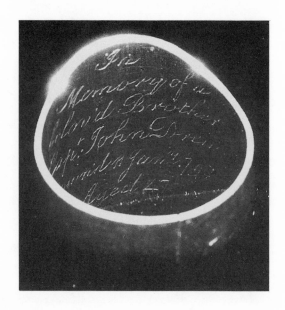

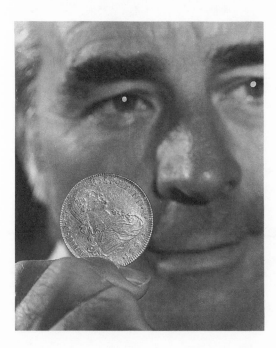

Harvey Harrington holds a gold Spanish coin dated 1795. He believed the coins to be but a tantalizing foretaste of the treasures to be recovered from the remains of *De Braak*. (*The Whale*)

Claudia F. Melson, Curator of Registration for the Delaware Bureau of Museums, with three containers, probably Iberian in origin, recovered from *De Braak*. The large 50 gallon water jug is identical to one recovered from the wreck of H.M.S. *Pandora*. (*Claudia Melson*)

Dozens of spirit bottles after cleaning and cataloging. (*Claudia Melson*)

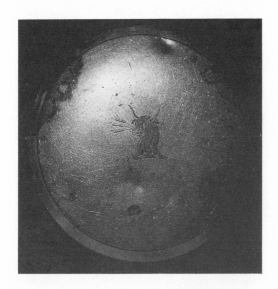

The back of a gold watch, the personal property of De Braak's ill-starred commander, Captain James Drew, bearing the Drew family crest, the head of a bull with three sheaves of wheat in its mouth. (*Delaware State Museums*)

The Cashman barge and crane rig that would wrest *De Braak*'s bones from the mouth of Delaware Bay, where they had rested for 188 years. (*Claudia Melson*)

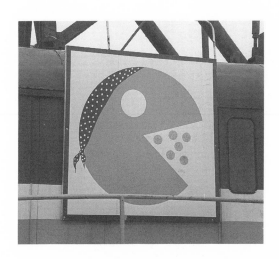

The pirate Pac Man chasing gold coins, mounted on the side of the recovery crane. *(David V. Beard)*

Hundreds of onlookers begin to assemble
on the shores of Cape Henlopen on the
morning of August 11, 1986 to view the
recovery of *De Braak*. By midday the crowd
of spectators swelled to 14,000. (*The Whale*)

For a brief moment during the rushed recovery, as De Braak dangled helplessy from her lifting cables, disgorging tons of sediments and artifacts back into the sea, she appeared to many as a ghost ship in the night. (*Delaware State Museums*)

Archaeologists and volunteers attempt to systematically sort through the debris aboard the hull the day after the recovery. (*David V. Beard*)

One of the points along the hull severly damaged by cables during the recovery of August 11. (*David V. Beard*)

Beard hoses down the hull to prevent drying out and wood shrinkage as Dr. John Kern looks on. (*David V. Beard*)

Beard gingerly cleans an artifact found in the debris as Delaware archaeologist Charles Fithian looks on. (*David V. Beard*)

Deputy Directory of Delaware Division of
Historical and Cultural Affairs Dean Nelson
retrieves a salior's shoe. (*David V. Beard*)

A concretion reveals a wine bottle and fine china, documented for the first time aboard a Royal Navy warship of the 18th century as being used by both officers and crew. Was this change in social habits a consequence of the levelling effects of the Great Mutiny? (*David V. Beard*)

Following the hull recovery, salvors attempt to remove all large items from the site, including the unused cradle. (*David V. Beard*)

The mysterious U.S. Lighthouse Service spar bouy (*top*) and stone anchor (*bottom*) found lying adjacent to the hull rest aboard the deck of the salvage barge. The buoy was permitted to rust into a useless pile of flakes before research into its origins could be undertaken. Had *De Braak* actually been found and marked before 1933? *(Claudia Melson)*

Dr. John Kern stands beside "Jaws," the giant clambucket that would be used to tear the bottom of Delaware Bay apart in a futile search for the mythical treasure of *De Braak*. (*David V. Beard*)

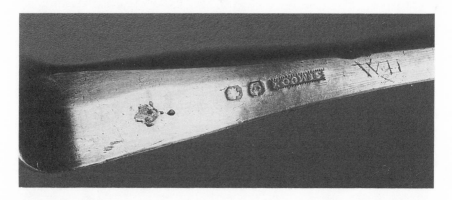

The initials "WH" inscribed on this silver fork suggest that it may have belonged to William Hurlston of London, one of *De Braak*'s midshipman, who was lost on May 25, 1798. (*Delaware State Museums*)

This Monmouth Cap, a hat style quite popular among English seamen of the 18th century, is only the second of its kind ever recovered intact from an English shipwreck site. (*Delaware State Museum*)

Thousands of sheathing tacks, each with the Royal Navy broad arrow stamped on the undersides of their heads, were recovered from the spoil dredged up by "Jaws." (*Donald Shomette*)

Two cranes maneuver on the shores of Roosevelt Inlet to remove the hull of *De Braak* from the barge. (*Marc Clery*)

The starboard hull of *De Braak* in the cofferdam home in which it would remain for four years. Soon after this picture was taken, the coffer was completely filled with water and the hull was totally immersed. (*Delaware State Museums*)

Lawn sprinklers keep *De Braak*'s battered hull wet to prevent wood shrinkage as the coffer fills with water. (*David V. Beard*)

Charles Fithian studies the "as fitted" Admiralty draft of *De Braak*. (*Donald G. Shomette*)

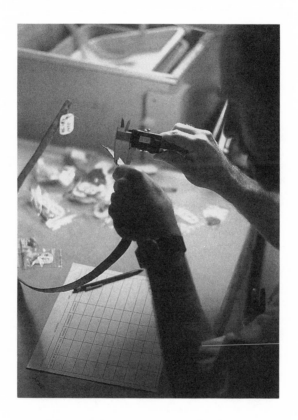

Fithian employs computerized calipters to take precision measurements of ametal barrel hoop. (*Donald G. Shomette*)

The author examines one of three anchors recovered from *De Braak* and housed at the former fish rendering factory which served as Sub-Sal's headquarters. (*John Brewer*)

Diver John Brewer holds a SHARPS Gun, a sonic high accuracy ranging and positioning system provided by the National Geographic Society to conduct ultrasonic mapping of the hull. The test was carried out within the confines of the coffer-dam environment at Lewes, and provided nearly a half million XYZ measurement points within less than two days. (*National Geographic Magazine*)

The Zwaanendael Museum shortly after the opening of the *De Braak* Exhibition. (*Donald G. Shomette*)

Lewes Mayor Al Stango, Tiddo Hofstee, Acting Ambassador of the Royal Netherlands Embassy, and Delaware Secretary of State Michael Harkins (*left to right.*) cut a ribbon officially opening the *De Braak* Exhibition at the Zwaanendael Museum. (*The Whale*)

Twenty years after Delaware Governor Russell Peterson witnessed the D&D Company's ill-fated quest for De Braak, he presents a commemorative speech at the opening of the De Braak Exhibition at the Zwaanendael Museum. (*The Whale*)

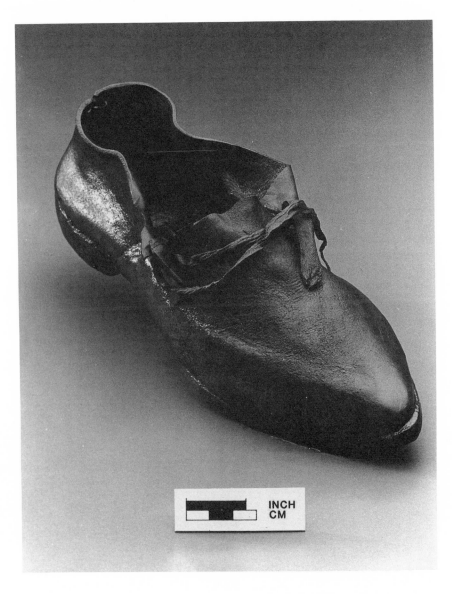

A shoe recovered from *De Braak*, one of approximately 150, showing the transition from buckles to laces. The buckle from this government issue shoe was removed and replaced by a lace, probably by its fashion-conscious owner. (*Delaware State Museums*)

This sheave, manufactured by Royal Navy contractor Walter Taylor in December 1791, was one of hundreds studied by the author in an effort to discover the cause of *De Braak*'s capsizing. (*John Brewer*)

The famous "fouled anchor" insignia of the Royal Marines which graced a marine shoulder belt. (*Delaware State Museums*)

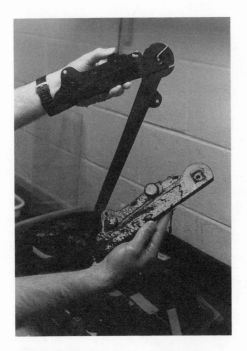

One of the more interesting navigational items recovered was this ebony Hadley's quadrant, or octant. Invented by John Hadley in 1731, the device completely superseded the backstaff and crosstaff by 1750 and remained in service into the 19th century. (*Donald G. Shomette*)

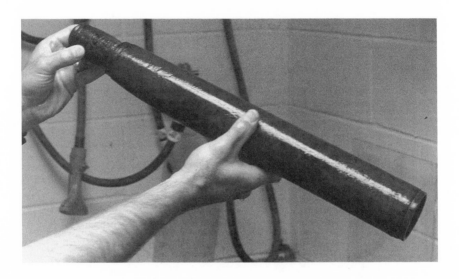

This mahogany telescope, with boxwood components, was so well preserved that wood specialist Harry Alden was moved to compare it to a Queen Anne or Chippendale chair. (*Donald G. Shomette*)

This black basalt teapot and creamer set (*above and facing*) is believed to have belonged to one of *De Braak*'s officers, possibly even Captain Drew himself. (*Delaware State Museums*)

A ceramic pipkin, probably used by one of *De Braak*'s officers for tea. (*Donald G. Shomette*)

T   W   E   L   V   E

The Right Know-How

For the next fifteen years, little attention was paid to the alleged treasure wreck lying off Cape Henlopen, Delaware. After all, there had been more important things to worry about, such as the Great Depression, World War II, inflation, the Communist menace, and the Korean War. Few folks had time or money to squander on pie-in-the-sky projects. By 1952, however, with America's newfound prosperity, the cycle of dreams and schemes inevitably began afresh. Again, the same old stories surfaced, albeit with a patina of veracity enhanced by the passage of time. Once again, the gold bug bit deep.

Of course, there were some new twists to the legend, such as the rumor that old Gilbert McCracken had brought one of the Spanish survivors of the *De Braak* disaster home with him. By the light of a flickering tallow candle, the Spaniard had actually shown him several gold bars plucked from the ship before she went down—all that had been saved from a treasure then calculated to be worth as much as $80,000,000. Among the first to have their interest piqued was a consortium of local businessmen and salvors from Lewes and Georgetown, Delaware. This latest team of aspirants was composed of Archie and Weldon Brittingham, Captain Henry Buckaloo, the veteran *De Braak* hunter Captain Charles T. Johnston, and a colorful character—explosives expert "Dynamite" Rod King.[1]

Of the five salvors, Johnston and King were undoubtedly the most likely to stand out in a crowd. Johnston had been a professional salvor for nearly half a century and, with his mane of white hair and sunburnt face, he looked it. As a child, he had personally witnessed the destruction of scores of ships on the cape in both the terrible "Blizzard of '88" and the "Storm of '89," never dreaming that his own life would one day revolve around shipwrecks and marine disasters. As a salvor, he was considered one of the best in the business. And, having personally participated in the Chapman Expedition, he was also one of the most knowledgeable salvors, not only about the shipwrecks of Delaware Bay, but also about HMS *De Braak*.

Johnston and King had been a good match from the beginning. The latter had entered the business in an oblique manner. His first job, in fact, had been as an assistant to a local county engineer, a lackluster and tedious position with little promise for adventure or advancement—until, that is, the day when his boss had ordered him to find a replacement for the district explosives engineer. Try as he might, King had been unable to locate a candidate for the position and, in exasperation, had volunteered himself for the dangerous work. He got the job and was soon involved in blasting ditches for farms, as well as occasionally demolishing derelict shipwrecks and underwater obstructions in local waterways. He enjoyed his work immensely, eventually becoming one of the best explosives experts on the Eastern seaboard. Within a short time, his skills in derelict removal had caught the eye of Charles Johnston, who promptly offered him a job. Soon King was working for Johnston, blasting and removing obstructions and wrecks from the Gulf of Mexico to the Great Lakes, under contract to federal, state, and private concerns.[2] Now, the two salvors, working in concert with the Brittinghams and Buckaloo, would lend their expertise to a search for the old Royal Navy brig lying off Cape Henlopen.

The team took on a hard-hat diver and veteran of the Colstad effort named Harry Morgan to conduct underwater investigations. They acquired a converted ex-navy minesweeper for use as a search vessel and diving platform.[3] And then, for thirteen weeks, they carried out an intensive search. In the end, like their predecessors, their own survey proved as costly as it had been fruitless. During one dragging operation, for instance, they had snagged a U.S. Navy submarine-detection apparatus operated by the naval unit stationed near Fort Miles, guarding the mouth of the bay. Federal authorities immediately declared the sensitive area off-limits to further search.[4] Despite such failures, a few in the group, including King, refused to admit defeat and continued to putter about Henlopen from time to time, always hoping to hit the big one. Others, such as Buckaloo, assumed something of a paternal attitude toward the elusive wreck.

In 1954, King began to seriously consider mounting another major effort. Snowy-haired Johnston, with more than fifty years of salvage work under his belt, was considerably less optimistic. Speaking for himself and several of his Lewes colleagues, he told William S. Dutton of the *Saturday Evening Post*:

> We think that all of the outsiders who want to try [to find the wreck] have now tried. That leaves the *De Braak* among what you might call the sea's lost hopes. But Rodney King thinks he has the old gold ship spotted. He's been exploring off Cape Henlopen with a mine detector. Maybe it's copper coins he's located, but folks here think it's something better. Our notion is that, so far, that lost hope has just lacked the right know-how about shipwrecks.[5]

Johnston's estimation of *De Braak*'s allure fell substantially under the mark, however, for outsiders would not be denied their chance, and many would still try their luck. In 1955, two Pennsylvanians, Robert Howarth IV, of Wallingford, and Dr. William H. Boyce III, of Philadelphia, led the the way by applying for and being granted a lease on the submerged land area where they believed *De Braak* to lie. That yet another group was preparing to conduct a search was perhaps not surprising, but what was significant was that Howarth and Boyce were the first to attempt to protect their interests by securing an exclusive salvage lease for a given body of water in Delaware. The area covered, 4,750 feet by 6,070 feet, just east of Cape Henlopen, was substantial (albeit well off the mark). Their actions triggered an immediate response both from the United States government and from those whose interests in the purported treasure wreck were more pecuniary.[6]

When Howarth and Boyce sought to secure a lease, they applied to the Delaware State Highway Department, which at that time legally controlled all Delaware lands above and below water that was not already assigned to the jurisdiction of some other state agency or to the federal government.[7] In January 1955, a week after the uncontested lease had been approved, the United States Navy stepped into the picture, issuing a draconian edict. The area intended for survey and salvage, the two would-be salvors were told, lay directly within the navy's harbor defense zone, off Fort Miles, on Cape Henlopen. Furthermore, in a statement issued by Lieutenant Edward T. McGuire, commander of the zone unit, the navy declared the area to be completely restricted for national defense purposes.[8]

At the same time that Howarth and Boyce were being hit with navy restrictions, their leased rights came under attack from another quarter. Captain Henry Buckaloo, who was livid over the state's having issued an exclusive lease, claimed that he too had a permit for the same area, but from the U.S. Army Corps of Engineers. Although he had also been quickly and quietly restricted by the navy, Buckaloo was infuriated at the highway department's assumption of authority to issue a lease in the first place. Unmoved, the highway department, which, as one observer caustically noted, "wasn't losing any sleep over the matter," informed Buckaloo that it had already secured an opinion from the Delaware State Attorney General's office before issuing the lease.[9] Indeed, the whole affair was viewed with some amusement by officials of the highway department, for whom the *De Braak* treasure hunt was classed with the Flying Dutchman. "Mention the De Braak to anyone in the office of the chief engineer of the Highway Department," one wag noted, "and you'll get smiles—cynical smiles."[10] Although the following year Howarth would apply for and receive a permit, and would dive several times on a site he claimed to hold *De Braak*, the hunt for the elusive warship temporarily faded from the news.

Nevertheless, such cycles of interest in *De Braak*, while taken with a grain of salt by some in the state bureaucracy, continued to seem significant to others. Among the more seriously concerned institutions was the Zwaanendael Museum in Lewes. The ornate building which houses the museum had been erected by the State of Delaware in 1931 to commemorate the tercentenary of the first European settlement in the state. The building had, in fact, opened its doors in 1932, the same year in which the Chapman Expedition began. A small-scale adaptation of the town hall of Hoorn, Holland (birthplace of Captain David Pietersen de Vries, founder of the 1631 settlement on the Delaware), the ornate brick structure featured stepped gable ends, a carved Dutch doorway, red and white shutters in the Dutch Renaissance Style, and exquisite ornamentation. It was the perfect repository for collections pertaining to the history of Lewes, Cape Henlopen, and Delaware, with the Dutch-American linkage evident throughout its design. Over the vestibule door was displayed the town crest of Hoorn, while a portrait of Queen Wilhelmina of The Netherlands, at age eighteen, hung elsewhere. Colonial artifacts, Indian relics, cannonballs from the British bombardment of Lewes during the War of 1812, Irish coins found washed up on the beach near Rehoboth, and an old iron ladder from the Cape Henlopen Lighthouse were also on display. But the museum's most prized holding, a battered old sea chest, was donated by Randolph McCracken and was claimed to have belonged to none other than Captain James Drew.[11]

As holder of the Drew sea chest—the only artifact believed to have survived the sinking of *De Braak* (albeit without historical provenance)—the modest little museum became a major attraction for all would-be salvors, a veritable mecca for the *De Braak* faithful. Yet, like most of the salvors themselves, the museum was woefully short of hard data on the disaster. By 1955, however, even before acquiring the chest, the resurgence of interest in the vessel and its history caused museum officials to begin the first serious effort to sift fact from fiction. They were, unfortunately, obliged to rely upon nonprofessional assistance, the consequences of which would significantly influence the course pursued by many *De Braak* hunters over the next three decades.

The services of a competent naval historian were sought, and Donald Stewart, of Baltimore, was eventually enlisted to research the ship and its history. Stewart was neither a qualified naval historian nor a researcher of the required caliber. But he had an impressive line in historical patter, making up facts as needed and citing sources that he was certain no one would or could check. The staff of the Zwaanendael, completely taken in by Stewart, welcomed him aboard. His first assignment was to produce a sketch of what *De Braak* had probably looked like for the museum's collection. Pleased with the attractive results of his draftsmanship, the museum, with little evidence to go on, next asked him to conduct some primary research. After several months, a summary report was submitted. Although no one doubted its accuracy then, Stewart's "study" amounted to little more than a contrived concoction of misinformation, factual distortion, and outright falsehoods. Stewart alleged that he had drawn his information from correspondence with major archival sources in Europe, as well as from a variety of personal contacts. Many of his references, however, never existed.[12] But it all sounded great!

Why Donald Stewart chose to produce such misinformation and to perpetrate such a hoax is still a mystery. More than two decades later he would become deeply involved in one of the first major treasure-wreck hunts in the State of Maryland, suggesting a pecuniary motivate for his actions in Delaware. That his chicanery succeeded in confounding many would-be salvors for the next thirty years is a testament to his talent for fooling those who were too willing to be deceived. His "research" letters were made available by the museum to any and all who sought them, and, until 1983, his data were taken as gospel.

Stewart's misinformation, however, meant little to Howarth and Boyce, who had been forbidden by the navy to work their lease zone. After the two Pennsylvanians had neglected to put up the monthly fee ($25) for the salvage rights, they were informed, in July 1956, that their lease had run out for failure to make payment.

Almost as soon as the Howarth-Boyce lease had expired, another contender sought to succeed them. In July 1956, an unnamed salvor contacted the Delaware State Highway Department, through a Wilmington, North Carolina, attorney named Edgar L. Yow, seeking exclusive salvage rights to *De Braak*. With Howarth and Boyce out of the picture, the highway department's chief engineer, Richard A. Haber, immediately approved the lease on condition that (1) Yow's client paid a monthly fee of $25 for the lease; (2) Yow's client turned over ten percent of the gross recovered from the site to the state; and (3) the U.S. Navy agreed to permit the treasure hunt off Cape Henlopen. On July 17, Yow was formally notified that the lease sought by his client would be approved, provided that he could secure the navy's approval. The state of Delaware, it would appear, had no intention of trespassing on federal jurisdiction or of acting as an intermediary between the salvor and the U.S. Navy. Securing the latter's approval was a matter for negotiation between Yow's client and the Department of Defense.[13] The problems of dealing with the navy were daunting, however, and apparently far more than the mysterious aspirant from North Carolina was willing to tackle. The pursuit of exclusive salvage rights by Edgar Yow and his client was abandoned.

For the next seven years *De Braak* would be left undisturbed in her silt-covered bed—until her repose was interrupted by a revolution, a veritable renaissance in undersea technology, which swept the nation and the world. Since 1943, when two French seamen, Emile Gagnan and Jacques Cousteau, had invented the self-contained underwater breathing apparatus, or SCUBA as it was later called, divers had been able to explore shallow seabeds unencumbered by the bulky hard-hat, surface-supplied air diving suits of the nineteenth and early twentieth centuries. All that a diver needed to do before plunging in was to strap a tank of compressed air onto his back, stick a breathing regulator into his mouth, and place a mask on his face and fins on his feet. By the early 1960s, the new sport of scuba diving had spread across Europe and America and was soon taken up by tens of thousands of diving enthusiasts. One of the principal spin-offs of the new sport was that underwater treasure hunting became a national pastime of unprecedented proportions. Now, every weekend diver with access to a small boat could search for lost gold and silver, or, at the very least, could tear a few portholes from better-known shipwrecks. A few began to employ surplus mine detectors for underwater searches, while others used increasingly sophisticated locating devices. Scuba diving had opened the seas to the masses. Treasure wrecks and purported treasure wrecks were being discovered at a dizzying rate.

Once again, interest began to focus on *De Braak*. In September 1962, a group of New York and Pennsylvania sport divers led by William Strube of Marietta, Pennsylvania, descended on Lewes for the purpose of locating *De Braak*. Strube's team included six divers—George Glick, Robert Howry, Mike Greineder, Richard Earhart, Gordon Donaldson, and George Derian—and was equipped with an eighty-three-foot vessel as its search craft. The team worked diligently well into November, but with no luck. Operations were finally called off when the boat nearly capsized in heavy seas.[14]

Strube and his associates were not discouraged. In June of the following year they returned, this time with the latest electronic equipment, including a magnetometer, used to sense the presence of ferromagnetic anomalies, such as cannon and anchors, on the bottom. As the summer progressed, they were joined by at least six more divers. But they fared no better than the year before. Although Strube had fielded the "finest group of divers available on the East Coast," he could not find *De Braak*.[15]

At the same time that the treasure hunters of the Delaware coast were scouring the waters off Cape Henlopen for a Napoleonic-era warship, a team of professional archaeologists working in the far-off Mediterranean was adapting the revolutionized diving technology to the excavation of the oldest known shipwreck in the world. The new science of underwater archaeology had been born, and it was advancing along a slow but certain collision course with the ghost of HMS *De Braak*.[16]

Widow's Walks

On June 9, 1965, one of the most unlikely trio of adventurers to set off in quest of *De Braak* appeared in Georgetown to attend a public hearing on their request for state approval of a salvage permit. The three men were Louis F. DeCerchio, a Philadelphia pharmacist, William T. De Feo, a South Philadelphia dentist, and Mario "Bud" Busa, a Pennsylvania plastics manufacturer.[1] Among the three, it had been DeCerchio who, years before, had first been irresistibly drawn into a lifelong fascination with the ship and her purported treasure. Like many before him, he had developed his own theories about the wreck and its whereabouts without bothering to scratch the historical record very deeply. Principal among his theories was the belief that *De Braak* had not succumbed to a gale, but had been upset by a mere gust of wind because of her improperly stowed cargo—an enormously valuable cargo consisting of gold and silver.[2] It had not been difficult to draw the other two into his obsession, with its promise of wealth. Together they formed the D & D Salvage Company specifically to locate and recover the *De Braak* treasure. Corporate offices were established at the 1631 Marina, Pilot House Road, on Roosevelt Inlet in Lewes,[3] not far from the site of Gilbert McCracken's homestead.

D & D Salvage did not go into the Georgetown hearings alone, but was counseled by a "resident agent," a savvy local attorney named George Tunnell. The commission they were to address had three hard-nosed members: A. Dean Betts, of Georgetown, and Mae Hall McCabe and Charles Mills, both of Rehoboth. This triumvirate had been specifically appointed by Governor Charles L. Terry, who had invested the commission with a wide range of powers under the law to fix purchase prices and rents and to manage other terms and conditions pertaining to subaqueous bottomlands. Any and all permits for underwater treasure hunts on state-owned bottomlands would be granted only if approved by the commission.[4]

DeCerchio's presentation was succinct. His company, he said, was "absolutely certain of the location" of *De Braak*'s remains. In fact, one of D & D's divers, Robert Howarth, now a resident of Florida, who had made his own attempt on the wreck, claimed to have actually been on the site four times and to have seen it on six more occasions. Howarth, it was noted for the record, had removed the by now almost mandatory piece of teak as well as other items to confirm the site's identity. The wood had reportedly been subjected to a series of scientific tests at the University of Wisconsin and its date estimated at sometime between 1778 and 1818.[5] DeCerchio made no bones about the wreck's potential value, stating flatly but effectively that *De Braak* had carried approximately $2,500,000 in silver and £80,000 worth of gold. "Numismatically speaking," he informed the panel, "the present day value of the coins alone could be in the vicinity of $8 million."[6]

In a businesslike manner, D & D proposed to submit a written agreement, promising the state twenty percent of all treasure trove. Furthermore, all artifacts and items whose monetary value was exceeded by their historical significance would be turned over to the state archivist, if the permit were approved. In return, the company would receive an exclusive search permit, good for three years, covering nine square miles of territory off Cape Henlopen.[7]

To substantiate its credentials for undertaking such a project, the company submitted a letter of support from Leon de Valinger, Jr., Delaware State Archivist and Director of the Delaware State Museum, in Dover. In the letter, De Valinger explained the historical significance of *De Braak*. "Locating the wreck," he wrote,

> and salvaging its cargo and remaining parts of the vessel would be important historically for the state and the nation. DeCerchio and his colleagues have visited the Delaware State Archives and have shown they possess a better fund of knowledge and demonstrated a more practical approach to the problem than any other group known to us. They appear to be adequately equipped and financed to fulfill the terms of the salvage proposal.[8]

The state, he went on, would benefit not only from a percentage of the profits, but also from "the historical importance of the expedition."[9] DeCerchio also informed the committee that his group had enlisted the "voluntary professional advice" of George Bass, of the University of Pennsylvania, a pioneer in the field of marine archaeology.[10]

It was just as well that D & D claimed the support of such authorities because the company soon found its application challenged by veteran *De Braak* hunter J. Rodney King and a local contractor named Melvin L. Joseph. Represented by their own Georgetown attorney, George A. Bramhall, the pair protested the granting of a permit to D & D on the grounds that DeCerchio, De Feo, and Busa were all from out of state. His own group, King pointed out, was composed of local residents who had been searching for the wreck for thirteen years and could therefore claim "prior privileges to salvage rights."

D & D's attorney, George Tunnell, retorted that King had been granted permission to hunt for *De Braak* in 1952. But in 1956 Howarth had received an unchallenged permit. Therefore, he reasoned, King's supposed privileges had no legal standing. As for expertise, besides Howarth, the company had secured the services of two more divers, Captain Peter Chase, of Florida, and William Smith, of Philadelphia.[11]

The commission viewed D & D's request favorably, despite King's challenge, and passed their recommendation on to Governor Terry. By July 27, the governor had agreed, in principle, to the conditions under which the permit would be granted. But there were still several obstacles to be overcome by the would-be salvors before they could begin operations—not the least of which was the United States Navy.[12] On August 2, Governor Terry had taken the politically expedient precaution of sending a copy of the information provided by D & D to Admiral John S. McCain, of the navy's eastern sea frontier command, based in New York City. In doing so, Terry was seeking to avoid any unexpected conflict with the navy, such as over any plans the Defense Department might have for the Cape Henlopen area. He was well aware of the importance to Delaware of the money provided by the federal military establishment and was not inclined, therefore, to upset the navy. He had thus taken the precaution of requesting Tunnell to draft a proposal spelling out the specific conditions of the agreement as well as the impact of the salvage effort on the area. Then he informed the lawyer that D & D's project design would have to be approved by both the state and the navy before he would grant an exclusive three-year permit.[13] D & D had no choice but to accept the governor's terms.

The last major obstacle to D & D's securing a permit was finally overcome when the navy gave its tacit "happy voyage" blessings to the plan—but with certain stipulations. There would have to be a "slight change in the boundaries of the hunt," so as not to endanger some of the delicate underwater hydrophonic devices which had been deployed in the area. Furthermore, the overall territory which could be investigated would have to be reduced from nine miles to four. The navy would permit the hunt to be conducted from

> the tip of Cape Henlopen north on longitude 75 degrees, 5 minutes, 50 seconds, to a point 38 degrees, 48 minutes, 49 seconds latitude, then east to a point which is one and one-eighth miles at 75 degrees, 4 minutes, 20 seconds longitude; thence a line from this point extends a distance of three and a half miles into the southeast quadrant at an angle of 160 degrees from true north, this to a point which is 38 degrees, 45 minutes, 30 seconds latitude, thence west to land.[14]

D & D's lawyer was less than thrilled with either the navy's dictates or the governor's revised version of the agreement, which accompanied the terms. After one year, Tunnell was told, the approved area would be reduced to one square mile, and Delaware would receive twenty-five percent of the net value of any cargo and the rights to jewelry, gems, and other precious stones. All items of historical significance, except coins, gold, silver, and copper, would also belong to the state.[15]

Again the salvors had little choice but to agree to the terms. Tunnell negotiated as best he could in a last ditch effort to secure the best possible conditions for D & D. He assured the navy that his clients knew "almost exactly" where the wreck lay, which, fortuitously, was within the allocated area. On August 3, he confidently announced that his clients expected to begin actual field investigations in a week, after the agreement was signed. Once the site had been pinpointed, he stated, they intended to dig a channel on each side of the wreck. Then, with the aid of sand pumps and tidal action to clear the site, they planned "to lift the De Braak with a secret mechanism."[16]

While negotiations with the navy and the state continued, D & D, eager to get going, having already spent a reported $80,000 on research, equipment, and fees, began making dry runs off Cape May, New Jersey, to test their gear. The actual area in which they intended to work was soon revealed when buoys were laid out to mark the recovery zone. DeCerchio was so optimistic about the project as preparations were made that he refused to call the effort a "search." He informed the press that some of his divers who had already visited the wreck site, including chief diver William Smith, knew exactly what to look for since much of the site was already exposed. "Of course," he added, "nothing is certain except death and taxes. But all things being equal, we hope to bring up the De Braak by the middle of October."[17]

News of the treasure hunt began to attract first national and then international attention. When word reached DeCerchio, De Feo, and Busa that a spokesman for the British Admiralty had pooh-poohed the treasure story, calling the ship's loss "not a glorious page of history but an obscure event," they remained undaunted. They countered by citing some of Donald Stewart's misinformation, such as that "deep within the Royal British Navy Archives is a letter revealing that the De Braak's captured Spanish treasure had been transferred off Cape Hatteras onto another British warship, the Northumberland, about a month before the De Braak sank."[18] But there was still an enormous booty aboard the old warship, and they would soon be able to get at it. Indeed, less than a year later, Busa would loudly proclaim that D & D actually possessed "a copy of the *De Braak*'s manifest and it says clearly the ship carried gold worth at the time of its sinking around 2½ million pounds [sterling]. . . . Why even if we just find coins, who can tell what they would be worth in the coin market?"[19] But not everyone was impressed by the fruits of archival research or the dusty records ensconced in British repositories. Some who had already tried their hand at finding *De Braak* and failed, such as Archie Brittingham, were mildly amused by the whole thing. "Anyone," Brittingham scoffed, "can buy that information for only $7 by writing to the British Admiralty in London. They'll send you all the details."[20]

D & D's optimistic hopes for an early start faded as negotiations with the navy and the State of Delaware dragged on. The navy had added a new demand for a $20,000 bond to be posted in case the salvors damaged any sensitive undersea acoustical equipment. Delaware now wanted twenty-five percent of the monetary rewards instead of twenty percent, as well as all historical artifacts. As always, it was the lawyers who profited most, for not until March 1966 would an agreement be reached.[21] Amazingly, the spirits of the company principals were not dampened by the incessant delays. During the winter of 1965–66, soundings were taken and wood samples from the wreck thought to be *De Braak* (said to be teak, of course) were retrieved. Bud Busa, president of D & D and now the corporate spokesman, optimistically predicted that 1966 would be the "year of the big gold strike." The company had finally secured permission from the navy and the state, leased a $40,000 dredging vessel, and converted a seventy-five-foot ex-navy minesweeper for salvage work. By April 1, Busa promised, the move down to Lewes with all the heavy equipment and vessels would begin. By May, he predicted, salvage operations would be fully under way.[22]

A week before the scheduled start of work, however, D & D's problems were renewed with interest: the weather refused to cooperate; the water was still too cold for extended diving operations; the dredge which had been leased was in such a dilapidated condition that it had to be completely overhauled and new engines installed; and the old minesweeper was acting up as well. It began to look as if operations would not be initiated at Lewes before mid-May. Then, when work finally did begin, the results were anything but rewarding, as breakdowns and equipment failures continued to harass the project.[23]

In late June, skepticism over the existence of the alleged treasure arose again when Jackson Jenks, director of the Naval and Undersea Museum at Newport, Rhode Island, irritated over what he considered a travesty of history, called the Delaware press "to set the people of Delaware straight on the De Braak." The treasure was as phony, he said, as the yarns about "those widow walks of New England houses." Jenks was determined to debunk the treasure legend, "I'll give any diver $1,000," he challenged, "if he can prove to me that the De Braak, if it is still in existence on the bed of the ocean, has a cargo of gold and silver."[24]

Then the Smithsonian Institution entered the fray. On June 28, Howard I. Chapelle, Curator of Transportation at the Smithsonian and an internationally recognized authority on ship design and maritime history, publicly declared that *De Braak* had carried no gold or silver and was "of little importance in marine archaeology." He pointed out that, although he had seen documents revealing that she had indeed taken a Spanish ship, that vessel had not carried gold or silver. Spanish treasure ships never crossed the ocean alone. "It's just ridiculous to think that this [brig] sloop ever captured a Spanish treasure ship," said Chapelle. As for the British salvage effort, it was indeed true that a halfhearted attempt to raise the warship had been made, but the project had been abandoned almost at once. "England," he said, "could have used all the gold she could have gotten her hands on in 1798. Believe me, if there were gold on the De Braak, the English would never have given up the job."[25]

Chapelle had long nourished an interest in *De Braak*, having been an observer on one of the expeditions in the 1930s. He had followed the progress of the numerous efforts to locate her thereafter, and, over the years, his conviction that there was no treasure to be found had only been reinforced. Then he became resolved to prove it. His first move was to contact the British Public Record Office, in London, to inquire about the Royal Navy's historical data on the vessel. The PRO not only replied, but recommended that Lieutenant Colonel M. E. S. Laws, a retired British Army officer who was an expert on ordnance and an experienced researcher, be hired to conduct a thorough evaluation of the Admiralty records. Colonel Laws, a resident of Sevenoaks, Kent, agreed to the partnership and immediately began the first comprehensive archival survey of *De Braak*'s historical record ever conducted.

The team's investigation began with the British Admiralty records, housed in the PRO, combining them for all data even remotely relevant to *De Braak*'s career in the Royal Navy. Meanwhile, a second search would be carried out at the National Maritime Museum in Greenwich, on the outskirts of London, for any possible drafts made of the warship at the time of her refitting. Such drafts, Chapelle knew from many years of experience, were typically made whenever any of the navy's warships were repaired or refitted, and these were housed in the museum's superb Admiralty Draughts Collection. The investigation bore fruit, when it was learned that regular inventories of the vessel had been made while she was in British service and that no pertinent records had been posted as either missing or stolen. Happily, the team discovered that there were very few gaps in the brig's official record except for the actual logs lost when she went down. Unfortunately, for the archaeological work which would be undertaken two decades later, the Plymouth Dockyard's internal records, primarily those relating to the vessel's repairs, surveys, and refitting, had been entirely destroyed during World War II.

Nevertheless, Chapelle and Laws succeeded in piecing together the mosaic of *De Braak*'s Royal Navy service career. They were elated to discover not only her lines, "as fitted," from when she was converted to a brig, but also her original configuration as a Dutch navy cutter, taken while in drydock. These plans consisted of the lines of the vessel, her deck-and-hold plan as a Dutch cutter, and a sheer plan displaying outboard and inboard profiles, as fitted for service as a Royal Navy brig.[26] The team followed *De Braak*'s career from the date she was entered on the Royal Navy's lists to the day she broke off from the Atlantic convoy. They documented her tragic demise and began to follow the paper trail which Captain Drew had left behind him in the official files. They assembled the data pertaining to the sale of the single prize that *De Braak* had taken prior to her loss on the Delaware. They left precious few stones unturned and, in the course of their investigation, destroyed many of the myths which had grown up around the wreck.

Typical of their debunking effort was the dispelling of the notion that *De Braak* had been made of teak. Although many salvors had displayed wood fragments which they claimed were teak, Chapelle countered those claims with the historical record: the warship had been built of oak. In response to Jenks's monetary challenge to any and all would-be salvors, the curator smiled and said, "I don't think he'll ever have to pay off that $1,000 reward."[27] Chapelle and Laws eventually published their research in 1967 in the prestigious *Smithsonian Journal of History*. In this work, step by step, they methodically dismantled the legend of HMS *De Braak* by putting flesh on the bone of history and placing the ship (and her final voyage) in its true historical perspective. Finally, they decimated the long-standing tale of treasure trove. Unfortunately, their work would be entirely ignored by the average fortune hunter, blinded by his own lust for gold.

Leon de Valinger, who, as Delaware State Archivist, had wholeheartedly supported D & D's efforts, refused to comment on either Jenks's challenge or the findings of Chapelle and Laws except to say that the documents shown to him by the salvors revealed that "there was gold on the De Braak." As for D & D, the team was too deeply engrossed by the increasing number of mechanical difficulties with the equipment to muster up much response to either Jenks or Chapelle.[28] They were committed to the hunt, and neither facts nor skepticism would hinder their expensive, headlong pursuit of a myth.

By the dog days of August, it was apparent to everyone that the early boasts of the D & D team's ability to locate the treasure quickly had been wishful thinking. The site which they had been working, although indeed a wreck, seemed less and less likely to be the vessel they had been seeking. Still, the local press kept a watchful eye on operations—just in case. Passengers on the Cape May-Lewes Ferry were advised "to keep a sharp watch to the southeast," for some fortunate soul might have the "luck to witness the discovery of a brand new-old wonder of Wonderful Delaware—the treasure ship De Braak."[29] D & D, however, was soon seeking a more promising target. The search, even so, was proving anything but romantic advanture, as D & D spent most of its time taking soundings and sand borings.[30] And, like most of its predecessors, the young salvage company was finding Cape Henlopen to be a virtual graveyard of sunken ships. Each new find was heralded in the press as the *De Braak*, only to be quietly forgotten when evidence failed to verify the claim. By the end of 1966, the treasure salvors of D & D had precious little to show for their work, other than yet another site which Busa steadfastly believed to be the *De Braak*. The next season, he assured everyone, would be the big one.

In April 1967, operations were resumed. "Lots of ancient wood is coming up from Davey Jones's Locker," the ever-optimistic company spokesman informed the press. But no gold. The hunt had gotten off to a slow start that season owing to poor weather conditions, but the wreck encountered at the end of the previous year seemed encouraging, even though it lay amid "countless wrecks in the graveyard." The purported hulk, company press releases stated, was embedded in a trough in the ocean floor, far deeper than the salvors had expected. Divers systematically probed several hundred square feet of the site by hand in seventy-eight feet of water, with less than five inches of visibility. Again, fragments of teak and a few chunks of oak were reportedly found on the site. Then, on July 12, De Feo and DeCerchio admitted that their calculations were a bit off. The site, it was revealed, had not been a shipwreck at all, but solid rock. "It completely befuddled us," declared one of the company's embarrassed founders.[31]

Still undaunted, the salvors decided to use the very latest in remote-sensing technology, an aerially deployed rubidium magnetometer, to locate the right site. The gear had been specifically developed by the Gulf Oil Company for exploratory work in locating magnetic anomalies in the earth. It seemed only natural to D & D that such equipment could also be used for detecting sunken ships. To deploy the instrument, an airplane belonging to the Aero Service Corporation, a division of Litton Industries, was secured. By midsummer the aerial survey had begun. The low-flying aircraft quickly pinpointed a large concentration of magnetic anomalies at the confluence of the Delaware Bay and the Atlantic. One of the most tantalizing of these, however, corresponded to a potential wreck located earlier in the season by boat, a mile and a half off the site of the old Cape Henlopen Lighthouse position. The target was thoroughly documented on the mag's strip chart recorder.[32]

The salvors were exhilarated by the data, which, conveniently for the media, seemed to meet every speculative and historical geographic criterion they could apply to it, no matter how twisted. A more definitive look, with a DC–3 to run another survey in order to chart the complete parameters of the site, was quickly scheduled. De Feo informed the press that it was undoubtedly *De Braak*'s guns, sixteen twenty-four pounder carronades, that had been picked up by the mag.[33] The wreck, he said, lay in seventy-four feet of water and beneath ten to fifteen feet of sand and mud. By late July, a hands-on investigation of the site was being carried out.[34]

That the site was indeed a shipwreck and not another "large rock" was soon ascertained when a variety of ship fittings and other well-worn, decomposing artifacts were recovered. Most were unidentifiable to the treasure hunters. They began to make the rounds of museums, the Army Corps of Engineers, and the Department of the Interior in an effort to identify the items. On August 12, De Feo and several of his associates visited the Zwaanendael Museum and left behind pictures of the recently recovered artifacts, which proved to be a crance iron, a deadeye and strap, and fragments of iron "from old ships." But nothing was verified as being from *De Braak*.[35]

Having found little satisfaction in the verdicts of these experts, De Feo even considered visiting the Smithsonian Institution, then thought better of it. But the amount of evidence indicating that the vessel in question was not the hoped-for treasure ship was simply too great for even D & D to ignore. The company was eventually obliged to report that the wreck appeared to have been a sailing ship of the nineteenth century, with construction indicative of the Civil War period. The admission was particularly hard to make since over $125,000 had been spent thus far on the project.[36] Nevertheless, the salvors simply moved on to another prospective site, barely 400 to 500 yards off the beach of Cape Henlopen State Park and 1,000 yards southeast of Cape Henlopen Point. This time the site lay in only thirty feet of water. It mattered little to the salvors that the position conflicted considerably with both the historically reported distance of one mile offshore and D & D's own calculation that the ship lay in sixty feet of water. The team's leaders simply did some more handy calculations and declared that the coastline had changed drastically.[37]

By the beginning of October, the salvors were satisfied enough with the site to announce publicly that a barge and crane were being brought in "to dig up all this rubble." The dredge company, however, immediately cancelled the barge's insurance, which had the effect of proscribing any operations at all. D & D responded by purchasing its own barge and crane. Then the weather refused to cooperate. The seas began to grow rough and the skies opened up. On November 20, Busa despondently announced that "the old weather witch," having shut down many operations in the past, would again work her magic. "So we might as well close up shop until the spring."[38]

The following season of 1968 began with company morale and finances improved by the addition of two new partners, veteran *De Braak* hunters Dr. William Boyce and Robert Howarth. Both of the new directors sought total anonymity, rather than publicity, as some of the original principals had begun to suffer ridicule. Bill De Feo, for instance, was heralded by his patients as a "treasure-hunting romantic." There was always the danger that if things really turned sour, there might be a loss of patronage. Nevertheless, by June full operations had resumed.[39]

Another barge, 110 feet long and 35 feet wide, had been secured, as well as a large crane with a two-story boom. The barge was firmly stationed over the site (marked by three modest clorox bottles) with a two-and-a-half-ton anchor. On the nearby shore, two big navy radio towers loomed over the operations, which were, of necessity, now carried out as economically as possible. Even with the fresh infusion of money from the new investors, funds were in short supply. An old Mako speedboat was employed as a runabout and service craft, which perhaps represented the level to which the corporation had sunk. As one visitor to the site noted, the peripatetic boat had "once probably [been] a seaworthy and shipshape vessel but now barely qualifie[d] in either category."[40]

On Sunday, June 21, 1968, diving began on the site. Two lifeguards, Dan Wiltz, a twenty-three-year-old from Louisiana, and his twenty-two-year-old assistant, George Gomez, an off-duty soldier, were now serving as company divers. As soon as they had begun to examine the area, they had found several pieces of metal. Two days later, in the late afternoon, the barge was maneuvered into a more favorable position and the crane took its first bite. Sporadically, over the next several months, salvage would continue. It would be interrupted by sour weather, mechanical failures, and, on one particularly disastrous occasion, by the sinking of both barge and crane. But there continued to be not the least hint of treasure.[41]

Down to the Wire

The executive officers of D & D Salvage had become nervous. By early November 1968, the company's exclusive, three-year franchise was about to expire and neither *De Braak* nor her alleged treasure had been found. Although the company's latest site, off Fort Miles Beach, seemed promising, renewal of the permit, which the company had once considered a given, was now open to question. On Tuesday, November 19, 1968, John M. Karanik, Acting Director of the Delaware Water and Air Resources Commission's Underwater Lands Division, publicly announced that the following day would be the deadline for permit applications from companies wishing to compete with D & D for the right to hunt for the treasure. Only one other application, submitted by a Dover man named Tom Kleles, had been submitted, but at least two more were expected within the hour, and three additional companies had expressed a strong interest. What worried D & D, though, was that if any of the applicants sought to hunt in the same area that the salvors had been allocated, the government had decreed that "the applicant who bid the highest bonus to the state would undoubtedly be awarded the lease."[1] The right to hunt for *De Braak* would be determined by a bidding contest, with proceeds to the state coming directly from the recovered treasure. D & D saw the move as a threat to the overall potential income from the site—when discovered—and as a direct affront to the years of money and labor which they had devoted to the project.

Fortunately for D & D, the commissioners had been deeply impressed by the considerable effort exerted by the company. As one journalist later put it, the commissioners' "attitude was one of moral obligation" to D & D for the past three years and the fortune spent on the project to date.[2] Not until March 20, 1969, however, was the final verdict of the commission leaked to the press. Nine days later, Busa formally announced that Delaware's new governor, Russell W. Peterson, had renewed D & D's permit. He also stated that this time the company would employ a "monster" crane with an eleven-cubic-yard clamshell bucket, which would be working in a 200-square-yard area less than 500 yards off Fort Miles Beach (now known as Cape Henlopen Beach).[3]

D & D's plans were not to be immediately realized. By spring, negotiations with a New York dredging firm had fallen through. Finally, on May 12, Busa announced that work would resume within the month, pending an agreement with another salvage company near Lewes. Within three weeks, he promised, the firm would send a rig capable of dredging six cubic yards of sand at a crack, at a cost of $1,600 a day plus manpower. "They claim they can do what we want in a five day period," declared the plastics manufacturer from Pennsylvania. The company, however, had grown wary of the whims of the "Weather Witch" and had decided to allow for a full fifteen-day operation in anticipation of time lost due to sour weather.[4]

Not until midsummer, however, despite Busa's optimistic predictions, were operations again resumed—but at a far greater expense than anyone had expected. Owing to the high cost of underwater work and the inordinately heavy equipment charges, D & D had literally run out of cash. The company had been obliged to sell an additional portion of its venture to four enterprising Pennsylvania men, all of them amateur divers. The leader of the quartet, Albert Schall, a twenty-nine-year-old service manager of an auto agency in Philadelphia, had soon brought three of his friends into the project: Kent Carliss, a twenty-seven-year-old automotive engineer; Tracy Bowden, a thirty-year-old electrical systems engineer; and Thomas Vallejo, a thirty-six-year-old excavation contractor. The group had become interested in D & D's efforts more than a year before, when Schall had purchased a car from DeCerchio. Although he was no longer an officer in D & D, but noticing that Schall and his friends were all wearing diving watches, DeCerchio had begun to discuss diving, and then the hunt for the long-lost treasure ship, with the men. By the onset of the 1969 season, the four divers, who were soon known as "the Treasure Divers of Delaware Bay," had reached an agreement with D & D to manage field operations. The company would provide advice and the expertise gained from past experience, as well as half of the treasure. In return, Schall and his associates would manage the day-to-day operations—and, most importantly, they would finance the final excavation effort.[5]

Fieldwork began in earnest on August 1, this time with the "Treasure Divers of Delaware Bay" at the helm. They had raised enough money to pay for no more than one week's barge and crane rental. But they were certain that that would be enough. Unhappily for them, diving conditions were anything but ideal, with visibility reduced to only three inches. "You have to have your nose at the end of the light," exclaimed Schall in frustration, "or you can't see your hand on your mask."[6] Within a few days, however, the wreck site began to surrender some of its secrets, as the clam bucket groped at her through the sands. Now, amid the tons of sediment being dumped on the barge deck, a variety of artifacts, such as deadeyes and other components of a ship's rigging, began to appear. And of course, there were even fragments of the ever-popular "teakwood."[7]

Until the morning of August 5, the tale of HM Sloop-of-War Brig *De Braak* had been, for Governor Russell Peterson, just another Delaware yarn spun for the tourist trade. Although he had personally signed the lease-extension permit for D & D, he had paid scant attention to the company's headlong pursuit of the ship's alleged treasure. It had, in fact, been only sheer coincidence that he and his wife had chosen the very same week when the salvors had resumed work to vacation on the beach at Fort Miles State Park. To the delight of both Peterson and his wife, they discovered that from the vantage point of their little cottage in the dunes they could observe the most minute proceedings of the salvage work being conducted only a few hundred yards away.[8] The governor had watched the salvors' progress with increasing interest through a telescope mounted on the upper deck of his cottage. By the morning of August 5, despite rain squalls and high seas, he had resolved to get a closer look at the proceedings. With the assistance of Francis D. Reardon, a local Delaware River pilot, Peterson and his wife, accompanied by several members of the ever-present media, had sallied forth to pay an impromptu visit to the site.[9]

Upon boarding the barge, the governor was immediately impressed by the tumulus of artifactual debris piled up on the deck. There were mounds of rusted chain, deadeyes, and wood fragments. Delighted by the visit of such an important personage, the salvors proudly showed him a rusted "bayonet," a ship's wooden pulley block, a crumbling pickax, and a corroded padlock. Fascinated, Peterson began to poke around the piles of rubble, listening intently as Bowden attempted to explain the stage reached by their operations thus far. The clam bucket had been digging about a dozen feet into the bottom, alongside the hulk, and a break through the hull was expected to occur imminently. The problem, however, was that time was running out. The team simply didn't have enough money to keep the project afloat for more than another day. "The biggest thing we've got going for us now is hope," Carliss declared. "The British . . . wouldn't have come clear across to here to try and raise it [*De Braak*] unless they knew there was something pretty valuable in the hold."[10]

That evening Peterson had returned to his cottage, his curiosity aroused. The four young salvors, however, were desperate—more desperate than he knew. Ensconced in their motel room back in Lewes, they were more convinced than ever that they were on the verge of breaking through the hull and into a treasure-filled hold. They had made calls to their associates in Pennsylvania, pleading for additional funds. "We thought we'd know for certain about the gold in three days," they told their friends. "But now it looks like a much larger vessel than we expected with a large number of compartments to be checked out."[11] But for all their efforts and despite their certainty that they were no more than a few feet away from fabulous wealth, they could raise little more than sympathy. By 11:00 P.M., all avenues seemed to have been exhausted. Then Carliss hit upon a bold scheme: they would make a direct, personal appeal to the Governor of Delaware for emergency state assistance. Certainly, the chief executive of the state could arrange for some form of funding or might at least have connections to those who could rescue the project in its hour of need. Within minutes, Carliss, accompanied by a young history teacher, Judy Ann Feldam, who had been working with the group, was en route to Peterson's secluded retreat.[12]

When the astonished governor answered the late-night knock at his door and admitted the young couple, Kent Carliss wasted little time on formalities. The project was going to close down, he said, just as they were about to make the big strike. "We're all sure of its worth. If we had more money of our own, we'd put it into the project right now," he told the governor. But they did not; moreover, unless D & D issued a certified check for an additional $3,100 to the dredge company, the entire effort would be for naught. Then he came to the point: Could the governor find the salvors several thousand dollars? Six thousand would just about cover them until the big strike was made.[13]

Peterson, although undoubtedly a bit stunned, took the highly unusual request seriously, for here were men who had given up everything in pursuit of a dream. He was, however, also a sensible man. He thus questioned the young salvor's certainty that *De Braak*, and not just another shipwreck, had been found.

"There's nobody at this point willing to confirm that we are digging on the De Braak," Carliss replied, "but it's definitely a teakwood vessel. And there were only two teak vessels in the British Navy at the time; one was on the other side of the world when *De Braak* sank."[14] Again, the old saw about teakwood was aired. Whether Carliss was ignorant about *De Braak*'s history or simply believed in her mythology is unknown. As Chapelle had already demonstrated, there were no eighteenth-century Royal Navy warships built of teak. Yet the tone of sincerity in Carliss's presentation had deeply impressed the governor, although he was well aware that "doubters" had denied the existence of any treasure aboard *De Braak*. "On the other hand," he responded, "suppose it did carry silver and gold? Look at the possible tourist lure. Also, there's the adventure of beating the so-called 'curse' that has been keeping the De Braak hidden in the sandy bottom of the ocean off Cape Henlopen!"[15] By midnight, Peterson had decided to call in an expert to identify the site as soon as possible. In the meantime, he would summon State Archivist Leon de Valinger and State Development Chief Thomas Evans to discuss the feasibility of securing additional funds to continue the salvage effort.[16]

With the governor (at least temporarily) behind the project, Carliss was confident that he would be granted the additional measure of time and money needed to locate the treasure. Indeed, through the efforts of Thomas Evans, enough funds were collected from private sources to pay for an additional day's investigation. The McClean Dredging Company, which had been providing the barge and crane at $3,100 a day was persuaded to donate a second day's use of the equipment. Peterson, however, had wisely not left up to D & D the business of securing an expert to identify the site. At his direction, the Smithsonian Institution was asked to provide the services of an expert in the field of underwater archaeology.[17]

On the afternoon of Wednesday, August 6, the Smithsonian Institution's specialist in marine archaeology (later to become State Underwater Archaeologist for South Carolina), a reed-thin young fellow named Alan Albright, arrived at Lewes and that same afternoon, accompanied by Governor Peterson, Evans, and De Valinger, visited the barge anchored over the purported wreck of *De Braak*. He had brought along a copy of the study that his colleague, Howard Chapelle, and M. E. S. Laws had published. Like Chapelle and Laws, Albright was convinced that the old warship had not been carrying treasure when she went down. But scientific objectivity required an open mind—and a thorough inspection of the on-site evidence.

Carefully, Albright began to poke through the debris piled up on the deck, examining an odd collection of spikes, blacksmith's tongs, horseshoes, ax heads, and miscellaneous components of ship's rigging. He asked the salvors if there were any cannons, cannonballs, or such identifiable items as buttons from military uniforms, but they replied in the negative.[18] After rummaging through a few more artifacts, Albright announced that there was nothing in the collection to verify that they had belonged to *De Braak*, although some artifacts were possibly of the same era. De Feo, aware that the expert's opinion all but doomed D & D's future efforts on the site, argued "that other maritime experts had told them otherwise and the evidence they had confirmed that they had found the De Braak."[19] "Anybody who gives a definite answer on stuff like this," retorted Albright as he fingered a rusting relic, "is in for trouble. They're just trying to impress someone."[20]

Albright's verdict was the kiss of death, and Tracy Bowden was incensed. He refused to believe that the ship was not *De Braak* simply because they had failed to locate any cannons or other artifacts of the type which Albright said were needed to verify the site's identity. Fighting a rearguard action, Bowden pointed out to Peterson that the man from the Smithsonian *had* indicated that the site was possibly a vessel of the correct era. And weren't the decks of the barge and the old U.S. Army dock at Lewes piled high with artifacts from the site? Didn't that count for something? Indeed, how could the wreck not be *De Braak*?

On August 21, D & D, still reeling from Albright's verdict but refusing to accept defeat, announced that it would again resume excavation work in September, this time with an even larger rig, a 100-ton dredge. Money to pay for the equipment rental would somehow be found. By the end of the following month, De Feo promised, D & D would either prove or disprove, once and for all, the site to be that of *De Braak*. The adverse publicity generated by the

Smithsonian verdict, however, had resulted in even more public skepticism over the site. One critic suggested that the wreck was a ship called the *Minnie Hunter*, which had been lost near the shore in 1883. Indeed, several vessels, including one called *Juneau*, lost around 1800, and a pilot boat, also lay in the immediate area. De Feo rebutted the argument, claiming that his divers had actually located the *Minnie Hunter* site some 800 yards north of where they had been dredging and only 150 yards offshore well before the current work had begun.[21]

One of the principal results of Albright's opinion, backed up by the Chapelle and Laws study, had been the final debunking of the teak myth. De Feo was quick to embrace the "new" data, announcing that the University of Wisconsin had identified some of the wood and various artifacts to be of white oak dating from the eighteenth century. A British lock which had been recovered had been sent off to England to be identified. When questioned about some of the other artifacts, De Feo had finally admitted that remnants from the *Minnie Hunter* as well as other nineteenth- and twentieth-century materials had also been brought up from the wreck, but claiming that these might "have been washed over to the site where we were working."[22]

Skepticism about the wreck's being *De Braak* continued to grow and had become more than a mere nuisance to the salvors. One argument which kept popping up was that the location where D & D had been working was dry land in 1798 and therefore could not possibly be the site of *De Braak*, but rather, of a much later vessel. De Feo countered by publicly revealing just how and why the company had decided to dig there. He said that a thorough study of maps and nautical charts from the period of the Dutch occupation onward had been a major component of the company's research. With a series of overlays, D & D had been able to predict a probable location for the remains of *De Braak*, marking the site with an *X* on a modern chart. When the magnetometer surveys were carried out, the wreck had been located only twenty yards from the coordinates of the mark. When asked why it was lying in much shallower water than the historical record suggested, De Feo had simply shrugged and declared that the water must have been three times deeper in 1798 than in 1969![23]

Schall, Bowden, and Vallejo refused to quit, continuing to work on the site without the support of a crane or barge. Airlifting became the method employed in the tedious business of clearing the wreck of the many tons of overburden. By November, the trio had reorganized and formed their own company, Tracy Bowden Associates, which was financed by a group of Philadelphia and New Jersey businessmen. D & D therefore had to work in partnership with another corporation, rather than proceeding under the less formal arrangement of earlier days. Nevertheless, the relationship between the two organizations was outwardly amicable. Yet, despite the enthusiasm evidenced by the young treasure hunters, the fickle weather of the Delaware Capes frequently dampened their zeal. "There is supposed to be a curse on this ship," said Schall melodramatically, "and sometimes you wonder if it isn't true. Every time we get the [airlift] pipe down and the boat is moving well over the spot we want cleared, the weather changes."[24]

Frustrations mounted, although the team kept publicly stating that they were on the site of De Braak. As their despair grew, however, they began to sound more desperate, as when Schall said that if they could "raise any old ship intact it would be worth the effort."[25] But again, another season had ended as it had begun, with grandiose statements about the prospects but little in the way of product.

At the beginning of 1970, the alliance between D & D and Tracy Bowden Associates turned to bitter rivalry. The power to grant another season permit to hunt for De Braak now rested with the State Water and Air Commission. And as on many previous occasions, it would be a commission composed of political appointees, rather than experts in history, archaeology, or cultural resources management, who would award the franchise. D & D's permit would expire on March 3, and it was anyone's guess what would happen after that. On February 11, John C. Bryson, executive director of the commission, noted that a decision on the one-year permit would have to be made by the 24th of that month. The number of applicants in 1970 amounted to only two: D & D Salvage and Tracy Bowden Associates.[26]

First off the mark was the Bowden team, who said that they would employ an airlift and would be ready to start in June, if granted the permit. D & D, by then cash poor, had also quietly resolved to use an airlift instead of a clam-bucket dredge, but, in an attempt to out-maneuver Bowden, had refused to disclose their site-clearing method. Both firms had, in fact, decided upon air-lifting because of a new element in the state's decision-making process: concern for the environment. "There are shellfish beds in the area," noted Bryson, "and we can't allow natural resources to be damaged, particularly since [the salvors] have not proven there is anything of real value down there."[27]

The environmental impact of dredging in the area was not the state's only concern, however. Slowly, almost imperceptibly, an appreciation for the archaeological potential of De Braak began to take root. Again, it was a scholar from the Smithsonian Institution who put things into perspective. In early April 1970, the archaeological significance of Delaware's most famous shipwreck was addressed by Mendel Peterson, the Smithsonian's Director of Underwater Exploration, during the annual spring dinner meeting of the Lewes Historical Society. Peterson, a pioneer in the field of underwater archaeology and author of a book on the subject entitled History under the Sea, had been asked to give a lecture on underwater exploration to the society in the Cape Henlopen High School auditorium. Employing much of Chapelle's and Laws's material on *De Braak*, he intrigued the audience with his own fresh comments on the value of the ship that placed it in a truly cultural context.[28]

For the first time, the sunken ship was discussed, not in terms of the treasure it might yield, but as a time capsule. Referring to his own experiences in the West Indies and Bermuda, Peterson noted that historic shipwrecks had frequently yielded records, equipment, and portions of cargo which had remained intact but segregated from similar materials of other eras by the sea. He noted that *De Braak* was potentially "important as a naval antiquity or as a material representative of the late eighteenth century." Indeed, the artifacts recovered from the shipwreck off Fort Miles Beach by D & D were no less important, for they also represented a moment frozen in time. Yet they could not, in themselves, be considered evidence that the vessel was *De Braak*. Indeed, he noted, the waters of the Delaware Capes held enormous archaeological potential because of many such shipwreck sites there. In concluding, he pointed out that Delaware waters were pregnant with possibilities and awaited underwater exploration.[29]

With respect to the salvors, Peterson's words fell on deaf ears. By May 22, D & D, who had finally been informed that they would once again be awarded the franchise, over the protests of Tracy Bowden Associates (now working on a treasure hunt in Puerto Rico), had declared that operations would resume in a month. The McClean Company of Baltimore had again been contracted to vacuum the entire area around the wreck site with an airlift, in lieu of the clam-bucket approach, which "might destroy valuable artifacts or the wreck itself." A failure by company officials to submit the necessary papers, however, caused a three-month delay. As a consequence, it was not until August 22 that D & D's new lease was signed by Governor Peterson.[30]

Again, as in the past, lack of capital had become a problem for the salvors. Although Bud Busa spoke boldly of beginning work by the end of August, there was little money available to pay for the necessary equipment. The company began negotiating with Tracy Bowden Associates to conduct the actual fieldwork. Albert Schall, perhaps representing the Bowden team's view, noted acidly that "D & D is having so much trouble among themselves that they can't decide what to do." He expected that infighting among the founders of D & D would likely result in the replacement of Busa as president, and he doubted that anything more would be done on the site.[31] His prediction would prove to be accurate.

The death knell for D & D's quest for *De Braak* was finally sounded the following year. On July 21, 1971, William T. De Feo, dentist, resident of Broad Street, Philadelphia, and company secretary, once again stated that he expected yet another renewal of the search permit even though work had not progressed during the preceding year. It was then revealed that the company had never posted either the required $1,000 lease fee or the $15,000 performance bond in 1970. The permit, it was disclosed, had never actually been issued. "They never went down to the wire with it," stated one bemused state official. D & D's search for HM Brig *De Braak* was finally over.[32]

People with Blinders On

After five years of frustrated effort, D & D Salvage Company's expensive search for the remains of *De Braak* had failed miserably. Ironically, the treasure hunters had managed to snag not only the attention of the news media, but that of the American publishing industry and the public at large as well. As a result, the story of the warship and its supposed booty became more deeply embedded in the national psyche than ever before. Its influence on the new world of avocational underwater treasure hunting was profound.

In 1965, Lieutenant Harry Rieseberg, an adventure writer who specialized in books on treasure hunting, teamed up with one A. A. Minkalow and published a melodramatic compilation of the richest targets a treasure hunter could hope for. Unfortunately, much if not all of the work was pure fiction. Nevertheless, Rieseberg's work, *Fell's Guide to Sunken Treasure Ships of the World*, though meeting with little critical acclaim, garnered an enormous readership. Within a short time several editions of the work were published. Almost overnight, it became a veritable bible for thousands of armchair treasure seekers. And, of course, among the more absorbing inclusions was a less-than-scholarly, but tantalizing, account of the loss of *De Braak* and her purported booty. According to Rieseberg's questionable (but rarely questioned) documentation, the warship had gone down with 1.5 million in gold ingots, silver doubloons, and $85,000 in Spanish specie, on May 10, 1798. Relying upon folktales, a dab of fact, and his own creative imagination for references, he stated that the warship had been built of oak and teakwood in 1797 for the Dutch Navy, had been captured by the French, and was later taken by the English. Her crew was comprised of eighty-six seamen and thirty-eight officers, and she was armed with sixteen brass carronades. She was, he claimed, a full 125 feet in length, thirty feet abeam, high pooped, and had sailed down the Thames in 1798 bound for the Caribbean bearing letters of marque. According to Rieseberg, *De Braak* was more than successful. Within a short time she had captured six Spanish prizes and transferred their treasures to her hold. Then, off the Delaware coast, she took a seventh, the *St. Francis Xavier*. Captain Drew promptly transferred the *Xavier*'s treasure to his "frigate" and set sail for Halifax. A terrible storm, however, blew up and sank his ship in Old Kiln Roads. A salvage expedition to recover the treasure had been launched in 1799 but was stymied by poor weather. In 1814, a British syndicate tried again. In 1877, a Philadelphia doctor tried his hand. Additional efforts to find and raise the ship, said to be resting in ninety feet of water, were made annually from 1880 to 1893, in 1932, 1935, and 1937.[1]

That the vessel had not been built of teak in 1797, was not administered by thirty-eight officers, had not entered the Thames in 1798, failed to approach the dimensions given, had not taken seven ships laden with treasure, and did not sink on May 10 mattered little. Rieseberg, purportedly a retired naval officer, seemed entirely ignorant of the fact that a commissioned Royal Navy man-of-war could not serve the Crown and as a privateer simultaneously. It was, however, a rousing good tale.

The publication blitz had begun. Accuracy in reportage was not mandatory to reach print.

By 1967, even as D & D was zealously bouncing from one wrecksite to another proclaiming each to be the vessel they sought, *De Braak* became grist for the sensationalist paperback trade. In one pulp book, entitled *Finders Keepers*, the bold promotional banner promised: "You can find millions in lost and buried treasure!" and offered insider tips on how to locate money, gold, and jewels. Between the covers, of course, was a personal account by an east-coast skin diver named James Howe who had "researched" the wreck of *De Braak*. Howe claimed, incorrectly, that the vessel had been lost on June 10, 1798, with $8 million in Spanish treasure aboard, barrels of specie, eighty tons of copper, 800 pounds of gold, tons of silver, forty-two crewmen, and 100 Spanish prisoners.[2]

In 1970 Rieseberg reprised his 1965 success with another treasure book entitled: *Fell's Complete Guide to Buried Treasure Land & Sea*. He now claimed *De Braak* had foundered on March 25, 1798 in fourteen fathoms of water a mile off the Cape Henlopen Lightship. This time, she was reported to have gone down with $15 million in gold and silver bullion and specie, seventy tons of copper ingots, and "80,000 pounds of English gold taken on at Jamaica for the Bank of England." He even threw in a consignment of diamonds for good measure.[3]

Rieseberg's widely-read account was pure fantasy. Indeed, it was the stuff of swashbuckling daydreams. Unfortunately, it was believed by many in its entirety, and its information, fictitious as it was, was acted upon by a few.

Further credibility was lent to the treasure legend the following year, when a well-known adventurer, underwater explorer, self-proclaimed archaeologist, and professional treasure hunter named Robert F. Marx, in an otherwise fairly accurate survey of vessels lost in American waters between 1492 and 1825, claimed that *De Braak* had gone down with seventy tons of copper ingots "and a large amount of gold and silver bullion and specie." Much of Marx's reputation rested on his claim, accepted by many at the time, to have discovered the wreck of the famed Civil War ironclad *Monitor* in forty-three feet of water off the beach at Cape Hatteras, North Carolina. He was also well known for his highly publicized discoveries of several Spanish galleons and their vast treasures and for his almost single-handed excavation of the sunken pirate stronghold of Port Royal, Jamaica. With his national following, his imprimatur lent an air of truth to the *De Braak* treasure story, an already inflated legend.[4]

In 1971, the same year that Marx's *Shipwrecks of the Western Hemisphere* appeared, another hugely successful book, *The Treasure Diver's Guide* by John S. Potter, Jr., was also published. This work, although also filled with misinformation, had an enormous appeal for a nation increasingly enamored of sunken-treasure hunts. In Florida, such treasure hunters as Burt Webber and Mel Fisher had captured the public's imagination with highly touted and well-publicized discoveries, if not with actually finding great wealth. Endorsed by such cult figures as Kip Wagner, the man who had found the 1715 Spanish Plate Fleet off the Florida coast, Potter's book sold out almost as soon as it appeared and soon had gone through several editions.[5] The book concentrated on treasure wrecks still to be found. One of the most popular sections detailed the *De Braak* saga right down to the D & D recovery attempt. It was, in fact, the culmination of years of accumulated historical errors, garbled facts, and misinformation—and Potter even added a few new myths.[6]

According to him, *De Braak*'s guns were bronze carronades which had been used to prey upon Spanish shipping from July 1797 to May 1798, as "she played the lone wolf in the Caribbean and Bahamas." The raider had captured "at least three Spanish *patches* [advice boats] and *naos* [merchantmen]," all of which carried precious metal. Overburdened with treasure and seventy tons of copper, she had easily fallen victim to a sudden squall and sank with thirty-eight crewmen aboard and 200 prisoners shackled below decks. Her total value at the time, he calculated, was somewhere in the vicinity of five to ten million dollars. Never mentioning the recovery effort of the *Hind* and the *Vixen*, Potter described how the *Assistance* had supposedly carried out unsuccessful salvage work with a diving bell for two full months before giving up.[7] Had he investigated the *Assistance* logs, he would have found no mention whatsoever to any diving operations. But then, few today would accuse the author of being a slave to fact.

The following year, Potter claimed, a second attempt was made, this time by a Royal Navy frigate called *Resolute*. The frigate, having brought "the stripped and lightened hull of another ship in tow," had attempted to loop a chain beneath the sunken brig. Attaching it to the second vessel at low tide, the British had tried to carry out a "tide-lift," that is, to use the force of the flood tide to pry the hull loose from the Delaware muds. The chains broke, according to Potter, because of the inordinately heavy treasure ship and her great, burdensome booty. It was a wonderful story, but there had been neither a Royal Navy ship named *Resolute* in commission at the time nor a second major salvage attempt.[8]

Potter's story combined and elaborated on many tales circulating throughout the treasure-hunting community, but the publicity generated by his book had a stunning effect. Soon the *De Braak* legend had become grist for the mill of men's adventure and treasure-hunting publications of all kinds. Lurid titles like "Delaware's $40 Million Treasure Jinx" appeared on the covers of scores of magazines sold in drug stores and newsstands across the nation.[9] The net effect was the popularization and further elaboration of the *De Braak* legend on a national level. Few could resist its attraction, for less than a mile or so off the sunny Delaware beachfront, many were led to believe, were millions of dollars in treasure awaiting the bold. It was assumed, as it had been in the 1930s, that all anyone needed was a little industry, some capital, a salvage permit, and the will to tackle the Weather Witch and the Delaware Jinx. The legend had become not only self-perpetuating, but it was also growing in proportion to every news story written about it.

One of the first people to publicly embrace the bogus "histories" following the failed D & D effort was Edward E. Westlake. This particular would-be salvor was an inmate (Number 107145) in the Michigan State Penitentiary. Serving a ten-year term for robbery and in his sixth year of incarceration, Westlake passed the time by reading about sunken treasure ships, and *De Braak* had caught his fancy. Inspired by the literature available in the prison library, where he spent most of his time, he had resolved to make his own attempt. The quest, he later stated, changed his life. "The next time I rob anything," he quipped to a television interviewer, "it'll be the treasure from the old ship, the De Braak," which he estimated to be worth $15 million.[10]

Westlake was not discouraged by the failures of D & D Salvage and many others or by the authoritative argument of Chapelle and Laws that *De Braak* carried no treasure. Nor did he see his own incarceration as anything but a temporary obstruction. Persuaded by the popular tales of the warship's fabulous wealth, he felt absolutely certain that she had gone down with a king's ransom in gold and silver. Without outside help, however, his quest would amount to little more than a daydream. Then, in 1970, he had met and been befriended by an engineer named Robert N. Riggs, who had been teaching a college extension course in physics at the prison. Riggs, president of his own engineering company based in Crystal, Michigan, had been intrigued by the inmate's scheme to recover the treasure and eventually was drawn into an agreement to support a search. Together, the two would-be adventurers began to plan their expedition in what certainly must have been the strangest environment for a treasure hunt ever to be concocted—a state prison.[11]

With Riggs's help, the project began to take shape. A stock corporation called Manta Ray, Inc., was formed, with Westlake as president. More than $10,000 was raised for the initial stages of the hunt, and the partners anticipated that "a lot more money [would] be coming in from people who are interested in the venture." Several researchers, it was announced, would be sent to London to study the British archives. An old, 130-foot, ex-navy minesweeper had been acquired for field operations, which the two unlikely partners announced would soon begin.[12]

Westlake, a "quiet, sincere man" in his fifties, had been a model prisoner. Scheduled for early release in October 1971, he had applied for a salvage permit in January of that year to William F. Moyer, manager of the Wetlands section of the Delaware Department of Natural Resources. In light of the recent recovery efforts, Moyer had little choice but to take the application seriously. He informed Westlake of the department's conditions for a salvage permit, including the proviso that "the U.S. Coast Guard, the Army Corps of Engineers and the Defense Department [didn't] object."[13] Although still hampered by having to conduct his affairs from the confines of his cell, Westlake had not been put off. He was more than a little anxious to secure a permit quickly, fearing that others might attempt to beat his group to the punch. In a letter to Moyer, he informed the Delaware official of his concern, stating that failure to move rapidly had already cost him the salvage rights to another treasure ship, the *Nuestra Señora de la Concepción*, lost off the Dominican Republic, to veteran salvor Burt Webber. The permit had to be issued, and soon, or all might be lost.[14]

Moyer's reply to the inmate informed him of exactly what the State of Delaware expected from a salvage agreement if the operation were successful: twenty-five percent of the net value of all cargo recovered. In addition, the salvors would have to agree to give the State Division of Historical and Cultural Affairs "all rights to any item of historical significance, artifacts and documents relating to the sunken vessel."[15] Nothing would be heard from Manta Ray, Inc., for the next nine years.

Two more years passed before another candidate would consider entering the ever-expanding ring of *De Braak* hunters. In 1973 Steve Snyder was a thirty-eight-year-old aeronautical engineer, specializing in the design and manufacture of sports parachute equipment. The success of his company, Para Flight, Inc., of Cherry Hill, New Jersey, had brought him enough financial independence to enable him to pursue other interests on a grand scale. One of those interests was HMS *De Braak*.[16]

Snyder was a Philadelphia-born entrepreneur who had been reared on the *De Braak* legend. Like many, he had been intrigued by treasure hunting and all the mystery and romance that went with it. Once, he had even hunted for deep-sea treasure off the coasts of Florida and the Bahamas, but it was not until the demise of the D & D Salvage Company project off Cape Henlopen that his interest in finding Captain James Drew's famed brig actually blossomed. Soon after D & D had given up, Snyder met Terry Crowe of Newark, Delaware, who had worked for a while on one of the expeditions. Crowe's tales quickly kindled the engineer's imagination. "The more we talked about De Braak," Snyder later recalled, "the more interested I became."[17] He began conducting his own research and then formed the HM De Braak Salvage Corporation, hiring a lawyer in Wilmington named John Babiarz to advise him on applying for an exploratory permit. Quietly and methodically, he had also begun to acquire sophisticated electronic equipment for the search.[18]

Unlike many of his predecessors, Snyder had few illusions about the wreck. He was well aware of Chapelle and Laws's study as well as the numerous previous efforts to locate and salvage the ship from 1798 on. He had familiarized himself with the lore and traditions surrounding the disaster and had done a considerable amount of archival research as well. "I know all about the legends and folk stories—and the actual history of the De Braak," he would say with a grin. "I am not deluded by the legends and myths." A careful, even cautious man, he was betting on his "scientific, realistic, preparatory homework" to see him through. He studied the ever-migrating coastline of the Delaware Capes and the shifting patterns of the ocean floor. He knew the history backward and forward, and he was patient.[19]

Snyder developed a three-stage plan. First, he would employ "special electronic equipment" capable of locating a shipwreck and telling him which among the many wrecks in the area was De Braak—although he never revealed exactly what kind of discriminating shipwreck locator he would use. The second stage entailed securing physical diagnostic evidence. "And then comes the time to dive and raise the ship." He was prepared to invest up to $1 million in the project.[20]

As with all of his predecessors, however, Snyder's permit application proved to be a lengthy process which did not enter its final stages until November 1974. By then the weather had deteriorated, making operations impossible until the following spring. The delay proved pivotal. During the winter of 1974–75, while his application was passing through its final stage of processing, Snyder had begun to have second thoughts about the project. "We came up with additional historical documentation," he later stated, "that the effort we were about to make . . . the chances of its being productive were minimal. . . . The ship did not carry the treasure it was said to. It basically contained cocoa beans and other commercial goods." Although he was quick to acknowledge that De Braak was certainly of great historical significance to Delaware, it was of little value financially—and therefore of little interest to him.[21]

Steve Snyder's hunt for *De Braak* was over before it began. Unlike many treasure seekers before him, his extensive research had saved him trouble and expense. Yet no lesson was learned, either by the general public or the treasure-hunting community, as the *De Braak* saga continued to grow in the popular press.

By 1980 at least nine major, documented expeditions had been undertaken to locate the wreck of *De Braak* (another three had been planned but not carried out). All but the original British salvage attempt had been motivated solely by a desire to recover the allegedly vast treasure she held. Each attempt had failed, but all had contributed to the legend. A folklore of sorts had even evolved from the salvage efforts themselves. At least thirty expeditions, went the story, had tried and failed to raise the fabled warship. Millions of dollars had been spent, many vessels had been destroyed, and at least twelve men, by one count, had lost their lives in the effort. Of course, most of the failures were chalked up to such forces as the "weather witch," ghosts, and the *De Braak* jinx, all of which added appreciably to the mystery of the wreck. And it was all rubbish. But the treasure hunters continued to arrive.

In August 1980, Donald F. Stewart, who had formed his own historical consulting organization called the Atlantic Ship Historical Society and a treasure salvage company called Sea Limited, announced his plans to locate and salvage *De Braak*.[22] Stewart, however, was simply too slow off the mark. Later in August, before he could organize his search, a Key West, Florida, firm called Seaborne Ventures, Inc., appeared in Delaware to test the waters around Lewes. Unlike many of the companies created specifically to hunt for *De Braak*, which had combined modern technology with amateur talent, Seaborne was led by a veteran treasure hunter with years of experience. Dennis Standefer, president of the company, had by his own account been successfully involved in treasure hunting since at least 1957. As the leader of a professional treasure-hunting corporation called Fathom Expeditions, Standefer had mounted extensive search-and-salvage operations in Mexico and along the Central American coast in pursuit of sunken Spanish gold and had become something of a treasure hunter's "guru."

One of Standefer's more notable campaigns had been to locate Captain Henry Morgan's famed pirate ship *Oxford*, thought to have been lost off Ambergris Cay, Belize, in 1669. The expedition had found instead a wreck that Standefer claimed to be HMS *Yealdham*, supposedly lost in that vicinity in 1800.[28] Another of his efforts had been the 1968–69 search for HMS *Leviathan*, which Standefer said had been sunk off the Yucatan coast in 1799 with $200,000 in precious metal and gems. By 1969, Fathom Expeditions was able to report that the wreck had been discovered four miles south of San Fernando de Omoa and that a thousand coins had been salvaged.[24] The discoveries of the *Yealdham* and the *Leviathan* loomed large in Standefer's career, having enhanced his status in the treasure-hunting community and earning him a place in Potter's *Treasure Diver's Guide*.[25] But historians were less impressed, knowing that there had been neither a *Yealdham* nor a *Leviathan* serving under commission in the Royal Navy on the dates Standefer cited.[26]

Factual accuracy mattered little to investors in treasure-hunting expeditions, however, as most of them were swept away by the glamor and mystique of the hunt and the charisma of the promoters. Such expeditions were particularly attractive when their target was a wreck off the Delaware coast, for *De Braak* was no longer the state's only treasure ship to lure salvors. Thanks to the notoriety of Potter's book and others, local lore about two purportedly coin-laden ships, the *Faithful Steward* and the *Three Brothers*, had also spread and begun to rival tales of the famous *De Braak*.

Since at least the 1930s, beachcombers had been picking up copper and gold coins along a narrow stretch of Delaware oceanfront called Dewey Beach (known to many beachcombers as "Coin Beach"), near Indian River Inlet and somewhat south of Rehoboth Beach. Many locals claimed that the coins came from either the wreck of the *Faithful Steward*, lost on September 2, 1785,[27] or the *Three Brothers*, said to have gone down in about 1775.[28] The allure of three potential treasure-bearing shipwrecks almost within shouting distance of one another had not gone unnoticed by Standefer. When he arrived on the scene in August 1980, it had been with the avowed intention of locating all three, as well as an unidentified fourth wreck lying further south of Indian River Inlet. Financed by a former associate of J. Rodney King named Mel Joseph, a wealthy Georgetown building contractor, and a well-heeled Atlanta, Georgia, family named Rollins, the chief executive of Seaborne was prepared to pull out all the stops. After all, one of his principal backers, Joseph, had also supported Mel Fisher, the world-famous discoverer of the richest wreck in American waters, the *Nuestra Señora de Atocha*. Standefer entered the Delaware arena with what can only be described as panache.[29]

Seaborne, having begun its efforts with a quiet, unannounced reconnaissance of the waters off Lewes, had promptly located a promising site thought to be *De Braak*. Following his initial investigation, Standefer was confident enough to apply for an exclusive salvage permit from the Wetlands Office, not only for the supposed *De Braak* site, but also for three wrecks in the other two sectors. Standefer and Joseph planned first to go after the *Faithful Steward* and the *Three Brothers*, between Dewey Beach and Indian River Inlet, as well as the unidentified wreck lying a mile and a half below the inlet. Their application for the *De Braak* site, however, was not uncontested. There were, in fact, two other firms competing for *De Braak*: Edward Westlake's Manta Ray, Inc., and another rival called Sting Ray, Inc., which had initially backed Seaborne.

But Westlake's group, which decided to wait until spring before applying, and Sting Ray, which was unable to raise enough capital, dropped out. Seaborne won by default. By the week of October 8, which in the past had been considered too late in the season to begin operations, three exclusive leases, covering one and a half square miles each and costing $1,000 apiece, had been issued to the Florida treasure hunter. Delaware's share of the take was to be the usual twenty-five percent.[30]

Standefer, moving swiftly, began assembling the necessary equipment and personnel at the Ocean House in Lewes. His activities, of course, were closely monitored by the local press, and not everyone was delighted. One group of sport divers from nearby Bethany Beach confronted the Wetlands Office with their concern that Seaborne's leases would tie up substantial portions of the oceanfront, limiting their recreational use. The Wetlands manager, Bill Moyer, who had authorized the leases, diplomatically defused the potential conflict before it could erupt. A compromise was reached, satisfactory to both parties, which would allow diving within 300 yards of the operations being conducted by Seaborne's salvage vessel.[31]

Standefer's array of equipment was formidable. He announced to the press that he would be employing not only a magnetometer, to detect magnetic anomalies on the bottom caused by large concentrations of ferrous metals, but side-scan sonar as well. This relatively new form of sonar, developed in World War II and refined by Dr. Harold Edgerton of the Massachusetts Institute of Technology, was deployed by dragging a sensor on a cable behind a boat. The sensor, or "fish," sent sound waves out and then received a return, or echo, which was relayed to a strip-chart recorder aboard the boat. The echo was then converted into line imagery on the recorder. In this fashion, a discrete profile of the seabed and anything protruding above the bottom, such as might be caused by a shipwreck or even a mound resulting from a deteriorated vessel covered by silts, could be located. Systematic deployment of side-scan sonar had already helped to locate several historic wreck sites, including that of the Civil War ironclad *Monitor* (miles from where Marx had earlier claimed to have found it). Standefer was betting that the system might be literally worth its weight in gold.[32] To facilitate excavation of the four shipwreck sites (three of which had yet to be found), Seaborne had rented from the ever-reliable McClean Dredging Company, of Baltimore, a 275-foot barge at a cost of $3,000 per day. The barge, which was expected to arrive during the second week of October, would serve as a platform from which clam-bucket dredging of probable sites could be carried out. The project's cost was expected to reach about $500,000.[33]

Standefer's research had apparently been as limited as that of most of his predecessors, and he relied heavily on the same old folktales. He first sought and secured the services of veteran *De Braak* hunter Archie Brittingham to discover the whereabouts of the venerable McCracken bible and to provide his own "valuable information" about the wreck. Brittingham was able to locate the bible in Salisbury, Maryland, and had arranged for Standefer to see it. One important source for background data on recent salvage attempts, however, had mysteriously disappeared.[34] On October 7, the Zwaanendael Museum in Lewes reported the theft of two books. These were not expensive books, having cost a total of only seven dollars, and one, *Shipwrecks off the New Jersey Coast* by Walter and Richard Krotee, was little more than a popular wreck-diving publication (complete with an inaccurate but zesty account of *De Braak*). The other, however, was a red vinyl notebook filled with yellowed newspaper clippings collected over the previous fifty years by the museum, all concerning *De Braak* and the many efforts to recover her treasure. The data, which was for the most part irreplaceable, would have been an invaluable asset to any one trying to locate the wreck. Despite the efforts of the town police, the books could not be found.[35]

The public image of its own research presented by Seaborne was that of a knowledgeable, nuts-and-bolts outfit, and company publicist Barry Schatz, a former Key West reporter, was quite effective in maintaining that image. During one of the firm's early press conferences, he had casually handled photostats which, he implied, had come from British archives and contained "all manner of reports on past attempts to raise the De Braak." But his data were no better than anyone else's had been. The teakwood-hulled ship, he stated confidently, was 125 feet long and lay exactly one mile off Cape Henlopen in precisely eight-seven feet of water. According to a Halifax newspaper report, he said, the ship had capsized and sunk after returning from a successful cruise of the Spanish Main. Sinking with her had been a fortune in gold and silver, precious stones, and £80,000 in gold specie taken aboard at Jamaica for transportation to England. Indeed, the wreck was so valuable, claimed Schatz, that the Admiralty had, as recently as 1979, submitted an "unprecedented" claim to Seaborne for thirty percent of whatever treasure the company might recover, and Schatz boasted that he had a letter to prove it.[36]

"What's so neat," the spokesman said on the day after the theft of the Zwaanendael scrapbook, "is the confusion of information and misinformation about the *De Braak*. It may be one of the most enduring legends of the mid-Atlantic coast. . . . It is the legend that has kept this thing alive. The legend has kept people going after it.[37] (What might not have occurred to the publicist was that he himself was adding to an already sizeable body of misinformation.)

Detailing the project's methodology, Schatz informed the media in early October that Seaborne had already located a vessel believed to be *De Braak*. "We don't have complete proof," he admitted. "But it's worth going after." The site in question was protected by strong currents and murky waters, and it was partly covered with sand. When the time was right, however, a barge would be anchored over it, and a gigantic clam bucket would scoop up the wreck remains and dump it on the open deck of the barge for sorting. "It sounds pretty reckless," boasted Schatz, "but if we do the sounding correctly and the De Braak is out there, then it's going to be found. Nobody ever had this kind of equipment before."[38]

Unlike previous expeditions, whose success or failure had hinged on the treasure alone, Seaborne recognized the "great artifactual value in anything that [could] be brought up," some of which also had great monetary value. A single carronade, Schatz pointed out, was worth as much as $15,000 in the antiquities trade. In further contrast to earlier endeavors, Seaborne's plan was fiscally sound. "The sacrifice we've made so far is nothing compared to [that of] a lot of people," he said, in an oblique reference to the D & D effort. "We don't intend to make that kind of sacrifice. We've got the equipment to tell us, before we start, whether we're being foolish or not."[39]

Standefer had decided to begin test-dredging operations off the Dewey Beach site on Thursday, October 9. When Schatz informed the press of the company's strategy, he noted that treasure hunters normally did not expect to find much treasure close to shore. Nevertheless, Seaborne would rehearse its operations by working the site for several days before moving up to Cape Henlopen for the big one, HMS De Braak. The following day, the same Bethany Beach divers who had opposed Seaborne's lease became caught up in the publicity frenzy and volunteered their services to the treasure hunters.[40]

Without a hitch, the McClean barge was towed into position and anchored a mere twenty yards from the beach, stern pointed shoreward, bow toward the open sea. It mattered little to the project director whether or not a shipwreck lay below (for there had been no verification of one), but only that operations got under way as quickly as possible.[41] Within a short time, the gigantic clam bucket had bitten into the sandy bottom, gouging out massive holes, and had brought its load to the surface to be deposited and sifted on deck. That Saturday, a team of reporters and cameramen from a local television station arrived on the scene to begin filming the treasure hunt for a local show called Prime Time, to be aired in December. As if on cue, the first major artifacts, two gold five-guinea pieces and a handful of copper coins, were found. The following day, while the cameras were running, another two gold five-guinea pieces and more coppers were plucked from the mud. By October 13, a total of nearly 200, badly deteriorated coppers, four gold coins, dated 1752, 1756, 1759, and 1766, a handful of brass and silver shoe buckles, a brass navigational divider, a few brass spikes, some copper sheathing, and some bits of slate and iron had been recovered.[42]

Bill Moyer, of the Wetlands Office, was impressed by the finds. "The coins," he exclaimed, "look like they just fell into the water yesterday," and were worth between four and five thousand dollars.[43] Despite the excitement of the state, the media, and everyone else, the salvors seemed strangely unimpressed by the recovered items. There were many artifacts, but no timber from a ship-wreck. At a cost of $15,000 in barge rental alone, the return so far had not been profitable. "We found a lot of junk," said Schatz, almost dismissively, on October 13. "If we don't find something big soon," he promised, "we'll move up to the De Braak site off Lewes."[44] But first the wreck had to be relocated with the side-scan sonar and then verified. As the search got under way, the barge was ordered up to Lewes, where its catch basin could be enlarged to facilitate the recovery of even greater amounts of dredge spoil. Upon verifica-tion of the wreck by divers, the barge would be towed out and anchored over the site, and dredging could begin.

Company officials appeared to remain unconcerned about the impending winter season, which, as they were surely aware, had closed down many op-erations before theirs. When questioned about the "weather witch's" ability to summon "her airborne broom corps" to abort Seaborne's efforts, Schatz replied sarcastically, "The elements are always against you. But that doesn't mean we need to bring the Bermuda Triangle north, does it?"[45] Nevertheless, everyone quietly feared that the oncoming season would claim its due, and, sure enough, the side-scan survey was conducted with great difficulty because of the weather. Since the sensor had to be towed by a small runabout on the open sea, turbulent conditions made reliable data assemblage all but impos-sible. Nevertheless, Schatz announced, the wreck earlier believed to be that of *De Braak* had been found. Workers had recovered some wood, thought to be mahogany, a "brass navigating device," a few brass spikes, and some ballast stones. But, owing to weather conditions, further side-scan work became im-possible. Even worse was the fact that, in three weeks of "survey," Seaborne had been able to use its magnetometer only seven times.[46]

The project came to a standstill. Not only had the "weather witch" begun to harass the salvors, but a deep split had developed between Standefer and his principal backer, Mel Joseph, over differences of opinion about the project's course. Standefer was anxious to publicly deny the schism claiming that all differences had been resolved. But the breach was too great.[47] On Monday, October 20, Standefer announced that because of rough seas and high winds, Seaborne Ventures would be suspending all operations until the following sea-son. "We figured this anyway," he said, attempting to put the best face on the situation before leaving for the Caribbean and another shot at instant wealth. "We didn't expect to complete all that we had to do. After all, we're much, much happier than when we began. It's unusual to start and in a matter of two days find gold." He would be back, he promised, as had all the salvors before him, in the spring.[48]

As he prepared to depart from Lewes, Seaborne spokesman Barry Schatz was asked to define what drives a treasure hunter. His reply was provocative and telling. "Gold and gleaming wealth," he said,

> have always been a powerful motivation. The entire Spanish New World was built on that obsession. In fact, the Spanish destroyed three of the world's most innovative civilizations because of it—the Aztecs, the Mayans, and the Incas. But there is more than the gleam of gold here. It is the lure of the past itself, the desire to link the present to a bygone time. It's the same kind of catharsis that an artist seeks. And like the artist who must believe in the importance of connecting his work, a treasure hunter is an optimist, a man who believes in the importance of himself to the flow of time. All the treasure hunters I know are big egotists. I don't mean that in a bad way. They are people who are driven. They are people who would appear to have blinders on. That's what causes them to hope, sometimes against all hope, that there's as much gold in a ship's store as there is in its legend.[49]

PART THREE

The De Braak *is home.*

Kevin McCormick, August 11, 1986

S I X T E E N

A Beautiful Small Wreck

By the age of fifty-one, Harvey Harrington, a native of Scituate, Massachusetts, had seen a lot of the world, but little of it from a first-class seat. His formal education had lasted only nine years, but he had made do. As a commercial diver, he claimed to have had more than two decades of wide experience working on pipelines, bridge piers, and underwater construction sites. To make a living, he had salvaged sunken timber logs, built sewer outfalls, and even dredged for gold and silver residue dumped from jewelry-grinding and polishing operations. He was only occasionally given to boasting, but was not averse to telling tall tales. He claimed to have once worked for the world-famous underwater explorer Jacques Cousteau and to have served during World War II as a special instructor at West Point, when he could not have been more than fifteen years old. Yet, like most working-class folks, he had dreamed of a better life. And one of his most cherished fantasies was of finding lost treasure.[1]

Harvey Harrington's dream of recovering forgotten treasure trove was purportedly born in 1969 when, while working in Central America, he had been shown jewels allegedly found by turtle fishermen salvaging a Spanish galleon wreck in Panama. He had never forgotten the experience, and in 1977, after moving to Boise, Idaho, he began researching shipwrecks—not just any wrecks, of course, but treasure wrecks. Soon, his interest became focused on three specific ships: the pirate ship *Whydah*, lost off Cape Cod in the early eighteenth century, the steamer *Republic*, and the most famous of them all, HMS *De Braak*.[2]

There is something magical in the allure of a sunken ship, be it a noble Spanish galleon, the majestic *Titanic*, or a lowly tramp steamer—especially in the mind of a landlocked, transplanted New Englander. The name *De Braak*, however, was more than magical to Harrington, who had soon begun to concentrate his attention on this one vessel. Perhaps it had become the very symbol of the lost warship: a container of exotic things, a traveler from far-off places on a forgotten wartime mission during a heroic age. Perhaps the lure was simply the alleged treasure itself. Whatever the attraction had been, it was enough to motivate the graying diver to consider launching his own effort to find *De Braak*, but not until 1983 was he ready to begin actively looking for investors and to apply for a search permit from the State of Delaware.[3] Soon, he was talking to potential backers: a mineral magnate in California, an Idaho rancher, an opera singer with oil wells in Boise, a real estate broker in Tucson, and a wholesaler in Kansas City. Then, while on a visit to Attleboro, Rhode Island, where he had begun prospecting for industrial gold and silver residue in Ten Mile River, Harrington met Louis Calcione, a fellow prospector and a native Rhode Islander. The would-be treasure salvor had soon broached the subject of *De Braak* to his new acquaintance. Calcione was intrigued and had volunteered to introduce Harrington to two friends in the construction business, Ralph LaPadula and George Peloso, both of whom expressed great interest in the potential venture. By fall, after several meetings, their shared curiosity about *De Braak* and their enthusiasm over the possibility of finding her had become self-sustaining. For Harrington, however, a spark had been ignited that would not be extinguished until the legendary ship was found.

In November 1983, Harrington began his quest in earnest when he, Peloso, and LaPadula met with the elderly Richard T. Wilson, the sole surviving veteran of the 1935 Colstad Expedition. Wilson, a successful real estate broker in Warwick, Rhode Island, was now over seventy years old. Although his own experience was long behind him, his memory of the treasure hunt of nearly half a century earlier had not dimmed in the least.[4] Wilson's tales of his adventures and his knowledge of the site stirred the imagination of his three guests. He had shown them a piece of wood, supposedly teak, which he claimed had been recovered from the wreck. He had described a coin, dated 1786, which was said to have fallen out of the boot of a hard-hat diver who had been exploring near the wreck. But must important to the trio was a map Wilson had shown them: based upon the McCracken data, the location where he believed the wreck to lie had been marked, as well as the spot where the coin had come from. For his three visitors, this was heady stuff. Here before them was the proverbial treasure map, with an actual "X" marking the spot. All that was missing was a parrot and a skull-and-crossbones. For Wilson, there was the assurance, warmly offered by his guests, that he would receive a share of any profits realized on the site by the trio.[5] For the three would-be adventurers, the meeting had planted a seed which would grow to bear bitter fruit.

While Harrington, LaPadula, Calcione, and Peloso negotiated the terms of their alliance, the Delaware Department of Natural Resources and Environmental Control (DNREC) approved Harrington's permit request, which had been submitted some time earlier. The permission did not come cheap. The search permit alone would cost $1,500, and an additional $7,500 security bond was required. To avoid any conflict with the state (which would again claim twenty-five percent of the value of any goods recovered within its coastal waters), a lease had to be taken on the section of bottomlands in which the wreck allegedly lay and would require an additional $20,000 security bond.[6]

In January, with the search permit approved in his name—and in his name only—Harrington's alliance with LaPadula and Peloso broke down, and he returned to Boise to pursue his fund-raising from different sources. Contact was soon made with Joseph Wise, of Tucson, Arizona, who had expressed an interest in the project several months earlier. Wise introduced Harrington to Gary Steingrebe, a California accountant who secured a $50,000 loan from the trust fund of a schoolteacher and an additional $25,000 investment for Harrington's project. On February 17, 1984, a joint-venture agreement was formally signed by Harrington, Wise, Steingrebe, and the teacher.[7] Their company, called Sub-Sal, was legally incorporated in Reno, Nevada, on March 15, 1984.[8]

Time was by then of the essence, for Harrington's search permit would soon expire. With funds finally in hand, he headed east to begin organizing the hunt. He had already decided on the search method, and it was not unlike others that had been tried on the Delaware. The difference would lie in the talent employed.

Harrington was well aware that the Delaware Capes and Bay were second only to the Outer Banks of the Carolinas as a graveyard of ships. Indeed, the bottom of Delaware Bay, as Chapman, Colstad, and the rest had discovered, was littered with several centuries' worth of shipwrecks, many of them containing ferrous metals. To search for De Braak with a magnetometer would undoubtedly provide more than a few red herrings, the pursuit of which was a luxury Harrington could ill afford. Dragging, of course, had proved totally ineffective and time-consuming. There was only one alternative.

When De Braak had gone down, as Harrington knew from historical accounts, her masts had remained visible above the water for some time afterward. Harrington, therefore, had calculated the likely height of the masts, and, allowing for the probability that the ship had come to rest on the bottom at a slight angle, he hypothesized that she lay in waters sixty to ninety feet deep. On the basis of the British salvage records, which stated that the hull lay in thirteen fathoms of water, Harrington was certain that if he followed the eighty-foot coastal contour, he would encounter his target. And if De Braak did lay at that depth, there was little chance of shoaling or complete site burial. Although the hulk would undoubtedly have deteriorated as a result of ship worms and the unrelenting forces of tidal currents, her collapsed remains would certainly still present a substantial profile on the sea floor. Thus, he had decided to rely principally upon side-scan sonar in his search.[9] Harrington contracted with Alan Bieber, of Ocean Survey, Inc., to operate an array of scientific equipment, including a side-scan unit. Bieber, a marine research specialist from Lyme, Connecticut, charged fees that were appropriately high, given his credentials. The side-scan unit could cost as much as $35,000, and, as he later informed the press, "I don't work cheap."[10]

In April, with a boat rented from the University of Delaware's College of Marine Studies in Lewes, Harrington and Bieber set out to find the grave site of HMS *De Braak*. Bieber's surveying method was meticulous and painstaking. His Klein side-scan "fish," a torpedo-shaped device towed on a cable behind the boat, emitted regularly pulsing sound waves through the water column to the ocean floor and then received and amplified their echoes. The results were instantly transmitted to a graphic recorder and were then printed out in the form of outlines. The contour of the bottom, as well as objects sitting on or protruding from it which the sound waves struck, were thus revealed. While the images could be marvelous, it was the interpretation of the data that was tricky. "It's kind of like a blind man trying to figure out what an elephant looks like by sense of touch and hearing," explained Bieber.[11]

Beiber divided the two-square-mile search area into grids. Then he began searching in overlapping patterns, dragging the "fish" at uniform depths, based on that of the water he was surveying. By the end of April, a total of thirteen definite shipwreck sites were thought to have been located. One Sub-Sal employee who later viewed the strip-chart data remarked that "some of the areas appeared to our equipment more like a debris field than a seabed."[12] On April 26, Harrington and Bieber evaluated the data and reduced the total to three possible sites which most closely approximated the historical record of *De Braak*'s dimensional characteristics. One wreck particularly caught Bieber's attention. The site lay about a mile east south-east of the Lewes Breakwater in seventy-five to eighty feet of water, and it was dangerously close to the main shipping channel leading into Delaware Bay. The strip-chart image of the site was quite well defined, indicating a mound about sixty feet long, twenty feet wide, and six feet high. Its stern end was oval, and the hull outline suggested a vessel of the eighteenth century. "It looked like what you might expect a wooden hull to look like after nearly two hundred years on the bottom of the sea," Bieber said. "It seemed to be in the right stage of deterioration."[13] He quickly wrote on the edge of the printout: "Beautiful small wreck."

Before a hands-on investigation of the three sites could proceed, the weather turned sour and the next week's forecast was for more of the same. With side-scan unit, boat, and diver costing $2,000 a day, Harrington had no choice but to halt operations. He would not, however, resume them as soon as good weather returned. Instead, he spent the next six weeks securing additional funds from his partners and applying for a salvage permit from the state, on the assumption that one of the three sites was *De Braak*. He then hired the thirty-eight-foot fishing boat *Seneca*, Captain Donald Evans commanding, and two New Hampshire divers, Thomas McGehearty and Timothy Lena, while retaining the services of Bieber. For Evans, the opportunity of employment on such a project meant a chance for adventure. When asked what he thought about working for Sub-Sal, he had replied: "Beats the hell out of fishing, and the pay is steady."[14]

On June 21, on-site investigations of the three wrecks finally began. The first wreck proved to be a modern barge, and the second a schooner. Bieber's "beautiful small wreck," however, was another matter. Although the specific elements of the wreck were at first unidentifiable, reconnaissance dives revealed an almost vertical row of disintegrating timbers and cast-iron ballast bars jutting about three feet off the sea floor. Scattered around the murky bottom were various loose artifacts which were hard to see at first. Anxiously, Harrington directed his divers to bring up something identifiable. Lena recovered only a piece of wood, but McGehearty brought up a bottle with a crooked neck, which, from the indented pontil, appeared to be blown glass. Even more interesting was his discovery of the ship's bell, still mounted in its belfry, and a number of sizable objects encrusted in a matrix of coral and hardened sediment, which McGehearty thought might be cannons. The following day, a small anchor was recovered. Harrington compared it to several pictured in Mendel Peterson's dated but classic handbook on underwater archaeology, *History under the Sea*, and thought it quite similar to a British naval anchor of the eighteenth century.[15]

It was soon apparent, to Bieber at least, that Harrington would need an expert to verify the identity of the wreck, most of which was still beneath the bottom sediments. Such verification would be an important prerequisite to securing a state salvage permit—and more financial support down the road. Bieber recommended that Harrington consult John Perry Fish, of Falmouth, Massachusetts. Fish was a maritime historian, an accomplished diver, and a partner (with Arnold Carr) in the Historical Maritime Group of Cape Cod, which claimed to have data on over 8,000 shipwrecks stored in its computer banks.[16]

Harrington agreed, and shortly thereafter Fish joined the investigation. He brought with him a dark, stocky, bearded professional diver named Joe Amaral. Reared in Taunton, Massachusetts, thirty-five-year-old Amaral had been diving for almost two decades. He had also served a stint in Vietnam as a paratrooper, had worked as a diver on a North Sea oil rig, and had been running a charter boat service on Cape Cod when Fish asked him to join the team on the Delaware.[17]

Fish and Amaral provided just the combination Harrington needed. Fish first looked at the small anchor which had been recovered by McGehearty. He noted that the acute angle of the crown, or the point where the arm joins the shank, suggested a Spanish-style anchor which had been employed by the Royal Navy until the end of the eighteenth century. If Fish's assessment was correct, the wreck was clearly of the right period. But it was his and Amaral's thorough investigation of the site itself which revealed even harder and more convincing data. After a number of dives, it had become apparent to Fish that the wreck's hull lay canted on her starboard side at a roughly thirty-five-degree angle and that scores of artifacts were scattered about. Most of the portside fabric had deteriorated, but some of the interior partitions and components had survived intact beneath the silt and sand. With Amaral's assistance, Fish produced a rough site map on which were noted the positions of a dozen or more cannons, encrusted muskets, a waist-high water jar, a ship's stove, dozens of blown-glass bottles, a rudder assembly complete with heavy copper chain, and two-foot-tall bilge pumps. The vessel's remains were oriented in a northwest-to-southeast direction, with the bow at 150 degrees.[18]

Ironically, the diagnostic data assembled by Fish plunged Harrington into a quandary. He needed proof that the wreck was *De Braak*, but to recover anything without a salvage permit would be a violation of Delaware law. How, then, could the site be identified without diagnostic evidence being recovered? Harrington boldly decided to hoist one of the guns onto the *Seneca*'s deck where it could be studied close-up, in broad daylight, and inspected for the presence of a foundry mark and date. After a cannon had finally been recovered, Fish cleaned and examined its trunnion. He quickly discovered the inscription "Carron 1796" and the Royal Navy's mark, a broad arrow, which was used to denote all navy property in the eighteenth century.[19] The piece was a carronade.

At first, there seemed to be little doubt that the vessel was HMS *De Braak*. Then the ship's bell came up, bearing the distinctively cast inscription "La Patrocle 1781." The confusion was soon displaced by excitement, however, when Amaral discovered a thirty-eight-pound clump of silver coins and doubloons, 206 in all, that had been fused together by the long-term electrolytic action of the sea, as well as a beautiful foot-tall chalice with bearded mermen for handles. Here, at last, was actual treasure trove. The objects had been found in the stern of the wreck, adjacent to a conglomerate of fused pig-iron ballast, cannonballs, and coral growth. If Harrington had felt any doubts about the ship's identity when he read the bell's inscription, he quickly dismissed them. He was now certain that he had discovered *De Braak*.[20]

Although Harvey Harrington knew that he had clearly violated Delaware law by removing artifacts from the site, he decided to return only the anchor to the bottom, keeping the coins, cannon, bell, and chalice. But was the wreck that of *De Braak*, as suggested by the carronade and anchor, or was it another ship named *La Patrocle*, as suggested by the bell's inscription? By the end of July, John Fish had also become convinced that the wreck was *De Braak*. When he compared his own data to photocopies of the 1797 Admiralty drafts of *De Braak*, meticulously redrawn by his wife, Mardi, which showed the bilge pump rising through the deck adjacent to the mainmast, he seemed to be viewing a schema of what he had seen in partial form on the bottom. They were, Fish was certain, one and the same.[21]

It was at this point that Harrington's problems really began to snowball. Back in Rhode Island, his former associates, Calcione, LaPadula, and Peloso, had learned of his efforts to locate *De Braak* without them. Inflamed by what they construed to be an act of treachery, they had formed a corporation of their own, called Worldwide Salvage, and then had promptly applied for a permit to salvage the wreck. The permit request specifically sought an exclusive salvage lease on 3.4 square miles of coastal waters. The state informed Worldwide that no more than a mile could be leased because of environmental considerations, primarily to do with potential disturbances to the shellfish beds. Worldwide countered by declaring that they intended to use only airlifts in their salvage operations, not the destructive clam-bucket method favored by earlier salvors. The supervisor of Delaware's Wetlands and Underwater Lands Branch, William F. Moyer, sitting in the catbird's seat, informed both Worldwide and Sub-Sal that neither contender would be granted a lease unless a completed application form which met all criteria had been submitted.[22]

Fearing that he might be deprived of his find and worried about the possible consequences of having raised artifacts without permission—an act which could certainly jeopardize his salvage-permit application—Harrington sequestered the carronade in twenty feet of water some distance from the wreck, in a small waterway called No Name Creek. The coins were secretly sent off to be professionally cleaned and appraised.[23] But the rivalry between Sub-Sal and Worldwide could not be concealed from the media. When Worldwide submitted its formal application, the $1,500 fee, and a $20,000 performance bond, the contest between the two firms became public. It was soon being reported that the wreck was worth $300,000,000. Ignorant of what Harrington had actually found, Worldwide claimed that the wreck lay buried under twenty to thirty feet of silt and that they knew exactly where it was. (They even had a piece of teak to prove it!)[24]

Before a salvage permit could be granted to Sub-Sal, Harrington had to prove that the wreck he had located was indeed *De Braak*. Therefore, in mid-July he invited Moyer to visit the site with him. With the state official looking on and entirely unaware that a carronade had already been recovered, the treasure hunter raised a second one. The piece was still packed with hemp and a charge, ready to fire. Harrington solemnly pretended that it was the first artifact to come up. When the piece was finally brought to rest on the deck of the boat, a small conger eel slithered from its mouth.

Carefully scraping away the encrustation of two centuries from the trunnion, the salvors revealed the Royal Navy's broad arrow, the serial number S–175, and the Carron imprint. Moyer was both impressed and elated. That Harrington had located the remains of an ancient warship was now a proven fact. Although he was privately convinced that it was *De Braak*, Moyer carefully avoided publicly committing himself to that view. Soon after, however, he announced that the State of Delaware was prepared to negotiate a salvage lease for an area of 1.6 square miles. The state's share would be the usual twenty-five percent of the total value of all treasure and artifacts recovered.[25] "The stage was then set for a three-year salvage operation," as one later agent for Delaware wrote, "that would end in one of the worst maritime archaeological disasters in recent history."[26]

To promote his own efforts and interests, Harrington hired a lawyer named Bob Woolf, best known as a bargaining agent for basketball star Larry Bird, film critic Gene Shalit, and singer Livingston Taylor.[27] Yet the treasure hunter, who had worked for many years in the diving industry, was still justifiably concerned about Worldwide's ability to challenge his right to salvage the wreck site, so he moved to secure additional protection. Acting on the advice of an admiralty lawyer, Harrington legally attempted to have *De Braak* placed entirely in Sub-Sal's custody, by "arresting" the wreck and her cargo. Such a move entailed filing an action in accordance with existing admiralty law against the ship itself in the admiralty district court, in Wilmington. But "arresting" the wreck and its cargo, on behalf of the government, the site would technically come under the jurisdiction of the United States district court, and sub-Sal would be its agent. The procedure, although arcane, had been employed throughout the Western world for hundreds of years and formed the very basis of salvage law. Thus, a suit, *Sub-Sal, Inc. vs De Braak, Her Appurtenances, Furniture, Cargo, etc.*, was quickly filed, and, on July 26, Chief Justice Walter K. Stapleton signed an order designating Sub-Sal the wreck's legal custodian.[28]

The prospects for treasure hunting in the United States seemed bright. Only the week before, a book entitled *Treasure Coast* had appeared, recounting the *De Braak* tale, myths and all, and exciting even greater public expectations of a sizable treasure haul. Then it was reported in the media that the famous pirate ship *Whydah*, one of the ships in Harrington's past daydreams, had been located by treasure hunters off Cape Cod. The world, it seemed, would soon be awash in treasure.[29]

Harrington moved quickly to further consolidate his authority over the site. At his request, the court appointed Dr. Terry Edgecomb, a professional friend and an acquaintance of Harrington's from New Hampshire, to serve the arrest warrant on the vessel. This was a punctilious legal expedient, steeped in tradition, which the court deemed necessary. On July 28, Edgecomb dived on the site and attached a plastic, watertight envelope tethered by a short span of rope to a carronade. The document read: "A warrant shall issue for the arrest of the *De Braak*, her appurtenances, her furniture, her cargo and apparel." Thus had Edgecomb formally effected the legal possession of the wreck until any and all possible claimants could be determined. Sub-Sal, Inc., had thereby achieved custody over the remains of one of the most famous Royal Navy warships ever lost in American waters.[30] Harrington's legal action was not without logic or historical precedent; indeed, the laws of salvage above and below the high seas had been rooted in the same protocol for hundreds of years. Without such formal procedures, noted one admiralty lawyer, "even the Queen of England could come in" and claim a right to the booty captured by one of her country's ships, even though it lay at the bottom of the sea.[31]

Harrington was finally ready to go public with his discovery. On Monday, July 30, he called a press conference at the University of Delaware's College of Marine Studies. A collection of artifacts recovered from the site, including a few cylindrical spirit bottles, a platter, a broken bowl, an X-ray made at the nearby Beebe Hospital of a musket, showing its trigger guard, trigger mechanism, and flint to be intact, were all displayed to the media. But the most attention-getting artifact on view proved to be the stubby carronade raised during Moyer's visit, displayed in a "preservative" bath. The presentation received national coverage, and everyone involved in the project became an object of media attention. Don Evans, Captain of the *Seneca*, was perhaps the most jocular. Discussing a visit to Drew's monument, he reported, half in jest, "We sat down, had a long talk with him one night. We [even] brought him a bottle of rum."[32]

John Fish, the authority on whom the most attention focused, was far more serious. "Everything we have found fits *De Braak* to a T," he informed the *New York Times*.

> I've spent a lot of time on shipwrecks, but I've never seen anything like this. We have not found any treasure yet, but we are confident that it is there.... What we don't know is how much. It could be worth as much as five million dollars. It could be as much as five hundred million dollars.[33]

The parameters of value for the site, accepted without question by the press, had thus been reset. The figures would be repeated again and again over the next two years in practically every news report issued about the wreck. Not a word, however, was even whispered about the recovery of a thirty-eight-pound lump of coins or a foot-tall chalice.

The treasure hunters concluded their press conference with a twenty-minute videotape. Reporters watched, rapt, as on the screen, John Fish maneuvered about the bottom, sliding between ancient ribs, passing the rudder post, a bilge pump, cannons, ship's stores, and a giant pottery jar. Divers chattered excitedly over the communications link with the surface. More than thirty dives had been made to inspect the site, it was announced, but the most exciting moment had occurred when the "surveyors spotted a metal ingot, which may be silver—or only pewter." The three divers, working only at slack tide and using only scuba gear, had spent a total of thirteen days investigating the wreck, and each visit had revealed new discoveries. Although Fish was the most informative of the project members, he was also the most restrained. Even if little treasure was eventually found, he said seriously, he would still consider the site "a very interesting find from a historical standpoint," a find which he felt should be investigated with archaeological thoroughness.[34]

Joseph Wise was asked if he expected to get rich from the site. "Either rich or broke," he said, laughing. "And we're working very hard at both," interjected Harrington.[35] Within hours, the story was being prepared for publication in newspapers across the nation. When interviewed by telephone, Harrington proclaimed his discovery to be "one of the greatest finds in the world."[36]

Soon afterwards, for the second time, the issue of history and archaeology versus the objectives and the methods of treasure salvage on *De Braak* was debated in the public forum. That *De Braak* was potentially a site of great historical and archaeological significance had eluded the attention of everyone in Delaware's state government. It had not escaped the critical gaze of the professional archaeological community. In the October 9th issue of the *New York Times*, the first hint of conflict between archaeologists and the ship's salvors was aired. When informed of the recovery effort underway, Donald Keith, a nationally known marine archaeologist, then a research associate at the prestigious Institute of Nautical Archaeology at Texas A & M University, had commented, somewhat prophetically, "We're a science, and treasure hunting is a business. Sometimes the interests of science and business collide."[37] But the prospects for conflict between business and archaeology that lay ahead seemed to be of little concern to the State of Delaware as, on August 1, Governor (and presidential hopeful) Pierre S. Dupont, IV, granted Sub-Sal, Inc., a one-year lease with exclusive salvage rights to the remains of HMS *De Braak*.[38]

S E V E N T E E N

One in Ten Million

Harvey Harrington moved swiftly. As soon as the lease and salvage rights were approved, permitting Sub-Sal, Inc., to proceed with the planned recovery of *De Braak*, he appointed Terry Edgecomb to superintend diving operations. An additional six divers were hired, along with the services of a seventy-seven-foot steel-hulled fishing boat called *Mariner*, Captain Robert McIlvane commanding, at a cost of $200,000. The vessel, owned by Frederick Krapf, of Wilmington, was no stranger to her mission, for she had been employed a number of years earlier by Mel Joseph and Dennis Standefer in their own search for the lost man-of-war. *Mariner* was soon undergoing outfitting for deep-water diving and salvage operations. Several air compressors, an underwater communications system, a decompression chamber, a diesel-powered crane, and a diving platform were added to the ship's equipage before she steamed down the Delaware River to join the expedition. All the while, John Fish had been making dives on the site twice a day to plot the wreck.[1]

With high-velocity currents, daily tides sweeping through at speeds of up to seven knots, and a summertime underwater visibility range of zero to four feet at best, the wreck site provided an exceptionally hazardous environment in which to work. Its eighty-foot depth all but dictated that decompression diving be used to accomplish Harrington's optimistic goals. In order for each diver to get in one hundred minutes of bottom time, a period of up to thirty-one minutes in the decompression chamber was necessary. Teams of dry-suited divers, hired from the New England area and the Louisiana oil fields, would be supplied with air through a hookah, a surface umbilical system providing a low-pressure demand air feed. A second line supplied electricity for the lights on the $3,000 Kirby-Morgan diving helmet, and a communication line permitted direct voice contact with the surface. On occasion, when observation and photography were necessary, or when slack tides permitted, scuba diving could be done, but only during optimum conditions or as necessity dictated.[2]

Harrington's plan of operations called first for the removal and recovery of fragile objects, such as glassware, resting on the sand and sediment over and around the wreck site. Next would come most of the heavy carronades, which, unless removed, might pose a hazard to divers digging around them. Then would come the excavation to recover the alleged treasure itself. When all operations had been completed, the exposed hull would be reburied to insure its protection, said the salvors, until such time as the science of wood preservation had advanced far enough to recover the hull without risking its loss or injury from exposure to the air.[3]

Fish worked relentlessly to provide at least an acceptable site map of the wreck's exposed portion, for a great deal depended upon his handiwork. Sub-Sal was well aware of a contingency clause in their lease forbidding the recovery of any artifacts whatsoever until the Division of Historical and Cultural Affairs had declared itself satisfied with mapping procedures. Thus, for two weeks, before actual salvage work could begin, the first survey of the site had to be carried out by Fish and Edgecomb. Their effort did not go unrewarded, however, for the positions of ten carronades (referred to by the salvors as "short cannons") and a long, 6-pounder bow chaser were plotted.[4]

The impact of the impending salvage of Delaware's most famous shipwreck upon the 2,500 citizens of Lewes was, at first, stunning. The sudden surge of reporters, camera crews, and interested tourists caught the little town by surprise. The Zwaanendael Museum staff was besieged by questions and telephone calls. Local businesses dependent on tourism noted a ten- to twenty-percent increase in profits. But not everyone bought Sub-Sal's story of having actually located *De Braak*. "It's kind of like the boy who cried wolf," remarked one longtime resident who had become inured to the almost cyclical event.[5] Others were even more cautious. "I'll tell you what," asserted a skeptical Henry Marshall, the seventy-three-year-old director of the Lewes Historical Society. "I wouldn't want to bet any money that they have really found it. I've seen too many [attempts] in my time."[6]

Near the end of August, after permanent moors had been established, with some difficulty, and a spate of bad weather had passed, salvage operations began in earnest. Now *Mariner* could tie up each day to a four-point mooring system, anchored at one corner by a 1,000-pound locomotive wheel. The triple cable complex needed for underwater air, lights, and communications was attached to the line by magnetic clips, thus permitting divers to make a safe, expeditious descent directly to the site. To facilitate salvage and provide at least a rudimentary form of locational control, the salvors established an arbitrary sixty-three-foot baseline across the site. Fish wanted to excavate the wreck in a controlled manner by utilizing the baseline, which ran nearly parallel to, and eighteen feet, six inches from, the starboard side of the keelson. The team's initial efforts to erect a workable grid, employing such ready-made equipage as military-surplus bed frames, however, failed miserably. Therefore, a number of four-by-eight grid units had to be constructed of PVC pipe and connected to the baseline. Each section was color-coded to help divers maintain their bearings in the eternal twilight of the bottom.[7]

When work on the site finally began, not surprisingly, Harrington focused his investigations primarily on the stern section of the wreck. It was, after all, from there that the coins had been recovered. Despite the wreck's thick covering of boring sponges, often as tall as two or three feet, which tended to mask the site and impeded artifact identification *in situ*, the work proceeded relatively smoothly. Then the flow of artifacts began. At first, they were principally found on the surface of the sea floor. Most were items that one would have expected to find in the officers' quarters, which were located in the aft section of the ship. By the end of August, more than 200 artifacts had been brought to the surface.[8]

Salvage operations continued, but under the most arduous conditions. Difficulties with the currents and tides obliged the team to work mainly during the two-hour periods at the turn of the tides. Nevertheless, Harrington and his men put in twelve-hour days, seven days a week, and their recovery of artifacts continued without any letup. The items brought up ranged from the mundane to the exotic: copper nails and spikes incised with the King's broad arrow, lead scupper tubes, a salt cellar, a china bowl and dish, a fifty-gallon Iberian water jar, dozens of "rum" bottles (some still corked and bearing the embossed letters "GR" for George Rex, eighty percent of which were intact), fragments of sailcloth, a telescope, a silver fork, leather shoe soles, a platter, fragments of a compass, a sheave dated 1792 and bearing the initials "WT," a brass sword hilt with ornamentation clearly incised in the leather scabbard, a crystal decanter (with stopper in place), and a bottle with the word "ketchup" etched across its face. From what may have been the munitions room came musket balls, flintlock trigger mechanisms, trigger guards, a pair of matched pistols, a bronze hammer used by gunsmiths to avoid sparking in the gunpowder room, a twenty-four-pound cannon ball, and a cannon firing mechanism with the name "H. Nock" and the date 1795 etched upon its surface. All heavily encrusted objects of unidentified service and type were simply labeled "EO" (encrused object).[9] "I've never seen a site yield so many valuable artifacts so quickly," declared one amazed state agent. "And so much of it displays the King's broad arrow."[10]

Once collecting on the surface had been completed, excavation with a six-inch airlift system commenced—sans screening or outflow management. That no effort was made to screen or monitor spoil brought up in the airlift proved to be a serious error. One state official later noted that, "considering the extreme environmental conditions, there can be little doubt that many small artifacts were lost or contaminated other parts of the site, further confusing the archaeological record."[11] Those small artifacts which were spotted, however, were extracted from the bottom by hand, placed in four-by-eight-foot wire baskets or nylon-mesh bags, and then brought to the surface. Heavy items, such as carronades, anchors, the ship's stove, and large, unidentified encrusted objects, had to be specially rigged for lifting by crane.[12]

As the work progressed, a diagram taped to the communications room door, which showed the wreck and the location of significant large artifacts, grew more detailed every day. (On one end, someone had wishfully sketched a small treasure chest.) Despite the team's efforts to maintain regional provenance, however, most of the locational data could be recorded only in relation to the blanket-sized horizontal planes of the four-by-eight grid sections. When the specific positions of significant finds were noted, they were relayed verbally to the surface through the communications lines and recorded on tape for later documentation. These recordings, unfortunately, would never be transcribed or analyzed.[13]

Still, the state had insisted that the recovered artifacts be labeled and inventoried so that some degree of archaeological control could be imposed on the salvage operations. Wise had ordered a small computer, to be used for documenting the items brought up, as well as a book on silversmith marks to help the team identify certain items. Various museums and historical organizations were asked to evaluate other artifacts. To some of the salvors, the failure to recover actual treasure was disappointing. To others, artifacts and treasure were one and the same. "How do you determine the value of a drawer latch or the sole of a shoe?" asked Wise. "Sure, there are collectors and we'll have to find them, and there may be some auctions, but we really aren't sure what we'll do with the items yet."[14]

As artifacts were recovered at an increasingly steady rate, they were assigned catalog numbers and tentatively inventoried, first aboard ship as they came up, and then again on shore. For the first time, the State of Delaware had actively sought to protect the site as a cultural unit and an archaeological resource, unlike efforts in earlier years, primarily to insure a proper inventory. After all, Delaware wanted its share. The salvor's lease, therefore, while broadly worded, nevertheless stipulated that a representative of the state be aboard the salvage vessel at all times when excavation was under way. Responsibility for this task at first fell to the Delaware State Police. But, during the weeks that followed, as the quantity and quality of cultural materials recovered made it apparent that greater expertise was necessary, DNREC decided to hire an underwater archaeologist to monitor Sub-Sal's daily operations. Hence, a graduate from East Carolina University named James Robert Reedy, Jr., was employed to observe salvage activities, make regular dives to inspect the progress of work on the site, record and catalog artifacts, assemble artifact-provenance data, and address the issue of artifact stabilization. Despite the terms of his assignment, Reedy's work was frequently of necessity, carried out ashore, where he attended to the conservation of the artifacts, rather than aboard the operations platform. His opinion of the salvors methodology was gushingly laudatory. Indeed, he considered the work of Harrington and his men to be better than that of many professional archaeological teams he had known "I wouldn't even call these guys treasure hunters. They have a real feeling for the material they're gathering—for the history behind the De Braak."[15] Their lack of concern for the more mundane or poorly preserved artifacts, however, suggested otherwise.

Reedy purchased several children's wading pools made of plastic, filling them with water and depositing the ever-enlarging collection of artifacts in them to prevent their drying out. These measures however, were wholly inadequate. Within a year, many artifacts had dried out, deteriorated, rusted, or had begun to turn to dust. Others, either accidentally or intentionally, escaped being processed altogether. Almost all of the smaller items were lacking a locational provenance, making an archaeological interpretation of their functions and spatial relationships (in some cases, their very identities) virtually impossible.[16]

Owing to both the salvors' priorities and the selective nature of the retrieval process, many artifacts which were of historical or archaeological significance, but which had not been recovered whole, were lost. In some cases, artifacts thought to be of no monetary value were discarded altogether before they could even be brought ashore. When De Braak's galley stove was discovered amidships, for example, it was hoisted aboard the salvage vessel, but the salvors, considering it little more than an unwieldy piece of junk and of no obvious monetary value, threw it over the side on their way back to Lewes. Out of ignorance, the salvors had disposed of one of only two such items, known as Brodie Stoves, ever recovered from an eighteenth-century shipwreck site. (The other stove had come from the site of HMS Pandora, a 24-gun man-of-war sent to hunt down the mutineers from HMS Bounty, lost on August 29, 1791, on Australia's Great Barrier Reef. Ironically, the Pandora wreck site, which had been identified in 1977, was undergoing meticulous excavation by archaeologists at the very same time the De Braak was being torn asunder.[17])

The physical remains of De Braak's crew and prisoners fared little better than the Brodie Stove. Harrington prohibited his men from retrieving, discussing, or documenting any human remains encountered during their work. A number of bones located near or beside the carronades (which caused some among the Sub-Sal team to speculate that they belonged to Spanish prisoners chained to the guns by Drew) were deliberately delivered up to the currents and lost forever. By this means, the salvors destroyed the very evidence which might have identified the remains. They had also denied scientists, such as biological anthropologists and forensic pathologists, access to information about eighteenth-century life at sea which could only have been derived from human remains.[18]

Salvage operations continued at breakneck speed, but it was not until the end of August that Harrington would be rewarded, albeit briefly, in his headlong pursuit of treasure. On August 29, chief diver Joe Amaral made a discovery which fueled both Harrington's imagination and the national news media's interest in *De Braak* once again. While conducting excavations on the starboard side of the wreck, Amaral discovered a small cache of English guineas. Then, an even more exciting find came to hand. Topside, Harrington was manning the communications console when he heard the diver exclaim: "Oh, my God! I think this is it, boss!" Then silence, until Amaral piped up again, this time even more excitedly, "I have a shiny one here in my hand. I have another one. And there's another. I'm going for the gold!"[19]

The discovery of the hoard was enough to trigger an epidemic of treasure fever as nearly one hundred coins, primarily Spanish gold doubloons dated from 1792 to 1796, were recovered from the area over the next few days. Each coin weighed about an ounce, bore the likeness of Charles IV, King of Spain and the Indies, and had mint marks from Mexico City and Lima. Harrington said nothing about this find in his daily reports to the press, preferring instead to bide his time until exactly the right moment.[20]

Then, just three days after his initial strike, Amaral made another exciting find: an eighteen-karat gold ring. While working on the bottom, he had found the ring and casually slipped it into his glove along with several gold pieces he had picked up with it. Returning topside, Amaral knew that he would be obliged to spend at least half an hour in the decompression chamber before he would be able to examine his discovery more closely. Immediately after boarding *Mariner*, therefore, he quickly handed over the ring and coins to his mates, even as he was being stripped of his bulky dry suit and helmet. Without wasting a moment, he slipped into the ten-foot-long decompression cylinder, and the double-locked door closed behind him.[21]

In the chamber, breathing pure oxygen for half an hour, Amaral's body was repressurized to a depth of forty feet so as to purge his blood of nitrogen buildup. The minutes ticked by slowly in the coffin-like cylinder, but outside he could hear a growing commotion. Curious, he watched his colleagues gesturing excitedly through the little window in the chamber. Finally, upon emerging, Amaral was permitted a closer look at the ring he had so casually slipped into his glove. The piece was missing a stone from its shallow setting. But clearly engraved in ornate letters upon the inside of the band were the words: "In Memory of a belov'd Brother, Capt. John Drew, drown'd 11 Jany. 1798, Aged 47."[22]

The discovery, said to be James Drew's mourning ring, seemed to verify the site's identity without a doubt. Reedy later declared the odds against such a find to be astronomical, "like one in ten million."[23] Although the authenticity of the ring and the account of its recovery were later questioned by some, particularly since its discovery came at a most opportune moment in Sub-Sal's economic history, the incident commemorated by the ring was, sadly, true.[24]

As later events would reveal, the recovery of the ring proved to be the watershed in Harrington's salvage effort. It occurred at a most perplexing point in the company's fortunes, for just when the treasure seemed to be within reach, Sub-Sal's money had all but evaporated. The very last of the $375,000 invested by Steingrebe's teacher, as well as $75,000 provided by another one of Steingrebe's investors was gone.[25]

To make matters worse, a suit had been filed in the U.S. district court on September 7 by Worldwide Salvage's legal counsel, Schab and Barnett, requesting that a temporary restraining order be issued to halt the project. Although the motion was denied on September 13, the lawsuit was permitted to go forward. The case was assigned to District Court Judge Caleb Wright, a crusty native of Georgetown, Delaware, and a specialist in admiralty law, who had specifically requested the assignment. The complaint against Sub-Sal was serious. Worldwide claimed that it had been information provided by Calcione, Peloso, LaPadula, and Wilson (principally the McCracken map bearings shown to Harrington in the fall of 1983) which had guided Sub-Sal to the site. Harrington, they charged, had broken an oral agreement with them to share the treasure and they wanted full redress. Specifically named as codefendants were Governor Pierre S. DuPont IV, DNREC Secretary John E. Wilson, Sub-Sal, Inc., and Harvey Harrington. The federal court promptly named George A. Ellingwood protector of the site. Ellingwood was a lieutenant on leave from the Scituate Municipal Police Department and, interestingly enough, Harrington's half-brother.[26]

In view of the lawsuit and his mounting financial difficulties, Harrington felt that the time had come to exploit the positive publicity and fund-raising potential of the coins and ring found a few days earlier. The president of Sub-Sal was by now well aware that simply mentioning treasure was enough to draw the press out in droves. On September 17, he dramatically proved this when he called a press conference at the De Braak Inn in Lewes. More than 100 members of the national news media, including the major television networks, arrived, eager to gobble up whatever morsels the salvors offered. Everyone attending the press conference was required to sign in and present his or her Social Security number and a driver's license as proof of identity. No one ever blinked.

Beneath the glare of television lights, the exhibits were spread across a blue velvet backcloth and included a telescope, a sheave, thirty-five Spanish doubloons, and thirty-four English guineas. The *pièce de résistance*, however, was the ring, enclosed in a miniature treasure chest wrapped in a cotton cloth. Two Lewes police officers and several shotgun-wielding security guards from Confidential Services in Lewes stood guard over the proceedings.[27] Coyly, Harrington suggested that the coins, which he claimed had been found on Septem-

held Sub-Sal's offices as well as several large, empty rooms which were basically off-limits to state personnel. The entire facility was in a state of disorder with various types of waste evident throughout. The place not only needed cleaning and organization, but even worse, few of the artifacts stored there had been attended to, and little or no effort had been made to stabilize any of them except for those that appeared to be marketable.

Melson immediately sought to wrest order from chaos, but with a nearly zero-dollar budget, her task was Herculean. She quickly instituted a regimen of draining, hosing down, and refilling the freshwater tanks on a regular basis to begin leaching the chlorides from the artifacts and to prevent fungal growth. Then began the slow, meticulous work of sorting and classifying the approximately one thousand artifacts that had been recovered in 1984 and of checking the inventory made that year against every item stored in the warehouse. The exercise became a learning experience for the young curator, who was initially unfamiliar with many of the maritime objects she would handle. But the arduous process of taking measurements, cross-referencing information, and quantifying the items in all of the artifact categories increased her knowledge of the collection a thousandfold. Indeed, within a year, Claudia Melson would become more familiar with the artifactual remains of HMS *De Braak* than anyone alive.

Her procedure was simple but effective. Since establishing provenance had been of little importance to the salvors and their inventory's accuracy was doubtful, Melson's quantification efforts became crucial. If an inventory description read "ceramics," she would break that category down into specific types and amounts, then start the evaluation process from there. Most of the artifacts had been tagged with white, waterproof, plastic slats that were typically used to tag trees and had been procured from a local nursery. A unique sequence of numbers had been written with a waterproof pen on each tag, which was then tied to each item with stainless-steel wire provided by a local airport. Small items, unfortunately, had been placed by the salvors in ziplocked bags, many of which contained several unrelated artifacts. Thus, each item in every bag had to be restored and renumbered. Furthermore, in the case of ceramics, duct tape had often been attached to the item, with numbers then written on the tape. Melson was obliged to remove each piece of tape, owing to its discoloring effect on the ceramic, and place each object in a newly numbered bag.[20]

During its 1985 season, Sub-Sal focused primarily on improving the efficiency of its artifact-recovery operation. With the new airlift-and-sluicing system in place, many artifacts which would have been lost the year before were soon being recovered—albeit with their provenance often undetermined. The flow of artifacts thus more than trebled Sub-Sal's 1984 recovery total and would have overwhelmed any less well-organized curator, but Melson held her for the salvors' removing the artifacts from the site in a "professional manner."[33] Harrington could not help but have been pleased at the state's visible support in court.

Throughout the rest of September, salvage continued on a round-the-clock basis as operations swung into high gear. Although another carronade and a long gun had been recovered and hoisted aboard *Seneca*, there was hardly any more gold or silver recovered from the stern. Gradually, as the salvors were able to ascertain that the coins and the ring had come from an extremely small area, "the size of a large blanket," as one writer later put it, the suggestion that they might have been stored in a chest, possibly in the captain's cabin, gained acceptance.[34] As the ship's upper sections slowly collapsed, it was reasoned, the rotting chest and its contents had fallen through and come to rest on the hull. The theory rapidly expanded to include the alleged treasure, which, it was firmly believed, had also fallen from the cabin to the bottom of the hull. It had then become enmeshed in a concretion of fused, corroded metal and coral deposits along the keel near the stern. The estimated size of the conglomerate was immense—approximately thirty feet long, twelve feet wide, and up to six feet thick—and, so far, it had successfully resisted the assaults of determined divers armed with underwater jackhammers. Other expedients, such as the use of dynamite primer cord, were considered as possible means of cracking the anomaly, but were dismissed by the state.[35]

Still the artifacts continued to roll in, even as an increasingly dark chain of events began to threaten operations. Harrington's economic and legal difficulties loomed larger with every passing day. A number of employees were laid off without having been paid. One disgruntled worker leaked information to Worldwide that certain items, such as the ship's bell, a pewter chalice, and some coins had been recovered without the state's knowledge. Worldwide, of course, would lose no time in rushing to exploit any such violations of Harrington's agreement with Delaware. In a panic, Harrington immediately ordered the items (which had, in fact, been secretly sent off for cleaning and appraisal) returned to headquarters. On October 10, a thirty-pound clump of oxidized silver coins, containing almost 200 Spanish pieces of eight, was taken back down and "rediscovered." The ship's bell and chalice then mysteriously appeared on Reedy's inventory, which by then was being kept aboard *Mariner*.[36]

Affairs worsened: When one former employee received an anonymous death threat, both he and his wife were escorted to the state line by Delaware State Police to ensure their safety.[37] On another occasion, the U.S. Customs Office in Rhode Island received an anonymous telephone tip that coins recovered from the wreck were about to be smuggled to Panama. The call quickly led to a state police reconnaissance of the purported smuggling craft, a nondescript schooner tied up at the Lewes waterfront, and then a search of the vessel by the Coast Guard. Nothing, of course, was found. Finally, a death threat was made against Harrington and the crew of *Mariner*, through another anonymous call, this time to the state police barracks in Georgetown. Some employees of Sub-Sal became convinced that organized crime had gotten mixed up in their affairs.[38]

Charges and countercharges were traded between Sub-Sal and Worldwide with increasing venom. Harrington was nervous. Almost immediately after the ring's discovery, he had ordered the security around the Fischer Enterprise grounds, his headquarters in Lewes, to be tightened. A new fence was installed around the property and guards were hired to protect the gate. An armored-vehicle company was lined up to transport any precious metals from the warehouse to a vault in Wilmington. Fearing an outright attack on their operations, Harrington's employees began to carry semiautomatic weapons. Paranoia began to feed upon itself. "It's sort of like the Wild West over here," declared Norman Barnett, a lawyer for Worldwide. "It's an ongoing saga."[39]

But it was Judge Wright who put the whole situation into perspective. "A lot of this cloak and dagger thing... is not warranted. Nobody knows who [the threats] come from. This is something that you find in a little town like Lewes. It is a small town, and these people can think of all kinds of fairy tales."[40] The whole episode, as far as he was concerned, was melodramatic and childish.

Yet the anonymous calls had an effect, for Harrington himself soon became viewed by the state attorney general's office with a jaundiced eye. On October 26 state police, acting on a tip, arrived armed with shotguns and search warrants at the fish fertilizer factory. After searching the premises and finding nothing out of line, they invited Harrington to go with them to Lewes to verify the contents of the safe-deposit box in which the gold and silver coins were supposed to be kept. It was then discovered that Harrington had sent more than one hundred coins, plus several pieces of jewelry that had been kept in the box, to Massachusetts for appraisal and sale by a company called Crystal Coin. Further investigation revealed that coins had also been sent as collateral for an $85,000 loan to the First National Bank of Boston. Since Sub-Sal's contract with Delaware stated that "the lessee shall store all artifacts recovered under this lease, whether of a base or precious nature in a manner prescribed by the division of History and Cultural Affairs," and would only have the right to sell gold, silver, diamonds, coins, jewels, and other items "deemed not historical," there as an obvious violation of the agreement. Only the written approval of the DCHA could have allowed Harrington to do as he had done, and he could produce no such letter. Not surprisingly, the Delaware State Attorney General's office considered Harrington's act to have been a clear breach of contract and directed that *Mariner* be boarded by state police and searched. Henceforth, it was announced, the police would remain aboard at all times to inventory any artifacts brought up.[41]

Sub-Sal's fortunes plummeted even further when, on October 30, World-wide filed a brief claiming that Harrington had been skimming treasure from the wreck and that his company's security was practically nonexistent. Judge Wright responded by ordering that a hearing be held on the issue of Sub-Sal's security measures and procedural practices. During the hearing, which was convened on November 13, Judge Wright learned of Sub-Sal's chicanery with the chalice and bell, and of the coins being used as collateral for a loan without the state's knowledge. He was deeply upset, and his interrogation of James Reedy did little to reassure the judge about Sub-Sal's operational procedures.[42]

When the hearing was over, Judge Wright ruled that the State of Delaware and Sub-Sal, Inc., would henceforth share control over all safe-deposit boxes in which items from the wreck were stored. Furthermore, nothing could be removed from the boxes unless representatives of both parties were present, nor could coins or any other artifacts be sold, transferred, pledged as security, or removed from the state without a court order. Harrington was instructed to keep detailed records of the costs incurred by the salvage operations so that they might be considered when the court ruled on Worldwide's suit against Sub-Sal. As for the judge's opinion of the alleged treasure, he stated, "I, quite frankly, have always felt that there wasn't much down there."[43]

Harvey Harrington's luck was no better at sea than ashore. On October 7, a crisp, clear Sunday morning, a near catastrophe occurred which almost ended operations entirely. At about 5:00 A.M., northwest of the wreck site, a 700-foot Dutch tanker had just dismissed her Delaware Bay pilot when she inadvertently began to drift out of her sea-lane. Suddenly, she was bearing directly down on the little salvage boat, which was firmly moored over the wreck. Before anyone knew what was happening, the tanker had come within a few feet of *Mariner*, severing one of her cables. Below, a diver crouched watching in terror as the tanker's enormous twin screws passed barely fifteen feet overhead. Although his three supply lines remained firmly attached to the down cable, the helpless diver was brutally tossed about. *Mariner* and the tanker had avoided collision by only five feet.[44]

Within a few days, *Mariner* was decommissioned and Harrington was obliged to rely entirely upon *Seneca*. Operations, however, were by then dictated by the weather and diving occurred only sporadically. One more significant recovery was made, consisting of 3,000 pounds of cannonballs, six and 24-pounder shot, and a large amount of grapeshot in an intact wooden "crate," the ship's shot locker.[45]

Facing the prospect of closing down operations for lack of funds, as well as a costly lawsuit presided over by a judge whose opinion of him had become less than favorable, Harvey Harrington continued to troll for financial support. His publicity coup, at least, had begun to pay dividends. By November, he had persuaded a pair of Massachusetts real-estate developers to invest in the project. The two investors, after signing a letter of intent, turned over $95,800 to the persuasive, debt-ridden Harrington, who promptly used it to forestall the company's immediate insolvency. Then, when a quarrel arose with Harrington over what their share of the alleged treasure would be, the investors filed suit in Delaware's District Court for breach of contract.[46]

Inevitably, as company morale deteriorated, a personnel flight began. Joseph Wise, Sub-Sal's vice-president, was the first to resign, having grown disillusioned over the treasure fever orchestrated by Harrington. When funds were no longer available to cover the costs of his travels between Delaware and California, Gary Steingrebe was the next to leave. By December, Harrington had fired Edgecomb and, soon afterward, the rest of the company's thirty-five-member staff.[47] As the year ended, following five months of diving, the company was left with an enormous debt. Although more than a thousand artifacts had been recovered, little of the purported treasure had actually been found. The most disastrous blow fell when the State of Delaware refused to renew Sub-Sal's salvage lease. Harvey Harrington, however, wasn't through— at least not quite yet.

E I G H T E E N

One Very Large Artifact

January 1985 began auspiciously enough for Harvey Harrington. Undeterred by setbacks and still hard at work trying to attract new investment by promoting the *De Braak* project as a source of possibly millions of dollars' worth of sunken treasure, he followed every promising avenue. One such course led him, by way of his wife, Patricia, to her thirty-four-old nephew, Kevin McCormick, a financial advisor in the Hanover, Massachusetts, investment firm of Davenport Associates. Through McCormick's efforts, Davenport Associates was persuaded to lend Sub-Sal $35,000. Having been promised a position as Sub-Sal's business manager, McCormick was soon prevailed upon by Harrington to develop a business proposal for the raising of no less than $1,000,000 to subsidize the recovery of *De Braak*'s alleged booty.[1]

Although McCormick's first efforts failed to generate the hoped-for funding, word of the venture soon reached the ear of a shrewd, high-rolling, Laconia, New Hampshire, businessman named L. John Davidson. Davidson had already lived a life packed with experiences, adventures, and investments. A graduate of Harvard and a veteran of the Air Force, he had, among other endeavors, built and sold houses, prospected for gold and uranium, worked as a real-estate developer, sold recreational property, invested in several gold-mining ventures, and was by then on his way to making a fortune in resort-home development on Lake Winnipesaukee, New Hampshire, when he learned of the *De Braak* project.[2]

Characteristically, Davidson set his sights not only on investing in the project, but on controlling it. After an unsuccessful attempt to persuade Davenport Associates to help raise funds for the project, he made a concerted effort to take over Sub-Sal and to secure the salvage rights for himself. The moment was propitious. With the State of Delaware becoming increasingly alienated by the antics of Harvey Harrington, Davidson knew that Sub-Sal would require a major face-lift before the company could ever hope to resume operations. In later describing his attempted takeover, he wrote: "My job was to create a different image to the State of Delaware and to restore confidence that the project would run in an orderly way to a responsible and proper conclusion."[3] Indeed, he was convinced that without both a massive infusion of money and his own "credentials" to offset the negative effects of Harrington's behavior, the project would simply die of attrition. Having been a staunch financial supporter of the Republican party in New Hampshire, his first move was to call in some political debts, using his connections to facilitate his power play.

Davidson called upon New Hampshire's governor at that time, John Sununu, who was also "a treasure ship buff," to provide a personal introduction to the newly elected Republican governor of Delaware, Michael Castle. The introduction, he explained, must stress not only his financial assets and ability to consummate the project, but his strength of character as well. "Significant among the personal credentials," he later stated,

> was my respect for tradition and the law as such apply to the nature of my land development in northern New England i.e. the restoration of most of the Main Street of Andover, Massachusetts, the restoration of Quechee Village in Vermont, the theme of our land plan and the responsible use of open spaces in New Hampshire. In conversation it also was helpful that I was an antique collector of long standing and a modern European history major at Harvard.[4]

Sununu's support was secured when he and Mrs. Sununu visited the *De Braak* site while he was in Delaware to chair the Republican Governors' Conference. The introduction was made and the takeover proceeded unhindered. By July, Davidson's own New Hampshire-based corporation, Drew and Associates, had bought out Wise and Steingrebe's forty-five-percent interest in the company for $85,000. Another $120,000 went to pay off Sub-Sal's outstanding debts. Within a short time, Davidson had taken complete financial control of the company and had become its chief executive officer. Harrington, who still owned forty percent of the stock, and Steingrebe's schoolteacher-investor, with fifteen percent, could do little to oppose him.[5]

Once he had attained control, Davidson moved swiftly but judiciously. His first act was to hire Kevin McCormick, who had resigned from Davenport Associates, to superintend offshore operations. Aware of the importance of Harrington's field experience and knowledge of the site, Sub-Sal's new commander offered the company's former president a one-year, $65,000 contract to serve as offshore manager of diving and salvage. Although Harrington accepted, it was no doubt with something less than zeal, for he would no longer control the salvage operations. Next, Davidson organized a meeting with Harrington, Sub-Sal's Wilmington-based lawyer, Michael J. Bayard, and Delaware's deputy attorney general, Michael Foster, to renegotiate the company's lease on the site, which had expired in July. With a new and apparently credible commander at Sub-Sal's helm, the lease was readily approved.[6]

Meanwhile, after the sad experiences of the previous year, the State of Delaware was finally beginning—however belatedly—to take a more serious interest in the historical and archaeological significance of the *De Braak* site. Authority over all salvage operations was granted to the Delaware Division of Historical and Cultural Affairs. State funds were also allocated for offshore monitoring and data management to the University of Delaware's Center for Archaeological Research. Not surprisingly, James Robert Reedy, Jr., was released from his position. H. Henry Ward, an archaeologist at the Center, was designated the state's principal agent. Unfortunately, Ward was neither a certified diver nor experienced in marine archaeology. To remedy this weakness and to insure that control over recovery data from the wreck site itself was exercised, the state began to search for a professional marine archaeologist to serve as Delaware's offshore agent and to work with the salvors in conducting mapping operations on the site.[7] Then, on August 5, 1985, almost immediately after the meeting between the deputy attorney general and the salvors, yet another state employee was assigned to the project.

When Claudia F. Melson, curator of registration for the Delaware Bureau of Museums and Historic Sites was called in to the office of agency chief Dean Nelson, her boss, she had little idea of what she was in for.

"Guess what you are going to be doing for the next two months," Nelson, challenged her.

Claudia shrugged.

"Putting numbers on all the artifacts salvaged from the *De Braak*," he said with a grin.[8]

Her mission would prove to be a daunting challenge, but one that the history scholar relished. That she was capable of performing the task went without question. In her curatorial capacity she was already responsible for the files on and the registration of over 150,000 items housed in over a score of state-administered historic houses and museums, ranging from furniture, silver, and textiles to a piece of moonrock. Her broad expertise, honed from a decade of experience, encompassed the management of every type of resource, from the Victorian clothing and furnishings exhibited in the governor's guest house to the lithics recovered from archaeological digs.[9] But *De Braak* would be different. Although Melson could not have foreseen it, the two months that she expected to devote to the project would stretch into years, and the collection that she would manage would eventually amount to more than one-sixth of the state's entire holdings then under her care.

Like the state, Sub-Sal, under Drew and Associates, had also been busy since its renegotiated lease had been approved. John Davidson hired the former state agent, James Robert Reedy, Jr., as a consultant to Sub-Sal.[10] Then, with Harrington's grudging assistance, Davidson began to search for a salvage vessel to lease for the 1985 season. Owing to a decline in the oil industry and the shutdown of many offshore-drilling operations in the Gulf of Mexico, Davidson and Harrington began their search in Louisiana, where it was said that such vessels could be hired at bargain rates. Failing there, however they were eventually obliged to settle for the lease of an eighty-nine-foot stern fishing trawler called *F/V Sea Star*. Over five weeks of precious summer weather and $75,000 were required before she was outfitted for the work, not only with the necessary equipment for large-scale diving operations (such as air compressors, a decompression chamber, and communications gear), but also with a sophisticated sifting system.[11]

The onboard artifact-sifting, or retrieval, system had been designed by Harrington as a modification of and supplement to the simple airlift system employed the year before. The new unit provided a surface airlift system, sucking up sediment through a six-inch PVC conduit hose connected to an input nozzle on the ocean floor. The system spewed out sediments topside onto a modified gold-mining-sluice assembly with a complex of screens and baffles set up on the ship's deck. The sluicing was done in three stages, the first of which entailed the trapping of denser objects in hard metal bars. The sifted flow then proceeded across a long inclined screen, where artifacts were collected by the salvors. The third sluice component was a simple tailings box. Here, even objects as small as straight pins or the hands of a pocket watch could be retrieved.[12]

On September 10, 1985, after a delay of nearly nine months, salvage operations on the remains of *De Braak* were finally resumed. Almost immediately, *Sea Star* was revealed to be, at best, an unstable operations platform when anchored. Worse, Harrington's retrieval system was both slow and difficult to operate on the deck of a pitching vessel. Barely a cubic yard of sediment per hour, far less than Davidson had hoped, could be sucked up from the bottom. The system was constantly being blocked by rocks and debris, making frequent, time-consuming shutdown necessary in order to flush it out and repair it. Operating expenses were soon running to $50,000 per week. Davidson was infuriated, especially when he discovered that Harrington spent more time off the project than on. Yet the salvage was nevertheless proceeding at an unprecedented rate.[13]

As before, all objects recovered were transported to shore for later processing. Again, airlifting was conducted upon grids laid down at the beginning of the season. This year, however, the system had been substantially upgraded. *De Braak*'s keelson was employed as a baseline, and a system of interlocking, four-by-six-foot grid units were laid out over the areas of excavation. Once a unit had been completely excavated, the grid could be readily and rapidly moved to another sector. Each grid section was assigned a trinomial identification, employing a color, a number, and a letter (e.g., Green 4A). This system was a vast improvement over earlier ones, permitting horizontal controls over artifact recovery. Unfortunately, it did not solve the problems pertaining to vertical provenance.[14]

As before, heavy objects, such as ballast and shot, were brought to the surface in baskets or rigged for individual lifting. Despite an increased concern for maintaining locational controls, difficulties continually cropped up owing to the artifacts' lodging in the airlift lines, as well as to slumping in excavated areas, which caused artifacts to migrate.[15]

Near the end of the season, Davidson began to focus more and more on the large, dense mass of metal and concreted deposits in the center of the wreck site. It was a substantial mass by any standards, and it posed a serious impediment to excavation. Overall, the giant concreted anomaly measured twenty-five feet in length and ten feet in width, with a radius that ranged from eight to twenty-four inches. Close examination revealed a considerable matrix of intact timbers, which were thought to be fragments of collapsed hull or interior decking, as well as several boxes and crates. Davidson believed the mass to be a concentration of artifacts formed by the gradual collapse of the gundeck and interior bulkheads. When a cache of silver coins was discovered near the mass and its proximity to several other recovered valuables was noted, the salvors became even more interested in the mysterious conglomerate. Then more artifacts, including gold and silver coins, the tiny hands of a pocket watch, and a two-inch gold chain were recovered.[16] After these finds were made, Davidson's men enthusiastically attacked the mass, chipping away at its bulk with hydraulic hammers. Fragments were transported to shore for analysis and further reduction. Timber sections, which represented substantial portions of the architecture of the vessel but were of little interest to the salvors, were merely moved and deposited elsewhere on the bottom with the aid of *Sea Star*'s lifting gear. Some sections were removed with less than gentle handling, and much of the intact fabric of *De Braak*'s architecture was severely damaged.[17]

Meanwhile, Claudia Melson had arrived at Sub-Sal's headquarters on the beach at Lewes. She was given a tour of the beachfront warehouse in which the artifacts were being stored. Perusing the outwardly shabby facility, Melson noted its being readily accessible from the waterfront where Sub-Sal's boats occasionally moored. In fact, from the nearby beach she could easily view the salvage work under way barely a mile offshore.[18] The warehouse itself, a ramshackle two-story building, looked like the set of a grade B war movie. Once part of a shellfish-processing factory for fertilizer production, it had been leased to the University of Delaware, which had then sublet it to Sub-Sal. Inside the concrete-and-cinder-block structure, Melson found six eight-by-fifteen-foot cinder-block tanks, which would provide quite suitable wet storage for the larger artifacts, such as the carronades and long guns, small anchors, ballast pigs, and barrel staves, already recovered from the site.[19] On the south side of the building were several small compartments, currently being employed as storage rooms, that she resolved to put to immediate use. The second floor held Sub-Sal's offices as well as several large, empty rooms which were basically off-limits to state personnel. The entire facility was in a state of disorder with various types of waste evident throughout. The place not only needed cleaning and organization, but even worse, few of the artifacts stored there had been attended to, and little or no effort had been made to stabilize any of them except for those that appeared to be marketable.

Melson immediately sought to wrest order from chaos, but with a nearly zero-dollar budget, her task was Herculean. She quickly instituted a regimen of draining, hosing down, and refilling the freshwater tanks on a regular basis to begin leaching the chlorides from the artifacts to prevent fungal growth. Then began the slow, meticulous work of sorting and classifying the approximately one thousand artifacts that had been recovered in 1984 and of checking the inventory made that year against every item stored in the warehouse. The exercise became a learning experience for the young curator, who was initially unfamiliar with many of the maritime objects she would handle. But the arduous process of taking measurements, cross-referencing information, and quantifying the items in all of the artifact categories increased her knowledge of the collection a thousandfold. Indeed, within a year, Claudia Melson would become more familiar with the artifactual remains of HMS *De Braak* than anyone alive.

Her procedure was simple but effective. Since establishing provenance had been of little importance to the salvors and their inventory's accuracy was doubtful, Melson's quantification efforts became crucial. If an inventory description read "ceramics," she would break that category down into specific types and amounts, then start the evaluation process from there. Most of the artifacts had been tagged with white, waterproof, plastic slats that were typically used to tag trees and had been procured from a local nursery. A unique sequence of numbers had been written with a waterproof pen on each tag, which was then tied to each item with stainless-steel wire provided by a local airport. Small items, unfortunately, had been placed by the salvors in ziplocked bags, many of which contained several unrelated artifacts. Thus, each item in every bag had to be restored and renumbered. Furthermore, in the case of ceramics, duct tape had often been attached to the item, with numbers then written on the tape. Melson was obliged to remove each piece of tape, owing to its discoloring effect on the ceramic, and place each object in a newly numbered bag.[20]

During its 1985 season, Sub-Sal focused primarily on improving the efficiency of its artifact-recovery operation. With the new airlift-and-sluicing system in place, many artifacts which would have been lost the year before were soon being recovered—albeit with their provenance often undetermined. The flow of artifacts thus more than trebled Sub-Sal's 1984 recovery total and would have overwhelmed any less well-organized curator, but Melson held her own.[21] The eleven weeks of excavation which comprised the season produced more than 3,700 artifacts. These were classified and placed in the appropriate tanks, plastic trash cans filled with fresh water, and other containers: leather items in one, wooden sheaves in another, cannonballs in a third, and so on. A fish-tank filter was adapted to recirculate the pool water through a bucket of insulation batting to help reduce bacterial growth in the containers that held organic artifacts. Chloride levels in the tanks were monitored, and the water changed regularly. Incremental water changes were necessary to begin leaching out destructive sea salts absorbed by the artifacts during nearly two centuries of immersion. Water samples were regularly taken to the University of Delaware's College of Marine Studies in Lewes, where chloride levels were measured and recorded.[22]

These efforts to at least stabilize the growing collections were admittedly limited, despite being carried out on an enormous scale. However, additional state funds for the preservation of artifacts (seventy-five percent of which would end up in the hands of the salvors, who had made little effort to stabilize the collections) was out of the question. Nevertheless, Melson, assisted by Elaine Ippolito, a well-known local artist, and from time to time by student volunteers from the University of Delaware, and advised by such nationally known archaeological conservators as Curtiss Peterson, gave it her best shot.

Melson was equally systematic in both her initial evaluation and her subsequent treatment of the collections. Her first task was to deal with the large number of black-glass bottles which had been brought up. Many contained coral and other marine growth on their surfaces, so these artifacts were placed in a ten-percent solution of citric acid, which caused the concretions to slough off within a few days. The bottles were then returned to the freshwater pools to continue their desalinization. After a year, they would be removed and air-dried. The same process was carried out on decorative glassware. After being dried, the glass was coated with clear fingernail polish, registration numbers were applied, and then it was given another coating of polish. The glass was then stored in acid-free boxes and Styrofoam egg cartons.[23]

Most of the ceramics were found to have been stained by the inordinate levels of iron oxide at the wreck site. These artifacts were soaked in a solution of oxalic acid. Many, of course, had not been recovered intact. Broken edges had to be meticulously cleaned, with brushes and dental picks used to remove the concretions which had accumulated around them.[24]

The treatment of metal artifacts was high on Melson's list of priorities, for these were among the quickest to suffer harm from extended periods of exposure of air. Most were cleaned by electrolysis, with a low-voltage electrical current being sent through a solution of sodium hydroxide in which the artifact had been placed. To facilitate the treatment of larger items, such as three ship anchors, the carronades, and other dense objects, individual wooden boxes were constructed as containers. Although the smaller items could be "cooked" in a variety of plastic dishpans during a process that took only a few days, the larger artifacts might take months or even years to be treated. Once the items had completed the electrolysis stage, they were scrubbed with very fine steel wool and then coated with Incrolac to keep them from tarnishing. Silver, pewter, and brass flatware cleaned up rapidly, revealing such details as smithery marks, graffiti, and the initials of crew members.[25]

Melson's expanding category files reflected all aspects of both work and life aboard *De Braak*, but especially prominent was the Royal Navy's broad arrow, which was incised on almost every ship-related object, from the captain's dinner bell to simple sheathing tacks. The flow of artifacts seemed infinite and included almost every item one could imagine being used aboard an eighteenth-century man-of-war, and then some. Lead objects ranged from fishing sinkers and sounding leads to scuppers and even a kitchen sink (complete with bronze plug). There were navigational items, such as the barrels and lenses of a telescope; compasses and dividers for map reading; and medical supplies, including a syringe, a bottle of pink medicine, part of a tourniquet, and a bronze mortar and pestle. There were dice and dominoes made of bone; pieces of a game that was popular in the eighteenth-century Royal Navy, called "Crown and Anchor;" and a miniature cannon (thought to be part of a timepiece) which could actually fire a charge. Personal items, such as a bone or tortoise-shell comb, a straight-razor case, five toothbrushes, and assorted shoes in various styles (some with buckles, others with laces), revealed the more human side of everyday life aboard a Royal Navy ship.[26]

The record-keeping procedures required to maintain an accurate inventory also constituted a major task. A ritual of checking and double-checking artifacts and lists was conducted every day. New discoveries of proper, and occasionally obsolete, artifact nomenclature and usage were made daily, and some portion of each day had to be spent photographing artifacts and stapling contact prints onto individual catalog worksheets. Relevant information, such as provenance data, dimensions, descriptions, maker's marks, graffiti, and so on, then had to be extended on the sheets before they were filed in numerical order, by type and category.[27]

Melson's own attitude toward her low-profile, often frustrating work on an artifact collection which, it appeared, would end up at the project's conclusion being sold or allowed to decay, was philosophical. The satisfaction lay in "seeing whats-its and thingamajigs become known and properly named parts and pieces of eighteenth-century shipboard life," she later noted.

> It is dealing with one very large artifact in which men lived and worked and died during the course of duty. And finally, it is the realization that new and accurate knowledge can be added to the record books and journals that was never available before. The real treasure of H.M.S. *De Braak* is the wealth of information that we can gather from this ship.[28]

N I N E T E E N

To Raise a Ship

As the second season on *De Braak* wound down, the relationship between John Davidson and Harvey Harrington grew strained. Davidson had little respect for his partner's managerial capabilities and held him personally responsible for the project's technical difficulties. For his own part, Harrington considered Davidson a martinet who was quick to interfere in fieldwork and unjustly critical of the airlift operation. Having lost control of his company, Harrington had begun to explore other entrepreneurial avenues, hoping to capitalize on his celebrity as the man who had found *De Braak*. More and more frequently, he left the day-to-day job of managing offshore work in the capable hands of David Agatha, a veteran commercial oil-field diver from California.[1]

If nothing else, Harvey Harrington had learned one lesson from the *De Braak* project—namely, that the mere mention of treasure was enough to attract money. Thus, he sought to exploit this tendency and use his relationship with Davenport Associates to form a new corporation called the Indian River Recovery Company. Late in 1985, together with Richard W. Hennesy, Davenport's director of operations, Harrington moved to arrest six well-known shipwrecks (that is, known to the sport diving community) along the New Jersey and Delaware coasts. In November, claiming that the said shipwrecks contained the *potential* for hundreds of millions of dollars in gold, Harrington's new company began to sell high-risk investment units for $2,500 each. Within a few months, a total of forty-one units had been sold to thirty-five investors.[2] As a result of his new venture and the declining fortunes of the *De Braak* project, Harrington's interest and participation in the work diminished, all the more so as his relationship with Davidson worsened.

Davidson, in turn, was fed up with Harrington, who had publicly presented himself as a diver of great experience, but had never—at least in Davidson's presence—even dove on the site. He accused Harrington of being a terrible business manager who padded the payroll "with every member of his family." Worse, claimed Davidson, was that

> upon signing a contract to be the offshore manager, [he] undertook to use the
> income with which I was providing him to salvage other wrecks prior to any

disagreement with me. It was only upon my discovery of his clandestine activities and refusal to give on the wreck as offshore manager that I became disenchanted with him.[3]

The season's work, which had cost Davidson $837,000, had resulted in the recovery of only fifty-seven gold and forty-nine silver coins. Much of the blame for that negligible haul he assigned to Harrington and his faulty airlift operation. In December, on the grounds that his excessive absences from work offshore had violated their contract, Davidson fired Harrington.[4]

The slack provided by the onset of winter allowed John Davidson time to regroup and to reconsider his operational tactics. Although 3,700 artifacts had been recovered, the total amount of coinage had been negligible. His curiosity about the mysterious concreted mass lying in the center of the wreck, however, had become an obsession, claiming more and more of his attention each day. Both airlifting and battering the conglomerate with hydraulic hammers had proved ineffective and expensive. In mid-December, a meeting between state officials and Sub-Sal personnel was convened to discuss the status of salvage work and, more specifically, to address the problem of the concreted mass. The conference was, if not pivotal, then at least instructive with regard to where Sub-Sal was headed in its efforts to wrest treasure from the site. Attending the meeting were officers from both the State of Delaware and Sub-Sal, as well as three archaeological consultants, all of whom had many years of experience in marine archaeology. John Broadwater, one of the senior archaeologists, was then director of the Yorktown Shipwreck Archaeological Project at Yorktown, Virginia, and a nationally recognized authority on English shipwrecks of the eighteenth century. Prior to the meeting, he had made an exploratory dive at the *De Braak* site, to examine and assess the giant anomaly lying amidships, and he had come to the meeting prepared to make some recommendations.[5]

The second archaeologist was Walter Zacharchuk, a former director of underwater archaeology for Parks Canada. he was already well known and respected in archaeological circles when the State of Delaware asked him to be a consultant on the *De Braak* salvage. His best-known work had been on the pioneering archaeological excavation of the wreck of the French frigate *Machault*, lost in 1760 in the Gulf of St. Lawrence.[6] The *Machault* project, which began in 1969 and concluded in 1972, had been carried out in an environment quite similar to that of the Delaware. The excavation had required more than 5,200 hours of diving time and had not only documented a major historic wreck *in situ*, but also led to the recovery of significant components of the ship and its contents. Zacharchuk, surprisingly, had since left the Canadian Park Service to do consulting work for Mel Fisher's Treasure Salvors, Inc., of Key West, Florida.

The third archaeologist was David Beard, a twenty-nine-year-old graduate of the underwater archaeology program at East Carolina University in Greenville, North Carolina. Beard, who spoke in a quick, clipped manner, with a deep southern accent, had studied under some of the foremost marine archaeologists in the United States, and had replaced Reedy as a consultant to the state on December 4, 1985. He contributed an archaeological professionalism which had been hitherto sorely lacking.

As the meeting commenced and discussion focused on the problem of the giant anomaly, someone suggested (to John Broadwater's horror) using "surgical" explosive charges to crack the concreted mass open. It was not a new concept and had been suggested to a state official by Harrington in 1984. Although the idea had been rejected by the state then, this time it was given serious consideration. "It was determined," one state agent later wrote, "that in light of new information about the nature of the site in general and the mass in particular this technique would be acceptable to the state if it were used in a controlled manner, and with the understanding that it would be discontinued if the results were detrimental to the archaeological integrity of the site to an excessive extent."[7] Although both Broadwater and Beard objected loudly, no one paid them the least bit of attention. In their minds, the very concept of an archaeological "salvage" of De Braak for profit was incongruous, and the idea of employing explosives appalling.

Meanwhile, Davidson began to explore avenues less traveled by his predecessors. Perhaps, he thought, there was more to the De Braak story than legend; perhaps what was needed was more archival research. Thus, in March 1986, Davidson flew to London to seek the assistance of a professional researcher named Gillian Hughes, whose task would be to sift through the British Admiralty records. Incredible as it might seem, only after sinking more than a million dollars into the De Braak project did Davidson feel compelled to undertake such an investigation—and one, moreover, that had already been conducted by such authorities as Chapelle and Laws. Indeed, it seems altogether likely that neither Harrington nor Davidson had ever read the account of this research published by the two experts in 1967. Among other avenues of research, Davidson had specifically charged Hughes with discovering whether or not De Braak had ever called at ports in either Jamaica or the Bahamas; what actual cargo besides cocoa and copper the prize ship Don Francisco Xavier had been carrying; and what, if anything, the court martial records had to say about the warship's loss. Not surprisingly, the researcher merely traversed the same archival paper trail which Chappelle and Laws had followed almost twenty years before.

Hughes' findings offered little support for the treasure hypothesis and even less new data. She found no evidence of De Braak's calling at any Bahamian or Jamaican ports, nor any evidence that the price ship had carried treasure other than 200 tons of copper. Nor could Hughes find any court martial records relating to *De Braak*. Still, Davidson refused to accept the paucity of evidence supporting the treasure legend, choosing instead to turn his attentions to a more positive suggestion made by Zacharchuk. The Canadian archaeologist speculated that if *De Braak* had in fact been carrying gold and silver, it might well have slumped onto the seabed as the upper section of the wreck decayed and collapsed. The treasure could then have eventually worked its way down into the sand beneath the wreck, according to Zacharchuk, although just how it could have done so was never clear.[8] To Davidson, Zacharchuk's explanation seemed a stroke of genius that explained why so little treasure had been recovered in the previous two years of intensive salvage work. Counter-explanations offered by Broadwater and other state agents to the effect that so few pieces of precious metal or stone had been recovered because, as the archival evidence indicated, there simply had never been any treasure to begin with were dismissed outright by Davidson.[9]

The head of Sub-Sal seized upon the hypothesis as hungrily as a squirrel would an acorn. Indeed, he thought, why not simply raise the hull, move it to one side with a barge-mounted crane, and use a clamshell bucket to scoop up whatever treasure lay beneath the wreck? Within a short time he had hired Zacharchuk to be Sub-Sal's company archaeologist,[10] and, by mid-April, an intensive analysis of the *De Braak* hull had begun, not for archaeological purposes but, rather, to prepare the wreck for a possible move.

In May, Beard made several preliminary dives to assess the conditions of the site. Surprisingly, visibility had improved markedly over that of recent months owing to a drought. Cold water temperatures had reduced algae growth, and it was still too early in the year for planktonic bloom to have clouded the site. Thus, visibility now extended to a stunning twenty feet on occasion, usually during high tides, and five to ten feet at low tide.[11] The opportunity to record the site on videotape was simply too good to pass up, even for the salvors. More than four-and-a-half hours of film were thus shot, but, unfortunately, owing to "the poor quality of the hard-wire video system used and the divers' unfamiliarity with ship construction and related artifacts, their video tapes, both visually and narratively, [were] gradually of little use in reconstructing the site" archaeologically.[12] Beard's work on the site was somewhat facilitated by the salvors' grudging acknowledgment that he was the best-qualified individual available to map the wreck. Since the salvors had failed to produce anything like a site map during the second season, as required by their lease, an agreement was quickly negotiated whereby Sub-Sal would provide divers on a regular basis to assist the archaeologist, on condition that his work not interfere with salvage operations.[13]

Beard's work, unlike the salvors', was carried out with only scuba gear. He was thus restricted to working during the slack-tide windows, usually lasting between thirty and forty minutes, when currents were negligible. Therefore, only two or, at most, three dives could be made each day. Like his predecessor, Beard worked from the baseline established in 1985, but instead of merely roughly sketching in the larger components of the wreck, he began to document and draw each section of the ship's fabric and structural features. As the picture began to develop, it became apparent that approximately forty percent of the starboard side up to approximately a foot and a half below the lower deck, or approximately twenty percent of the entire original structure, had survived intact. Concentrations of artifacts, such as large numbers of lead sounding weights located in the bosun's stores in the extreme bow, as well as rolls of leading sheathing and even spare windowpanes found in the carpenter's stores in the starboard bow, were sketched in. Newly discovered larger artifacts which could be removed by hand, such as pieces of furniture, bottles, and gunstocks, were carefully mapped in before being moved.[14]

Davidson was buoyed by the progress as he planned his next step. By early June he had negotiated with a marine construction company owned by J. M. Cashman, of North Weymouth, Massachusetts, to furnish a 150-foot barge, two auxiliary barges, a seagoing tug, and a crane capable of raising 300 tons, with 168 hours of crane time guaranteed. He had also hired an engineer from the same company as a consultant. Next came the pitch, to be delivered at a day-long conference on June 2 with Dr. John Kern, director of Delaware's Division of Historical and Cultural Affairs, to talk over the possibility of moving the hull.[15]

The meeting between Kern and Davidson was also attended by McCormick, Beard, Zacharchuk, the Cashman engineer, and several state officials. The salvors got right to the point: Zacharchuk proposed that the hull be placed on a cradle, lifted and moved at least fifty feet away in order to permit a thorough dredging of its former site for treasure and whatever other artifacts might be discovered. Beard suggested that, if the hull was moved, a frame should be placed on top of the wreck and a wide strip run under the hull to prevent artifact spillage. Kern opposed the plan vigorously, holding out for the more conservative approach of excavating the site by airlift and employing adequate archaeological survey measures. But, in the end, the Delaware officials were swayed by Zacharchuk's proposal, on which he had boldly elaborated with the further suggestion that, if the hull was going to be moved, it might as well be brought to the surface where it could be studied and recorded at leisure.

At the conclusion of the conference, Davidson emerged triumphant. He had not only gotten the state's approval on moving the hull via cradle (secured and cushioned during the actual recovery), but, more importantly, he had won permission, pending a written project design, to excavate the hull site, with a clamshell bucket.[16]

Beginning on June 12 and continuing throughout June and July, divers worked energetically to remove the last of the carronades from the site, as well as a number of large components of the port hull, which had collapsed onto the sand. They also needed to clear away all of the old traveler lines and the remains of the shattered PVC grid (which had been destroyed when the dive boat's anchor dragged across the site), even as Beard hastily struggled to map and measure as much of the wreck as possible. Smaller artifacts were still being brought up, many of them bearing intriguing initials, inscriptions, or graffiti. When the handle of a pewter spoon crudely engraved with the name "Mitch" was recovered, it was quickly checked by Melson against the ship's muster, on which several seamen named Mitchell had been listed. A wooden, hand-held mirror (sans reflective glass) bearing the initials "A. J." could not be traced to anyone on the muster list, adding yet another item to the growing collection of *De Braak* mysteries. Many of the objects recovered were unique and many more were curiosties, such as a bootjack designed for removing low-heeled boots, an Iberian water jug, or a hair comb belonging to one of the Spanish prisoners. Given all the artifacts that had been found June, Beard was convinced by the end of June that *De Braak* would never yield any treasure. "It would," be assured his colleagues matter-of-factly, "have been found by now."[17]

Taking advantage of the good weather, the Sub-Sal divers began to prepare the hull for recovery. Using high-pressure water jets attached to a diesel-powered pump that was mounted aboard *Seneca*, they began clearing a forty-foot section of the bow. Before any lifting could be done, several feet of sterile, non-artifact-bearing mud had to be removed so that the overall weight to be raised was reduced. This operation revealed, for the first time, the ship's actual ceiling and hull planking, the starboard edge, and the port side to the stern post. By the time this phase had been completed and the entire perimeter of the ship's remaining fabric had been exposed, it was clear that the hull was intact along the whole length of the keel. Once the perimeter had been delineated, steel pipes, painted white, were driven into the seabed five feet from the ship's edges and at ten-foot intervals around the hull. The pipes, it was hoped, would serve as guides for the clamshell-bucket excavation around the hull.[18]

The next step called for seven channels to be carved with high-pressure water jets through the ocean floor beneath the wreck, and a one-inch-diameter flexible water probe strung through each channel to pass messenger cables under the hull. The cables would later be used to thread one-and-a-half-inch, fabric-covered steel lifting lines, which would serve as slings when the hull was raised. (In the meantime, Davidson had concluded contract negotiations with Cashman, guaranteeing the latter $115,000 and three percent of the net gained from any treasure recovered in return for the barges, tugboats, crane, and crane time.[19]

By the end of June, the plan to raise *De Braak* had begun to draw public attention—and criticism. On June 30, a Wilmington newspaper reported that if the wreck were raised, it would either be placed on a barge where it could be salvaged, moved to shallower, less turbulent waters closer to shore, or brought ashore for salvage and preservation. The news immediately aroused the opposition of some area recreational divers. One sports diver, a Wilmington attorney named Peter Hess, was quoted by the press as opposing any effort to raise "probably the foremost underwater archaeological site in Delaware" and as proposing that the site be made into an underwater preserve. Although his efforts would prove useless against the well-organized salvors, his sentiments were shared by a growing number of professional archaeologists and sports divers.[20]

Davidson plowed ahead, undeterred by public sentiment, but Delaware state officials were growing increasingly concerned. In late July, Kern requested that a comprehensive operations plan for the salvage be submitted to him in writing. Davidson immediately drafted a response entitled "Outline of Procedures for the Salvage of *De Braak* Hull and Artifacts," dated July 27, 1986. Two days later, Davidson and Kern met to discuss the outline.[21] Davidson's project design called first for a comprehensive excavation around the hull with a clamshell bucket, then for cables to be passed under the hull, creating a set of slings. The slings were to be fastened to two block-and-tackle units hung from the crane by two massive cables, each four and three-quarter inches in diameter. Buoys on sixty-five-foot lines would be attached to the bow and stern ends of the wreck prior to the lift. The equal height of the buoys could then serve as a guide so that balance could be maintained during the transfer of the hull to the cradle. Three-foot-long, two-by-six-inch wooden spacers would then be placed between the slings and the hull, at its starboard edge, to spread the load and minimize the possibility of damage. Then, and only then, could the hull be slowly raised to a point less than a dozen feet off the bottom, swung sideways, and lowered onto the specially built steel cradle. The fifty-by-twenty-foot cradle, which would be lowered to the site prior to the recovery attempt, would be designed to support two-thirds of the hull at its center of gravity. Davidson calculated that there would be barely an eight-foot overhang at the stern and about a dozen-foot one at the bow. To prevent the spillage of artifacts and sediments still resting in the hull as she was brought up, the wreck would be covered with a shroud of porous fabric or wire-mesh screen. The ship would then be raised at a rate of no more than one and a half feet per minute to minimize any unforeseen consequences of the lift and to prevent damage to the fragile components of the hull itself. The whole operation was projected to require approximately sixty minutes.[22]

Once the remains were safely on board one of the Cashman barges, 2,600 cubic yards of sediments from the site would be dredged up with a fifteen-

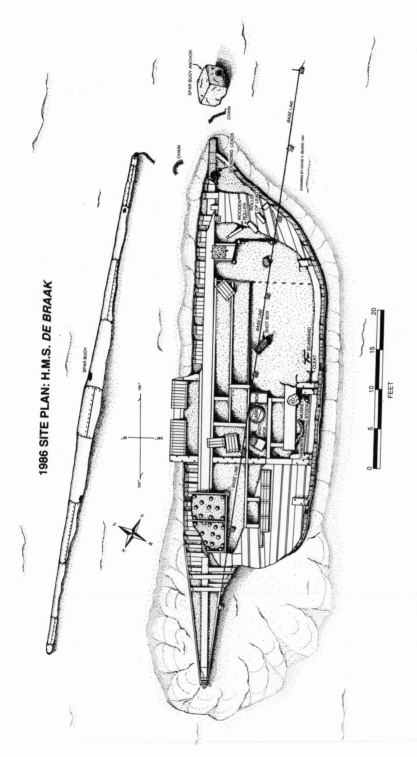

1986 SITE PLAN: H.M.S. *DE BRAAK*

Underwater archaeologist David Beard's site plan for the *De Braak* wreck site shortly before "the pick." Note the proximity of the mysterious spar bouy to the wreck. (*David V. Beard*)

CONJECTURAL STAGES OF *DE BRAAK* COLLAPSE

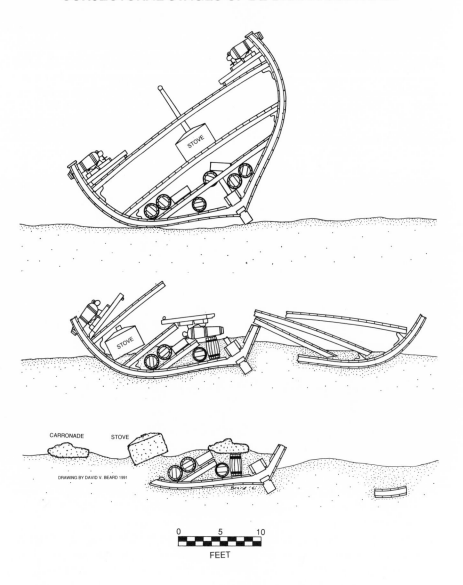

Beard's schematic showing conjectural mode of wreck disintegration. (*David V. Beard*)

cubic-foot clamshell bucket and processed either on the auxiliary barges or at Sub-Sal headquarters. The recovered hull would then be excavated by state archaeologists and the Sub-Sal team. The process would begin with washing away the muck and sand with seawater and screening out the larger debris of all kinds, including the bigger artifacts; the team would pick through the pebbles, shells, and dross by hand, extracting smaller artifacts and any treasure that had thus far eluded discovery. The entire operation, Davidson optimistically concluded, would take less than two weeks.[23]

Davidson was adamant that the vessel be raised "at the earliest possible time" and transported aboard the barge to the Fischer complex. Early raising of the vessel to a barge, he claimed, would also insure that the hull would not be damaged by the dredging operation. He agreed to provide adequate security for the hull and artifacts while they remained on the harbored barge. Kern was equally adamant on his own part that the division of Historical and Cultural Affairs supervise and secure adequate personnel for implementation of the recovery plan.[24]

By July 30, it had been agreed that, once examined, the hull would be returned to the deep.

> Immediately before the scheduled departure of the crane from the wreck site, at the conclusion of the proposed operations, the vessel on the barge will be transported back to the wreck site. The vessel will be lowered to the ocean bottom at the wreck site, lifted from its cradle, and covered on-site with scoops of ocean floor material deposited by the crane bucket. Reburial of the hull will protect it from structural decomposition which would otherwise proceed rapidly.[25]

In addition to the agreed upon methodology, it was determined that Walter Zacharchuk would "be retained by Sub-Sal throughout the entire duration of the crane operation to coordinate responsible implementation of archaeological recovery with the Division of Historical and Cultural Affairs.[26] The ground rules were the state's; their implementation was up to Sub-Sal, Inc.

On July 25 David Beard, who was just beginning to document the site systematically with still photographs, was obliged to terminate his efforts owing to the salvors ambitious schedule. His final shots, however, proved to be of great significance, for he managed to record several structural features which had not appeared on the admiralty drafts and had apparently been added by the ship's carpenters sometime after the plans had been drawn. There were still numerous artifacts to be documented, many of which had been recently recovered and were of great help to Beard in his efforts to identify several of the vessel's stowage compartments. Beard did his best to document all of these features and groups of artifacts by recording them on his still-evolving site map.[27]

Perhaps one of the most intriguing finds, however, did not belong to the wreck at all. On the port side of the hull, divers discovered a sixty-five-foot spar buoy with a large stone anchor and chain attached. Close examination revealed that the buoy was constructed from several segments riveted together. At the top end of the buoy, in relief, were the letters "USLSH," which, it was soon realized, stood for "United States Light House Service."[28] The discovery was significant, for the buoy had clearly been lost prior to 1939, when the Light House Service had ceased to exist. The number of speculations about and theories of the buoy's origins and its ending up in such close proximity to the wreck ran almost as high as estimates on the value of the *De Braak* treasure. One theory held that the wreck had been marked during the late nineteenth century as a navigational obstruction, since the buoy's design suggested manufacture during this era. Another hypothesis was that the buoy had been blown from another site during a storm and had become entangled in the wreck as it sank. The most likely theory, however, "and the one which made Sub-Sal somewhat uneasy," was that the mysterious buoy had been employed during one of the earlier salvage efforts, possibly the Pancoast, Chapman, or Colstad expeditions. The discovery of the buoy's stone anchor less than two yards off the wreck's bow lent some credibility to the theory, although nothing could be proved.[29] But for several of the salvors the implications were clear. It was just possible that one of the earlier expeditions had actually recovered the treasure and never reported their success—for obvious reasons.

All thoughts of having lost the treasure to a previous salvage attempt, however, were quickly forgotten when one of the more exciting finds on the site occurred. This time it was Dave Agatha who made the discovery. While inspecting the slings for the lift operation, he happened to reach into a depression between some planking and frames and there discovered thirteen gold escudos.[30] It was a wonderful omen. Davidson was convinced, now more than ever, that the legend of the *De Braak* treasure was true. All that now stood between him and a fortune was the hull of the legendary treasure ship herself.

On August 5 the clamshell bucket, which had been sarcastically dubbed "Jaws" by the archaeologists, took its first mouthful of sediments from the site around the wreck. According to the lease agreement, the salvors were not permitted to carry out excavations within twenty feet of the hull before its removal. Fortunately, Beard's investigations around the hull had already been completed, albeit hurriedly, for on August 7 the bucket ripped out the ship's sternpost along with part of the keel. The excavations were clearly anything but "surgical," as the salvors had promised they would be. The "accident" made it obvious to all that the giant clamshell bucket, had it been permitted to operate any closer to the site, would have caused incalculable damage to the remaining fabric of the hull and all that lay within it.[31] For the horrified archaeologists, however, this incident was but a foretaste of the future.

TWENTY

The Pick

The massive twenty-ton, steel-and-wood cradle onto which *De Braak*'s hull was to be shifted had been made by welding eight- and twelve-inch steel I-beams together. It was more than adequate to hold the 150-ton hull of the currently most famous shipwreck in America. On Saturday, August 9, the cradle was put aboard an auxiliary platform and conveyed to the site, where the Cashman barge and crane had been moored for the past several days. The following morning, at slack tide, the unit was carefully lowered to the bottom and positioned adjacent to the hull. A diver was then dispatched by Davidson to inspect the site. He soon reported over the communications console that the cradle had been deposited approximately thirty feet from the starboard side of the wreck. While on the bottom, he took a few moments to hunt for souvenirs of the day and brought up a section of a rare eighteenth-century navigational octant with a workable brass screw.[1]

Soon after the cradle had been deployed to Davidson's satisfaction, he returned to shore and called a press conference at this headquarters, where he outlined the procedures for the hull's recovery, loosely referred to by some of his personnel as "the pick." The final stage of the project, which he noted had thus far cost over two million dollars, was about to commence. *De Braak* would be lifted from her resting place by the crane, transferred to the cradle, and then raised to the surface at a rate of one-and-a-half feet per minute—no more and no less quickly.[2]

The sea was oil-slick calm early on the morning of Monday, August 11, as Davidson's divers suited up. Over the weekend, several newspapers had carried various accounts and rumors of handfuls of gold having been recovered from the wreck only a few days before. Press reports on the estimated value of the alleged treasure still fluctuated between five million and five-hundred million dollars.[3] That a media event of some significance was developing came as no surprise to state officials—nor that John Davidson was actively orchestrating one. From the outset, a festival atmosphere had pervaded the site, with the crane cabin decorated by a bright Pac Man figure wearing a pirate's bandanna and—appropriately—chasing gold coins.[4]

At 7:00 A.M., a diver was sent down to the cradle to await the lowering of the crane's block-and-tackle rig to which rings, linking the ends of the cables slung around *De Braak*, would be clasped. When all was in readiness, the blocks were slowly lowered, even as a stiff wind began to blow. By the time the blocks reached the diver, heavy swells were beginning to raise and lower the barge, causing similarly dramatic surges on the blocks. Try as he might, the diver could not rig the lifting cables to the crane's blocks.[5]

"I'm bouncing up and down here like a yo-yo!" he complained in exasperation over the communications link. Minutes later, he surfaced for decompression, totally exhausted and frustrated by the dangerous ordeal.

A second diver descended and was soon working feverishly, riding the same "bucking horse," bouncing up and down ten feet or more with each swell. A third diver, dispatched at 10:00 A.M., discovered that the rings had become hopelessly tangled and were rigged in the wrong order.[6] He persisted, and finally, the news that Davidson had been awaiting arrived from below. At about noon, the final ring had been slipped onto the block-and-tackle rig. Whether everything was secure enough to raise the ancient ship was another matter.[7]

Slightly before noon, John Kern had boarded the operations barge and been informed by Davidson and Zacharchuk of the difficulties encountered below. The tension was heightened when Davidson reported that a severe storm was on the way, which would impose a delay of at least seventy-two hours if operations were not concluded before the day was over. He had to decide whether to proceed with "the pick" or call it off until the storm had passed. Davidson made his choice without hesitation: *De Braak*, he stated emphatically, would have to be raised now; there was, as he saw it, simply no alternative.[8]

The media interest, which had been seeded by the weekend news reports, was by then growing gargantuan. Some 14,000 people, more than four times the normal number of visitors, had crowded onto the shores of nearby Cape Henlopen State Park to watch the proceedings, while dune buggies raced up and down the beach, vying for the best spot from which to view the historic moment.[9] By 12:30 P.M., several dozen pleasure and fishing boats filled with spectators had arrived and clustered around the starboard side of the crane barge. Within an hour their number had swelled to fifty and required three police launches to keep them far enough off-site. Several helicopters from Philadelphia television stations hovered overhead, taping the spectacle, for that evening's network news programs. Although high seas and heavy winds continued to build, still they came.[10]

John Kern looked woefully skyward at the hovering choppers. The formal position of the State of Delaware was quite clear. History was playing second fiddle to the so-called treasure, and, as a professional, the senior state official was anguished. "I hate to see this whole thing dictated by a media event," he said to no one in particular. "We have a two-hundred-year-old time capsule down there, and we could lose it."[11] But the momentum of events would not be hindered. "The pick" would soon be carried out, and there was little that Kern or anyone but the salvors themselves could do to stop it.

Soon after 3:00 P.M., Davidson ordered the crane operator to test the four-and-three-quarter-inch cables for equal tension. Slowly, the cables were tightened, then a jerk was felt, followed by slack. Inspection revealed that the ring attached to one of the cables had slipped off its hook on the block and could not be reattached. The cradle, it was now decided, was in the wrong place. It would be impossible to re-rig the cradle as well as the hull cables properly before foul weather hit.[12] David Beard, for one, was aghast. As he later wrote,

> The fact that the cradle had been fine in the morning and that a 300-ton capacity crane and a team of divers who were top-notch underwater riggers were standing by to correct any such problems did not deter these [Sub-Sal] officials from their new story. It was apparent that with all of the media coverage and spectators standing by, the salvors had no intention of postponing the lift until these engineering problems could be corrected.[13]

Davidson decided to delay "the pick" only until slack tide that night. The hull, he decided, would have to come up without the cradle. If spreaders and planks could be placed between cable and hull to prevent the cables from cutting through the timbers, he assured the nervous state officials, it could be brought up safely.[14] When word of the delay reached the surrounding flotilla of spectators and television crews, as well as the horde of onlookers ashore, the carnival atmosphere evaporated and was replaced by one of dismay.[15] Aboard the operations platform, however, Davidson and his team energetically began to prepare for "the pick."

Once he had decided to abandon the cradle-lifting operation, Davidson had also quietly decided against covering the hull with a wire shroud to prevent artifact spillage. Worse, he became determined that *De Braak* would be brought up as rapidly as possible, lest either the "embryonic" archaeologists, of whom Davidson thought little, or the state officials on board make some last minute objection. The weather would soon deteriorate, so speed was essential; the operation would thus have to be streamlined. Divers were again sent down, this time to place three-foot-long, four-by-four timbers weighted with iron pipes between the cables and the starboard edge of the wreck, in a jerry-rigged effort to distribute the stress on the hull.[16]

The state officials present were upset over the turn of events and Davidson's change of plans. They voiced their concerns that the cables would cut through the waterlogged hull like a sharp knife. Indeed, Kern pointed out that the procedural change would violate the terms of the legally binding lease agreement. Davidson responded curtly that he had not signed anything—his lawyers had signed the lease. "It was obvious to Kern," Beard observed caustically,

> that if he tried to interfere with the salvage operations, Davidson, a major supporter of the Republican Party in New Hampshire and more recently of former

Governor Pierre DuPont's bid for the presidency of the United States, would use his influence with the state's administration, also Republican, to see that Kern was stifled, if not fired.[17]

By early evening, the barge was lit by floodlights and the festival atmosphere prevailed once more, despite the onset of a misty drizzle. Hundreds of boats were again drawn to the scene, some circling the site with their lights focused on the arena of action. Marine police launches were again hard-pressed to keep onlookers at a distance. Helicopters buzzed overhead like so many mosquitoes. Charter-boat operators did a brisk business, charging fifteen dollars a head for ringside seats. The Delaware media event of the century was once more in full swing. Thoroughly disgusted, Kern backed down from a confrontation with the salvor and fled the scene on the next available boat to shore. Without Kern's authority, the remaining state representatives had no hope of influencing the course of events.[18]

At 8:30 P.M., with slack tide, the lift began. Movie cameras began to roll and still cameras clicked as if jolted into action by the sudden flip of a switch. The big diesel engine of the crane decorated with the pirate Pac Man roared to life, and the 100-foot boom was solemnly raised. The monster pair of drive wheels, at first slowly and then with increasing speed, began reeling in the centuries-old warship like a fisherman with a trout on his line. Below, the bones of a veritable legend were freed from the sucking mud that had imprisoned them for 188 years. Three minutes later, the keel of HM Sloop-of-War Brig *De Braak* broke the surface. Instead of the planned foot-and-a-half-per-minute lift, she had been raised at a hull-wrenching rate of thirty feet per minute. Then, as if on cue, a cacophony of cheers, applause, and boat-horn blasts erupted from the armada of spectator boats that surrounded the site.[19]

Suddenly, a friction brake on the crane failed. Operations halted while critical repairs were made. For nearly forty-five minutes the crane operator, Joe Soares, remained at the controls, his feet pressed tightly on the brake pedal. Salvors, archaeologists, and spectators alike seemed to hold their breath, for all the while *De Braak* was awash and beaten by the swells, with no doubt untold numbers of artifacts being swept unseen from her hull just below the surface and back to the bottom.[20] Finally, the diesel engine coughed back to life, belching black smoke. The lift resumed, and seconds later, a seventy-foot length of keel, with a twenty-two-foot-wide section of the starboard side of the hull attached, emerged from the black sea. Under the harsh glare of floodlights, the wreck hung, with its starboard side vertical about twelve feet above the water's surface, for several minutes. As the archaeologists watched in horror, cannonballs, other artifacts, and solid objects of all kinds and sizes splashed back into the bay along with a black, oozzy mixture of mud and water.[21] The loss was incalculable. Not only had the matrix constituting the primary cultural deposits of the site been lost, but most of the ship's interior partitions had also fallen out. "Those sections," Beard observed in disgust, "would have been of particular interest to maritime archaeologists, historians, and ship architects because they were constructed by carpenters after the rest of the ship had been built and therefore appear in no archival plans available for *De Braak*."[22]

The disaster became a catastrophe, as the four-by-four timbers used to distribute the stress of the cables on the hull began to fail. The cables began to cut through the hull, as one archaeologist described it, "like a knife through hot butter."[23] More artifacts fell into the water as the thick steel lines continued to slice into the soft, water-logged oak. Fortunately, as they cut through the hull they began to run into barrel staves and iron ballast, which soon jammed their progress. For a single, brief moment, the two massive cables strangling the hull in midair created a fleeting image of a ghost ship flying above the water with two masts and two sets of shrouds in full array.[24] If *De Braak*'s sinking had been a disaster, her raising, except for that single dramatic moment, had been historic humiliation.

The losses resulting from the rushed, inept recovery were enormous. *De Braak*'s keel had been cracked and her hull disfigured. Approximately six feet of artifact-bearing sediments, eight hundred cubic feet of silt and sand, had been dumped back into the sea. As John Kern later told the press, "Almost all of whatever might have been inside it while being raised from its grave" had been spilled from the wreck.[25]

Aboard the observer boat *Keena Dale*, Kevin McCormick, unlike the horrified archaeologists, was overjoyed. "It's just so much more than a piece of wood and copper," he said when the hull broke the surface. Just then, a small powerboat sped up to the *Dale* and her master handed over a bottle of champagne to the elated projected director. Another cheer went up.[26]

At 10:30 P.M., with artifacts, debris, and muck still sliding from the wreck into the deep, the hull was lowered onto a waiting barge that had been pushed into position by a tugboat. Then, as the hull was lowered, further damage was inflicted upon it. Because the barge was rising and falling with each heavy offshore swell, crane operator Joe Soares had to release his burden at precisely the right moment—an impossible task. "Poor timing by the crane operator and the already weakened condition of the timbers," noted one embittered archaeologist, "resulted in a longitudinal crack being made down the length of the hull, approximately 10 feet inboard from the starboard edge, when a swell rapidly raised the barge, accelerating the force of the impact at the moment it received the hull.[27] Then even more damage was inflicted when the extreme aft end of the keel was brought down on several metal floats which had been left on the barge deck by the salvors. The consequence was the cracking of the keel and deadwoods about twelve feet forward of where the sternpost had been (before being torn off during the earlier clam-bucket operations).[28]

There were no braces or other supports on the barge's bare deck to prevent further disfigurement of the hull. Nor did anyone seem to care. Again, a cheer erupted from the spectator fleet as triumphant divers on the salvage platform began to douse themselves with champagne. When they boarded the adjacent, slime-covered barge bearing the object of their long, hard labor, they did so as conquering heroes, and L. John Davidson stood the proudest of them all. A tall, bearded television cameraman, "with an intense look about him," was among the first to heap adulation on the salvor. Approaching the exhausted and emotionally drained chief executive of Sub-Sal, the man extended his hand and said: "I just want you to know that I am very proud to shake your hand. I travel every day around the country covering news events. I rarely get an opportunity to meet someone who to me represents the spirit of the people who once built this country."[29] Davidson was touched. In his own eyes, "the pick"—and the media event it had spawned—had been a truly great success. Nearby, a jubilant Kevin McCormick echoed Davidson's sense of triumph. "The *De Braak* is home." To which one state agent retorted morosely, "You may have won your treasure, but we have lost ours."[30]

That evening *De Braak* was hauled to the pier at Lewes where several state officials sought to board and examine her. Their reception was less than welcoming. "Actually," recalled Beard, "we were physically threatened by a drunken welder who had been put in charge of 'security' by Davidson."[31] The next day, however, they came to stay.

After a canvas tent had been rigged over it, and several hoses and lawn sprinklers set up to keep the hull wet, twentieth-century Lewes and the world at large got their first look at the ship which had made the little town famous. The legend was in reality anything but attractive. Indeed, the slippery, muddy hull appeared less than the stuff of legend. The shattered, mangled, slime-covered wreck was, indeed, even smaller than some of the sleek, well-appointed, modern pleasure craft from which spectators had watched its resurrection. Cannonballs, grapeshot, and musket balls were clearly visible, looking like pimples on the concreted matrix which still adhered to the hull itself.[32] In the harsh light of day, the incalculable damage inflicted on what could have been a truly remarkable archaeological resource was painfully evident. *De Braak* had been revealed for all to see, and the sight was anything but glamorous.

"On the bottom," John Kern commented sadly, "the hull was an envelope with artifacts in it. The contents of that envelope were lost in the raising. We lost the relationship of the artifacts to the hull."[33] Archaeological provenance had been sacrificed for the advantage of several days' time and the publicity of a magnificent media event. McCormick, of course, saw it differently. "The puzzle is still going on," he informed a reporter from the *New York Times*, "but a big piece of it came up last night," a piece, as he would soon publicly announce, that might be returned to the sea for reburial until it could be preserved.[34] But the disaster had not escaped everyone's notice, and some pundits soon began to refer to the recovery as the "De Braakle."[35]

Early on the morning of August 12, state archaeologists and the salvors began the meticulous process of searching the hull for any artifacts which might still remain aboard. Despite the holiday mood among the salvors, the archaeologists did their best to conduct the search systematically in order to document the local provenance of whatever still remained. The curator of archaeology for the Delaware Bureau of Museums and Historic Sites, Charles Fithian, who had been enlisted in the project only days before, explained the frantic pace of their activities: "We simply didn't know how long we were going to have access to the hull before they placed her back in the ocean like McCormick said they would."[36]

Under the overall direction of the Division of Historical and Cultural Affairs, primarily in the person of administrator Dean Nelson, and the on-site supervision of David Beard, the archaeologists first cleared the heavy cables and disarticulated debris from the wreck while hastily recording as many details of what they found as possible. Once this task had been completed, the hull was divided into five sections, principally along the lines of the main riders which were still in place. Local provenance was maintained by keeping any and all artifacts from each section together. With the salvors constantly pressuring the fifteen-to-twenty-man search team to hurry, however, a formal, comprehensive survey of the artifacts *in situ* proved impossible. Still, the work progressed. The sediments were sifted through screens by several teams, even as others combed the muddy hull on hands and knees looking for larger items.[37]

A tantalizing assortment of artifacts began to appear: a gold coin, a pewter spoon, a shot locker once filled with cannonballs for a 24-pounder cannon, a nearly perfect wooden sheave dated 1797, a fire broom with the thatch still preserved by pitch, a brass belt buckle bearing the famous fouled-anchor insignia of the Royal Marines, an ivory domino with eleven dots, a ceramic bowl, two shoes, some gun flints and musket pieces, a leather slipper with a green bow attached and still tied, and the most moving discovery—a human metatarsal bone.[38] Davidson was excited by the artifacts and more optimistic than ever. "This is a serious archaeological find," he declared. "We can never dismiss the fact that there may be treasure. The historical benefit is part of the fun of it . . . to be the first to solve a 200-year-old puzzle."[39]

Outside the fenced-off grounds of Fischer Enterprises, thousands of people began to mill about, drawn to the site by the national news media and hoping for a glimpse of the famous wreck. But only state officials and a few members of the press were permitted entrance by the armed guard at the gate. Many of the curiosity seekers soon became distraught. "Maybe we'd have a better chance to see it if it sank in Russia," protested one woman who claimed to have come from The Netherlands specifically to see the vessel which had once sailed under her native flag. Others took the brush-off lightly. "If we were enterprising," suggested one wag, "we'd rush to the hardware, buy a ladder, and charge 50 cents to climb up and look through my binoculars."[40] His comments were certainly in the spirit of the enterprise under way behind the fence.

By Wednesday, August 13, much of the public hoopla had died down, and the crowd had all but disappeared. The weather, with a hurricane expected off the Atlantic coast at any time, had deteriorated to such an extent that the crane and barge had to be brought in to the pier for safety's sake. "We were fearful this would happen," Davidson said in an effort to justify the haste with which *De Braak* had been raised.[41] In the interim, both he and McCormick began to consider their next move. For the next two weeks, weather permitting, they informed the press, divers would be sent to scour the bottom for the supposed fortune which had so far eluded them. Not all of the Sub-Sal team, however, were still convinced of the treasure's existence. Agatha, the company's intrepid chief diver and one who had paid over 150 visits to the wreck, suggested that some treasure might indeed be found, but added that he personally was "not too sure" about the existence of a "mother lode." In any event, the hands-on underwater search would have to be terminated in two weeks when the lease on the crane, which was vital to large-object recovery operations, expired.[42]

Still of particular interest to the salvors was the large, encrusted object that had fallen off the wreck during "the pick"—the same object which had proven impenetrable on the bottom. McCormick thought that the mysterious mass might very well hold the ship's bounty of gold, silver, and jewels, or merely more cannonballs and pig-iron ballast. Aware of the limited but increasing criticism of the procedures that had led to the loss of cultural materials during the lift (principally stemming from the archaeological community) and of his crew's concern over the lack of booty recovered thus far, Davidson pointed hopefully to the abyss from which *De Braak*'s tortured carcass had been hauled, where anything might still be found: "The real story of treasure and artifacts," he stated optimistically, "is still on the bottom."[43] As soon as the weather calmed, he promised, they would return. Not only would the large encrusted objects be recovered, but sizable portions of the port hull and other large artifacts would also be brought up in baskets and slings.[44]

Once the site had been cleared of large items by divers, Davidson said, the crane would be used to scoop up sand, muck, and shell materials on and about the wreck site with a clam bucket. Each bucket load would provide enough material to fill one and a half dump trucks. "Because of the large amount that can be lifted in one scoop," he said sincerely, but in total ignorance of the facts, "the process should actually help protect artifacts from damage. . . . The debris will be placed on barges and sifted."[45]

The salvors had previously made few pretenses of caring about archaeological interest or the historical value of the artifacts being recovered, other than those which were obviously worth a lot of money or were useful in attracting publicity. Now, the uneasy relationship between the archaeologists (representing the state) and the salvors began to unravel almost overnight. Henry Ward, who had been working on the project for the state, while earning a master's degree in archaeology at the University of Delaware, was incensed at the crude methods employed by the salvors. It mattered little to him that the state had permitted similar approaches in the past. "If someone tried to do to a Navajo pueblo what was done to the *De Braak*," he stated bitterly, "he would wind up in jail." David Beard called the project an "unmitigated archaeological disaster."[46] Charles Fithian did his best to maintain scientific objectivity as the crisis continued and twelve-hour days became eighteen-hour days, but he found that his normally easy-going temperament was taxed to the fullest. And the worst was yet to come.

On the afternoon of August 15, Delaware's Governor Michael Castle, accompanied by Lewes's Mayor Alfred A. Stango, visited Sub-Sal's headquarters for their first look at the hull. Castle had been attending a meeting in North Carolina of the Southern Governors' Association when the lift had been made and had heard of the recovery the following day on the morning news. "I was very disappointed not seeing the lift," he said in a joint press conference held with Davidson, as they viewed the lawn sprinklers dousing the contorted hull. As he fingered some of the more interesting artifacts, the governor's delight was obvious. "I'd love to have been there when they brought that up. I just thought it was one of the most exciting things to ever happen to Delaware."[47]

The governor's excitement was infectious. In a gesture of good will, Davidson publicly informed Castle, in all sincerity, that Delaware would get first choice of the artifacts recovered. Castle, ever the politician, but apparently unaware of Davidson's intention to rebury the hull, replied that the state and the salvors should work together to preserve the wreck entirely. He judiciously avoided the issue of just who would pay for or direct the expensive conservation effort. He conceded that it would be costly and declared with a wink that state officials would have to determine whether there was enough interest in the artifacts to warrant the expense of a *De Braak* museum. That state officials and Mayor Stango would like to display a sample of the 6,000 artifacts recovered thus far, and preferably in Lewes, was a given, however. "Any of these things may take money," cautioned the governor. "We're pretty tight with our dollars, and we'll try to make it pay off some way," possibly through charging admission.[48] (Davidson now quietly abandoned all thoughts of returning the hull to the sea.)

Castle was so thoroughly taken with the historic materials spread out before him that it came as no surprise when he warmly promised Davidson the state's continuing cooperation and assistance. For starters, Castle even agreed to help the salvors cut through the state's bureaucratic red tape so that a selection of artifacts could be taken to New York and displayed on the popular NBC *Today Show* and the CBS *Morning News*.[49]

The governor's message came across loud and clear to the state archaeologists and resource managers obliged to carry out the executive will. The salvors were now entirely in the driver's seat, and whatever they did would be officially fine with Delaware!

Mining *the* De Braak

In the days that followed the raising of *De Braak*, David Beard, Charles Fithian, Dean Nelson, and their colleagues worked frantically to clean, photograph, and record her damaged, distorted hull. Although actually only half a hull, or "ship on a half-shell," as one wag put it, since only the starboard side had been buried in the mud and protected from marine organisms, to the archaeologists groping on hands and knees along her muck-covered timbers, it was the very substance of history itself. For convenience of reference, the wreck was subdivided into five sections, each separated from the next by the riders attached to the ceiling planking. Incredibly, tons of *De Braak*'s iron ballast was found to be still concreted to the hull. A considerable amount of 24-pound shot was discovered still amidst the remains of the ship's shot locker, also concreted in place. Now even small items, such as peas, corn kernels, and coffee beans, which had miraculously survived 188 years of immersion, were being plucked from the grime.[1] The archaeologists' zeal in recording as much as possible as quickly as possible was not unwarranted, for on August 12 Kevin McCormick had publicly stated that once the excavation offshore was completed, Sub-Sal might be obliged to return the hull to the sea and cover it up until "future generations can find a better way to preserve it."[2]

L. John Davidson, however, preferred to focus his attention on preparing to recover the alleged treasure, which he was certain had somehow managed to elude discovery and still lay in the seabed. After all, hadn't Walter Zacharchuk, a bonafide archaeologist, said that it must have been under the hull all along? And if it wasn't, then it most certainly must have been part of the artifact-bearing glop and concreted matter which had slipped from the hull during the lift.[3]

Others were more skeptical about the likelihood of success. David Agatha, growing more cynical each day, suggested that unless a "cache of gold bullion or some other significant treasure store" were recovered soon, there would be no alternative but to call off the search. The lease on the crane was about to expire, and with expenditures surpassing two million dollars, the project seemed likely to close down.[4] One investor, Robert Steuk, saw the artifacts themselves as the only salvation. "The only sure way it [*De Braak*] pays is if we can come up with a good collection of artifacts that tells a story."[5] Such a collection could then be simply auctioned off to the highest bidder. If all else failed, the artifacts could at least be put on display and admission charged to see them, although it could take years to recoup expenditures by this means. Davidson, however, was more inclined to sell them off. "Somebody," he said, "would pay dearly for the ship's bell, the captain's ring." He even toyed with the idea of turning the tons of iron ballast into "handsome collector's items" by melting it down and recasting the metal in the shapes of various artifacts which had been recovered. These items could then be stamped with an official *De Braak* seal and sold. "What else do you do with ten tons of pig iron?" he asked.[6]

Unlike some members of his team, Davidson was still optimistic. Immediately after his joint press conference with Governor Castle, he had been elated to learn that the court battle with Worldwide Salvage had ended in Sub-Sal's favor. Harvey Harrington's lawyer had successfully argued that the discussions between his client and Peloso, LaPadula, and Calcione could not be considered as constituting an oral contract. Since the members of Worldwide had been unwilling to sign a contractual agreement or to provide financial support before the wreck was found, Harrington's lawyer argued, they had no claim to it afterwards. Indeed, since *De Braak* had actually been located approximately a third of a mile away from Wilson's coordinates, Worldwide had no case at all.[7]

On August 15, after a week-long jury trial presided over by Judge Wright, the jury of three men and three women had deliberated for five hours before finding that no partnership had ever been formed between Harvey Harrington and the members of Worldwide Salvage. Nor had Harrington located the wreck by means of Wilson's map, based on the McCracken data. It is not surprising that Davidson, who also wished to avoid any legal confrontations that might jeopardize his ownership of the ship and her artifacts, called the judgment "enlightened." Now, with the court fight over, he could concentrate entirely on the business at hand.[8]

After "the pick" was over, the weather, as predicted, had rapidly deteriorated as Hurricane Charley moved north. By the middle of the week, however, the hurricane had passed well out to sea, and on Saturday, August 16, diving operations resumed with an intensive scouring of the wreck site for materials which had slid off the hull during the recovery. Of particular interest was the large clump of concreted matter in which, it was believed, some of the treasure might be contained. But smaller items were also retrieved: porcelain, shoes, scores of broken barrel and key staves, an eight-foot section of tarred hawser, and a sword handle were soon recovered, raised in baskets, and added to the growing inventory of artifacts.[9]

On August 28, the mysterious conglomerate was finally recovered. When broken open, it was found to contain not treasure, but four tons of cast iron ballast and over 600 cannonballs. The mass had been created by ferrous oxides from the iron, which, when combined with natural sediments and calcareous concretions, had formed a nearly indestructible cement-like matrix. A reporter who questioned Beard about the mass was informed that it was anything but treasure. When the article appeared in a local newspaper, Davidson was livid and vowed that he "would kick [Beard's] ass" if he made any further comments to the press without clearance from Davidson. Although Beard was not employed by Sub-Sal, Davidson obviously believed that even state employees and contractors should come to heel at his command. When Kevin McCormick was questioned about the disappointing discovery, he answered evasively, "Being a business person, I planned the operation around there not being a treasure. . . . How can I be disappointed in more than 8,000 artifacts of historic value?"[10] But such profound disappointment could not be hidden.

As confidence in the existence of the treasure waned, criticism of the hull's botched salvage continued to mount. "Are the legends of fabulous treasure true?" asked the press. An editorial in the *New York Times* finally suggested what many in the archaeological community, including those who had been hired by the state, had felt all along: "The public interest would have been better served by leaving the wreck alone until it could be properly excavated by underwater archaeologists."[11] But such a conclusion had been reached too late, and Davidson, who was picking up the tab, proceeded with his plans, unperturbed by the censure. While his divers combed the seabed, Davidson brought in his latest weapon—an industrial sand and gravel separator. The device would be used to separate, as one local newspaper report put it, "muck and shell from artifacts and treasure" during the next phase of operations.[12] The plan was quite simple. Once the site had been cleared of large items by the divers, the crane, deploying a large clamshell bucket, would scoop up as much as 9,000 cubic yards of sediment from the seafloor about the wrecksite and deposit it on waiting barges for transport back to headquarters. During the first phase of retrieval, personnel stationed on the receiving barge would attempt to recover large or rare artifacts as soon as the bucketloads of sediments had been dumped. Once each barge was fully laden, it would be towed to the company pier at the fish-fertilizer plant. There it would be tied up to a second barge on which the gravel and sand separator was mounted.[13]

The separator had been leased from a neighboring rock quarry operation and cleverly converted by Zacharchuk to segregate artifacts from gravel, seashells, and sand. Employment of a manual screening method, as initially intended, would have permitted personnel to process only an estimated one and a half cubic yards of excavated materials per day. Zacharchuk's new device was, in Davidson's view a marked improvement. The earlier mechanism had been constructed of two four-by-ten-foot screening platforms covered with quarter-inch wire mesh. When the first bucket had deposited its load on one of the screens (on August 8, before "the pick"), the legs of the screen had buckled and sent personnel scrambling for safety as the clamshell caromed wildly about the deck.[14] But Zacharchuk's new method included modifying the gravel separator by the addition of a high-pressure sprinkler and a two-stage conveyor belt mounted aboard a grounded barge, affectionately dubbed "Devil's Island." After being deposited on the conveyor, the dredge spoils could be processed forty times faster than with the earlier system.[15] Indeed, the company's archaeologist claimed that between twenty and sixty cubic yards of sediment could be processed per hour. "It's not exactly archaeology," Zacharchuk said in one of the project's greatest understatements. "It's more like mining the *De Braak*."[16]

When the process began in earnest, Charles Fithian was astonished by the system. "It looked like a South American diamond mining operation," he later said. "The materials were being scooped up off the barge by a front end loader, of course after they had been driven around on for a while, and then dumped in a bin. Then all the stuff comes crashing down on the conveyor belt, breaking many fragile objects in the process."[17] As the materials were carried along the conveyor, Sub-Sal personnel would attempt to sort out artifacts before they reached the end of the belt. There the dross (plus any overlooked artifacts) were dumped in a pile for eventual redeposit in the sea. A complete cycle would take approximately two minutes, and the sorters quickly became exhausted by the demanding work. The process was an unforgiving one, for to miss an artifact could mean its loss forever.[18]

The screening-and-separation process began on August 20. Almost immediately artifacts of all kinds were plucked from the debris on the belt. Among the first items to appear were a unique monogrammed scrub brush with bristles still intact, copper sheathing nails by the hundreds, the bottom of a glass tumbler, bottle fragments, ceramic shards, pistol side plates, gunflints, lead shot, cannonballs, pig-iron ballast, a leather belt, and the jawbone of a young man "with nearly perfect and still sharp teeth." Davidson was particularly excited by the early recovery of an eight-escudo gold piece dated 1794 and bearing the portrait of Queen Maria I of Portugal, who had ruled from 1777 to 1816. But the coin proved not to be a promise of things to come, for over the next several weeks only one more gold escudo and two silver pillar dollars would be recovered.[19]

The present and future condition of what remained of the hull was of growing concern to state officials. On August 20, a meeting between state representatives and Sub-Sal was held to discuss the issue. The discussion revolved around the questions of what should be done with the hull, how much it would cost, and who would pay for it. McCormick had already publicly stated that it had yet to be determined whether the copper-sheathed hull could even be preserved at a "reasonable cost."[20] John Kern, of course, had let it be known that he, for one, had been terribly disappointed by the salvors' failure to follow the procedure that would have guaranteed a safe lift in the first place, but now that the hull was up, he was adamant about the need for making long-range plans to protect it. "The less time the ship's remains are above water," he had pointed out prior to the meeting, "the better."[21] No one bothered to mention that such plans might better have been made before the hull was raised in the first place.

Two days later, Delaware Secretary of State Michael E. Harkins, who administered, among other things, the Division of Historical and Cultural Affairs, personally met with the salvors to address again the issue of the hull's preservation and future. Two options were considered: return the hull to its saltwater environment, preferably somewhere close to shore; or excavate a large hole in the ground, line it with waterproof material, fill it with water, and immerse the hull in it until a comprehensive, long-range plan could be adopted.[22] There were disadvantages to both solutions, not to mention the short-term risks of simply moving the hull from its present berth to yet another new environment. Any further movement might inflict additional damage to its already fragile structural integrity. Placing it back in the sea would only prove a temporary expedient, for it would there be exposed to the destructive attack of marine biota unless the remains were completely reburied—a task almost as complex and costly as its recovery had been. Placing the remains in a containment system of fresh water, filtered and chemically treated to leach out the sea salts and inhibit fungal growth, would be the best plan, but that too could be costly.[23]

The long-term issue of preservation was one that neither side wished to explore too thoroughly, for, as Kern noted, preserving and restoring the hull would prove "very time-consuming and expensive." It had to be kept wet to prevent it from shrinking and from "flaking into wood splinters." Eventually, its frames and planks would have to be stabilized by being treated with expensive polyethylene glycol.[24] Again, the science of archaeology and the business of treasure hunting had become conflicting interests. Davidson, for one, was more interested in searching for loot than in stabilizing and preserving half of an ugly, mangled hull. He was a businessman, after all, and the partial remains of a damaged hull had absolutely no resale value. Few in the government seemed interested in allocating taxpayer money to an operation which could prove costly—especially since the state's share was only twenty-five percent of the goods—but the hull had become a responsibility that someone had to assume.

To his credit, Harkins bit the bullet and agreed to an expenditure of $10,000 to $15,000 to fund an immersion program immediately. A plan was quickly drawn up whereby the hull would be covered with a canvas shroud, beneath which a saltwater-spray system would keep the wood wet. The canvas would at once protect the hull from the elements and keep the moisture in. In the meantime, a search would be made for an appropriate location to which the hull could be transported and where long-term preservation work could begin. Once *De Braak* had been safely immersed in a specially built containment pool, the best mode of preservation could be determined. The plan stipulated, significantly, that the state would hold the title to the hull, which would not be considered part of Delaware's share of the wreck's hoard of artifacts. While the scheme eliminated the threat of Sub-Sal's interference with any actions that might be taken concerning the hull and gave the state full authority over it, the economic burden of caring for the hull now fell entirely upon Delaware.[25]

Relieved of all responsibility for preserving the hull—an ugly, unmarketable artifact if ever there was one—Davidson was happy to turn his attention to the dredging operation. His agenda for clam-bucket excavation of the wreck site was indeed ambitious. And as for financing the additional crane time needed, he would somehow find the money. But he was unhappy with the Cashman operations: By August 22 only five to seven truckloads of sediment had been recovered from the seabed for processing, ostensibly owing to poor weather as Hurricane Charley headed out to sea. But he was also dissatisfied with the company's performance, and there were of course, conflicts over money.[26]

On September 2, Davidson's dispute with Cashman came to a head when he filed a suit in U.S. District Court in Wilmington against the Weymouth Equipment Corporation, its subsidiary, the Sea Hunt Corporation, and Sea Hunt's president, James M. Cashman. The basis for Davidson's suit was that Sea Hunt, which had been paid $89,000 to provide equipment and salvage service and was promised another $25,000 upon completion of the project, as well as a three-percent interest in whatever was recovered, was supposed to have raised 2,500 cubic yards of sediments from the seabed, including the hull itself. Davidson charged, however, that the company had raised only 1,000 cubic yards, employed faulty equipment, damaged other gear used in lifting the hull, and then had abandoned the site before fulfilling its contractual obligations. Davidson claimed that Sea Hunt had thereby forfeited all rights to the final $25,000 payment and should pay damages to sub-Sal of $50,000, the amount paid a second contractor to finish the work.[27] (Davidson had, in fact, hired another contractor to complete the job, but he had also increased his overall goal, hoping to remove 250 truckloads of sediment over a period of only seven days. The recovered material, he calculated, would take a month to process and would no doubt yield the treasure he sought.[28]

By September, the sand-and-gravel screening operations had been moved ashore, with the sifting and sorting conducted in a sheltered building at the fish-fertilizer factory. This entailed the sediments being offloaded at a wharf in

Lewes and transported by truck to the warehouse before being processed. The processing work itself continued both day and night. Yet the results, for Davidson, were as disappointing as ever. Although a wide variety of artifacts was still being extracted by the screening operation, precious few of these were coins. What was worse, from the archaeologists' point of view, was that many of the artifacts which had been recovered intact were broken or otherwise damaged during their subsequent transfer.[29]

Even Davidson's optimism was sorely tested. He began to grow apprehensive that something might be overlooked during the dredging, and in October he dramatically increased the sediment-recovery volume again. Digging would now be carried out to a depth of fourteen feet in the area where *De Braak*'s stern had once lain and where numerous artifacts had been found. When this strategy failed to yield more treasure, he enlarged the excavation zone to include an area off the starboard side of the vessel's former site, where many coins had been found, to be dug to a depth of eight feet below the bottom. Again, the yield was minimal. Finally, Davidson doubled the overall dimensions of the dredging area, which by now was approximately the size of two football fields, but still without recovering any treasure.[30]

As the volume of sediment being brought up increased, work along the processing line continued without any letup, and some remarkable finds were made. In mid-October, for instance, one of the workers at the gravel screener plucked a wool-knit sailor's cap from the top of a pile of muck which had just been shoveled out of the machine's hopper. The floppy, round-crowned, wide-brimmed headpiece aroused only a temporary interest. Not until later, when it was identified as a Monmouth cap, a style quite popular among eighteenth-century seamen, was its significance recognized. Although the cap had been common in its time, only one other specimen from an archaeological dig, recovered during a waterfront excavation in New York, had ever been found.[31]

For some of the salvage team, the stress of the constant sorting was temporarily relieved on October 14, when they began the delicate task of moving the estimated fifty-five to sixty-five-ton *De Braak* hull to its new holding pond. A concrete-and-cinder-block containment area had been constructed near the company's headquarters at the fish fertilizer plant. The barge carrying the hull had to be brought up to the Lewes wharf, where *De Braak*'s battered remains would be transferred by crane to a state-owned military-surplus flatbed truck and transported to the plant. None of this proved to be easy.[32] To begin with, the stern had to be sawed off to prevent it from cracking and falling apart, owing to a major fault in the keel. Then two cranes, of fifty-ton and fifty-five-ton lifting capacity, respectively, were brought in and backed up to the pier where the barge was docked. The cable from the larger crane was fitted snugly around the hull's stern, while that of the lighter-capacity crane was rigged to the bow. The two machines proved totally inadequate for the job. A third crane, of thirty-five-ton capacity, was brought in, but could not effectively aid the first two. Due to the limited length of their booms and their lift mechanism, none of the cranes could be brought close enough to the barge docked at Roosevelt Inlet to be of any use. A reinforced dirt embankment had to be constructed to permit them access. Furthermore, the elevation of the barge itself posed a problem, so the work crews filled the barge's hold with water to sink it lower. But the available cranes still lacked the capacity to complete the job. The following day, two more powerful cranes, both with sixty-five-ton lifting capacities, were brought in, and finally, the hull was shifted from the barge to the truck.[33]

The procession through Lewes began, achieving a peak speed of six miles per hour. Davidson, McCormick and his wife, Carolyn, and several members of the salvage team, wearied by their round-the-clock ordeal, now rode upon the decks of *De Braak* for the last time, waving at astonished onlookers as the ship passed by in triumph. "We're sailing," quipped a delighted McCormick as the caravan passed beneath Lewes's lone traffic light at the intersection of Pilottown and Savannah roads. At Gills Neck Road, the motorcade was brought up short by the overhanging branches of a pair of trees. Then, with less than two inches to spare, the procession passed under.[34]

Upon reaching the containment, area, the hull was again lifted. A prefabricated wooden bed, its contours designed to provide the hull with support during the long stabilization and preservation process ahead, lay waiting in the empty pond. The hull was deposited in its bed with only inches of leeway to spare on its bow and stern ends.[35]

Despite these diversions, Davidson's attention continued to be absorbed by the search for the ever-elusive treasure—a search that was by now clearly fruitless. Frustrations were mounting. When two pillar dollars, which had evaded discovery and ended up in the pile of processed sediments, were found just before the mound was disposed of, Davidson ordered that the entire load be reprocessed. Salvage expenditures were approaching $70,000 per week, adding almost half a million dollars to the red side of the ledger. Davidson had been heard to quip, "There's going to be a limit to climbing the mountain to see the other side. We'll have to cut it off at some point;"[36] and by December, that point was finally reached. With financial support exhausted and winter coming on, he ordered the screening system dismantled and recovery operations cancelled until further notice.

Since completing "the pick," the salvors had dredged and screened more than 42,000 cubic yards of Delaware muck at a cost of a quarter of a million dollars to recover only a single pair of gold coins and seven pillar dollars. All told, over the long salvage effort approximately two and a half million dollars had been spent, according to company officials, on the recovery of only 650 gold and silver Spanish and Portuguese escudos and British guineas, pennies, and half-pennies—a bit of pocket change and, perhaps, a little booty from the captured Spanish prize. Approximately forty pieces of jewelry were recovered, including several rings, a black onyx and gold snuff box, pieces of a watch fob, and the back part of a pocket watch—again, little more than the personal possessions of a British crew of officers, seamen, and marines.

Unlike many others who had tried and failed to locate *De Braak*, the men of Sub-Sal and of Drew and Associates did succeed in recovering, in a most brutal fashion, the remains of one of America's most famous, historic shipwrecks, along with nearly 26,000 artifacts. But the legendary treasure was never found. Some maintained their faith even in the face of defeat. Davidson's belief in the existence of the fortune that never was could not be shaken. Somehow, he had been tricked, or perhaps he had erred, overlooking some important detail or failing to thoroughly excavate the right spots. Like many before him, he also vowed to return for another try. Perhaps next season. But it was never to be. Both the real *De Braak*, and the legend she inspired had been desecrated, drained, broken, and then all but demolished. The seabed surrounding her grave had been vacuumed clean. And in the wake of her resurrection there would be chaos, humiliation, recriminations, and a growing sense of dismay. Gradually, it began to dawn on America that a great national treasure—once a remarkable time capsule full of history—had been shattered for the sake of 650 coins. Davidson, who had committed a fortune to the effort, remained philosophical about the whole affair. "We have," he sighed in resignation, "produced far more for the public than had we left it alone."[37] Before the public would benefit, however, someone would have to pick up the pieces.

PART FOUR

When public and private interests conflict over limited resources, it is a fundamental function of government to safeguard the public interest.

Edward M. Miller, September 29, 1987

Mount Davidson

In October 1986, while John Davidson was still publicly expressing confidence that he would soon be striking the mother lode with his clam bucket, Kevin McCormick was optimistically estimating the value of the 650 coins recovered at between $500,000 and $600,000. Only another 1,500 to 1,800 coins, he predicted, would be needed for the project to break even. Despite the public show of confidence, however, it was clear to the inner circle of Drew and Associates that the effort was likely to end up a financial disaster and John Davidson, having personally accounted for sixty percent of the funding, would have taken the biggest hit of all. The issue of cost was becoming a sore point all around. By October 16, the State of Delaware, concerned over possible criticism of its handling of the affair, would publicly acknowledge an outlay of only $10,000 in state funds on the project, most of which had been paid to move the hull from the barge to the freshwater holding pond. The loss, unfortunately, was not only monetary.[1]

Despite the enormous price he had personally paid for his adventures, Davidson's public position on the disposition of the *De Braak* artifacts seemed upright. Time and again he was quoted by the press as gallantly promising to give the state a representative sample of the collection, even if the project failed to pay for itself. "We intend to give them," he vowed, "all the stuff it takes to make an interesting museum." What was rarely mentioned was that the state legally owned a quarter of the goods anyway.[2]

As early as September, while thousands of artifacts made their debut on Zacharchuk's industrial gravel separator, public attention had begun to focus more sharply on what their final disposition would be. Talk of building expensive museums filled the air. Governor Castle suggested that potential museum sites might include Cape Henlopen State Park, the grounds of the Cape May-Lewes Ferry Terminal, the Zwaanendael Museum, or even in a new library that the city of Dover hoped to build.[3] Such talk immediately provoked some jockeying for the right to exhibit any recovered treasure or artifacts. In nearby Georgetown, the first to stake its claim, even before the project had closed down, was the Delaware Technical and Community College. Under the leadership of its president, John R. Kotula, the college had already persuaded the owner of one major treasure ship collection to donate a reported $2,000,000 in gold and silver coins to the school for exhibit. In fact, Del Tech was already in the process of building an 1,800- to 2,000-square-foot display area in the college library, assisted by $30,000 in seed money provided by the State of Delaware, to house the collection. The donated artifacts had been recovered by treasure salvor Mel Fisher from the wreck of the famed *Nuestra Señora de Atocha* and allotted to his financial supporter, Georgetown businessman and former *De Braak* hunter Mel Joseph, as his share of the take.[4]

While awaiting transfer to the new facility, Joseph's collection had been temporarily stored in three safe-deposit boxes in the Mellon Bank in Georgetown. In the meantime Kotula, emboldened by the money that had already come from the state, aggressively lobbied for another million dollars in state aid with which to build an addition to the library in the hope that Joseph would donate more treasure—eight to nine million dollars' worth—to the building "museum." "Joseph can sell the stuff and make money," Kotula suggested, "but then he'd have to pay more taxes on it."[5] The college president publicly stated his opinion that the school had a good chance of getting as much as ten to twelve million dollars from the salvor if the state were to pay for the building. Acquiring the *De Braak* collection would add icing to the cake. "I think the library is the natural place for the museum," Kotula said about the *De Braak* artifacts. "I can see significant historical interest in the treasure. The library is centrally located for Sussex County and it's on the direct route to the beach."[6]

The race was on. In response to what appeared to be a substantial head start by Del Tech, Judith A. Roberts, president of the Lewes Historical Society, retorted that since *De Braak* had been discovered off Lewes, "it's Lewes's treasure." Mayor Stango was similarly vociferous: "I want the artifacts to stay here," he stated emphatically. Then Michael E. Harkins, Delaware's secretary of state, pointed out the obvious: "You're going to have a hard time getting the *De Braak* treasure out of Lewes and you're going to have a hard time doing something with the Del Tech treasure not connected with the school."[7] Nobody, of course, bothered to consult with Davidson.

Harkins, disturbed by reports about the potential deterioration of the artifacts themselves, was more concerned with their preservation than with where they might ultimately end up. On November 20, he presented a portion of his annual shopping list for the next fiscal year to the state budget director and Delaware's development office for review. His proposed "wish list" of $5.3 million included $570,000 for *De Braak*, $200,000 of which would be earmarked for expenses entailed by treating and otherwise stabilizing the artifacts. Looking ahead, Harkins estimated that construction costs for a museum suitable to house the ship and its artifacts, should one be built, could total as much as $3.2 million, but he clearly noted that the state had no plans to employ public funds for such an undertaking. To advocate such a commitment of taxpayers' hard-earned monies at a time when the condition and future disposition of the collection were both uncertain would have been political suicide. Instead, he began to promote the idea that foundation grants might be sought by private groups or that some wealthy individuals might be willing to build such a facility (in other words, let the private sector worry about the museum). Unfortunately, the secretary of state's budget request for funds to maintain and study the *De Braak* hull and artifacts would only be partially fulfilled and no wealthy benefactors would step in to pick up the rest of the tab.

In July 1987, Harkins revealed for the first time that Delaware had spent $115,000 to pay for the storage of the artifacts and the ship's hull at the Fischer Enterprises site and for a nautical archaeologist to assess and document the condition of the hull.[8] The announcement, fortunately, slipped by unnoticed, arousing little comment. By this time, the tenor of negotiations between the salvor and the state had begun to change. Having expended more than $2.5 million on that project, John Davidson, ever the businessman, now sought to minimize his financial losses. Since Delaware's twenty-five-percent share of profits, like the treasure itself, had failed to materialize, Davidson hoped to persuade the state that it would be to Delaware's advantage to accept a legal transfer of the entire artifact collection. "We're in sort of a holding pattern waiting for the state to decide on how we can work it out," he said in mid-July. "Our desire is to transfer the artifacts to the state and have them build a museum to accommodate them."[9] But there was more to Davidson's magnanimous gesture than devotion to the public weal, for he had discovered that under federal income tax laws he would have to pay a substantial amount in taxes if he made an outright donation of the artifact collection to the state. Therefore, Davidson was actually proposing to make a "wholesale cost transfer" to Delaware. It would be to his advantage to have the artifacts, or at least enough of them for a "first class museum," turned over to the state "at the least cost possible": that is, not what the project expenses had been, but what the transfer expenses might be. He could then write off the balance of his business losses as a tax deduction. Such a transfer, however, could prove to be very expensive for the state, which might have to pick up a tab of one to two million dollars. Harkins, sitting in the catbird seat, shrewdly claimed ignorance of the federal tax situation and the state's potential costs.[10]

In August, as Claudia Melson and Charles Fithian were desperately attempting (on an impossibly small budget) to stabilize and evaluate the enormous collection of artifacts at the Fischer warehouse, William J. Miller, Director of the Delaware River and Bay Authority, came to the rescue. With Harkin's support, the DRBA was able to provide a one-time grant of $75,000 to help with preservation and documentation, despite the artifacts' disposition still being in doubt. Although the money came at a critical moment, it was only a fraction of the amount needed to save much of the collection from its imminent deterioration. At the same time, Miller announced that the Authority's Cape May-Lewes Ferry Terminal grounds in Lewes, which had earlier been considered a potential site for the *De Braak* museum, was no longer a viable possibility. Plans already approved to expand the terminal would simply leave too little space for such a facility.[11]

The artifact collection, amassed over three seasons of unrestricted excavation on *De Braak*, was enormous. Well over 26,000 items had been recovered, almost all of them requiring immediate attention, namely, stabilization and documentation. The salvors, of course, had primarily focused on the more attractive artifacts, notably those found intact and deemed marketable. As a consequence, little corporate attention had been paid to the immense assemblage of imperfect, broken, disintegrating, or mundane items which comprised the bulk of the collection.

For Claudia Melson and Chuck Fithian, who were assigned to inventory, stabilize, and evaluate the collection as quickly as possible, one glance at the ground floor of the warehouse was enough to induce shudders. Two of the cinderblock holding tanks contained the warship's sixteen guns, stacked like cordwood. A third held over 400 iron ballast "pigs." Nearly a thousand pieces of cooperage were contained in two more tanks. A sixth containment area held scores of timbers, either ripped from the hull by the salvors at various stages of the operation or picked up elsewhere without their provenance having been recorded. A seventh tank, constructed to serve as added storage space, contained a heterogeneous collection of cabin window frames and windowpanes as well as shoes, brushes, and scores of miscellaneous items. At one end of the ground floor, adjacent to the tanks, lay a mound of dried concretion fragments that the salvors had intended, at some point, to break open by hand in search of overlooked treasures.

In several anterooms, which Melson kept locked, children's water-filled wading pools overflowed with shoes, textiles, copper drift pins, sheaves, case shots, pistol and musket stocks, side plates and trigger guards, octants and other navigational instruments, the ship's copper rudder chain, surgeon's tools, leather fragments, buttons, nuts, bolts, screws, combs, toothbrushes, razor cases, and myriad other item. In the corner of one of the anterooms lay a large laundry tub filled with over 400 cannonballs. Beside it sat a bucket full of lead bullets and grapeshot. Nearby stood several water-filled plastic garbage cans stuffed with hundreds of sheaves, blocks, and deadeyes. A third anteroom, furnished with a single table, a light, a space heater, and a wall of shelves overflowing with stacked artifacts, functioned as Fithian and Melson's "headquarters." In one corner sat a waist-high, fifty-gallon, earthenware water jar.

On a shelf beside it lay the ship's bell, with "La Patrocle" clearly engraved upon its surface, as well as boxes of ceramic and glass fragments, hinges, drawer pulls, pipe stems, unbroken bottles, and other odds and ends.

Outside and directly to the south of the warehouse was a formidable pile of spoil; the muck dredged up from the burial site of De Braak. The archaeologists called the mound "Mount Davidson" in ironic honor of the salvor who had built it—and who still maintained that overlooked treasure might be buried somewhere within it.

The inventory was daunting, especially given the unrelenting pressure on the archaeologists to complete the job before the salvors disposed of the collection. In August, immediately after "the pick" occurred, Chuck Fithian had been charged with doing just that. "Basically," he explained,

> my boss assigned me to the task of trying to document the De Braak hull and its associated collection—which was too large a task for anyone to do in the apparently brief time we thought we had. So what we attempted to do was to put together a top-level team of archaeologists and other scientists, culture material specialists, and historians who had expertise in critical areas of the collection that we needed to examine.[12]

Fithian set out to recruit the team himself, armed with only the DRBA grant. By October, he had secured the services of a footware specialist, D. A. Saguto, a professional historical cordwainer who constructed exact reproductions of shoes for museums, living-history organizations, and archaeological studies. Cheryl Holt, an archaeo-botanist from Alexandria, Virginia, was hired to analyze the hundreds of items of flora recovered from the wreck, primarily such footstuffs as beans, peas, and corn. Dr. Henry Miller, Director of Archaeology at historic St. Mary's City, Maryland, who specialized in faunal analysis, took on the task of evaluating bone materials.

The macroscopic and microscopic analysis of the many varieties of wood samples collected was to be conducted by art conservator and wood specialist Harry Alden, of the Henry Francis Du Pont Winterthur Museum. Ross Wilson, Keeper of Uniforms and Insignia for the Canadian War Museum, was contacted for data pertaining to the materials of the Royal Marine uniforms salvaged from De Braak. Kerry Shackleford, a journeyman cooper, and a specialist in historical cooperage analysis with the Colonial Williamsburg Foundation, and a consultant to the Yorktown Shipwreck Project, was asked to evaluate the ship's barrel staves as well as navigational instruments and other items. The task of analyzing the formidable collection of bottles and table glass was assigned to Wade Catts, Colleen Desantis, and Scott C. Watson of the University of Delaware, while the ceramics would be analyzed by Alice H. Guerrant, of the Delaware Division of Historical and Cultural Affairs. The architectural study of the key components of the hull itself fell to David Beard, the

the state consultant with more hands-on knowledge than anyone else of the single largest artifact. Documentation of the standing and running rigging was taken on by Fred Hopkins, Jr., Graduate Dean of the University of Baltimore, and myself. Fithian reserved the onerous task of analyzing armaments, both large and small, for himself.[13]

Although few of the researchers could have foreseen it, Fithian's emergency program for the documentation and analysis of the *De Braak* collection would last for not just a few weeks, but would continue for months and, in several cases, years. Without the brash showmanship exhibited by the salvors during the previous three years, little media attention would be drawn to the diligent efforts of the research team. Fortunately, Davidson had also temporarily withdrawn his attention from the project to attend to serious financial problems elsewhere, thus allowing the researchers some time to conduct their work. They would do so, however, with precious little support from the professional archaeological community. For after the botched recovery, and with the 20/20 vision of hindsight, many archaeologists had taken a foursquare position against the salvage operations and Delaware's decision to permit them in the first place.

John Davidson, despite all evidence to the contrary, continued to believe in the *De Braak* treasure. By December 1988, still toying with the idea of resuming a search for the elusive hoard of gold, he had resolved to hold on to his salvage permit for at least another year. "We don't think we did as thorough a job as might have been done," he informed the *Philadelphia Inquirer* during a long telephone interview from his home in New Hampshire.[14] His gold fever had proved to be incurable.

For those involved in the stabilization, conservation, and inventory process, the thought of more salvage work was a nightmare. Thousands of items in the collection were literally falling apart from lack of appropriate attention. By early 1989, a retinue of consultants had been taken on to assess the collections, but there were still no full-time personnel attached to the project. Both Fithian and Melson, who had been casually assigned to do the impossible, were being directed to attend to other pressing matters which had been ignored because of the *De Braak* crisis. They could no longer devote their expertise exclusively to the collection, but had to spend whatever time they could spare on assisting the various consultants. As a result, thousands of wooden objects, which had survived for nearly two centuries beneath the Delaware mud, now grew soggy and discolored, some even beginning to disintegrate. The leather shoe collection, the largest and finest of its kind in the world, was gradually turning to mush. Block and tackle, which had been recovered in some quantity, became soft and pliable in the free-water baths and began to lose their form and shape. Thousands of artifacts made of animal, vegetable, or mineral material were falling apart at a disheartening rate despite Melson's remedial attentions. Others simply disappeared.

The problem was simple: Delaware could not and would not allocate more funds for the costly conservation equipment, facilities, and personnel needed to preserve a collection of artifacts whose future disposition was unknown. As the state and John Davidson wrangled interminably over the collection, Fithian grew understandably perplexed. "We've done our best to stabilize the artifacts, but degradation is inevitable," he said. Michael Foster, who had believed that there would never be any profits derived from the artifacts in the first place, put the whole situation in a somewhat cynical, but nevertheless realistic, perspective: "If a fortune had been found, this thing would be moving along."[15]

By December, the situation had progressed from bad to worse: the Fischer Enterprises property, where the artifacts were being stored, had been sold to a real-estate developer. Although the developer refrained from setting a deadline for the state to vacate the premises, the need to resolve the issue of the artifacts' final disposition had become even more urgent.[16] Davidson and the Secretary of State were finally stirred to action, but without a mutually agreed upon valuation of the collection no progress could be made, by either side. The first move was obvious. The artifacts would have to be appraised by a qualified expert. Both sides concurred on sharing the cost of the appraisal. The state promptly proposed the names of three appraisers, and Davidson submitted two of his own. Agreement seemed close at hand.[17]

In the meantime, the question of what to do with the collection and, ultimately, how to divide it remained. How many actual artifacts would the state have to deal with? Michael Foster declared that if the collection was small, it might be housed and exhibited in the Zwaanendael Museum; if it was large and included the hull, however, a separate building would have to be constructed. (The state had, in fact, already begun to explore the possibility of of purchasing or leasing several pieces of private property in the Lewes area.) In any case, one thing was certain: whatever the solution might be, it was going to cost money.[18] Davidson continued to express his wish to simply transfer the entire collection to the state, which would then pick up the federal tax tab. Jeffrey D. Lewis, an executive assistant in the Delaware Department of State, voiced the state's official line: "I don't think it's the state's position to get into [Davidson's] tax situation."[19]

The prolonged wrangling was frustrating to the handful of professionals charged with cleaning up the mess left by the salvors. As long as bureaucrats continued to argue with Davidson over the legalities of who would do what, neither side was willing to address the sad condition of the collection. The consultants had thus come to focus their work on documentation rather than stabilization. Fithian grew more uneasy with every passing day. "As far as I am concerned, the collection is priceless," he declared. "The De Braak is part of the history of the people of Delaware, and you can't put a price on that."[20] The diligent work being done by Fithian and his colleagues gradually began to earn the sympathy and praise of their peers in the archaeological and historic-preservation communities, even as the bumbling of state officials further aroused their ire. Unfortunately, the irreversible damage done to the artifacts was growing worse by the week. James Delgado, Chief Maritime Historian for the National Park Service, while praising the archaeologists' efforts, summed up the situation concisely: "What these folks are trying to do is conserve one-third of a one-of-a-kind book of which two-thirds of the pages were torn out and muddied and many of them were burned. No matter what . . . there is no way the entire story of *De Braak* can be told."[21] John Davidson responded to the comment gruffly: "Sitting under the sand and continuing to rot is not the answer."[22]

Meanwhile work on documenting the hull continued unabated and with little public notice. In November 1988, at my instigation and with the support of Chuck Fithian and the Delaware Bureau of Museums and Historic Sites, an effort was launched to survey the submerged hull of *De Braak* in minute detail using a revolutionary technology. Specifically, the survey technology we hoped to employ was called the Sonic High Accuracy Ranging and Positioning System (SHARPS). This new system had only recently been developed by Martin and Peter Wilcox of the Applied Sonics Corporation, at the suggestion of Dr. Donald Frey of the Institute of Nautical Archaeology, for use on archaeological targets in the Mediterranean. Its primary purpose was to solve the problem of performing accurate measurement under water with an ultrasonic device similar to, but improving upon, existing underwater navigation systems. Working on the principle that very brief high-frequency ultrasonic pulses can be sent through relatively large distances of the water column, the Wilcoxes reasoned that they could set up a "net" of ultrasonic transceivers mounted around a submerged site and connected by cables to a power source and a computer topside. A diver would then carry a portable transceiver to be used as an electronic "pen." With the pen the diver could literally outline objects or selectively pinpoint and record the positions of discrete targets underwater. The pen's brief ultrasonic pulses would be received by the various transceivers at times corresponding to their relative distance, from the point of origin. Each transceiver would send a "pulse received" signal up a central cable to a computer, which would gather the distance data, determine the ranges, make the necessary triangulation calculations, and then display the resulting position points on a video monitor. With each point's XYZ coordinate recorded and simultaneously displayed, the sequential recordings could then be linked together to form a picture, the isometrics of three-dimensional features produced, and so forth. Up to ten pulses per second could be sent through the water column and recorded, either automatically or at the discretion of the pen "manager," that is, the diver or his surface control.

A prototype system, with software designed by Dennis Hahn and Dr. Glen Williams, had already been successfully field-tested by John Broadwater in a sheltered cofferdam environment surrounding a shipwreck site at Yorktown. Soon afterwards, through the generous support of the National Geographic Society, the Maryland Geological Survey, the National Oceanic and Atmospheric Administration, the University of Baltimore, the Woods Hole Oceanographic Institute, the Applied Sonics Corporation, and the U.S. Navy, I had the unique privilege of administering the first field tests of the system in an open-water environment. These tests had been conducted, with varying degrees of success, in February 1987 on the wreck of the steamboat *New Jersey*, lost in Chesapeake Bay in 1870, and on two nineteenth-century schooner wrecks, *Henrietta Bach* and *Dashaway*, in Maryland's Patuxent River. At one site, the *Henrietta Bach*, we had been able to accurately survey the bones of a 66.5-foot wreck in shallow water in a remarkably brief period of only fifty-five minutes, gathering a total of 1,038 points of reference, with precise XYZ coordinates for each point. Using traditional means, it would have taken weeks to assemble so much data.

It thus became our hope that the *De Braak* hull, leaching in its shallow bath of fresh water, could be just as effectively and rapidly surveyed as the *Bach* had been and that the data would provide David Beard with a significant corpus of new information to add to his own in-depth studies. Vital to the success of the experiment was Emory Kristof, a professional photographer with *National Geographic*, who was one of the leaders in the field of remote underwater exploration and a pioneer in modern deep-water photography. A big man, well over six feet tall, whose thick coal-black beard and piercing eyes were reminiscent of Blackbeard the pirate, Kristof had photographed the depths of the world's oceans, from the Galapagos Rift Valley of the far Pacific to the frozen waters of the Arctic. I had worked closely with him on several expeditions, including the 1987 field-testing of the SHARPS in the Chesapeake, and now found him more than willing to field-test the *Geographic*'s own new SHARPS unit for the first time within the controlled environment of the *De Braak* cofferdam.

Our survey team consisted of Kristof, Michael Cole, Keith Moorehead, and Joseph Stancampiano, all from *National Geographic*; Chuck Fithian and Claudia Melson from the Delaware Bureau of Museums and Historic Sites; and my own research group, which included Dr. Fred Hopkins, photographer Nicholas Freda, and diver John Brewer. On November 21, 1988, a frigid, clear day, all of us assembled for the first time on the Fischer Enterprise grounds. A systematic survey plan was laid out, based on our experiences in the Chesapeake, and then three SHARPS transceivers were deployed and tested around the interior edges of the cofferdam. Our primary objective would be to electronically trace and record literally every seam, timber, rider, and futtock exposed on the upper side of the hull and to document the precise location of every nail, spike, drift pin, and trunnel that penetrated it. After we were through, we hoped to produce an accurate, rotatable, wire model based on

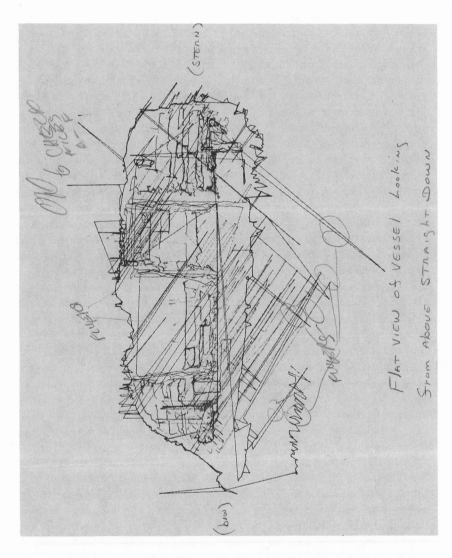

The preliminary hull feature plan, unedited, generated from the SHARPS survey of the *De Braak* hull. (*University of Baltimore*)

the computerized image of the area surveyed. Several months later, after the data had been processed and evaluated, the water would be temporarily drained from the cofferdam. A comprehensive photographic record of the survey area would then be made and a photomontage of the entire wreck produced. Once this material had been processed and digitized, we hoped to be able to put photographic flesh on a three-dimensional computerized model and to use it in future study, interpretation, and conservation planning—possibly even reconstruction. (If it worked within the confines of the *De Braak* cofferdam on a bona fide shipwreck, there was no reason why such a procedure could not work with a wreck site in open water as well. Perhaps a faster, cheaper, and more efficient methodology for surveying all aspects of underwater archaeological sites would be the result.

De Braak had been many things to many people. Now, for the first time, she would serve as a guinea pig for science. During the next two days, diver John Brewer and I, with surface support provided by Kristof and company, would become as intimately familiar with *De Braak*'s hull as Beard or any of the salvors had ever been. In the process, we would collect nearly half a million electronically generated data points while mapping and recording measurements of every feature on every square inch of the hull. The computerized data would later be processed and synthesized into appropriate graphic forms by the University of Baltimore's Academic Computer Center.

The process, not surprisingly, proved to be even more of a learning experience than we expected. Too late, we found that our system of repetitive mapping had been far too efficient. More than a quarter of a million XYZ reference points had been duplicated and had to be laboriously removed from the various computer files assembled during the survey, one by one. Numerous "flyers," or technical glitches that had slipped into our computer files required endless hours of editing and correcting by the university's resident computer expert. Our project design, we gradually realized, had been far too grandiose for our limited resources, and the end product was less than we had hoped for. The effort had, in fact, only partly succeeded in generating new data, more as a result of our flawed methodology than of any limitations on the stunning new technological tool for underwater survey being tested. Next time, we vowed, a better project design would be employed. Unfortunately, we would get no second chance. The expensive technology and talent, generously loaned to us by the *National Geographic* and the University of Baltimore, had been a one-time donation.

And all the while, a swirl of events had continued to cloud the future of *De Braak* and its myriad artifacts. In early 1989, L. John Davidson and the State of Delaware, after nearly two years of sporadic negotiating, finally reached at least one agreement: the well-known New York firm of Christie's Appraisals, Inc., would conduct the all-important valuation of the *De Braak* collection.

Christie's had an impeccable reputation, and its experts had acquired a considerable degree of experience in the course of appraising and selling recovered treasures and artifacts from such wrecks as the *Neustra Señora de Atocha* (1622), the *Santa Margarita* (1622), HMS *Feversham* (1711), HMS *Invincible* (1758), and a Dutch East Indiaman (ca. 1645), among others. *De Braak* would be in good company—and in good hands.

On Wednesday, March 16, three well-dressed appraisers from Christie's arrived at the vaults of the Mellon Bank in Lewes, where a cleaned selection of the most marketable artifacts, particularly the coins and jewelry, had been stored. The appraisers were Anthony M. Phillips, a specialist in silver and Renaissance jewelry; James Lamb, an expert numismatist and an assistant to the vice president of Christie's; and J. Brian Cole, an authority on armaments and ceramics. With Fithian and Melson present to answer any questions, the team set to work.

Lamb shed his jacket, rolled up his sleeves, and began to assess the 650 coins. He was impressed—at first.[23] "These are remarkably well-preserved," he said out loud, to no one in particular. Studying one bright coin, he noted: "This Lima gold piece still has its mint luster on it—never been used."[24] Luster, however, was one thing; rarity was quite another: almost none of the coins was uncommon for the period, and examples of most could be found in any good coin shop.

While Lamb was examining the coin collection, Phillips and Cole had begun to pass back and forth the famous Drew mourning ring, the authenticity of which had been questioned on several occasions. Phillips studied the piece through his jeweler's loupe, puzzling over something. It seemed odd that the ring was adjustable, a most uncommon feature in eighteenth-century bands. Eyeing the piece closely, Phillips speculated that the top might have held a panel for a lock of hair. He then delivered his verdict: "I think it's absolutely right."[25]

Later, the trio would visit the dank Fischer warehouse, where many of the less impressive artifacts were still housed. Looking rather overdressed there, they nevertheless began to poke through the dirty collection. The assessment was conducted over several days, but the entire collection, it was rumored, would not be appraised—only a "hit list" approved by Davidson. Even then, it would be three months before Christie's revealed the final estimate. On June 7, J. Brian Cole informed Kevin McCormick that those artifacts from *De Braak* which had been appraised were valued at $298,265, far less than the $500,000 to $600,000 estimated (for the coins alone) by McCormick. (The estimate did not include either the small collection of coins secretly recovered by Harrington in 1984 and still held in a Boston bank vault as collateral on his loan or the remains of the hull.) The appraisers had little experience in valuing some of the artifacts, most notably the largest of them all, the ship itself. They did, however, suggest that the hull might be worth as much as $50,000—if a buyer who wanted it could be found.[26]

Having failed to negotiate a direct transfer of artifacts to the state in a deal that would have been advantageous to himself, if not to Delaware, Davidson began to consider an outright sale. He was not pleased with Christie's appraisal. A spokesman for Sub-Sal claimed that the estimate did not reflect the full value of the collection. With Delaware still engaged in negotiations with the disgruntled salvor, Jeffrey Lewis, of the Department of State, sought to soften the blow, noting that the artifacts might indeed be worth more if they could be properly documented and marketed.[27] To do so, of course, would take money and time, both of which, in view of the deteriorating conditions of the collection, were in terribly short supply. Since an appraisal had finally been carried out, however, the long-overdue determination of the collection's disposition could now be made. Lewis informed the press that the state's archaeologists who had acted as conservators of the artifacts and had studied them, compiling a chronicle of eighteenth-century Royal Navy life, "now [planned] to place a dollar value on their historical and conservation efforts. We would like the entire collection."[28]

By this time, however, Davidson had put his own price on the collection (a far higher one than the appraisers'), but neither he nor the State of Delaware was prepared to publicly reveal the amount demanded. To do so, it was felt, might adversely affect the delicate negotiations. If and when any distribution of artifacts was made, it could only be done with the approval of the U.S. District Court in Wilmington, which, under Admiralty law, had jurisdiction over the site and everything recovered from it.[29]

As negotiations sputtered along, the Bureau of Museums and Historic Sites did its level best to head off mounting criticism of the manner in which Delaware had handled the *De Braak* affair. It was an unenviable task. Indeed, the whole issue of the "legalized looting" of shipwrecks, as historic preservationists called it, under the umbrella of Admiralty law, was already the target of intense attacks by professional archaeologists and anthropologists across the nation. The conflict between salvors and historic preservationists, in fact, had long been a familiar one in the chambers of Congress, where the issue had come up for debate almost annually since 1983. Now *De Braak* and, consequently, Delaware were likely to be made the focus of embarrassing national attention by historic preservationists on that most brightly lit stage—the floor of Congress.

At issue was not simply a small state's mismanagement or its simply having surrendered a historically important archaeological resource to a commercial enterprise. The problem was far more complex than that. At issue was the very capacity of a nation in its entirety and across its different regions to preserve or to abandon the physical remains of its own maritime past. *De Braak* had become a symbol of that issue.

Professor Richard A. Gould, of Brown University, in a scathing attack on treasure-wreck hunting in general, aptly observed that the United States might

"well be the only country left in the world where individuals and private companies can legally go out and loot shipwrecks." Moreover, he was extremely
critical of the national mindset which lionized treasure hunters whose success
was derived from the destruction of the nation's historic-resource base, and he
said as much as editor of a groundbreaking work on the theory and practice
of marine archaeology and anthropology entitled *Shipwreck Anthropology*.
"There is," Gould observed,

> a spurious romance about treasure hunting that garners far more public support
> than this activity is entitled to. Some of the worst offenders have been recently
> portrayed in heroic fashion by the media, without the opportunity for "equal
> time" by professional archaeologists and shipwreck historians.[30]

Daniel Lenihan, a nationally respected marine archaeologist and director of
the National Park Service Submerged Cultural Resources Unit, extended the
criticism even further to include the administrative policymakers of the states
themselves. "Unfortunately," he wrote, in a critical statement that might have
been levelled specifically against Delaware had it not been written before the
discovery of *De Braak*, "state administrations have too often been proven to
see wrecks much in the way that treasure hunters do—as just another economic resource in the unharvested sea."[31] Lenihan's colleague, marine archaeologist Larry Murphy, added even further fuel to the fire by observing that
shipwrecks "have become popular as mines in historic relics and as fodder for
the investment schemes of the modern-day treasure salvor."[32]

Although all of these criticisms had been published in 1983, at about the
time when Harvey Harrington was seeking support for his efforts on the Delaware, each one was also pertinent to *De Braak*, that is, to the salvors who had
all but destroyed her and to the state bureaucracy which had permitted the
destruction of a major archaeological resource. Now, it would be up to the
Bureau of Museums and Historic Sites to rectify the matter and put the best
face on an otherwise embarrassing affair. As before, the nearly impossible task
was dumped in the laps of Charles Fithian and Claudia Melson, aided by their
capable colleagues.

The bureau's approach was refreshingly candid, allowing the events to
speak for themselves. To its credit, the agency moved swiftly to air the whole
story publicly—and before the professional archaeological community.
Fithian and Melson, in collaboration with Curator of Exhibits Dominique
Coulet, artist Peggy Keene, and the rest of the bureau's staff, organized a full-
blown exhibition (and on a shoestring budget) at the Zwaanendael Museum.
The story of *De Braak*, her artifacts, and many of the findings made by
Fithian's tiny corps of specialists, were revealed to the public for the first time.
It was an impressive display. Even though the methods by which the recovery
of the wreck and its myriad components had been accomplished were brutal,

the artifacts themselves formed one of the most exhibit-worthy collections ever excavated from an eighteenth-century man-of-war. The exhibit mounted by Fithian, Melson, and their colleagues put no pretensions on display, only the truth.

On the evening of October 2, 1989, after weeks of preparation, a preview showing and reception was held at the museum for all those who had worked to document and preserve the collection. Through panel displays, diagrams, photographs, and many of the artifacts themselves, the story of *De Braak* was accurately told for the first time in its long history. Neither L. John Davidson nor Harvey Harrington was present at the preview. The news media all but ignored the event. Soon afterwards, the exhibition was formally and officially opened. A ribbon, hung across the front entrance to the museum, was cut by Tiddo Hofstee, of the Royal Netherlands Embassy in Washington, assisted by Lewes Mayor Al Stango and Delaware Secretary of State Michael Harkins. John Davidson basked in the glow of hearing such luminaries as naturalist-artist Roger Tory Peterson and others comment excitedly on the wonder of it all. Commemorative words were spoken by former Delaware Governor Russell Peterson.

L. John Davidson was pleased. Secretary of State Harkins was pleased. Governor Castle was pleased. Harvey Harrington was unavailable for comment. *De Braak*, it seemed, would live on after all. Her legacy, however, was not to be what everyone expected.

Bulldozed Gettysburg

The interminable negotiations over the disposition of the *De Braak* artifacts were largely ignored by the national media. As news, the dazzling finds which had momentarily captured the public's imagination in the summer of 1986 proved to be as shortlived as sound bites on the evening news. The excitement was gradually replaced by a growing realization of the magnitude of what had been lost during the archaeological fiasco on the Delaware. The legend of *De Braak* was being brutally laid to rest, it seemed to some, in exchange for some ill-defined tax dodge for the salvor. Her legacy had yet to be addressed.

In the process of being transmogrified from fabled treasure ship to a twisted heap of sticks, *De Braak* had become a symbol of sorts and a rallying point for historic preservationists across the land. Like *Atocha* and *Whydah*, her excavation and recovery for commercial profit had gained her a form of negative immortality; she became an example of how things ought not to be done. Yet the conflict between Davidson and the State of Delaware paled in comparison to the impact the wreck would soon have on the national scene, specifically in the United States Congress, where a battle had been raging for five years between historic preservationists and the commercial treasure-salvage industry.

At issue was the basic premise of admiralty law, which allowed commercial fortune hunters and treasure salvors, such as Sub-Sal, Inc., the right to excavate and salvage historic shipwreck sites in state and federal waters specifically to recover gold, silver, and other marketable commodities for profit. The heavy-handed manner in which *De Braak* had been excavated and raised (as permitted under admiralty law) and the salvors' subsequent use of the clam-bucket method to salvage her remains, had been brutal enough to deserve and receive national disdain. The destruction and loss of historic sites in the course of such undertakings was not, many began to feel, in the best interest of the public or of historic preservation, the salvors claims notwithstanding.

Even the *New York Times*, which in the past had monitored and occasionally lauded the efforts of such salvors as Pancoast, Chapman, and Colstad, now felt obliged to offer opinion pieces on the ravages of commercial treasure salvage. In an editorial provoked by the botched recovery of *De Braak*'s hull and the ongoing controversy over the *Whydah* and *Atocha*, the *Times* voiced considerable indignation.

> How to stop the destruction of historic wrecks is a question of increasing urgency. Finds like the Spanish galleon *Atocha* off Key West and the pirate ship *Whydah* off Cape Cod have whetted treasure hunters' appetites. Techniques like side-scan sonar have made wrecks easier to locate.
>
> But salvagers usually lack money to excavate wrecks with the care appropriate to archaeological sites. The goal is to strip them of precious objects quickly. The loot is dispersed, the historical information in the wreck is abandoned, and another irreplaceable time capsule is destroyed.
>
> Archaeological sites on land are already protected; why not those on the seabed? It's hard to devise a formula that rewards the salvor's necessary role in locating and working on a wreck while safeguarding the public's interest in a thorough excavation. Finding and retrieving wrecks is expensive. Melvin Fisher spent 25 years and $7 million in search of *Atocha*. Without the salvors, many wrecks would never be discovered. But once wrecks are found, state governments need a firmer say about excavation.
>
> Many states, like Delaware, protect a salvage's find from other salvors in return for a share—often 25 percent—of whatever is brought up. But since the state usually contributes little money to the expensive underwater operations, it is the salvor who calls the tune, often a rough one.[1]

In light of this growing concern for some means of protecting archaeologically important, historic shipwreck sites, the *De Braak* recovery could not have come at a better time. Since 1983, proponents of legislation designed to protect and manage such sites had been working hard, building on a base of important precedents that had been set at both the national and state levels. Their efforts followed in the footsteps of such landmark legislation as the Federal Antiquities Act of 1906 (the nation's first historic preservation law), the Historic Sites and Buildings Act of 1935, the National Historic Preservation Act of 1966, and the Archaeological Resources Protection Act of 1979.

As with many other preservation efforts, the conflict over historic shipwrecks had a long, tortuous history, with each episode laying the groundwork for the next. The first major skirmish erupted in 1965 when the remains of the 1715 Spanish Plate Fleet were discovered in Florida waters by a retired contractor named Kip Wagner. The find, given worldwide publicity in the pages of *National Geographic*, set off a veritable gold rush to the Florida coast, but it also had the more positive effect of stirring up concern in Florida over the need to protect the state's underwater cultural resources. The consequence was the enactment of the Florida Archives and History Act in 1976, by which ownership of all shipwrecks resting on or in submerged lands was vested in the State of Florida. Like similar laws enacted by many other states, Florida's Archives and History Act would not go unchallenged.

The fundamental issue, in what would become a Gordian knot of public, private, and commercial interests, was who had the power to make decisions concerning a resource: in this case, historic shipwrecks buried on or in a state's submerged lands. As Anne G. Giesecke, Legislative Director for the Underwater Society of America and a leading architect of federal shipwreck legislation, would later write:

> The public interest of the federal court under the admiralty system is to return goods to commerce and the interest of the states is multi-use resource management. As part of the public interest to be considered by the governing group are the interests of archaeologists, sport divers, and treasure salvors. Archaeologists see some shipwrecks as bits of history, sport divers see opportunities for recreation, and treasure salvors see monetary gain.[2]

Conflict was inevitable.

In June 1971, Melvin Fisher's Florida-based salvage company, Treasure Salvors, Inc., made the first dramatic recovery of gold artifacts from the wreck of *Nuestra Señora de Atocha*, nine miles off the Florida Keys. Florida granted Fisher a permit, similar to those granted to many *De Braak* hunters, giving Treasure Salvors, Inc., the exclusive right to search for and salvage the *Atocha*, with the state retaining rights to twenty-five percent of any profits realized. Between 1971 and 1975, artifacts worth approximately $6,000,000 were salvaged from the wreck. Then, in 1975, a long and complex series of legal disputes arose between the federal government and the State of Florida regarding jurisdictional authority over the site, sovereign prerogatives, and, most important, the validity of admiralty law. Fisher immediately instituted an action, under admiralty law, to "arrest" the wreck. The widely publicized dispute was finally resolved by the Supreme Court, which ruled in the federal government's favor (and, therefore, in Fisher's). The salvor's title to and possession of *Atocha*, under the accepted precepts and principles of the admiralty action taken by him, were affirmed.[3] Despite the protests made by outraged historic preservationists, Fisher's salvage rights were later reaffirmed in another case initiated by a rival salvor seeking to conduct his own recovery operations on the *Atocha*. As a consequence, salvage law and the salvors' rights to property abandoned at sea, including property from historic shipwrecks, were upheld. The principle that the finder of an historic shipwreck could legitimize the find by filing an *in rem* action in federal admiralty court was held to be legally valid.

Fisher's aggressive legal efforts further inflamed the conflict between historic preservationists and treasure hunters. The commercial treasure-salvage community claimed the right to invest their own money in searching for and salvaging sunken treasure ships for profit. Preservationists declared that such undertakings usually resulted in the destruction of historic and archaeologically valuable shipwreck sites. For the preservationists, it was an uphill battle.

In 1978, another one of Fisher's companies, Cobb Coin, Inc., sought to explore for and excavate treasures from the 1715 Spanish Plate Fleet within the three-mile limit of Florida's coast. After finding artifacts thought to be from one of the 1715 galleons, the company filed a petition in federal court seeking either to be declared owner in possession of the wreck or to be compensated for salvage services rendered to the vessel on behalf of the federal government. Florida intervened and filed a counterclaim to the site, seeking restitution of the artifacts recovered by Cobb Coin under the provisions of the Florida Archives and History Act. After an extended court fight, Cobb Coin's exclusive salvage rights to the wreck were affirmed. It was a landmark decision. Florida's Archives and History Act and its attendant regulations, the court ruled, conflicted with the basic principles of federal maritime law and violated the Supremacy Clause of the United States Constitution.[5] As Giesecke would later note: "The court's opinion gives a clear indication that where a state regulation of historic shipwreck resources conflicts with federal principles of admiralty and maritime law, the statute will be struck down as unconstitutional."[6] The impact of the Treasure Salvors and Cobb Coin cases upon the historic-preservation movement was devastating. "Because most antiquities laws (of those states that have them) are patterned after the Florida Archives and History Act," Giesecke observed in a 1983 review of the controversy, "in that they assert ownership by the state to all underwater cultural resources and utilize a permit system coupled with a fixed system of recovery, it seems likely that they too will be held invalid."[7] (The message, of course, had not been lost on Harvey Harrington, who sought control of the *De Braak* wreck through admiralty action, or on the State of Delaware, which was well aware of the controversy in Florida and dutifully struck to the letter of the law in its handling of the issue.)

The prospects for historic preservation of various sites, particularly of those known as "treasure wrecks," as archaeological resources, recreational areas, or historic preserves seemed dim. In 1982, nearly a dozen leading American archaeologists and anthropologists (including Professor George Bass, of Texas A & M University; Professor Richard A. Gould, of Brown University; Daniel J. Lenihan and Larry Murphy, of the National Park Service; Wilburn A. Cockrell, of the Florida Department of State; and Professor Mark Leone, of the University of Maryland) issued a statement condemning the destruction of historic shipwrecks in Florida waters. They noted that these sites, many dating from the sixteenth and seventeenth centuries, were an "irreplaceable resource for archaeology and anthropology" and were being legally and illegally looted on an unprecedented scale by professional treasure hunters and amateur divers. Casting down the gauntlet, they implored their colleagues to become involved in the crisis and to oppose such activities at every opportunity. "Our position," they wrote, is that the same scientific, legal, and ethical standards that apply to archaeology on land should apply to archaeology under water. Archaeology for gain, by selling gold and other materials taken from wrecks for personal or corporate profit, is not acceptable. Nor is any direct involvement by archaeologists in activities that foster a market in such antiquities. We urge our colleagues [to] refrain from working or consulting for treasure hunters and [to] avoid trafficking in gold and other loot taken from wrecks. Professional archaeologists will need to consider carefully any action they may take that could support treasure hunters, and they should consider the implications of anything they might do that affects these wrecks and the materials taken from them.[8]

Giesecke and others began to consider strategies for dealing with the issue at the national level. The only reasonable route to a solution was through federal legislation, which, at a minimum, would be obliged to address three basic questions: (1) What type of shipwrecks deserved protection? (2) Which level of government—state, federal, or a combination of the two—would be best suited to administer such a program of protection? And (3), if federally managed, what should the geographical scope of any protection be? Giesecke and others proposed that a viable approach would require a modification of admiralty law, an unconditional declaration of state ownership of historic shipwrecks from congress to the states, and federal regulation of activities affecting historic shipwrecks beyond the territorial area.[9] The preservationists and archaeologists moved swiftly to secure legislative support. By the fall of 1983, even as Harrington was gearing up for his assault on *De Braak*, H.R. 3194 was introduced by Congressman Walter B. Jones of North Carolina, for consideration by the appropriate committees of the U.S. House of Representatives. The bill was specifically designed to exempt those shipwrecks old enough for inclusion in the National Register of Historic Places from the provisions of maritime law. Wreck sites found on state lands would be managed by the states; those on other submerged lands would be managed by the Department of the Interior.[10] It seemed a straightforward expedient, but many critics considered the bill flawed and its passage was expected to be difficult.

The bill soon began making the rounds of the relevant Congressional committees. On September 27, hearings were held by the House Committee on Merchant Marine and Fisheries, chaired by Representative Walter B. Jones. It was immediately obvious that treasure-hunting advocates and commercial treasure salvors, led by Mel Fisher, were prepared to challenge the bill aggressively. The treasure lobby claimed ready support among members of the sport-diving community, many of whom feared the loss of their right to make recreational dives on shipwreck sites. Only two days earlier, on September 25, the treasure lobby had secured major organizational support when the Atlantic Alliance for Maritime Conservation was formed by thirty-five sport divers, diving shop owners, attorneys, lobbyists, salvors, archaeologists, and journalists, in large part to oppose the legislation. The organization was led by two archaeologists who had championed Fisher's fight for the *Atocha*, R. Duncan Mathewson III, Director of Archaeology for Treasure Salvors, Inc., and Cobb Coin, Inc., and Charles R. McKinney, an archaeologist with the U.S. Department of the Interior, as well as an Arlington, Virginia, archaeologist named Daniel A. Koski-Karell. Supported by such national sport-diving publications as *Skin Diver* magazine, the well-organized Atlantic Alliance quickly attracted a large constituency in opposition to the proposed legislation.[11]

Meanwhile, in the U.S. Senate, S. 1504, a companion bill to H.R. 3194, sponsored by Senator Lloyd Bentsen of Texas, began making the committee rounds. Unlike the treasure lobby, the archaeological and historical communities were far less well organized. Many were unprepared for the contest and seemed neither willing nor able to mobilize sufficient support for either bill.[12] The preservationists quickly became mired in minutiae, but however bogged down they might be, they were far from being defeated.

By August 1984, as Harrington was bringing up his first important artifacts from the bones of *De Braak*, the House Subcommittee on Public Lands and National Parks of the Committee on Interior and Insular Affairs had filed its report on H.R. 3194, now entitled "The Abandoned Shipwreck Act of 1984." Rewritten, the new bill provided for the transfer to states of titles to abandoned shipwrecks found in state waters and either substantially buried, (i.e., in coralline formations) or listed (or eligible for listing) in the National Register of Historic Places. State environmental and antiquities laws would apply to any activities that might affect such wrecks. Under the terms of the amended bill, the Advisory Council on Historic Preservation would be responsible for producing guidelines to assist states and the federal government in developing legislation to regulate and manage such resources and to allow for non-destructive "recreational exploration of shipwreck sites."[13]

On the Senate side, however, S. 1504 was being effectively stymied by Florida Senator Paula Hawkins, who had been corralled by the treasure lobby into vociferously opposing the bill. The battle was intensely fought both on Capitol Hill and in the national media. On August 20, the National Trust for Historic Preservation issued a special "Preservation Network Alert," urging constituents to enlist their senator's support to counter Hawkins's vocal opposition. The Society for Historical Archaeology begged its own members to voice their support for the bill.[14] *Skin Diver* magazine, read by thousands of sport divers across the nation, ran editorial after editorial in opposition to the bill, while the Atlantic Alliance courted the recreational-diving community at large and the sports industry it supported.

As the battle, over S. 1504 and H.R. 3194 raged on, *De Braak* began to attract the attention of historic preservationists at the highest levels of government. The Advisory Council on Historic Preservation, in its 1985 *Report to the President and the Congress of the United States*, noted:

> In Delaware, divers located the wreck of the 18th-century British vessel *De Braak*, one of the most exciting finds of recent years and one of the biggest discoveries ever of undamaged marine artifacts. The commercial salvors who discovered it are excavating *De Braak* under the direction of the State, which as required under Delaware law, will take 25 percent of recovered materials. The archaeological community and other interested parties are watching this job closely to determine whether commercial and scientific interests and the public good can all be served at the same time.[15]

For the first time, the President and Congress had been formally apprised of the proceedings on the Delaware. Thereafter, the negative impact of the events that subsequently transpired off Cape Henlopen did much to sway many in Congress toward support of the bill. The treasure lobby, however, was till a force to be reckoned with.

Although the bill passed in the House on September 10, Senator Hawkins's maneuvers effectively blocked the efforts made by others to pass the shipwreck legislation in the Senate. Proponents of the bill were stunned. Instead of causing them to abandon the effort however, the setback hardened their resolve, and despite overwhelming opposition from the treasure-hunt/sport-diver coalition, similar bills were reintroduced in every Congress thereafter. In 1986, for example, H.R. 3558 and S. 676 appeared with minor variations on earlier versions. These bills reaffirmed federal ownership of abandoned shipwrecks on federal lands, declared that the salvage laws did not apply to abandoned shipwrecks, and asserted U.S. titles to (and the right of title transfer to states) abandoned shipwrecks buried or embedded in submerged lands, in coralline formations on submerged lands protected by the state, or on submerged lands included in, or eligible for inclusion in, the National Register of Historic Places. The bills allowed for existing admiralty and salvage law to apply to all shipwrecks other than those covered by their own provisions and again directed the Advisory Council on Historic Preservation to develop guidelines to assist the states and federal government in carrying out their responsibilities. A strategically valuable addition to these bills, designed to insure that the rights of support divers to dive on shipwrecks were not infringed upon (and to weaken their support for the treasure lobby), was the provision allowing non-destructive recreational exploration and private-sector salvage of shipwreck sites.[16]

Eventually, opposition to the bills began to weaken, especially as their proponents began to gather a growing body of national support, including the Department of the Interior, the National Governors' Association, the National Trust for Historic Preservation, the Underwater Society of America, the National Council of State Historic Preservation Officers, the American Association of Museums, the Underwater Archaeological Society of Maryland, the Coastal States Organization, and many others.[17] Still, negotiations and the politicking continued. Senator Lowell Wiecker of Connecticut wanted to split all materials recovered from salvage operations between the state and salvor, which the archaeological community strongly opposed. The Society for Historical Archaeology, now taking a leading role in championing the legislation, retained a professional lobbyist named Helen Hooper to help win the battle on Capitol Hill.[18] Then, on June 18, 1986, Senators Wiecker and Gramm of Texas introduced their own shipwreck bill, S. 2569, which was essentially the same as H.R. 3558, and referred it to the Senate Committee on Energy and Natural Resources.[19] But passage in 1986 was not to be.

Proponents of the legislation continued to press on. On March 26, 1987, yet another bill, designated S. 858, "To establish the title of States in certain abandoned shipwrecks, and for other purposes," was introduced in the Senate. Entitled "Abandoned Shipwreck Act of 1987," the bill was sponsored by Senator Bill Bradley of New Jersey and co-sponsored by Senators Claiborne Pell and John Chafee of Rhode Island, Chic Hecht of Nevada, Bob Graham and Lawton Chiles of Florida, Lloyd Bentsen and Phil Gramm of Texas, Robert Stafford of Vermont, Daniel Inouye of Hawaii, and Frank Lautenberg of New Jersey. Barbara Mikulski of Maryland would later join the group supporting the measure.[20] The premise of the bill was that states have the responsibility for managing a wide range of living and nonliving resources found in their waters and submerged lands and that shipwrecks are included among those resources. As in earlier bills, it was deemed necessary to allow for the recreational and educational use of state waters and shipwrecks by sport divers and others, and, as irreplaceable state resources, for tourism, biological sanctuaries, and historical research. Provision was made to ensure that states holding title to shipwrecks pursuant to the proposed act permit reasonable access by the public to such sites. The bill also proposed that Congress declare as policy the need for states to fulfill their responsibilities (as stipulated by the Act) to develop their own appropriate, consistent policies to protect their natural resources and habitat areas, to guarantee the right of recreational exploration of shipwrecks, and to permit appropriate public and private sector salvage of shipwrecks, consistent with "the protection of historical values and environmental integrity of shipwrecks and the sites."[21]

In managing the resources subject to the provisions of the proposed act, states would again be encouraged to create underwater parks or similar areas by which provide additional protection for those resources. The federal Advisory Council on Historic Preservation, in consultation with public and private sector interests groups, including archaeologists, salvors, sport divers, historic preservationists, and state historic preservation officers, would be directed to publish, within six months of passage of the act, advisory guidelines for the protection of historic shipwrecks and properties. Such guidelines, it was proposed, should be available to assist states and the federal government in developing legislation and specific regulations with which to fulfill their responsibilities.[22]

Given that the United States would be asserting its title to any abandoned shipwreck that lay embedded in a state's submerged lands, in coralline formations protected by a state in its submerged lands, or in the submerged lands of a state listed in, or eligible for listing in, the National Register, the heart of S. 858 was its proposal for the effective transfer of U.S. title to the state on whose submerged lands the shipwrecks were located, other than those found on public lands of the United States (excepting the outer continental shelf), which would remain the property of the federal government.[23]

As S. 858 struggled along, the Oceanography Subcommittee of the House Marine and Fisheries Committee and the Subcommittee on National Parks and Public Lands of the House Interior Committee began separately considering a companion bill, H.R. 74, to pass on for full committee action. As always, hearings were again convened, over the objections of the bill's supporters, who argued that a sufficient record had already been established. Nevertheless, progress of any kind was better than none at all, and proponents took heart when the House subcommittees agreed to work closely with their Senate counterparts. Some pro-bill lobby groups were now even certain that final action would be taken by both the House and Senate early in 1988.[24]

On April 21, 1987, the Subcommittee on Oceanography began its hearings. The moment had finally arrived when *De Braak* would move to center stage. The salvage operations on the ship itself, which had garnered national attention less than a year before, would now become the focal point of a vigorous, militant, and well-crafted assault by proponents of the new "Abandoned Shipwreck" act. *De Braak* would serve as an example of everything that the bill's sponsors hoped to remedy. The sheer brutality of its recovery was a preservation lobbyist's dream.

The opening salvo before the subcommittee was fired by no less a personage than J. Jackson Walter, President of the National Trust for Historic Preservation. Walter's prepared statement, which would be repeated in late September before the Senate Subcommittee on Public Lands, National Parks and Forests by J. Revel Carr, Director of the Mystic Seaport Museum, was insightful, scathing, and effective. "Our experience in the maritime archaeology field and our legal analysis of the present situation," he began, "lead us to conclude that historic shipwrecks are, without doubt, the single most endangered category of historic resources in our nation today."[25] Shipwrecks, he went on to point out, were subject to salvage operations which failed to protect their value as archaeological sites and caused the loss of crucial data on the discovery, exploration, and development of the United States. Valuable information about maritime technology, international and interregional trade, and seafaring life was being lost forever. Salvage operations that failed to adequately map the underwater location of vessels and other objects forfeited the very information that trained scientists could gain from studying the relationship of such objects to each other. Where salvage techniques failed to recover all of a vessel's contents—both those objects that possessed market value and those of scientific value—archaeologists stood to lose pieces of the complex puzzle that constitutes the story of a vessel and its time. And when proper conservation measures were not applied to a recovered vessel and its contents, the rapid deterioration of ancient materials exposed to surface conditions denied archaeologists the ability to compare materials from one find with those from another and denied the citizens of the nation the opportunity to see artifacts and to learn about the wrecks through museum display.[26]

Passage of the "Abandoned Shipwreck Act," Walter observed, would remove many historic shipwrecks from the jurisdiction of federal admiralty law and delegate the management of such wrecks to the states in whose waters they were located. It was the uncertain applicability of admiralty law, in fact, which had placed many state officials seeking to protect the nation's interests with regard to historic shipwrecks in untenable positions. If they sought to impose what they believed to be appropriately archaeological requirements on an excavation, they faced the threat of being challenged under admiralty law. If they did not impose such requirements, they faced the threat of being criticized for failing to protect the nation's heritage. The sordid saga of *De Braak* was a perfect example of this no-win situation. Walter's analysis could not have been a better description of Delaware's predicament, nor of the state's civil-service professionals, who were held responsible for observing the letter of the law while also attempting to manage the state's historical and cultural resources within the ethical constraints of their professions.

Despite these problems, however, Walter was adamant about one thing. "States," he said,

> should be able to have a clear and undiluted input on shipwrecks found in their waters. Historic artifacts in water are no different from those found on land. If an historic artifact were found on dry land of a state there's no way it would be allowed to degrade. The same should go for artifacts in the water.[27]

Walter paused for effect. "Recently, despite the best efforts of state preservation officials," he continued.

> treasure salvors damaged, in a vain attempt to recover treasure, the H.M.S. *De Braak*, an English military vessel that sank off the coast of Delaware in 1798. Lifted by cables without benefit of a proper cradle, salvors ripped into the hull and dropped much of its contents and interior on the sea floor. The salvors then

employed a clamshell bucket to dump the remains of the vessel into a road construction rock sorter to sift for treasure. These techniques denied archaeologists the information they might have gained from a careful study of the exact location of artifacts on the ship. The threat of admiralty law litigation restrained Delaware's ability to condition the salvor's efforts. A successful admiralty law challenge would have placed control of the wreck in the admiralty courts and removed all state leverage over the recovery techniques. Such litigation would have also cost Delaware's taxpayers tens of thousands of dollars.[28]

Walter's closing summation was both dramatic and devastating. "As a nation," he concluded,

> we would not tolerate a commercial enterprise that bulldozed Gettysburg and then dumped the remains through a sifting machine to recover valuable objects. Yet this is exactly what current law allows treasure hunters to do to our nation's maritime legacy. This legacy is not the property of any syndicate of investors, daredevil treasure seekers, or even, well-meaning sportsmen. It is the property of the nation as a whole and the nation as a whole is not currently protecting its interests in the heritage of our historic shipwrecks.[29]

Walter's dramatic presentation before the House subcommittee did not pass unnoticed by the press. Instead, it was picked up by the news services and reported in newspapers across the nation. The fight for S. 858 had turned an important corner.

On September 29, further hearings on the proposed bill were convened before the Senate Subcommittee on Public Lands, National Parks and Forests. Testimony and briefer statements, both for and against S. 858, were tendered by many expert witnesses and interested parties. *De Braak* was never far from the center of debate and was frequently employed by both sides to support their arguments. For example, Wilmington, Delaware, attorney and sport diver Peter Hess, a vociferous opponent of the bill and the whole premise of state control over historic shipwreck sites, argued:

> State ownership of shipwrecks is not a panacea for historic preservation. In my home state of Delaware, the state's title to H.M.S. *De Braak* was undisputed. Although a state-permitted salvage operation was subject to an admiralty action, the federal judge gave the state complete discretion to oversee the archaeological aspects of the salvage operations. Despite this the state allowed highly controversial methods to be employed which resulted in substantial damage to the partial hull structure which was lifted to the surface. Without sufficient funds with which to properly preserve this fragile waterlogged wooden remains of the *De Braak*, the state is left with an albatross—and clear evidence that just because it owns the *De Braak*, there is no assurance that such historic shipwrecks will be properly protected or preserved.[30]

If Hess's well-crafted statement swayed any legislators after Walter's testimony, they were readily brought back into the fold by telling arguments submitted in written form by Edward M. Miller, Project Manager of the National Oceanic and Atmospheric Administration's USS *Monitor* National Marine Sanctuary. Miller began by citing the 1985 Advisory Council on Historic Preservation's report on *De Braak*, which had commented that it was "one of the biggest discoveries ever of undamaged marine artifacts." What, he asked, was the disposition and state of preservation of the artifacts only two years after the council's statement? What type of archaeological record had been made? How were the collections conserved? Were they located where future researchers could study them? How were they being interpreted? Had a report been published? Where could the public see the artifacts on display? How much had the "private enterprise" cost the taxpayers of Delaware and what had they received in return? How, indeed, had the public good been served by the salvage? "Perhaps," he suggested cogently, "the greatest irony of this *single* example is that the destruction of the archaeological site and even the actual recovery of the remaining hull structure was undertaken by the salvors on the 'rumor' that there was $500 million in gold and silver aboard." Would, he asked, such treatment of a similar eighteenth-century historical resource have been tolerated on land?

> Unfortunately, the cultural value of this fragile, finite, irreplaceable and non-renewable resource has all but been totally destroyed in preference to its alleged salvage value. Some may express sympathy for the salvors who "risked" $2.5 million of their own money in their "rush for the gold"—but we must ask ourselves who are the real losers in such cases? The State of Delaware will never know the full value of what was lost, either materially or archaeologically, due to the depredation of their maritime cultural heritage. It may be instructive to reflect on the difference in outcome between the *Mary Rose* Project in Great Britain with the *De Braak* Project in the United States. Generations of Englishmen will witness their cultural heritage in a maritime vestige of Henry VIII's England, but few, if any, Americans will remember the *De Braak* or the cultural depravity which destroyed it. The failure of the Federal, independent and private agencies charged by Congress with the protection and preservation of the national patrimony, to defend the public's interest in the case of the *De Braak* is mute testimony of the flawed national hierarchy concerning our maritime heritage. The continuing lack of coherent Federal leadership, consistent policies, and national legislation is sad evidence of the "pervasive 'out of sight, out of mind' syndrome" [concerning maritime resources] within government and even within historic preservation itself. When public and private interests conflict over limited resources, it is a fundamental function of government to safeguard the public interest.[31]

Although the debate would continue, and many more examples would be cited of historic losses occurring as a result of the quest for sunken treasure, none, perhaps, had been as appalling (or as effective in garnering support for passage of the Abandoned Shipwrecks Act of 1987) as the sad saga of HMS *De*

Braak. The bill's passage, of course, could not be attributed solely to the *De Braak* example, but it was without question of key importance in turning the tide of the legislature. Ironically, the brightest moment in the history of an otherwise nondescript sailing ship, lost while on a forgotten mission, had been the example of its salvage. But the example had been taken to heart.

On December 19, 1987, the United States Senate passed S. 858. On April 13, 1988, the bill, after a few false starts, finally sailed through the House of Representatives with a final roll-call vote of 340 to 64. On April 28, 1988, the Abandoned Shipwreck Act of 1987 was signed into law as Pub. L. No. 100-298 by President Ronald Reagan.[32] The legacy of HMS *De Braak* had finally, after nearly 190 years, been divined.

TWENTY FOUR

The Legend Revealed

When 3,000 archaeologists, anthropologists, historians, educators, cultural resource managers, conservators, museum curators, and others convened for the First Joint Archaeological Congress at the Baltimore Convention Center in early January 1989, it was billed by the media as the largest assembly of its kind in American history. The conference was jointly sponsored by the American Philological Association, the American Schools of Oriental Research, the Archaeological Institute of America, and the Society for Historical Archaeology. More than 130 sessions and 900 papers were scheduled for presentation over a four-day period, covering such diverse topics as underwater archaeology, satellite mapping technology, archaeo-botany, and even Platonic philosophy of law. Maryland Governor William Donald Schaefer and Senator Paul S. Sarbanes were scheduled to greet the nation's best and brightest, followed by keynote speeches and addresses by such leading national archaeological luminaries as James Deetz, George Bass, Hester Davis, and Brian Fagan.

It was an awesome assembly of academic elites from points all over the North American continent. To this high-powered group, who molded the intellectual theory, moral conscience, and national policy on archaeological and historical matters, Charles Fithian, Claudia Melson, and their colleagues would present the preliminary but important fruits of their research on HMS *De Braak*. Although the greatest legacy of *De Braak*, without question, had been her contribution to the passage of the Abandoned Shipwreck Act nine months earlier, Fithian and those who had worked with him to evaluate her remains believed that important lessons could still be learned from her collections. Despite the edict of their peers that archaeologists have nothing to do with collections recovered by treasure salvors, regardless of the circumstances, they stoutly believed that such artifacts could not be simply ignored or left to disintegrate. It was the hope of Fithian and the Delaware Bureau of Museums and Historic Sites that the scholarly work accomplished by the dedicated team would justify that philosophy.

Given the disdain with which most members of the archaeological community viewed anyone who was even remotely associated with treasure-ship salvage, the Delaware contingent expected a cool reception for their work, at best. Indeed, acceptance of their symposium, entitled "Archaeological Investigations of the British Warship H.M.S. *De Braak*," had been anything but a given. Opposition, on professional and ethical grounds, by the Society for Historical Archaeology, to any presentation by treasure hunters and their house archaeologists had already resulted in the highly publicized refusal to accept the submissions of at least one symposium on the *Whydah* Project. The *De Braak* abstracts, it was rumored, had barely squeaked through the peer review process, and then only on the strength of the presenters' reputations and independence from the salvors. But they *had* made the program.

On the morning of Saturday, January 7, Charles Fithian, conservatively dressed in a gray suit, fidgeted as the crowd began to filter into the room where the symposium would be held. He and the other presenters joked lamely among themselves about how small the audience was likely to be. In the next room down the hall, the "Father" of nautical archaeology, Dr. George Bass, was chairing a session on the recent discovery of a late-Bronze Age shipwreck—the oldest ship ever found—off Ulu Burun, near Turkey. Elsewhere symposia were being held on such popular research subjects as the archaeology of Colonial Williamsburg, underwater archaeology of the Great Lakes, the archaeology of Spanish America, and the archaeology of the Continental Shelf. Thus, with twenty-four concurrent sessions, the odds favored a light turnout at best. Despite the competition, however, the room continued to fill up, until even standing room was at a premium.

Given the long battle for passage of the Abandoned Shipwreck Act and the impact of her salvage on those proceedings, HMS *De Braak* was indeed a hot topic. For many here, the ship and its salvage had come to epitomize the systematic destruction of historic shipwreck sites by treasure salvors under the aegis of admirality law. Now that the issue had been resolved once and for all, however, several in the room publicly questioned the value of even studying the wreck and its collections. A few even castigated those scholars who had chosen to do so on the grounds that their work was akin to aiding and abetting the enemy. The challenge for Fithian and company, whose principal concern was to extract as much data as possible from the collections before they were sold off, was considerable.

Even the salvor, L. John Davidson, who was aware that the historic value of the collection far exceeded its worth in the marketplace, sought to downplay *De Braak*'s archaeological importance. Less than six months earlier, and despite his many prior public assertions to the contrary, Davidson had written a surprising denunciation of the archaeological significance of the ship;

> Reference to a time capsule on the bottom is a popular expression but not applicable to the *De Braak*. ... The quality of hull salvaged as compared with the

whole original ship that had already rotted and disappeared provides evidence that there was no time capsule for study except for what was brought up plus the encrusted areas. The ship was swamped when it sunk and for nearly 200 years had rotted and disappeared in great part. No reasonable person could assume that the lifestyle of the crew would be recreated from what was left.[1]

It was now up to Fithian and his colleagues, after more than two years of studying the artifact collection to prove Davidson's statement utterly false. Fithian's introductory remarks, presented to a somewhat unfriendly audience, would do much to set the tone and justify the proceedings that were to follow. "If you refer to the *De Braak* as controversial," he began,

> it would probably be the archaeological understatement of this entire conference. The *De Braak* represents the best and worst kinds of events that are happening in the realm of underwater archaeology. It is illustrative of the best in that it underscores what a sunken ship can tell you, what it can reveal about life at sea and the technology of seafaring. And it is characteristic of the worst in terms of the irresponsible destruction of a major cultural resource resulting from the pursuit of personal or corporate profit. Despite the damage and destruction, however, there are many questions that we can address through a thorough analysis of the collections in hand. Unhappily, because of the manner in which the project was conducted, there are many more that we cannot, principally the archaeological and anthropological ones. Yet, our business as archaeologists is to extract every piece of data from this marvelous collection, and place it within the context of the history, technology, and society of the age in which *De Braak* lived and died. We can never have it all, but as professionals we have to try.[2]

There was a respectful silence as the audience digested Fithian's simple philosophy and waited to see just how well his independent group of researchers would support his assumption.

Daniel Griffith, Deputy State Historical Preservation Officer and the first symposium speaker, intended to provide a candid preface to the session with his presentations, "H.M.S. *De Braak*: The Legend Revealed." He read his paper quickly and nervously, practically racing through a synopsis of the history of the old warship and the growth of her legend. He traced her origins, her abbreviated naval career, and the grim tale of her commercial salvage. The audience murmured uneasily as he spoke of the state's granting of the salvage lease that had led to the wreck's discovery. Many grimaced as he discussed the disastrous salvage procedures used to raise the hull and the terrible clambucket assault on the thousands of artifacts that had dropped into the seafloor during "the pick."[3] Griffith's summation of the state's policy, its goals of maximizing the retrieval of significant historical and archaeological data, and its desire to disseminate the findings through appropriate forums did little to alleviate the dismay evident among his peers. Many had come prepared for an academic lynching, and Griffith's straightforward account, unhappily, failed to disarm them. But the worst was over.

Claudia Melson's presentation then followed detailing her efforts to manage and stabilize the collection, and entitled, appropriately enough, "Keep It Wet." The talk, which emphasized her "triage" format for getting artifacts— everything from carronades to ketchup bottles—into wet storage as rapidly as possible, did much to win over the audience. She discussed methods of artifact transport, treatment, and documentation. She analyzed the successes and failures of sophisticated freeze-dry technologies employed on leather, wood, and fragile textiles. Her familiarity with every facet of the collection was demonstrated time and again. She described at length the more than 100 shoes and boots, both civilian and military issue, worn by the sailors and marines aboard *De Braak*. She discussed how the evidence in the collections revealed that the surprisingly fashion-conscious seamen had cut the buckles off their government-issue shoes and replaced them with stylish leather thongs and ribbons. D. A. Saguto's research on the *De Braak* shoe collection had provided the first significant evidence of shipboard fashion trends mirroring those just coming into popularity ashore, in an era of dramatic social change on both land and sea.[4]

The largest single artifact in the *De Braak* collection was, of course, the hull itself. David Beard's account of his combined hands-on and archival research revealed an enormous amount of information on the origins and architectural history of the ship. His opening statement, of a paper entitled "*De Braak*: An Architectural Study of an 18th-century Brig," was anything but subtle. Indeed, Beard boldly contradicted the conventional wisdom concerning the warship's origins. "*De Braak*," he stated in his clipped Arkansas accent, "was probably a cutter built by the British in the late 1770s." For the next half hour, he presented documentary, architectural, and physical evidence to support his claims. The audience was captivated (and the lynching postponed).

Although the original assumption, proposed by Chapelle, was that the vessel had been Dutch-built, Beard strongly disagreed. Pointing first to the Admiralty draughts, which revealed a much steeper rise of floors than the more flat-bottomed Dutch craft of the period, he countered Chapelle's claim. Then Beard noted that *De Braak*'s interior spaces and lines, prior to refitting, were very much like those of other Royal Navy brigs typical of that period, citing studies conducted on HMS *Irene* for comparative analysis. From his measurements and other analyses of the hull, he had discovered that certain dimensions, including those of hull timbers from the lower part of the ship, such as the keelson, keel, false keel, a hog, and various types of deadwood in the stern and bow, as well as the hull's stem and stern construction, were identical with or similar to those of other vessels of proven British construction. Typical of Beard's findings was that scarphs in the keel were exactly four and a half feet long, the exact length commonly indicated in British ship specifications.

Moreover, copper drift pins were incised with the name of an English firm, "Forbes," which had perfected the copper alloy blend for pin manufacture in Great Britain. Trunnel configurations were found to be the same as those of HMS *Dartmouth*, a British warship built in 1655, lost off Scotland in 1690, and rediscovered in 1973. There was, of course, the possibility that many of these components had been added during *De Braak*'s 1797 or 1798 refittings, but the sheer bulk of the data suggested otherwise.

Beard's architectural analysis had been thorough. He had determined that more than forty percent of the starboard hull, from the keel up to one and a half feet below the lower deck, had been preserved: the "embryonic archaeologist" so despised by Davidson had examined and recorded every accessible inch of it. Ceiling planking (referred to as "thick stuff" in period documents), strakes, shot lockers, foremast and mainmast step, riding bits, interior riders, hanging knees, futtocks, limber boards, wooden bilge pumps, scuppers, fishplates, drift pins, sheathing configurations, and even nail types and sizes had been documented and sketched for current study and for posterity. His work did not overlook the extensive damage caused by the hull's disastrous recovery and the subsequent injury inflicted before its transfer to the holding pond.

Examining the keel closely, the young archaeologist had also discovered signs of much older damage near the stern, probably sustained from a grounding of the ship, and he was eventually able to document the techniques employed to repair that damage. In the keelson, he had located the original hole for the mast, made when the vessel was still a cutter. In their haste to refit the ship in 1797, the British shipwrights had merely plugged the hole with a cast-iron ball rather than taking the time to fill and patch it. Beard found patches everywhere in the ceiling planking. These discoveries revealed much about shipyard procedures, for instead of removing whole dry-rotted planks, the carpenters had merely cut out the worst sections and then patched the planking with plugs of wood. He attributed such techniques to haste, shortages of wood, and the fact that shipwrights were allowed to keep prize pieces of timber for themselves.

Based upon his meticulous analysis of the hull and the architectural record of *De Braak* and ships like her, Beard concluded that the wreck was definitely HMS *De Braak* and that she was of British construction.[5]

But why had she capsized? Many believed the cause to lie in her standing and running rigging, for even Drew himself had complained that the ship was overmasted. That was a question which Fred Hopkins, Jr., and I had spent almost two years trying to answer. Our analysis of hundreds of blocks, sheaves, bushings, pins and related tackle recovered during the excavations offered some tantalizing possibilities and was the topic of our symposium presentation, entitled "The Machine is Wholly Untried: The Evaluation of Naval Blocks and Sheaves from HMS *De Braak*."

Until the middle of the eighteenth century, the production of blocks and sheaves (pulleys) for the Royal Navy was a relatively unsophisticated affair. Individually made by hand, naval blocks, which were needed for a variety of tasks, from hoisting sail and managing the ship to running out guns and raising the anchor, lacked uniformity of design, quality, and durability. Yet the importance of ship's blocks was readily illustrated by the fact that a seventy-four-gun ship required over 1,400 blocks of various types for both rigging and the handling of guns.

In the course of our research, Hopkins and I had learned that around 1756, a Southampton ship's carpenter named Walter Taylor had realized that if blocks and sheaves were better constructed, there would be fewer accidents at sea. Working in secrecy, Taylor and his son, Walter, Jr., developed manually operated machines to accurately saw, bore and turn the various parts of a ship's blocks, as well as an iron pin, or axle, design (to replace the earlier lignum vitae pins) on which the pulley revolved. Except for ship's guns, where sparking might cause an explosion, Taylor pins were almost universally adopted. Then, in 1770, the Taylor blocks were given their most important test by the Royal Navy when they were used to fully rig HMS *Centaur*. By using blocks of only half the size conventionally used, the weight of *Centaur*'s masts was reduced by 1,300 kilograms. The benefit to the Royal Navy was obvious. The Taylor family monopoly on Royal Navy block production was assured. Soon the manual block-making machines were converted to horsepower, and Taylor blocks became the standard. Then, in 1803, the Navy Board approved the installation at Portsmouth of a revolutionary steam-powered block-making machine invented by Marc Isambard Brunel. By 1805, the Taylor monopoly had been destroyed. The industrial age had arrived, and its impact on the Royal Navy was profound. During the Taylor-block era, the Navy's annual consumption of blocks was estimated at 100,000 and required 110 skilled workers to meet the demand. By 1808, Brunel's Portsmouth machines were producing 130,000 blocks yearly and required only ten unskilled workers.[6]

The *De Braak* collection of blocks, bushings, and sheaves (many featuring the Taylor imprint) represented the largest collection of its kind from the Taylor-block era and the last of a crafted product doomed to extinction by the advent of the Industrial Revolution. Our mission had been to examine and record the characteristics of every artifact in the tackle category, none of which had been recovered with any provenance noted, and thereby to establish a study collection. Our second objective had been to ascertain their deployment and uses aboard ship by comparing the artifacts with widely accepted standards of the period. And finally, we hoped to discover some clue as to why *De Braak* capsized.

The artifacts were divided into four groupings: sheaves, bushings, blocks, and miscellaneous items (pins, chain plates, washers, and gun tackle). Scores of features, including such variables as typological variations and commonalities, dimensional characteristics, typographic forms of die strikes, maker's marks, dates, place names, Royal Navy markings, design features, wood type, and so forth were meticulously recorded for every artifact. Each item was both drawn and photographed. Once the data was assembled, it had been turned over to the Academic Computing Center of the University of Baltimore and entered into a data-base management system called V.P. Planner. For each of the 262 sheaves and 280 bushings, no fewer than thirty-two variables were entered. Unfortunately, only nineteen blocks had been recovered, eleven in such a poor state of preservation as to be useless for study. Yet the data gathered from the collection was significant.

We had hoped that statistical comparisons and calculations of the data, using large test groupings, with published standards of the period in which *De Braak* had served (primarily extracted from David Steel's 1794 treatise, *The Elements and Practice of Rigging and Seamanship*), would produce data on the identification, possible provenance, and specific uses of the blocks. In fact, they were readily identified as main and foretopmast rope blocks, mainmast studdingsail ties, and as a mainmast studdingsail gaff-topping lift. Statistical correlation of the sheaves' dimensional characteristics with line size and probable associated block typology, however, presented us with a quandary: either (1) our sample was too small to test; (2) Steel's table data employed for comparison was inaccurate or had a completely different provenance; or (3) *De Braak* was over-sparred. Given our final computations, it appeared that the *De Braak* blocks and lines were possibly as much as two times the normal weight for a typical Royal Navy vessel of her size and rig. *De Braak* had originally been constructed as a single-masted cutter sometime prior to 1783, with a hull designed to mount the heavy long guns of the era. With the addition of another mast and other significant modifications made after her acquisition by the Royal Navy and the arming of the ship with carronades approximately half the weight of normal long guns of the same caliber, *De Braak*'s original center of gravity was altered radically. The British penchant for piling on as much sail as possible to get as much speed as possible from a vessel—despite the danger—was well known. Had the heightened center of gravity, caused by oversized rigging and a smaller on-deck weight been a major factor in the capsizing of the ship? Were other brig-sloops susceptible to the same over-sparring, rigging, and design flaws that may have done in *De Braak*? Sadly, without precise archaeological provenance of the artifacts themselves (particularly relating to the distribution and tonnage of the ballast), the only conclusions we could draw from the analysis of the blocks and tackle were hypothetical.

Fortunately, our research was ongoing. By the late summer of 1991 we had discovered through a comprehensive analysis of Royal Navy losses incurred between 1776 and 1869, some dramatic new evidence to support the flawed-design-and-over-sparring hypothesis. During this period, no fewer than 427 brig-sloops had been commissioned by the Royal Navy. Of that number, 135 (or 31.62 percent of the total in the brig-sloop class) had been lost at sea, sixty-eight by wrecking, twenty-seven by foundering, two by stranding, four by fire, one by scuttling, two by ice, six from battle related events, one by mutiny, one from prisoner insurrection, and twenty-three by enemy capture. The remainder had been sold, broken up, cancelled before completion, or disposed of by the Royal Navy in a variety of ways. Of the casualties, fifty nine had been lost within five years of their commissioning (ten before the end of their first year at sea), and 105 before the age of ten. Ninety seven of the total lost (a stunning 22.72 percent of the class total) had either wrecked, foundered, or been stranded as a complete or partial result of weather and/or sea conditions. Was the brig-sloop design and rig adopted by the Royal Navy unsafe? Did *De Braak*, one of the earlier vessels to be so rigged and armed, and the ninth of her class to be so lost, merely reflect an error, or combination of errors typical of the lot? The statistical evidence, together with our discovery of over-sized running rigging seemed to suggest just that.

De Braak, we later concluded, like nearly a quarter of her sister ships built or altered before and after her, had been a tragic victim of a most unfortunate combination of weather, gravity, and flawed design.

Charles Fithian was the next to speak, presenting the fruits of his own diligent analysis of the ordnance, side arms, and ammunition from *De Braak*. Although he first addressed the fourteen 24-pounder carronades and two six-pounder bow-chasers, certainly among the heaviest and most readily documented artifacts to be recovered, his attention centered more on their sundry components and the projectiles they fired. There were, he reported, two principal types of artillery projectiles found aboard—round shot and canister. The former was used to inflict structural damage on an enemy ship and, secondarily, to produce flying splinters that could injury the enemy's crew. Canister, composed of a wooden base with a cylindrical tin body in which were packed iron balls of a particular number and weight, was almost exclusively employed as an antipersonnel weapon. When fired at the crowded deck of an enemy ship, the effect produced would be similar to that of a shotgun fired into a densely packed duck pond. Although no intact unit of canister had been found, several wooden bases were recovered, as well as a number of wooden containers in which the ammunition was packed. There was plenty of grapeshot, also employed as an antipersonnel weapon, but without the characteristic base and vertical spindles.

Of greater importance, however, had been the presence of fixed ammunition for six-pounder canisters. Unlike the 24-pounder canisters, in fixed ammunition the final charge was actually connected to the projectile, enabling gun crews to charge their weapons in one step instead of two and thus increasing their firing rates. The presence of fixed ammunition aboard *De Braak*, Fithian was delighted to discover, constituted the earliest recorded use, other than for testing, of this type of ammunition at sea.

A number of instruments necessary to serve the ordnance were also intensively studied. There was a fragment of a six-pounder rammer head and the rounded head of a 24-pounder sponge, both employed in gun-loading operations. Vent covers, or aprons, which were normally secured at the gun's breech to prevent moisture from collecting, were also discovered and documented. Such items were particularly important since Royal Navy practice demanded that guns be capable of being charged and fired to prevent scaling, at any given time at sea, as well as for practice and in battle. Other important pieces of gear included two examples of rope wadding used to hold both charge and projectile firmly in the gun's breech, and a large double block, completely encased in concretion, from a set of side tackle employed for both running out and training the gun.

Of special interest to Fithian were fourteen brass gunlocks. Normally mounted at the gun's breech, the gunlock's flintlock firing mechanism was far superior to the slower-burning match of earlier times and permitted a more dependable and rapid rate of fire. In the course of his research, Fithian had discovered that the first experiments with such equipage had been conducted (successfully) by Captain Charles Douglas, aboard HMS *Duke* and *Formidable*, during the early 1780s, and had been readily accepted by the Navy Board soon afterward. Two discrete types of gunlocks—one for guns of 9-pounder caliber and up, and the second for smaller guns—had been authorized by the Board of Ordnance. The gunlocks recovered from *De Braak*, again much to Fithian's delight, proved to be the earliest examples of this new technology encountered to date at a Royal Navy shipwreck site.

Fighting, of course, was the supreme test of a warship's internal organization. Frequently, a naval contest required not only the exchange of artillery fire, but close fighting, boarding, and small-boat amphibious operations. In such instances, the ship's marine contingent was armed with a variety of small arms, including muskets, pistols, and such weapons as swords, knives, and hatchets. And there were also the personal side arms of the officers and crew to consider. The most common firearm in the *De Braak* collection was the redoubtable British Sea Service musket, a standard Royal Navy weapon since the 1750s. Produced in both long and short types, the Sea Service musket was easily recognizable by its distinctive stock and furniture. The Sea Service muskets found aboard *De Braak*, sans their long distinguishable barrels, which had succumbed to the elements, were of the type produced specifically for the British Admiralty and distributed to vessels on the basis of their rates and crew sizes. Specialized training in the use of small arms was given to certain members of the ship's company (usually referred to as small-arms men) by noncommissioned officers. Their purpose was to serve as sharpshooters, to repel boarders, to participate in boarding parties or amphibious operations, and, on rare occasions, to fight ashore. The marine contingent aboard Captain Drew's brig was armed with both short Land Pattern and India Pattern muskets. The

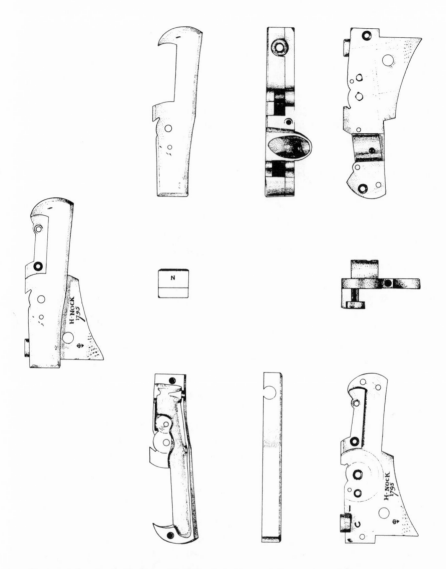

Fourteen brass gunlocks, all of the kind presented in these drawings, were mounted on the breeches of *De Braak*'s carronades, and proved to be the earliest examples of such ordnance technology discovered to date on a Royaly Navy shipwreck. The gunlocks were manufactured by H. Nock in 1795. (*Delaware State Museums*)

Land Pattern had been developed as a result of the British experience in North America during the French and Indian Wars. By 1768 the short Land Pattern musket had been adopted by Royal warrant and would serve as the standard shoulder arm for the British army until 1797, when the India Pattern was introduced. The demands imposed by the war with Napoleonic France, resulting in severe arms shortages after 1793, had dictated the development of the shorter and cheaper India Pattern and its subsequent adoption as the standard-issue musket until the conclusion of the flintlock era forty years later. It was thus not surprising to hear Fithian confirm that the collection of shoulder arms recovered from the wreck reflected the transitional phase between those eras.

Two types of Sea Service pistols were identified by Fithian. One type displayed stock furniture which was stylistically similar to that found on English muskets of the era. Most of these, it was discovered upon cleaning, were in such pristine condition that the English ordnance approval marks were clearly discernible. The second type of pistol, a quantity of which had been found aboard the wreck and which was certainly a component of the ship's armory, at least at the moment of her loss, was, by its shape, absence of British ordnance approval marks, and suggestive continental style, a more problematic sample. Its stock hardware, Fithian discovered, was very similar to that found on French 1733–34 cavalry marine pistols recovered from the wreck of the French warship *Machault* in the St. Lawrence. Its presence aboard a British warship aroused a spate of interesting speculations. One possible explanation was that these weapons had been captured pieces which, owing to the chronic British arms shortage, were readily adopted by the Admiralty and issued to *De Braak* during her outfitting and arming.

Although iron and steel artifacts had not, as a rule, endured very well at the *De Braak* site, Fithian was still able to extract valuable information from a variety of edged weapons found aboard. No blades or hilts had been recovered intact, but leather scabboards and the clips that held them had been. Analysis of these indicated that they had been used for the carriage of straight blade cutlasses approximately three feet in length. An examination of British cutlasses of the period (in the Tower of London collections) revealed that the average cutlass length ranged between thirty-one and thirty-six inches. Although British naval-officer dress had become standardized by 1785, an officer's choice of sword was still a personal matter. (It was not so for the enlisted man, whose saber was standard equipment.) Study of the scabbards suggested that they would have been adequate to carry the famous Figure Eight iron cutlass, a single-edged weapon which was the most commonly carried weapon in the Royal Navy.

There were also a variety of bayonet scabbards, suitable for use with a standard seventeen-inch, triangular Sea Service short Land or India Pattern musket bayonet. Fragments of, or components for, other edged weapons, such as knives, small swords, and dirks, were also analyzed. Some suspensory equipment, such as a sliding leather bayonet frog used for carrying a bayonet on a waistbelt, and identical to one recovered during the excavation of Fort Ligioner, a site from the French and Indian War era, was of special interest. Another piece of gear was a double frog waistband used to carry both cutlass and bayonet together. Significantly, it was of a type commonly used by soldiers during the eighteenth century, but which had never before been documented as having been used at sea. Although the provenance of these artifacts was almost nonexistent, owing to the method of salvage, period illustrations and documented Royal Navy practice during wartime suggested that edged weapons would normally have been placed amidships, either in containers or mounted randomly on masts, adjacent to, or over, gunports, or anywhere else they could be picked up easily to repel boarders.

The entire collection of small arms, edged weapons, and related accoutrements which had survived was neither large nor representative of the quantity probably carried by *De Braak*'s crew and marines. It did, however, include a small assortment of musket parts and sword hilts that were probably Spanish in origin. Stock fragments and stock furniture of a musket were identified as having come from a regulation Spanish infantry shoulder arm commonly used near the end of the eighteenth century. A regulation brass Spanish infantry or dragoon sword hilt, with parts identical to one documented for the year 1803, was also recovered. Like the discovery of the French pistol, those of the Spanish arms were viewed with keen interest.

Fithian cautiously accounted for the presence of these weapons in two ways: they might have been taken from the *Don Francisco Xavier* after her capture to prevent her crew from regaining their ship; or, like the side arms resembling the 1733–34 French pistol, the Spanish arms might well have been issued from stores of captured armament by the Admiralty when *De Braak* was being outfitted. Indeed, their similarity to regulation military types suggested an original source other than a captured merchantman.

Other expendable ordnance-related materials recovered included lead shot and gunflints, and some interesting calculations were made of the gunpowder needs of the ship. Although thorough examination of the cooperage aboard *De Braak* by Kerry Shackleford failed to verify the presence of containers used specifically for powder among the recovered artifacts, it was obvious that gunpowder would certainly have been carried aboard the brig in bulk as well as in cartridge form. Fithian's research revealed that the Royal Navy practice at the end of the eighteenth century was to require each ship to carry enough powder and ammunition to discharge each gun sixty to seventy times. Based on this practice, he calculated that in order to fire each gun sixty-five times, *De Braak* would have had to carry over 2,000 pounds of gunpowder—not including the amount needed for the small arms aboard.

Both lead shot and gunflints had been recovered in large quantities during the latter days of the salvage operation. Loads of shot in the hundreds and suitable for every caliber of small arms found on board had been inventoried. Approximately 1,000 gunflints had been recovered and analyzed as well, providing the researchers with interesting data on the British manufacturing techniques employed to produce them. Most had been produced from black flint, probably extracted from the mines of Suffolk and Kent, and included both English spall and the commonly adopted French blade traditions, knapped in specific sizes for cannon, musket, and pistol. The once common and distinctive English blade gunflint, believed to have been introduced as early as 1775, was not found, while a large number of flints knapped in the French blade tradition did turn up, the implications of which could only be a matter of speculation.[8] It was clear that Fithian's research, as productive as it had been, merely scratched the surface of what was still to be gleaned.

The next to speak was Harry Alden, an art conservator and specialist in wood analysis from the Winterthur Museum. Alden had been asked in May 1987 to identify eighteen samples of wood from the wreck, but he stayed on to study more than 440. His research went into considerable depth, for he not only sought to identify the enormous range of wood types found aboard De Braak (as well as the components of the ship itself), but also to chronicle their various rates of decay and to propose conservation measures for the future.

Alden had begun by categorizing all of the wood-based artifacts and then had proceeded to take samples from each, including armaments, cooperage, dunnage, navigational instruments, ordnance, rigging, the hull and its myriad member parts, and other miscellaneous items. He had sampled and analyzed everything from musket stocks to basketry. His findings were not only revealing, but they formed a comprehensive data base suitable for comparison with all similar British ship remains of the period. Sea Service muskets and pistols, for instance, which were originally thought to have been manufactured from a low-grade wood, such as ash or beech, proved to be of the highest grade of walnut. Ramrods were of ash and beech, and, surprisingly for British arms, also included a sample of hickory, an American wood.

The ship's cooperage encompassed an incredible variety of woods, including an unexpected tropical wood (removed from the Xavier?). Banding and hoops for barrels and kegs were composed of a mélange of hazel, willow, birch, beech, ash, and white oak. Bungs were of oak and red pine. Heading materials were white oak, pine, and beech. Lashings were willow. The staves themselves were red oak, beech, birch, red pine, and white oak.

Alden conducted macroscopic analysis of many if not most of the samples, including the ship's dunnage, some of which still maintained horizontal lenticels of bark. Here he found samples of cherry, walnut, small quantities of white oak, birch, sassafras, and even a tropical hardwood.

Navigational instruments included an ebony octant and a mahogany telescope with components of boxwood. The mahogany was so well preserved, with its original color and hardness intact, that Alden was moved to compare it to a Queen Anne or Chippendale chair.

One by one, he ticked off the list of his findings. Canister bases were made of elm, shot boxes of spruce and elm. Rammer heads were of the red oak group, and shot stands of white oak. Sponge heads were of elm and ash. Sheaves were invariably made of lignum vitae, belaying pins and parrels of ash, and deadeyes and blocks of elm.

Unhappily for those who still represented the Pancoast tradition of the teak-built ship, Alden discovered that *De Braak* had been constructed of everything but. "Samples," he stated,

> included beech which was found in the stern keelson. Elm turned up in the dead-wood. Live oak turned up in the major framing of the ship in addition to the white oak group. . . . A good part of the bulkheads and internal compartments of the ship and the shot locker was composed of the red oak group, Scotch pine, and Riga pine.

Alden was impressed with the macroscopic preservation of all of the wood samples: most were in a pristine condition, and seventy-five percent of them looked as if they had just been cut. Oil cells in the sassafras, after nearly 180 years of immersion, still emitted a fresh odor. Growth rings in white oak samples were as clearly visible as on the day they were cut. The sheaves of lignum vitae, a self-lubricating wood and the densest known to man (with the tensile strength of aluminum), were still so hard that more than sixty razor blades had been expended on attempts to cut the tiniest samples. Basket willow was "like new."

Alden had not stopped at simple identification, but had proceeded to initiate a pilot study, with one of his art conservation students at the University of Delaware, to assess the various conservation measures that could be used for the wood components in the *De Braak* collections. The study analyzed the various levels of water saturation in the different wood types, as well as their porosity and subsequent rates of degradation, all of which had to be identified in order to plan future conservation approaches and budgeting needs.

Alden's research, like that of many of the other specialists presenting their findings that day, was ongoing. He had continued to sample wood from the ship's dunnage, in hopes of discovering evidence of any unexpected landfalls where wood might have been taken aboard, and from the hull, to better evaluate how the wood was used in its construction. He had also begun to study other cellulose objects, such as rope and the flagging on barrel staves, while continuing to assist and consult on the conservation of waterlogged wooden objects for future display. He had already made an enormous contribution to the sum total of knowledge about *De Braak* and the tools and accoutrements of her period—and he had only just begun.[8]

De Braak's ability to sail and fight was one thing, while her ability to remain at sea and to sustain the life of her crew with a modicum of supplies and provisions was quite another. Fithian was well aware that the realities of day-to-day life of the men who had sailed, fought, and died with her (despite Davidson's convictions to the contrary) could still be discovered in the battered fragments of cooperage, ceramics, and glassware which they had used, as well as the evidence of the food they had eaten, the clothes they had worn and the physical remnants of the shipboard society they had maintained.

When Kerry Shackleford, one of the foremost authorities on early cooperage, received Fithian's call for help at his office in Colonial Williamsburg, he was still finishing up the documentation of cask and barrel staves from the wrecks of several British victuallers and warships sunk during the siege of Yorktown in 1781. For Shackleford, the prospect of examining similar materials from another British shipwreck of the same era was exciting, for it offered the prospect of expanding his already sizeable data base on eighteenth-century cooperage. During his study of the barrels, casks, and kegs recovered by archaeologist John Broadwater from one of the Yorktown wrecks (officially referred to as YO-88 and later identified as the Betsey), he had never received more than twenty to thirty barrel staves to examine at any one time. When he arrived at the Fischer Enterprise warehouse and was led to one of the eight-by-ten-foot containment blocks filled with nearly a thousand staves, he was stunned. "It was," he joked, "an interesting challenge just to get to the one on the bottom."[10]

Before he could begin to examine the staves, he determined that it would first be necessary to hand wash the entire collection, which had been stained red through and through by iron oxides from the wreck site. Soon after their first cleaning, he returned them to the water only to discover later that the red stain had leached to the surface and more washing would be necessary—every few weeks, in fact. Fithian promptly organized a volunteer program to keep the staves cleaned, but the process seemed endless.

Evaluation of De Braak's cooperage, Shackleford quickly learned, would be far more difficult than that of YO-88. Unlike the casks from the Yorktown wreck, which had been excavated intact, all of the De Braak staves and heads had been recovered without provenance and were unrelated, but they undoubtedly represented scores of containers. "It's almost puzzle time," the cooper quipped, resigning himself to the task.[11] Despite the daunting problems he faced, Shackleford approached the job methodically. He knew from experience that there were certain constraints on barrel and cask construction. The areas between the grooves and crows (where the extreme head of a cask fits into the container itself), between the groove and the end of the cask (called the chime), and between various components of the head itself were all constants. By measuring these and by recording the thickness and overall length of each piece, Shackleford would be able to sort out the "wad of sticks" lying in the tank. After taking multiple measurements of the entire collection, he entered the data into a data-base management program and began to sort further. Markings, graffiti, odd construction discrepancies, and other features noted during the examination were also systematically analyzed and entered into the program.

Shackleford was able to assemble 107 different units, that is, pieces attached to other pieces, and ended up with fifty stave groupings and over fifty heads that mended together. From these, he was able to partially reassemble at least twenty different containers. By careful computation and assessment of the remaining staves and head fragments, he determined that the collection held components for at least another sixty containers. These findings, given the lack of provenance and the ruthless fashion in which the wreck had been excavated, came as a complete surprise. "I would never have guessed," he reported, "that we could have so many from the site."[12]

The next objective was to determine the probable usage of the containers. Most appeared to have held liquid provisions, primarily rum, which was normally stored in the heavier and thicker casks made of white oak. There were at least ten half-hogsheads, which contained twenty eight gallons of liquid apiece; eighteen barrels containing thirty six gallons of rum each (or, occasionally, beer); a large, eighty-four gallon cask called a puncheon; and nine casks, of 126 gallons each, called pipes. Shackleford also noted the remains of at least six thin-staved containers, which would have carried salt pork or beef. Six containers appeared to have served as personal food tubs, mess kits, or as small drinking vessels called "tigs," recovered only from sites of the sixteenth, seventeeth, and eighteenth centuries. One unusual find, and an exact duplicate of several found at YO-88, proved to be a container for lead musket balls.

Shackleford surmised that so many heavier casks, such as the rum containers, had probably survived, while the lightweight pork and beef casks had not, because heavier casks were normally stowed in the deepest portion of the ship, thereby lowering the vessel's center of gravity. When *De Braak* sank in an upright position and quickly filled with mud and sand, the lighter containers on top were more exposed to marine biota. (The destructive recovery methods employed by the salvors did not increase their chances of survival.)

Based upon provision invoices for similarly manned vessels, and the amount of food and drink known to be needed by a crew of eighty-five men for six months, Shackleford determined that *De Braak* should have carried over 300 containers. Rum provisions alone, he estimated, would have totaled approximately 14,500 gallons. Thus he concluded that representative components of nearly a third of the provision containers (including casks which would have carried 5,500 gallons of rum, beer, and water) had been recovered. The cooper paid special attention to the identification of markings and designs branded on the casks, all of which would have been entered into the Royal Navy's invoice books (no longer extant) when *De Braak* had been provisioned at Plymouth. He observed that the Royal Navy's broad arrow marks were always stamped in the same place and appeared on all of the rum casks, but, for some unknown reason, not on the beef containers or lighter-weight pieces. He studied a concretion composed of stacked cask staves from a pipe of rum, called a "shook," which he concluded had been dismantled and numbered for convenient storage and later reassembly.

For Shackleford, there were some delightful discoveries. "One of the things I had hoped to find," he reported,

> literally jumped out. It was a change of technology which we saw only hints of at Yorktown. Traditionally, up until the 1750s, we had presumed that all of the material prepared for cooperage was split from the log rather than being prepared by any mechanical means, such as sawing. Two sites of the nine Yorktown sites contain staves that were sawn rather than split. We wrote it off as something oddball that was not common. Well, we could not write that off here, for without exception, every container is sawn.[13]

Shackleford knew that in constructing a cask, as a rule, the interior of a stave would be hollowed out or curved to facilitate bending and to increase the interior volume of the container. But none of the liquid casks from the *De Braak* site showed any evidence of hollow chafe to their interior surfaces. "What we think we are seeing," he said,

> is a change in the technology as we get closer to the beginning of the 19th century; the availability of sawn materials becomes more common in different parts of the country. We have yet to see that in any part of this country's [the United State's] cooperage. Obviously, it would stand to reason that the majority of the cooperage of this vessel is of European origins, particularly English.[14]

One of the most recognizable things that Shackleford observed was that all of the staves and cooperage had been new when the ship sank. Unlike those that had been recovered at Yorktown, which revealed signs of having been repaired, used, and reused many times, the *De Braak* collection had been in almost perfect condition when lost. Barely twenty percent of the liquid containers had been repaired with pegs (to prevent leakage), while 100 percent of the Yorktown collection had been repaired.

Shackleford was positive of the collection's value, despite the lack of provenance for many artifacts. "What we have gained from this site," he said bluntly,

> is the ability to continue our data-base collection of information about cooperage. In working in occupations and trades where you are reproducing containers and other products, one of the more difficult things to do is to have objects that you can definitely date, and cooperage is an extremely important one. We have no way at this point of definitely dating a container without question to its period. With sites like this we have that sewed up.[15]

No less important to an understanding of the quality and style of life aboard *De Braak* were Alice Guerrant's analysis of the ceramics and the evaluations made by Wade Catts, Coleen Desantis, and Scott C. Watson of the bottle and table glass recovered from the wreck. Guerrant's objective was to set her study in the context of one of man's most important social activities—the act of eating. "The high point of many people's lives," she began, "is dinner time, and a sailor's life at sea is no exception."[16] The "mess" was the focal point of each sailor's daily activities, the place where he ate his meals and enjoyed the opportunity for social interaction. The conflicts tensions, and social dynamics built up over months of living in close quarters at sea dictated that the crew be able to change messmates at least monthly. Usually, four to eight men messed together. Aboard *De Braak*, the crew would thus have been divided among seven to fourteen messes, not including the marines, midshipmen, or officers. James Drew, like most commanding officers, ate in his own quarters and at his own table, either alone or, occasionally, with an invited officer. The crew's diet was monotonous, usually consisting of boiled meat, boiled vegetables, boiled pudding, bread, and cheese. Drink was usually limited to grog, beer, and water, although lime and lemon juices were carried on long voyages to prevent scurvy.

The mess cook was responsible for collecting the provisions of food for the mess, as well as for preparing it and placing it in bags with the mess tally's identification. He delivered these to the cook, who would place them together in a cauldron for several hours. Later, the mess cook would collect his bags, divide their contents among the mess kits, and deliver the main meal of the day to his messmates. The commonly held view was that meals were eaten on wooden plates, or trenchers, with knives and spoons and that drink was taken from tin cups. Officers were better equipped. Although both officers and crew were obliged to purchase their own mess gear, either while in port or from the purser, the better-paid officers acquired fine pewter, ceramics, and even silver, if they could afford it. Frequently, in order to vary the monotonous shipboard diet of boiled foods, officers would purchase special drinks and fare that they could have baked, roasted, or broiled.

A total of 252 ceramic objects or representative pieces of them had been recovered from the *De Braak* wreck site. Unlike most ceramics found at land sites, there were very few of uncertain function. Equally important was the collection's representing a specific point in time when the ship sank (hence the validity of the "time capsule" concept), rather than the assortment of discards from different periods typical of a land site. Thus, the range of wares was narrower and, having been transported from Europe, included types which had not been recovered from nearby mid-Atlantic sites of the same era. Only twenty-seven percent of the ceramic vessels were of utilitarian form, while the great majority proved to be refined tablewares, quite the opposite of what was

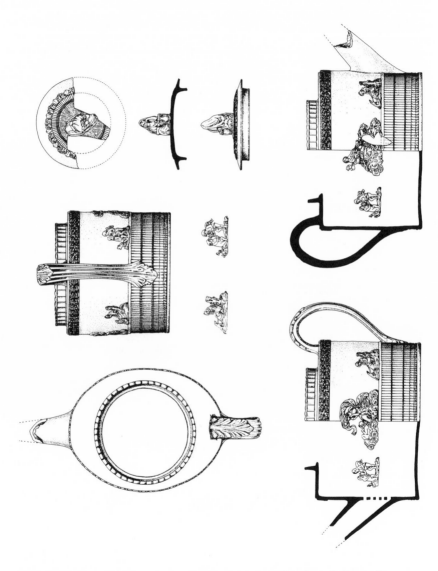

This black basalt teapot and creamer set is believed to have belonged to one of *De Braak*'s officers, possibly even Captain Drew himself. (*Delaware State Museums*)

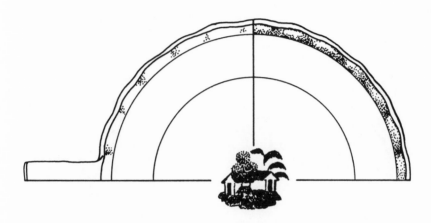

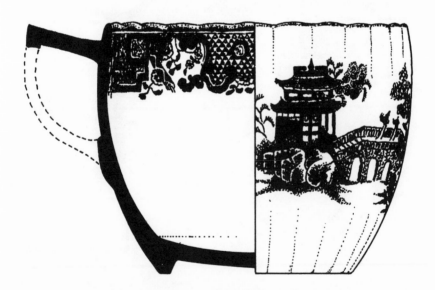

Fine china such as this cup and bowl served both officers and seamen alike, and may have been purchased by ship's purser William Wade before *De Braak* sailed on her final voyage. (*Delaware State Museums*)

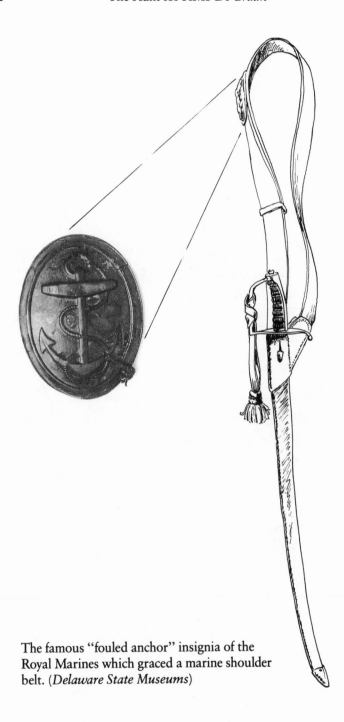

The famous "fouled anchor" insignia of the
Royal Marines which graced a marine shoulder
belt. (*Delaware State Museums*)

normally encountered on land sites—or what was expected aboard a man-of-war.

Twenty-six different vessel forms in sixteen different wares were identified, two-thirds of them creamware and pearlware, which were popular tablewares ashore. Surprisingly, many of the creamware plates, platters, and soup plates bore a wide range of mess marks scratched on their bases, indicating their use by the crew rather than the officers. All of the creamware, including dishes, basins, pitchers, a teapot, tea bowls, and saucers, was so similar in style that Guerrant concluded that they had been purchased all at once, probably in haste, for resale to the officers and crew aboard when *De Braak* had sailed on her last voyage.

The highly popular pearlware included green and blue shell-edged plates, soup bowls, and platters, four of which bore mess marks. The decorative variety of the full range of pearlware, particularly among the cups, tea bowls, and saucers, and bowls possibly from tea sets brought aboard by the officers and midshipmen for use or resale, was stunning. There were samples of many different and delightful patterns, including blue hand-painted patterns, floral patterns with mesh borders, house-with-fence patterns, a polychrome sprig pattern, blue transfer print patterns, and the famous Barilla pattern, which had not been documented in North America prior to 1796. Even English and Chinese decorative porcelains had been found, albeit in small quantities, along with the utterly utilitarian white salt-glazed and Delft or buff-bodied tin-glazed stoneware. One of the tin-glazed galley pots even featured the blue anchor mark of a French pottery.

The most elaborately decorated and beautiful vessels found were a black basalt teapot-and-creamer set. When first reported in the press, the set had been hastily and incorrectly identified as "mourning" pots, which were then linked to the death of James Drew's brother John. Among the more interesting finds were Iberian red-bodied, tin-glazed galley pots and several elaborately decorated bowls, with green, blue, and yellow floral patterns and geometric motifs. Initially, these vessels were believed to have been taken from *De Braak*'s Spanish prize. However, closer inspection revealed that one of the bowls had been on board long enough to have acquired a mess mark, so it had probably been purchased rather than taken as a piece of prize goods.

The remaining ceramics comprised coarse wares, most of them brown stoneware storage pots (identical to samples recovered from HMS *Pandora*), bottles, lidded pipkins, and ink bottles, as well as North American gravel-tempered were, Buckley ware, and even a type of Iberian coarse ware that was typical of the Mediterranean and had not been found on mid-Atlantic land sites. There were also conical-bottomed olive jars and castral and storage pots. The largest single item recovered was a huge oil jar, often found on land sites, which had been pierced near the bottom, probably for a spigot or bung,

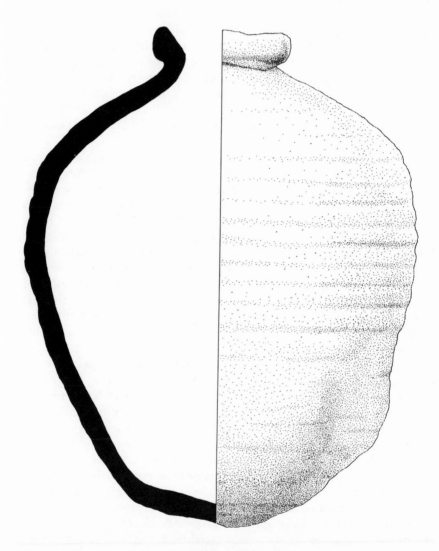

Two Iberian water jugs recovered intact from the wreck. (*Delaware State Museums*)

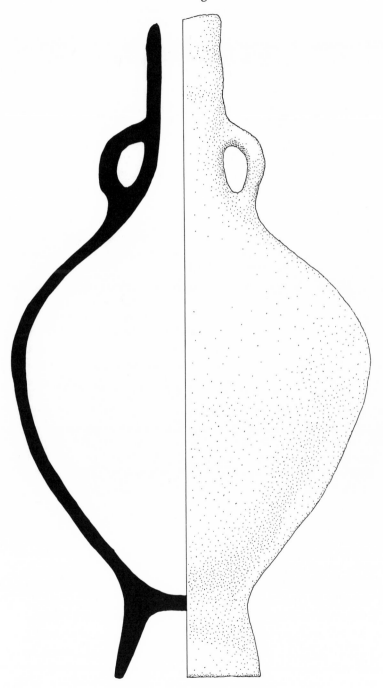

and reused as a water jar on deck. (A duplicate of this item had also been recovered from *Pandora*.) There were smaller collections of coarse, red-bodied
earthen wares of American or Northern European origin, employed as serving
vessels, in food storage and preparation, and for hygienic and medicinal purposes. A large number of matching cups, tea bowls, and saucers, and a pair of
teapots had been recovered, and Guerrant concluded that tea and other such
drinks might have been restricted to the officers. "On the other hand," she
suggested, "only one mug was located in the entire assemblage. What then
were the crew using to drink from? Since it seems clear from the mess marks
that the crew were in fact eating from refined ceramic plates, perhaps they
were also using fancy pearlware cups to drink their grog!"[17] But could this be
safely concluded she asked. After all, the use of tin cups in the Royal Navy was
well documented, and although none of these had been recovered, iron and tin
preservation on the site had been very poor. With the exception of a single
"tig," wooden drinking vessels, once commonly employed, had also not been
found, despite the good state of wood preservation.

A small number of storage vessels, ranging from six to sixteen and five-
eights inches high and used primarily for pickled or salted food, had been recovered. Very few food preparation vessels were found, however, reflecting the
primary cooking method of boiling each mess's food in a bag. Evidence of only
a few alternative cooking modes, including several pans probably used for
baking or mixing "duff," a kind of boiled pudding with raisins, had been
brought up by the salvors. The last class of ceramics recovered was for hygienic
and medicinal functions had been recovered. Ninety percent of these were galley pots or drug pots, but there were also three chamber points, probably from
the sick bay, as all able-bodied personnel were expected to use the head.

Guerrant compared the *De Braak*'s ceramics to those recovered from three
other excavated shipwrecks of the same period; HMS *Pandora* (1791), HMS
Orpheus (1778), and the American Revolutionary War ship *Defense* (1779).
De Braak's ceramic assemblage, she noted, had been primarily composed of
refined tablewares, in sharp contrast to those of other ships of the period. Although not enough information had become available yet on *Pandora*'s assemblage, those of *Orpheus* and *Defense* had clearly demonstrated a status relationship between their ceramics and the officers. The number and type of
ceramic vessels, as well as the areas where they had been recovered, reflected
the exclusive use of refined tablewares by officers of these ships. Wooden tan-
kards and plates used by the crew had been found aboard *Defense* but not
Orpheus. Some aspects of the ships' ceramics, however, were quite similar:
many of the most decorative pieces were in the latest styles. The *Orpheus* collection included a number of highly decorated creamware forms produced no
more then a decade before her loss. Although *De Braak* 's creamware was con-

siderably plainer, an equal degree of fashionable style was represented by her pearlware and besalt forms. Based on these and other comparisons, it seems probable that British naval vessels of the period were usually supplied with the latest fashion in ceramics. Yet these distinctive features of *De Braak*'s ceramics, in contrast to those of vessels sunk only a decade earlier, might have been due to changes in the navy's provisioning of its ships—or merely to the idiosyncrasy of the particular purser charged with provisioning *De Braak*. Only the archaeological excavation of other Royal Navy shipwreck sites of that era could provide the answer.

Guerrant's conclusions from her preliminary examination of the ceramics collection were instructive. There were, she deduced, clear distinctions between the mess equipment of officers and of crew, although the evidence indicated, for the first time on a ship-of-war of this period, that both groups were eating from the same types of dishes. Was this, perhaps, a consequence of the Great Mutiny? Still, officers did have access to a greater variety of food and drink and did use some distinctive vessels, such as tea sets and pipkins, for their service. There was less evidence of social distinctions found in the ceramics of *De Braak* than in any other items recovered. When ceramics had entirely replaced wooden ware, ratio of refined wares to coarse wares was skewed, as compared to that of other sites. The indicators of a weaker relationship between refined ceramics and higher social status was, Guerrant warned her colleagues, a reminder of the dangers of relying upon such indicators of status without considering the context of the site and the period. Most of the ceramic vessels appeared to have been purchased, probably by the purser, and brought aboard as food containers or for resale to the ship's men. Others had been brought aboard by the officers to suit their own particular tastes and needs.[18]

The analysis of the glassware by Catts, Desantis, and Watson was equally revealing. The trio had sought to identify the important functions of bottles and table glass, as well as evidence of such specific shipboard activities as ritual drinking by officers and of the use of glass containers for medicines and stores. With the help of contemporary British and American naval documents, secondary sources, and comparable glass assemblages, they had set out to chronicle the functions and social contexts of glass aboard *De Braak*. Their holistic approach to analysis entailed a major undertaking, for they would be obliged to study more than 350 glass vessels, including wine and beer containers, tumblers, decanters, condiment bottles, storage containers, table glass, medicinal vials and bottles, perfume bottles, flasks, and sand glasses.

Their first task had been to survey fifty-three whole and three broken English wine bottles in the collection. The word "wine" was a generic term for these types of bottles, which were often used or reused for fluids other than wine. Indeed, the presence of lead shot in several bottles indicated that they were cleaned out and recycled. The majority of the collection, it was pointed out, almost certainly came from the officer's mess or belonged to individual officers, but were definitely not part of the ship's general provisions.

Recent investigations by researchers Olive Jones and Ann Smith, they pointed out, had conclusively demonstrated that a considerable amount of liquor was commonly consumed by the officer class at mess, both ritually and in the course of dining. The officers' mess itself had both a military and a social function, serving as a place where officers were drawn together in a cohesive unit and as a social center where status and rank were reinforced. As the purser's records for one Royal Navy warship, HMS *Raleigh*, have revealed, large quantities of assorted liquors, including Madeira, Lisbon, and Tenerife wines, as well as port, sherry, brandy, beer, ale, and cider, were procured for the mess by individual officers—by the dozen, the gallon, and the cask. Most of the alcoholic beverages were stored, as Shackleford had pointed out, not in bottles but in wooden casks which were tapped to fill bottles and decanters for an officer's table.

Typologically, the dark-green English wine bottles had similar cylindrical shapes, featuring rounded shoulders, rounded or balched heels, down-tooled or flattened lips, and rounded cone, dome, conical, and parabolic basal profiles. Pontil marks were the result of using sand pontils. Utilizing the English wine bottle types alone as a means of dating the wreck, the three investigators arrived at a date between 1790 and 1820, and they were delighted to discover that similar conclusions had been drawn from bottles recovered from *Pandora*, half a world away.

One of the most exciting finds had been a wine bottle with a glass seal on the body, bearing the words "Marine Mess." Since *De Braak*'s fourteen-man contingent of marines did not include any commissioned officers of a rank high enough to have had his own bottle, Catts, and his colleagues concluded that the bottle must have been government-issued expressly for the marine contingent, making it the only known bottle of its kind in the world to date.

The collection also included thirty-eight British beer bottles, resembling, but subtly different from, the English wine bottles, as well as nineteen free-blown, cylindrical French wine bottles. The latter featured long, gracefully tapered necks, down-sloping shoulders, and rounded heels with no push-up marks. Although the presence of French wine bottles aboard an English man-of-war during a period of war with France might seem incongruous, it was not unusual. Inventories of American warships from the time of the Quasi-War with France revealed that substantial quantities of French brandy were carried. The *De Braak* collection offered the first evidence that the British followed the same practice.

A great variety of tableglass, including twenty-four stemmed drinking glasses, twenty-one tumblers, nine decanters, two firing glasses, one dessert glass, one salt-cast trencher, three cruets, two casters, and two condiment containers, had been recovered and was clearly associated with the officers' mess. Aboard American warships of the same period, such items, of the common rather than the high-style variety, were listed as standard-issue cabin furniture. Analysis of the *De Braak* table glass revealed that these pieces too were of the common variety, which suggested that they had also been standard issue for the Royal Navy officers' mess, perhaps owing to the high attrition rate from breakage of such objects aboard a man-of-year. Of the tableglass, two condiment containers were of particular interest. One was an intact cylindrical bottle decorated with a wheel-engraved shield-and-wheat design. Inside the wheel the word "KETCHUP" was engraved. The decoration, it was noted, was an imitation of the metallic engraved chains of the period, which identified a container's contents. There were numerous recipes for "ketchup" at the end of the eighteenth century, few of which resembled the condiment commonly used today. One recipe, from *The London Art of Cookery*, published in 1789, was quite popular with sailors and had consisted of mushrooms, cloves, and other spices mixed with beer (the staler, the better). Fragments of a second condiment bottle, probably for onion, were also recovered.

Both British and American warships, at the end of the eighteenth century, carried huge quantities of liquids and semiliquids as part of the ship stores, mostly in casks and kegs, either as hospital supplies or for general issue. Wine, particularly white wine, was commonly issued aboard British men-of-war. In 1798 the US Frigate *Constellation* carried hospital stores consisting of 32½ gallons of brandy, 98 gallons of sherry, 99 gallons of Lisbon wine, 47¾ gallons of port, 66 gallons of porter, one keg with five gallons of lemon juice, and three hogsheads carrying 400 gallons of vinegar. For a three-month voyage in the same year, the US Frigate *United States* carried 4,140 gallons of rum for crew rations. *De Braak*, according to Shackleford's calculations, carried more than 14,000 gallons!

The *De Braak* collection of ninety-three partial and whole storage bottles, that is, large cylindrical containers with the prominent "GR" seal of the admiralty, is one of the largest known assemblages of its kind from a single site. Several of the otherwise empty bottles still had their corks, implying the reuse of such containers. Research by Olive Jones and Ann Smith, as cited by Catts, et al., suggests that these containers were large pharmaceutical bottles: "As medicines are almost the only type of material being supplied by the army and navy that is suitable for storage in glass containers of that size, these were probably used for that purpose."[19] Jones has suggested that the bottles held a substance used in large quantities, but issued in small amounts. In 1798 the only liquid used by the British navy in such quantities was lemon juice, an antiscorbutic. As a prophylactic against and a remedy for scurvy, lemon juice, mixed with grog, was consumed by navy crews in prodigious amounts. It was

This Marine Mess bottle is the only one of its kind known to exist, but may have been standard issue by the British government to Royal Marine units during the Napoleonic era. (*Delaware State Museums*)

One of 93 large pharmaceutical
containers bearing the familiar
British Admiralty "GR" glass seal
(George Rex), this bottle is believed
to have carried lemon juice. Mixed
with grog, lemon juice served as an
antiscorbutic and was consumed in
vast quantities on long ocean
voyages. (*Delaware
State Museums*)

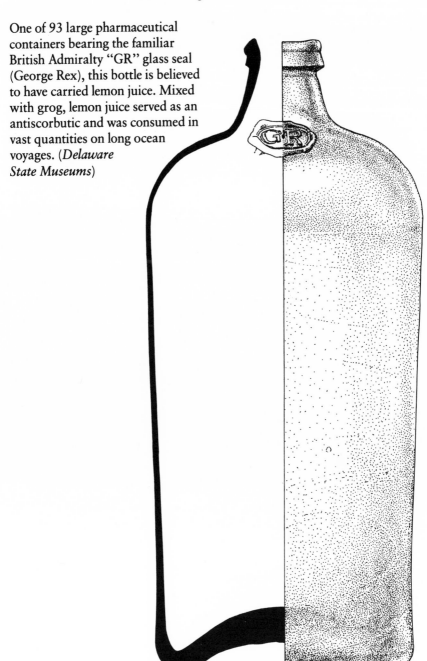

This condiment bottle contained the "ketchup" of the 18th century, a concoction quite popular with sailors of the period, consisting of cloves, other spices, and mushrooms, mixed with stale beer. (*Delaware State Museums*)

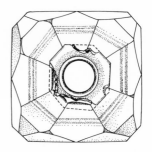

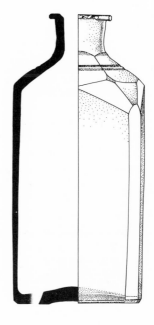

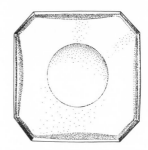

A decanter used by an officer to
store spirits. (*Delaware State
Museums*)

normally stored aboard ship in half-gallon bottles—like those bearing the "GR" seal of Admiralty property. Catts and company calculated that the *De Braak* collection represented 46.5 gallons of lemon juice. If each man aboard consumed 1.4 gallons on a six-month voyage (a rate of consumption documented in the Royal Navy records of the period), a total of 120.4 gallons would have been required for the voyage. The excavation, then, had resulted in the recovery of twenty-eight percent of the total that should have been aboard, a figure remarkably close to Shackleford's estimated percentage of the casks recovered.

Perhaps the most notable set of anomalies in the glass collection were six blue-green French flacons made of bubble glass. These dip-moulded wide-mouthed containers with bell-shaped bases were produced in a wide variety of sizes and forms. The flacons recovered from *De Braak* were of the type most commonly employed in serving and storing preserved and brandied fruits, pickles, anchovies, olives, and oils. What was unique about them was that such flacons were most commonly found on British military sites of the 1750s and 1760s, but rarely later and almost never on a shipwreck site.

As Guerrant had done before them with the ceramics, Catts and his colleagues made it abundantly clear that the *De Braak* glassware was extremely significant for the data it provided on the physical and social life of men aboard a late eighteenth-century Royal Navy warship. The abundance and integrity of the individual specimens meant that these artifacts constituted a first-rate comparative collection. Catts, Desantis, and Watson had already made unexpected and important findings and their work, like that of their colleagues, had barely begun.[20]

The *De Braak* symposium did much to defuse the hostility of the archaeological community—which had awaited the delegation from Delaware on that day in January 1989—and more to legitimize their work in the eyes of their professional peers. Unfortunately, it did little to resolve the issue of the artifact collection's final disposition.

At 8:30 A.M. on March 28, 1990, a front-end loader began to remove the earthen berm surrounding the cofferdam in which *De Braak* had been kept for nearly four years. The water which had covered the old brig's bones had only hours before been drained away. For those of us who had come to watch her removal to yet another temporary home that day, it was a gratifying event. The land on which Fischer Enterprises had stood had been sold to a real-estate developer. *De Braak* had to be moved, but unlike "the pick," everything went as smoothly as possible.

The hull had been covered with a large, blue, plastic sheet, weighted down by tires, to keep it damp during the operation, even as the loader carefully dismantled the coffer wall around it. Two cranes, one from First State Crane

Service and the other from Nanticoke Homes of Greenwood, Delaware, had been leased for the delicate lifting job. Under the direction of John Hayden of First State, *De Braak* was to be carefully raised and then set down on a huge flatbed truck. After being properly braced, she would be transported to the grounds of the Cape Henlopen State Park administrative center, only a short distance away. There, she would remain under a sprinkler system for nearly four months until a specially designed containment site could be constructed by Hayden's firm to house her for the foreseeable future. The move and the construction project had been budgeted at close to $100,000.

As the project proceeded, I walked about the former Fischer Enterprise grounds with Claudia Melson, Chuck Fithian, and Fred Hopkins, musing over the events of the last six years. All around us heavy excavation equipment was tearing up the earth and what was left of the ramshackled fish rendering plant that had served as Sub-Sal's headquarters. Another high-priced condominium would soon go up in its place. *De Braak*'s time here was over, and there would soon be little left to betray the fact of her four-year tenure. "Mount Davidson" had succumbed to the developer's bulldozer, while the detritus of three seasons of salvage lay scattered about in rusting profusion. The white, battered shell of the divers' decompression chamber lay partially exposed beneath a mound of freshly dug earth, while bits and pieces of broken equipment and the old fish rendering plant itself were ground into rubble.

At 1:50 P.M., the lift began, this time with mind-numbing caution and deliberation. Exactly two hours later, *De Braak* came to rest on the truck bed— a scant twenty feet from the cofferdam. By late evening, she had arrived at her new residence less than two miles away.

On July 30, 1990, *De Braak* was moved once again, this time into her custom-designed quarters on the Cape Henlopen State Park grounds. She had graduated by then to a specially constructed building with foam-plastic interior, a concrete floor, complete with a huge drain system in its center, and wet storage containers for miscellaneous timbers. Here, beneath an eternal spray of water, the carcass of legend could be kept wet until such time as she could be attended to in the manner she required. In the meantime, the State of Delaware and L. John Davidson continued to dance about each other, working out their steps over who would get what, how much it would cost, and who would bear the burden. They would continue their intricate waltz for the next year and a half. Gradually, the salvor became increasingly less inclined to negotiate.

On the evening of Thursday, February 6, 1992, I received a call from Chuck Fithian, who informed me that the issue of title to *De Braak* and her artifacts had at long last been resolved in the U.S. District Court in Wilmington by Judge Wright only two days earlier. Within a week I had obtained a copy of the court order. The U.S. District Court for the District of Delaware and the

State of Delaware, it seemed, after a "lengthy period of inactivity due, in part, to the disinterest of the parties in this case," after six years of delays and endless negotiations, had had enough. Accordingly, Delaware had moved for a summary judgment. Citing the federal Submerged Lands Act of 1988, which had established title to and ownership of all lands beneath navigable waters, within the boundaries of the respective states, including seaward boundries established in a line three miles distant from the coastline, and vested ownership of all resources therein to the states, Judge Wright had ruled that *De Braak* had been recovered from territorial lands belonging to the State of Delaware. Though the Act had given Delaware title to the land upon which *De Braak* had been located, it did not establish that title to the actual shipwreck and the artifacts resided within the State. The Court had instead relied upon the common law of finds. Cognizant that the application of salvage law involved the presumption that the owner of an abandoned vessel had not been divested of title, the Court had rejected the salvage law theory, and subscribed to the theory that the "disposition of a wrecked vessel whose very location has been lost for centuries as though its owners were still in existence stretch[es] a fiction to absurd lengths."[21]

The comon law of finds is based upon the concept of *animus revertendi* (the owner has no intention of returning), which, in Judge Wright's view, was the most appropriate law to govern in the context of the *De Braak* issue. Citing a number of precedents, noting that *De Braak* had been abandoned in 1798 and its location off the Delaware coast had remained unknown until 1984, the Court had concluded that the law of finds applied. Ownership of abandoned property, according to the common law of funds, he declared, is generally assigned "without regard to where the property is found [except that] when the abandoned property is embedded in the soil, it belongs to the owner of the soil." It was not necessary, however, for a property to be entirely buried in the soil for the embedded exception to apply. Though the *De Braak* hull had been partially embedded on land owned by the State of Delaware, Judge Wright had ruled that the embedded exception to the law applied and gave Delaware clear title to *De Braak* and its artifacts. "There is, he wrote in concluding,

> no issue of material fact in this case which would negate the State of Delaware's claim of title to the *De Braak* and its artifacts. The affidavit of William F. Moyers filed by the State of Delaware demonstrates that the *De Braak* was located partially embedded on land belonging to the State of Delaware pursuant to the Submerged Lands Act.[22]

As no other party had filed an affidavit to show that there was a "genuine issue of fact" for trial, the Court declared that the State of Delaware's Summary Judgement on the State's claim to title of *De Braak* and its artifacts be granted.[23]

The long waltz had finally come to an end.

APPENDIXES

The Landrake-Saltash Drew & Watkins Genealogy

Complement of HMS De Braak

Abandoned Shipwreck Act of 1987

Appendix A
The Landrake-Saltash Drew & Watkins Genealogy

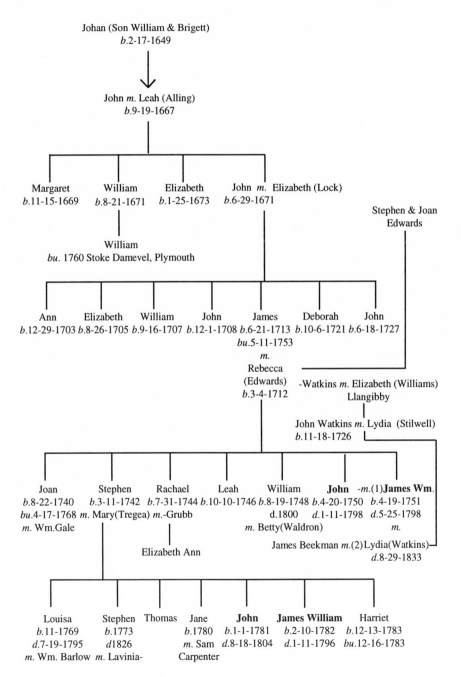

Note: Names in boldface are known Royal Navy Officers

Appendix B
Complement of HMS De Braak

Officers, Warrants, and Seamen 1797–1798

Name	Rate 1797	Rate 1798	Place of Abode
Albrook, Thomas*	Able	Seaman	Sweden
Amis (Annis), Stephen	Able	Seaman	Plymouth, Devon
Arundele (Arundell), William*	Able	Midshipman	Ireland
Bernard (?), John*	Seaman	Boy (?)	Colehampton, Devon
Biddle, Ambrose (?)	Able	Seaman	Birmingham, Warwickshire
Black, Angus	—	Ordinary	Rothua (?) Isle of Burke (?) [possibly Rothesay, Isle of Bute]
Breach, John	Ordinary	Ship's Barber	London
Brookbanks, William*	—	Seaman	Island of Jersey
Browne, William	2d Class Boy	Boy	Cirenster, Gloustershire
Burman, Thomas	Ordinary	Seaman	Biddeford, Devon
Burt, Thomas*	Armorer	Armorer	Plymouth
Buss, William*	Ordinary	Boy (?)	Chatham
Cooper, William (?)*	Cook	Cook	Bristol
Day, William (John)*	Able	Seaman	Ireland
Devenport (Davenport), Thomas*	2d Class Boy	Ward Room Steward	Birmingham
Dobson, William	Ordinary	Ordinary	Brough, Westmoreland
Dove, Isaac	Quartermaster Mate	Quartermaster	Ipswich, Suffolk
Doyle, Mathew	Seaman	Seaman	Bunting Cap, County Wicklow

Drew, James*	Commander	Commander	Saltash, Cornwall
Edward, Edward*	Ordinary	Seaman	Plymouth
Griffith, Thomas	Master	Master	Plymouth, Devon
Groves, Alexander	Coxwain	—	–
Harrison, James**	Ordinary	Ordinary	Poole
Hazel (Hapall), George	3d Class Boy	Boy	Plymouth Dock
Hearle, William*	Able	Midshipman	Plymouth
Hickson, Thomas*	Lieutenant	Lieutenant	Ireland
Hill, William	—	Seaman	Woodbury near Exeter
Howard, William*	Carpenter	Carpenter	Plymouth
Hudd (Hoad), James*	3d Class Boy	Boy	Bath, Glamorganshire
Hurlston (Harlston), William (?)*	Midshipman	Midshipman (Listed as "William")	London
Hyfield, John*	3d Class Boy	Midshipman	Weymouth
Jacobs, John	Able	Seaman	Hamburgh
Larkins, Thomas	Ordinary	Landsman	Dublin
Leach, John	Seaman (?)	Ordinary	Port Glasgow, N.B. [Scotland]
Levellin, John (Levellam, Joseph)	Carpenter's Crew	Seaman	Plymouth
Lingum (Lingham), ALexander	Ordinary	Seaman	Glenar, County Limerick
Little, William	Seaman	Seaman	Westbury near Bristol
Mahane, Michael (?)	Able	Seaman	Waterford, Ireland
Man (?), W (?)	Able	—	—
Mann (Munn), John*	2d Class Boy	Boy	Colehampton, Devon
Marshall, John	—	Seaman	Le Havre-de-Grâce
Mason, John	Able	Seaman	Plymouth, Devon
May, John	Ordinary	Seaman	Reoruth, Cornwall
McParson, Archibald	Able	Quartermaster	Greenock, N. B. [Scotland]

Michele (?), James (Samuel Michell))	Quartermaster Mate	Yeoman of the Powder Room	New York
Mills, John*	Seaman	Ordinary	North Britain
Mitchele, (?) (Mitchell), Richard*	Clerk	Captain's Clerk	Bristol
Morris, John*	Able	Seaman	Saltash
O'Neil (O'Neal), John	Able	Captain's Clerk	Rath Hale, County Limerick
Palser, Joseph (Palser, Joshua)	Seaman	Ordinary	Tilbury, Gloustershire
Patrick, Hugh	Ordinary	Seaman	Greenock, N.B. [Scotland]
Pissele (?), John	3d Class Boy	—	—
Poter (Potr), Henry	Ordinary	Ordinary	Plymouth
Ralph, James (?)	2d Class Boy	Boy	(?) Cornwall
Randele (Randell), William*	Able	Carpenter's Crew	Plymouth
Redman, Edward (?)*	Carpenter	Ship's Carpenter	Plymouth
Rumbold, William (?)*	Gunner	Gunner	Gosport
Satterly, William*	Carpenter's Mate	Carpenter's Crew	Plymouth
Sweet, John*	Able	Seaman	Plymouth
Thomas, James	Yeoman of the Powder Room	Boatswain's Mate	Bristol, Gloustershire

PUBLIC LAW 100–298 [S. 858]; April 28, 1988

ABANDONED SHIPWRECK ACT OF 1987

Section 1.   Short Title

This Act may be cited as the "Abandoned Shipwreck Act of 1987."

Section 2.   Findings

The Congress finds that—

(a) States have the responsibility for management of a broad range of living and nonliving resources in State waters and submerged lands; and

(b) included in the range and resources are certain abandoned shipwrecks, which have been deserted and to which the owner has relinquished ownership rights with no retention.

Section 3.   Definitions

For purposes of this Act—

(a) the term "embedded" means firmly affixed in the submerged lands or in coralline formations such that the use of tools of excavation is required in order to move the bottom sediments to gain access to the shipwreck, its cargo, and any part thereof;

(b) the term "National Register" means the National Register of Historic Places maintained by the Secretary of the Interior under section 101 of the National Historic Preservation Act (16 U.S.C. 470a);

(c) the terms "public lands," "Indian lands," and "Indian tribe" have the same meaning given the terms in the Archaeological Resource Protection Act of 1979 (16 U.S.C. 470aa–47011);

(d) the term "shipwreck" means a vessel or wreck, its cargo, and other contents;

(e) the term "State" means a State of the United States, the District of Columbia, Puerto Rico, Guam, the Virgin Islands; American Samoa, and the Northern Mariana Islands; and

(f) the term "submerged lands" means the lands—

(1) that are "lands beneath navigable waters, as defined in section 2 of the Submerged Lands Act (43 U.S.C. 1301);

(2) of Puerto Rico, as described in section 8 of the Act of March 2, 1917, as amended (48 U.S.C. 749);

(3) of Guam, the Virgin Islands and American Samoa, as described in section 1 of the Public Law 93–435 (48 U.S.C. 1705); and

(4) of the Commonwealth of the Northern Mariana Islands, as described in section 801 of Public Law 94–241 (48 U.S.C. 1705).

Section 4. Rights of Access

(a) Access Rights. —In order to—

(1) clarify that State waters and shipwrecks offer recreational and educational opportunities to sport divers and other interested groups, as well as irreplaceable State resources for tourism, biological sanctuaries, and historical research; and

(2) provide that reasonable access by the public to such abandoned shipwrecks be permitted by the State holding title to such shipwrecks pursuant to section 6 of this Act, it is the declared policy of the Congress that States carry out their responsibilities under this Act to develop appropriate and consistent policies as to—

(A) protect natural resources and habitat areas;

(B) guarantee recreational exploration of shipwreck sites; and

(C) allow for appropriate public and private sector recovery of shipwrecks consistent with the protection of historical values and environmental integrity of the shipwrecks and the sites.

(b) Parks and Protected Areas.—In managing the resources subject to the provisions of this Act, States are encouraged to create underwater parks or areas to provide additional protection for such resources. Funds available to States from grants from the Historic Preservation Fund shall be available, in accordance with the provisions of title 1 of the National Historic Preservation Act, for the study, interpretation, protection, and preservation of historic shipwrecks and properties.

Section 5. Preparation of Guidelines

(a) In order to encourage the development of underwater parks and the administrative cooperation necessary for the comprehensive management of underwater resources related to historic shipwrecks, the Secretary of the Interior, acting through the Director of the National Park Service, shall within nine months after the date of enactment of this Act prepare and publish guidelines in the Federal Register which shall seek to

(1) maximize the enhancement of cultural resources;

(2) foster a partnership among sport divers, fishermen, archaeologists, salvors, and other interests to manage shipwreck resources of the States and the United States;

(3) facilitate access and utilization by recreational interests;

(4) recognize the interests of individuals and groups engaged in shipwreck discovery and salvage.

(b) Such guidelines shall be developed after consultation with appropriate public and private sector interests (including the Secretary of Commerce, the Advisory Council on Historic Preservation, sport divers, State Historic Preservation officers, professional dive operators, salvors, archaeologists, historic preservationists, and fishermen).

(c) Such guidelines shall be available to assist States and the appropriate Federal agencies in developing legislation and regulations to carry out their responsibilities under this Act.

Section 6.   Rights of Ownership

(a) United States Title.—The United States asserts title to any abandoned shipwreck that is—

(1) embedded in submerged lands of a State;

(2) embedded in coralline formations protected by a State on submerged lands of a State; or

(3) on submerged lands of a State and is included in or determined eligible for inclusion in the National Register.

(b) The public shall be given adequate notice of the location of an shipwreck to which title is asserted under this section. The Secretary of the Interior, after consultation with the appropriate State Historic Preservation Officer, shall make a written determination that an abandoned shipwreck meets the criteria for eligibility for inclusion in the National Register of Historic Places under clause (a)(3).

(c) Transfer of Title to States.—The title of the United States to any abandoned shipwreck asserted under subsection (a) of this section is transferred to the State in or on whose submerged lands the shipwreck is located.

(d) Exception.—Any abandoned shipwreck in or on the property of the United States is the property of the United States Government. Any abandoned shipwreck in or on any Indian lands is the property of the Indian tribes owning such lands.

(e) Reservation of Rights.—This section does not affect any right reserved by the United States or by any State (including any right reserved with respect to Indian land) under—

(1) section 3, 5, or 6 of the Submerged Lands Act (43 U.S.C. 1311, 1313, and 1314); or

(2) section 19 or 20 of the Act of March 3, 1899 (33 U.S.C. 414 and 415).

Section 7.   Relationship to other Laws

(a) Law of Salvage and the Law of Finds.—The law of salvage and the law of finds shall not apply to abandoned shipwrecks to which section 6 of this Act applies.

(b) Laws of the United States.—This Act shall not change the laws of the United States relating to the shipwrecks, other than those to which this Act applies.

(c) Effective Date.—This Act shall not affect any legal proceeding brought prior to the date of enactment of this Act.

Source: *United States Congressional and Administrative News, 100th Congress, Second Session 1988, Volume I, Laws P. h.*—*100-243 to 100-418 [STAT. 1 to 1574].* West Publishing co., St. Paul, Minnesota.

NOTES

One

1. No fewer than thirty-eight vessels have been recorded as lost at or in the immediate vicinity of Cape Henlopen, Delaware, prior to 1798. The earliest documented shipwreck occurred in 1652 when a party of fourteen Englishmen were wrecked and then rescued by local Indians. As many as 150 vessels may have been lost without record in these same waters during the period 1631 to 1798. Prior to the year 1900, more than 233 vessels had been documented as lost in the same vicinity. E. B. O'Callaghan, ed., *Documents Relative to the Colonial History of the State of New York; Procured in Holland, England and France*, 15 vols. (Albany: Weed, Parsons and Company, 1853–1887), 12: 201, 215; Donald G. Shomette, "Shipwreck Profiles of the Delaware Coast: Delaware Breakwater to Fenwick Island" (report prepared for Nautical Archaeological Associates, 1981).

2. The site of Lewes Town (pronounced Loo-iss) was first established by a party of thirty-two Dutch settlers led by Peter Heyes under the sponsorship of Captain David Pieterson de Vries. The settlers arrived in April 1631 at Lewes Creek (now Roosevelt Inlet) aboard the ship *Walvis* with the objective of establishing a whaling industry. Named Swanendael (Valley of the Swans), the settlement was almost immediately destroyed by Indians. When De Vries arrived in December 1632, he discovered that the massacre had wiped out the colony to a man. Remaining for three months, he renamed the place Hoorn, after his native city in Holland. The creek became Hoornkill (later corrupted to Horekil and then Whorekill). In 1658, under the auspices of the West India Company, the Dutch established a second colony there called Sekonnessinck. In 1664 the colony was again devastated, this time by English forces under the command of Sir Robert Carr. By 1670, however, Dutch settlers had again filtered back to the banks of Horekil and established a third settlement which they named after the creek. Three years later, this settlement was also destroyed, this time by invading Marylanders sent by Governor Charles Calvert. In 1683, with resettlement again underway, the site was conveyed by the Duke of York to the government of William Penn. Whorekill was renamed Lewes in honor of the town of Lewes, England. The county was named Sussex, after Sussex County, England, and Lewes became its seat of government. In 1791 the county seat was removed to nearby Georgetown, but Lewes continued to serve as a minor commercial and

maritime entrepôt for Delaware until the beginning of the 20th century. [Virginia Cullen], *History of Lewes, Delaware* [1956], Rev. ed., NSDAR, 1981, 1–7; C. A. Weslager, *The English on the Delaware: 1610–1682* (New Brunswick, NJ: Rutgers University Press, 1967), 38–39, 176–202; Donald G. Shomette and Robert D. Haslach, *Raid on America: The Dutch Naval Campaign of 1672–1674* (Columbia, SC: University of South Carolina Press, 1988), 183, 243–50; Leon de Valinger, "The Burning of the Whorekill, 1673," *Pennsylvania Magazine* (October 1940): 473–87.

3. The tradition of the rescued *De Braak* sailors has been rendered in numerous variations, most of which seem to be of relatively recent origin. The earliest published version which specifically mentions wrecked sailors being offered succor appeared in the *Sun*, of Baltimore, on July 25, 1887. The McCracken account did not appear in print until the 1930s, although it was almost certainly a well-known tradition prior to 1887. An article in the *New York Times* on April 29, 1879, the earliest nineteenth-century account located to date claiming treasure to be aboard *De Braak*, noted that the story was "handed down from generation to generation" and was frequently related to summer tourists by the "rough old wreckers" of Lewes. The tale evolved to such an extent that, in 1954 William S. Dutton would write in the *Saturday Evening Post* that a sheet of paper enclosed in the McCracken family Bible

> bears the faded handwriting of Gilbert McCracken, a famous Lewes ship pilot of old days. It says that a Spanish prisoner was washed ashore alive, clinging to the sea chest. Pilot McCracken came to his aid and took him to his home for the night. By the glimmer of a tallow candle, with the gale still raging without, the Spaniard told of a fortune in coins and gold bullion aboard the sloop. It was the booty from two captured Spanish ships home-bound from South America. The man had held some gold bars in his own hands. William S. Dutton, "The Shipwrecks They've Seen!" *Saturday Evening Post* (13 Feb. 1954): 78.

Examination of photoprints of the hand-written data from the McCracken family Bible revealed no such account. The *Sun* (25 July, 1887); *New York Times*, 28 April, 1879; McCracken Family Bible, photocopy, *De Braak* File, Delaware State Museums, Dover.

4. The *Sun*, 25 July 1887.

5. In 1887, Jacob A. Marshall, Katherine's son, claimed to have in his possession a half-doubloon from the wreck, "which his mother gave him as a family piece." Ibid.

6. Ibid.; St. Peter's Episcopal Church Record Book (transcript, Delaware State Museums, Dover). David V. Beard notes that crew members of *De Braak* who had been washed ashore were buried in a sailor's cemetery, which now lies beneath the parking lot of the Delaware River Pilots Association in Lewes. David V. Beard, "HMS *De Braak*: A Treasure Debunked, a Treasure Revealed" (M.A. thesis, East Carolina University, 1989).

7. See Landrake-Saltash Drews and Watkins connections (Genealogical Chart [photocopy], *De Braak* File, Delaware State Museums, Dover). The Drew family crest was documented by British heraldry experts in London at the request of

Claudia Melson, Curator of Registrations for the Delaware Bureau of Museums and Historic Sites (now the Delaware State Museums), from an engraving on a gold pocket watch recovered during excavations of the *De Braak* wreck site in 1986. The family connection was confirmed in 1988 when Elizabeth Carrick, a descendant of the family of James Drew's wife, Lydia Watkins Drew, produced a letter from Lydia to her sister, Elizabeth, dated September 30, 1819, which bore the Drew family crest. The family seal was noted by Maunsell Van Rensselaer, Lydia's nephew, as proof of the family's Irish ancestry. Paul Brodeur, "The Treasure of the *De Braak*," *New Yorker* (16 Apr. 1988): 58, 59; Maunsell Van Rensselaer, *Annals of the Van Rensselaers of the United States, Especially as They Relate to the Family of Killian K. Van Rensselaer, Representative from Albany in the Seventh, Eighth, Ninth and Tenth Congresses* (Albany: Charles Van Benthuysen & Sons, 1988), 223; Claudia Melson (pers. comm.). For the Drew genealogy, see Appendix A.

8. N. A. M. Rodger, *The Wooden World: An Anatomy of the Georgian Navy* (Annapolis: Naval Institute Press, 1987), 252–53.

9. Sir Lewis Namier and John Brooke, *The History of Parliament: The House of Commons 1754–90*, 3 vols. (London: Oxford University Press, 1964), 2: 400.

10. Rodger, *Wooden World*, 255–56.

11. G. J. Marcus, *A Naval History of England: The Formative Years* (Boston and Toronto: Little Brown and Company, 1961), 50.

12. Gillian M. Hughes, Notes and Collections (*De Braak* File, Delaware State Museums, Dover). HMS *Burford* was built at Chatham Dockyard and commissioned in 1757. She was 162 feet in length and 44.5 feet abeam, and 1,424 tons burden. On March 31, 1785, she was sold out of service. J. J. Colledge, *Ships of the Royal Navy*, 2 vols. (Newton Abbot, Devon: David and Charles, 1969) 1: 96.

13. See Marcus, *Naval History of England*, 365–66, for discussion on the career ladders in the Royal Navy of the Georgian era.

14. G. M. Hughes, Notes. HMS *Edgar* was a fourth-rate, 1,297-ton man-of-war. Built by Randall at Rotherhithe, she was 155 feet in length and 44 feet abeam. Commissioned on November 16, 1758, *Edgar* would end her days in August 1784 by being sunk as a breakwater at Sheerness. Colledge, *Ships of the Royal Navy* 1: 183. HM Sloop-of-War *Hound*, of 267 tons burden, was 92 feet in length, and 26 feet abeam. Built by Stowe and Bartlett at Shoreham, she was commissioned on May 22, 1745, and sold out of service on October 27, 1773. Ibid., 272. HM Sloop-of-War *Tamar*, of 343 tons burden, was 96.5 feet in length and 27.5 feet abeam. Built by Snook at Saltash, she was commissioned on January 23, 1758. Renamed *Pluto* on September 23, 1777, she was converted to a fireship and captured by enemy forces, probably French, on November 30, 1780. Ibid., 547.

15. Rodger, *Wooden World*, 263.

16. Ibid., 260; Marcus, *Naval History of England*, 368.

17. Lt. James Drew Certificate, 1771, G. M. Hughes, Notes.

18. Benjamin Highborn to John Adams, December 10, 1775, Adams Papers, Massachusetts Historical Society, reprinted in *Naval Documents of the American Revolution*, 8 vols. (Washington, DC, 1964–), 3: 33.

19. Ibid.

20. Graves's recommendation for Drew's promotion was approved by the Admiralty on September 27, 1775. *Commissioned Sea Officers of the Royal Navy 1660–1815*. British Admiralty, 3 vols. (London, 1954), 1 (A-F): 269; *Naval Documents of the American Revolution*, 1: 1166; 3: 35n. *Scorpion* was originally purchased by the Royal Navy in January 1771, under the name *Borryan*, and renamed *Etna*. Initially fitted out as a fireship mounting eight guns, she was 294 tons, 94.5 feet in length, and 27 feet abeam. Later refitted as a sloop-of-war, she was recommissioned as *Scorpion* on August 10, 1771. After considerable action in American waters during the Revolution, she was sold out of service in North America on December 27, 1780. Colledge, *Ships of the Royal Navy*, 1: 27; "The Present Disposition of His Majesty's Ships and Vessels in Sea Paye, Admiralty Office, 1 December 1775," Admiralty Records 8/51; *Naval Documents of the American Revolution*, 3: 1400

21. Pitcairn Jones, *Sea Officers List, 1660–1815*, (London: 1815).

22. Ibid. HM Sloop-of-War *Otter* was a brig-sloop of 202 tons, 79 feet in length, and 25 feet abeam. Her armament included eight 18-pounder carronades, and fourteen 4-pounders. She was built by Hills at Sandwich and commissioned in 1780. In 1800 she was converted to a fireship, and on December 16, 1801 was sold out of service. Colledge, *Ships of the Royal Navy*, 1: 400. HMS *Powerful*, of 1,627 tons burden, was 168.5 feet in length and 47 feet abeam. Built by Perry at Blackwall, she was commissioned April 3, 1783, and broken up at Chatham in May 1812. Ibid., 1: 433.

23. *Commissioned Sea Officers*, 1 (A-F): 269. HM Sloop-of-War *Echo*, of 342 tons, was 101.5 feet in length and 27.5 feet abeam. Built by Barton at Liverpool, she was commissioned October 2, 1782, and broken up in 1797. Colledge, *Ships of the Royal Navy*, 1: 181.

24. See HM Sloop *Echo* Captain's Logs (9 February 1789–21 May 1790), Admiralty Records 51/297 (Public Record Office, London), for Drew's voyage.

25. HM Sloop *Fly* Captain's Log (29 May 1790–31 May 1791), Admiralty Records 51/344 (Public Record Office, London). *Fly*, a vessel of 300 tons, was 96 feet in length and 36.5 feet abeam. Built at Sheerness Dockyard, and commissioned in 1776, she foundered off Cape Flattery, Newfoundland, in 1802. Colledge, *Ships of the Royal Navy*, 213; W. P. Gosset, *The Lost Ships of the Royal Navy, 1793–1900* (London and New York: Mansell Publishing, Limited, 1986), 36.

26. HMS *Fly* Captain's Log, Admiralty Records 51/344.

27. Brodeur, "Treasure of the *De Braak*," 60.

28. Rodger, *Wooden World* , 60.

29. David Erskine, ed., *Augustus Hervey's Journal* (London: W. Kimber, 1953)

30. HMS *Fly* Captain's Log, Admiralty Records 51/344

31. Rodger, *Wooden World*, 130.

32. Brodeur, "Treasure of the *De Braak*," 60.

33. Ibid.

34. Rodger, *Wooden World*, 75–76.

35. A. B. C. Whipple and the editors of *Time-Life* Books, *Fighting Sail* (Alexandria, VA: Time-Life Books, 1978), 63.

36. Van Rensselaer, *Annals of the Van Rensselaers*, 145–146. The Watkins homesite was situated on the grounds where the Battle of Harlem Heights had been fought on September 16, 1776.

37. Brodeur, "Treasure of the *De Braak*," 59. Van Rensselaer writes:

> "The seal of Capt. Drew in my possession shows that they [the Drews] were of the Irish branch, which intermarried in the 17th century with the Maunsells, which may account for his acquaintance with my aunt (Lydia)." Van Rensselaer, *Annals of the Van Rensselaers*, 223.

Van Rensselaer's supposition seems much more reasonable than those which suggest that Drew met Lydia on his 1791 voyage. According to the ship's log kept by Drew, *Fly* left Spithead on May 21 and stayed at Portsmouth Harbor until June 10, when she finally sailed for the western hemisphere. On July 23 she was at Greggett Harbor and then commenced cruising the coasts of Labrador and Newfoundland. On November 1, she sailed for home in company with HMS *Salisbury* and *Rose*, and arrived at Plymouth on November 14, 1791. The voyage had provided absolutely no time in which a relationship between James and Lydia could have blossomed. HMS *Fly* Captain's Log, Admiralty Records 51/344.

38. The Reverend Moore's son, then thirteen-year-old Clement C. Moore, would become the author of "'Twas the Night before Christmas." According to Brodeur, one of Lydia's other cousins was married to Aaron Burr. Burr married twice, the first time on July 2, 1782, to Theodosia Prevost, widow of one British Army officer and sister to two others, who was already the mother of five children. Burr's second marriage, in 1833, was to a former courtesan from Rhode Island named Eliza Bowen Jumel. Van Rensselaer, *Annals of the Van Rensselaers*, 146–222; Brodeur, "Treasure of the *De Braak*," 59; Philip Vail, *Aaron Burr: The Great American Rascal* (New York: Award Books, 1973), 47, 50, 234–36.

39. Last Will and Testament of Captain James Drew, (transcript, *De Braak* File, Delaware State Museums, Dover).

40. *De Braak* Chronology, compiled by Claudia Melson (*De Braak* File, Delaware State Museums, Dover).

41. Captain James Drew to Navy Board, 1793–1795. Drew Transcripts, (*De Braak* File, Delaware State Museums, Dover).

42. See James Dugan, *The Great Mutiny* (New York: G. P. Putnam's Sons, 1965) for a complete account of the Easter insurrection.

TWO

1. James Dugan, *The Great Mutiny*, 305.

2. In the Royal Navy of Georgian England, major vessels were classified by rate. First-rate vessels mounted one hundred guns or more; second-raters carried ninety to ninety-eight guns; third-raters carried sixty-four to eighty guns; fourth-raters mounted fifty to fifty-six guns; fifth-raters mounted thirty-two to thirty-six guns; and sixth-rate sloops-of-war carried from fourteen to twenty-four guns. Two-masted brig-rigged vessels, such as *De Braak*, although not technically fitted as sloops-of-war, were rated as such for commission and wage purposes and were employed in much the same service.

3. The question of whether *De Braak* was built for or merely purchased by the Admiralty of the Maas (Rotterdam) has been addressed by two reputable Dutch Naval historians. A 1964 investigation by Commander J. F. Van Dulm, Chief Naval Historian, Ministeris van Defensie, Marine, concludes that "the cutter 'de Brak' . . . of 14 guns was bought in the year 1781 by the Admiralty of the Maze [Maas]." A different finding was reported in 1973 by Dutch naval historian J. C. Van Ooesten, who wrote that the vessel had been specifically built for the Admiralty. Howard Chapelle of the Smithsonian Institution and his colleague Colonel M. E. S. Laws accept the view that she was Dutch built. J. F. Van Dulm to Paul E. Smith, (March 26, 1964), and J. C. Van Ooesten to J. B. DeSwort, (July 24, 1973), *De Braak* File, (Zwaanendael Museum, Lewes); Howard I. Chapelle and M. E. S. Laws, "H. M. S. *De Braak*: The Stories of a 'Treasure Ship,' " *Smithsonian Journal of History* (Spr. 1967): 58.

4. Beard relates that through a personal contact with David Lyons, Head of Inquiry Service at the National Maritime Museum, London, on January 7, 1989, he was informed that a deposition by Lt. Johann Von Grootinwray noted that the vessel was once English and had been captured by the French during their "last war," which would have been the Anglo-French conflict during the final days of the American Revolution. Lyons personally related the same information to this author on January 11, 1990. The recovery, in 1984, of a ship's bell bearing the name *La Patrocle* from the wreck of *De Braak* strongly supports Lyons's statement. No Royal Navy vessel bearing that name was ever commissioned, nor has any vessel matching *De Braak*'s pre-1795 configuration, rig, size, and tonnage been noted in British Admiralty records as having been captured. Thus, it seems likely that if the vessel were, indeed, a British-built bottom, as Beard is inclined to believe, she could have served originally as either a privateer or a merchantman. No documentary evidence, however, has been found to date by this author which supports Lyons's information. David V. Beard, "Treasure Debunked," 3; David Lyons (pers. comm).

5. *De Braak* plans, Registration 6346, Box 65, (Admiralty Draughts Collection, National Maritime Museum, London); Chapelle and Laws, "H.M.S. *De Braak*," 58; Beard, "Treasure Debunked," 81–82.

6. Chapelle and Laws, "H.M.S. *De Braak*," 58; Van Dulm to Smith (March 24, 1964); Robert Haslach (pers. comm).

7. Van Ooesten to DeSwort, (July 24, 1973).

8. Captain Grootinwray was from Hellevoetsluis, at the mouth of the Maas. He died on January 20, 1799, at Rotterdam. His name appears in official records in several forms: Johan Von Grootinwray, Johan Grotenray, and Johen Arnold van Grootenwray. Van Dulm to Smith, (March 26, 1964).

9. Ibid.; George Le Favre, *The French Revolution from 1793 to 1799* (Washington: Columbia University Press, 1964), 14.

10. Van Dulm to Smith, (March 26, 1964).

11. The Batavian Republic was established in the Netherlands in 1795 by the invading armies of revolutionary France. Although officially independent, it was in fact under the control of 25,000 French soldiers. During the republic's brief existence, the nobility lost their privileges and many fled to England. Although a

constitution was adopted, the republic ended in 1806 when Napoleon I made his brother, Louis, King of Holland.

12. In late 1796 a document entitled "The State of the Naval Forces of the Republic of Batavia, Vendemaire 12, Year 5 [October 3, 1796]" reported that *De Braak* was among thirty Dutch ships in English ports at the time of the invasion of Holland by France. In *The General Register of the Naval Forces of the Netherlands, Subsequently, the Batavian Republic, from 1795 to 1811*, it is noted that *De Braak* had been outfitted with fourteen cannons, had been purchased by the Admiralty of the Meuse [Maas], was in England at the beginning of the war between Holland and France in 1795, and had been confiscated by the English on March 4, 1796. Transcripts (*De Braak* File, Zwaanendael Museum, Lewes).

13. Navy Board to Admiralty (September 30, 1795), Navy Board Out Letters, Admiralty Records 2/374 (Public Record Office, London). *Zeeland* [*Zealand*] was first rated by the British at sixty-six guns and later at sixty-four. Officially seized January 19, 1796, she was formally renamed *Justitia* and commissioned as a Royal Navy vessel in October 1803. In October 1815 she was converted to a convict ship. On February 11, 1830, *Justitia* was sold out of service and broken up. *The Times* (London [September 19, 1796]); Colledge, *Ships of the Royal Navy*, 1: 622. *Braakel* was first noted after her capture as a fifty-six-gun man-of-war, but after her official confiscation on March 14, 1796, at Plymouth, she was described as a fourth-rater of fifty-four guns. At 1,010 tons, she was taken into service, commissioned in June 1799, and saw employment as a troopship. On September 29, 1814, she was sold out of service. *The Times* (London [September 19, 1796]); Colledge, *Ships of the Royal Navy*, 1: 86. *Tholen* was rated at thirty-six guns, *Pyl* at sixteen guns, and *Miermin* at fourteen guns. The discrepancy in ratings between the publicly reported gun carriage and the ratings listings may stem from the Royal Navy practice at this period of not including carronades in the gun rates of certain vessels. *The Times* (London [September 19, 1796]).

14. *The Times* (London [March 8, 1796]).

15. *Fortune* was a brig-sloop of 280 tons burden. Built by Stewart at Sandgate, she was eighty-five feet in length, twenty-nine feet abeam, and mounted fourteen 4-pounders. She was purchased while on the stocks in August 1780, and was wrecked at Oporto on June 15, 1797. Colledge, *Ships of the Royal Navy*, 1: 218.

16. Chapelle and Laws, "H.M.S. *De Braak*," 58; Spencer, Pybus, and Gambier to Lord Dundas (July 18, 1795), Navy Board Out Letters, Admiralty Records 2/374 (Public Record Office, London).

17. Chapelle and Laws, "H.M.S. *De Braak*," 58.

18. Ibid.

19. Ibid., 59.

20. Chief Surveyor of the Navy to the Navy Board (September 1, 1796), Admiralty Records 106/1935 (Public Record Office, London).

21. Navy Board to Admiralty (September 8, 1796), Admiralty Records 106/1222, part 25.

22. Ibid.

23. Navy Board to Admiralty (September 10, 1796), Admiralty Records, 106/2088 (Public Record Office, London).

24. *De Braak* plans, Registrations 6346 and 6347, Box 65, (Admiralty Draughts Collection, National Maritime Museum, London); Beard, "Treasure Debunked," 88–90. Unfortunately, the records covering the period *De Braak* was being refitted at Plymouth are not extant. The present day victualing establishment, the Royal William Victualing Yard, was opened in 1831. Records for the period after that date are held there, but nothing was transferred from the superseded victualing yard at the Barbican, where *De Braak* was refitted, one and a half miles away. C. J. Squires to Claudia Melson (February 20, 1988), *De Braak* File (Delaware State Museums, Dover).

25. *De Braak* plans, Registration 6347; Beard, "Treasure Debunked," 88–90.

26. Ibid.; See William N. Boog Watson, "Alexander Brodie and His Firehearths for Ships," *The Mariner's Mirror*, 54: 4 (Nov. 1968): 409–11, for a complete discussion of the development of the Brodie Firehearths.

27. In 1780, William Falconer described sheathing as "a sort of casing or covering laid on the outside of a ship's bottom, to protect the planks from the pernicious effects of the worms: particularly in hot climates, as between the tropics. Sheathing either consists of a number of boards or deals of fir, or of sheets of lead or copper; which last is a very late invention, having been only experienced on a few of His Majesty's frigates: it seems, however, to answer the purpose much better than the fir-planks." William Falconer, *An Universal Dictionary of the Marine: or, A Copious Explanation of the Technical Terms and Phrases Employed in the Construction, Equipment, Furniture, Machinery, Movements, and Military Operations of a Ship* ([1780], repr. Devon, England: David and Charles Reprints, 1970), 261. For a complete synthesis of the history and importance of copper sheathing in the Royal Navy, see R. J. B. Knight, "The Introduction of Copper Sheathing Into the Royal Navy, 1779-1786," *The Mariner's Mirror*, 59: 3 (Aug. 1973): 299–310.

28. Navy Board to Admiralty (October 11, 1797), Admiralty Records 106/2088. The Navy Board first proposed that *De Braak* be armed with ten 6-pounders and manned by a crew of eighty-six. The Admiralty asked if she might not be better armed with carronades instead of the traditional long guns. After some deliberation, the Navy Board agreed and suggested that she be armed with sixteen 24-pounder carronades. Chapelle and Laws, "H.M.S. *De Braak*," 59.

29. Charles Fithian, "To Fight and Conquer: The Armaments of H.M.S. *De Braak*," (paper presented at the First Joint Archaeological Congress, Baltimore, MD, 1989) tape recording; Charles Fithian, pers. comm.; Chapelle and Laws, H.M.S. *De Braak*," 53; Whipple, et al., *Fighting Sail*, 60.

30. Whipple et al., *Fighting Sail*, 60; Fithian, "To Fight and Conquer."

31. Chapelle and Laws, "H.M.S. *De Braak*," 59. Wages aboard a Royal Navy warship officially began when the captain and crew assigned to her were entered into the muster and pay books. No seaman could receive pay unless assigned to a vessel. Officers were placed on half pay while not actually engaged. *De Braak*'s official service began on June 13, 1797. Navy Board to Admiralty (June 13, 1797), Admiralty Records 106/2088.

Three

1. On June 26, 1797, Drew requested that one James Wall be appointed the ship's first lieutenant. Drew to Evan Nepean (June 26, 1797), Admiralty In Letters, Admiralty Records 1/1719 (Public Record Office, London); Chapelle and Laws, "H.M.S. *De Braak*," 59.

2. Navy Board to Admiralty (October 11, 1797), Admiralty Records 106/2088; Fithian, "To Fight and Conquer"; *The Times* (London [September 30, 1796]).

3. Marcus, *Naval History of England* , 410–411.

4. Drew to Nepean (September 13, 1797), Admiralty Records 1/1719; Drew to Nepean (September 27, 1797), Admiralty Records 1/1719.

5. *The Times* (London [December 16, 1797]).

6. *The Times* (London [December 18, 1797]).

7. *The Times* (London [December 21, 1797]).

8. *The Times* (London [December 19 and 20, 1797]).

9. *The Times* (London [December 19, 1797]).

10. *The Times* (London [December 20, 1797]).

11. *The Times* (London [December 25, 1797]).

12. Navy Board to Mr. Marsden (December 11, 1797), Admiralty In Letters, Admiralty Records 1/1719; Navy Board to Admiralty (December 16, 1797), Admiralty Records 106/2088.

13. Admiralty to Drew, December 24, 1797, Admiralty Records 2/135.

14. *The Times* (London [December 22, 1797]).

15. Admiralty to Drew (February 8, 1798), Admiralty Records 2/284, part 201.

16. John Drew was born April 20, 1750. At the age of thirteen, in 1763, he entered the Royal Navy as a captain's servant aboard HMS *Bellisle*. He would later serve aboard HMS *Solebay* as an able seaman and as a midshipman. On September 19, 1777 he received his lieutenant's certificate. In 1778 he began service aboard *Sultan* and, on February 6, 1783, was promoted to post captain and given command of *Seahorse*. Five years later, in 1788, he commanded *Squirrel*. In 1790 he was given *Trusty*, and in 1794 *Melampus*. His final command came in early 1795 when he was assigned HMS *Cerberus*, a new fifth-rate, thirty-two-gun man-of-war. *Cerberus* was 135 feet in length, thirty-six feet abeam, and 796 tons burden. Built by Adams at Bucklers Hard, she had been commissioned in September 1794 and would serve with distinction until sold out of service on September 29, 1814. Jones, *Sea Officers List*; Lieutenant's Passing Certificate, John Drew, Admiralty Records 107–6, 107–7 (Public Record Office, London), 201; Colledge, *Ships of the Royal Navy*, 1: 113.

17. *The Times* (London [July 14, July 18, September 28, and November 23, 1796; October 16, November 30, and December 4, 1797]); *Steel's Royal Navy List*.

18. *The Times* (London [January 15 and 16, 1798]).

19. *The Times* (London [January 16, 1798]). HMS *Hindustan* was an ex-East Indiaman originally named *Born*. She had been taken into the Royal Navy in 1795 as a fourth-rate fifty-four-gun man-of-war, and was 1,249 tons burden, 160 feet in length and forty-two feet abeam. In 1802 she was converted into a storeship and two years later, on April 2, 1804, was accidentally burnt while in Rosas Bay, San

Sebastian, a mile from the Fort of Ampurius and the Church of St. Peter. Cooledge, *Ships of the Royal Navy*, 1: 268; Gosset, *Lost Ships of the Royal Navy*, 41. HMS *Penguin* was originally a Dutch vessel named *Komet*, which had been captured off the Irish coast on August 28, 1795, by HMS *Unicorn*. Rated as a sloop of 336 tons, she was 93 feet long, 29.5 feet abeam, and mounted two eighteen-pounder carronades and four nine-pounder long guns. On July 27, 1809, *Penguin* was sold out of service. Colledge, *Ships of the Royal Navy*, 415.

20. *The Times* (London [January 16, 1798]).

21. Ibid. Acting Lieutenant James William Drew was born October 20, 1781. St. Nicholas Parish Register of Births, St. Nicholas Church (Saltash, England).

22. *The Times* (London [January 16, 1798]).

23. Admiralty to Drew (February 8, 1798), Admiralty Records 2/284, part 201; Admiralty to Pender (February 23, 1798), Admiralty Out Letters, Admiralty Records 2/1099; Admiralty to Vandeput (February 24, 1798), Admiralty Records 2/135, parts 99 and 100. HMS *St. Albans* was a third-rate sixty-four-gun man-of-war of 1,380 tons, 159.5 feet in length, and 44.5 feet abeam. Built by Perry at Blackwall, she was commissioned on September 12, 1764. In September 1803 she was converted to a floating battery, and in June 1814 was broken up. Colledge, *Ships of the Royal Navy*, 1: 479.

24. Admiralty to Drew (February 8, 1798), Admiralty Records 2/284, part 201; Admiralty to Pender (February 23, 1798), Admiralty Out Letters, Admiralty Records 2/1099.

25. Admiralty to Drew (February 8, 1798), Admiralty Records 2/284, part 201.

26. Drew to Nepean (February 18, 1798), Captains' Letters "D," Admiralty Records 1/1720 (Public Record Office, London).

27. See Dugan, *The Great Mutiny*, for the most complete account of the mutiny published to date and the roles of the crews of *Saturn* and *Ramilles* in the uprising.

28. Drew to Nepean (February 18, 1798), Captains' Letters "D," Admiralty Records 1/1720; HMS *De Braak* Muster Book, Admiralty Records 36/12890; *De Braak* Pay Books (January 9, 1801), Admiralty Records 35/211.

29. HMS *De Braak* Muster Book, Admiralty Records 36/12890; *De Braak* Pay Books (January 9, 1801), Admiralty Records 35/211.

30. Drew to Nepean (March 2, 1798), Captains' Letters "D," Admiralty Records 1/1720; Drew to Nepean (March 7, 1798), Captains' Letters "D," Admiralty Records 1/1720. Vessels listed by Drew as under his care included the ships *Day*, *Speculation*, *Phoenix*, *Commerce*, *Venus*, *British Queen*, *Dove*, *Lamb*, *Friendship*, and *Pomona*.

31. See HMS *St. Albans* Captain's Log (26 May 1797–16 September 1798), Admiralty Records 51/1272 (Public Record Office, London) for full particulars of the convoy's tribulations in crossing the Atlantic.

32. Pender to Admiralty (March 26, 1798), Captains' Letters "D," Admiralty Records 1/1720.

33. HMS *St. Albans* Captain's Log (April 1 to April 4, 1798), Admiralty Records 51/1272.

34. Chapelle and Laws, "H.M.S. *De Braak*," 57, notes that the pay for the entire Halifax garrison was "far less than $30,000."

35. *The Daily Advertiser* (New York [May 24, 1798]).

36. *Country Porcupine* (Philadelphia [June 14 and 15, 1798]).

37. HMS *St. Albans* Captain's Log (May 24, 1798), Admiralty Records 51/1272; *The Daily Advertiser* (New York [May 29 and 30, 1798]); *Claypool's American Daily Advertiser* (Philadelphia [May 28 and 29, 1798]); *Norfolk Herald* (May 26, 1798). Off the Chesapeake, the ships *Juno* (Captain Beard) and *Richmond* (Captain Simpson) turned in for Norfolk. *Helen* (Captain Patterson), which had been fired upon by *Triton*, put in for York River. The ships *Sidney, Carlisle, Active*, and *Ranger* pressed up the bay for Baltimore. The ships *Carolina* and *Maria* and the brig *Pallas* turned southward for Charleston. Pender's habit of seizing suspect enemy vessels or ships believed to be laden with French goods was again evinced when he stopped, searched, and seized the American merchant brig *Batchelor* (Captain Gad Peck), off the Highlands of New Jersey, and sent her to Halifax as a prize. *Claypool's American Daily Advertiser* (Philadelphia [May 26, 28, and 30, 1798]); *Norfolk Herald* (May 6, 1798); *The Daily Advertiser* (New York [May 30, 1798]).

38. *Norfolk Herald* (May 25, 1798); *Claypool's American Daily Advertiser* (Philadelphia [May 28, 1798]). Ten of the convoy vessels accompanied Pender as far as Sandy Hook: the ships *Severn* (Goodrich), *Swan* (Woodham), *Alliance* (Wood), and *America* (Mallaby), all from Liverpool for New York; the bark *Adriana*, initially bound for Philadelphia but landed at New York to avoid French cruisers; the armed ship *Nancy* of Boston, and the merchant ships *Packet* and *Delight*, bound for Boston; the barque *Neptune*, bound for Portsmouth; and the ship *Accepted Mason*, bound for Wiscassett. Another of the convoy vessels, the *Penelope* (Morrell), from Bristol for New York, had parted company with the fleet in longitude 63°30′ W, latitude 35° N, and had arrived on May 18, a full week ahead of both Pender and Drew. *Claypool's American Daily Advertiser* (Philadelphia [May 26, and 30, 1798]).

39. *Norfolk Herald* (August 29, 1798).

40. Ibid.

41. *De Braak* was in Old Kiln Road (Whorekill Roads) by 4 P.M., Friday, May 25. Pender had been off Cape Henlopen that morning. Considering the closeness of their arrivals, it would have been impossible for *De Braak* to have traveled as far south as the West Indies, Jamaica, or the Spanish Main to conduct raids on Spanish shipping, as treasure hunters would later claim, and still have arrived on the Delaware at almost precisely the same time as the fleet with which she had set out. Cf. *The Daily Advertiser* (New York [May 28, 1798]); Beard, "Treasure Debunked," 15–16; and HMS *St. Albans* Captain's Log (May 24, 1798), Admiralty Records 51/1272.

42. The report by Vincent Low, the first published account of the disaster, stated that *De Braak* fell in with the prize, en route from Río de La Plata with 200 tons of copper and a consignment of cocoa, "about 25 days ago." This would have placed the time of capture at May 3. That *De Braak* actually fell in with the *Xavier* on or about April 30, however, is attested to by a certificate issued to Lt. Thomas Griffith by Drew to take command of the prize. Drew instructed Griffith: "You are hereby required and Directed to repair on Board the St. Francis dehaveren alias Commerce De Londros prize to His Majesty's Sloop Braak under my command taking all possible care not to part company and should you by any unavoidable accident, you

are to repair to Cape Henry in the Chesapeak and there wait my arrival for further orders. Given under my Hand on Board His Majesty's Sloop Braak at sea the 30th day of April 1798. . . James Drew." Drew completed his directions by providing Griffith with signal instructions. *Claypool's American Daily Advertiser* (Philadelphia [May 28, 1798]); Drew to Griffith (April 30, 1798), Certificate of Service, Masters (c. 1800–1850), D–G, Admiralty Records 6/167 (Public Record Office, London). The value of Drew's prize was referred to in Captain Skidmore's account of his encounter with *De Braak*, which was published in Norfolk several days later. *Norfolk Herald* (May 29, 1798).

43. Drew to Griffith (April 30, 1798), Certificate of Service (see note 42).

44. *Claypool's American Daily Advertiser* (Philadelphia [May 28, 1798]); *New York Times* (April 29, 1879); *The Sun* (Baltimore [July 25, 1887]).

45. *The Sun* (Baltimore [July 25, 1887]).

46. *Claypool's American Daily Advertiser* (Philadelphia [May 28, 1798]).

47. Ibid. Until 1984 and the excavation of the *De Braak* wreck site, the action which occurred on board at the moment of loss could only be speculated upon, although it was noted in 1887 that Allen reported that when the brig careened, the guns shifted to the leeward on the deck and helped drag her down. *The Sun* (Baltimore [July 25, 1887]).

48. Phineas Bond to Lord Grenville (May 28, 1798), Special File Proposed Salvage of *De Braak*, Admiralty Records 1/5121/3 (Public Record Office, London); *Claypool's American Daily Advertiser* (Philadelphia [May 31, 1798]).

49. *The Sun* (Baltimore [June 25, 1887]), indicates that fifteen Spaniards had been taken off the Spanish prize and transferred to *De Braak*. Several prisoners purportedly floated ashore and escaped.

Four

1. *The Sun* (Baltimore [July 25, 1887]).

2. See *Naval Documents Related to the Quasi-War between the United States and France: Naval Operations from February 1797 to October 1798* (Washington, DC: Government Printing Office, 1935) 87–88, for complete text on "An Act More effectual to protect the Commerce and Coasts of the United States." Even before the onset of the "quasi-war," French cruisers and privateers, employing the coastal sounds of Maryland and New Jersey to hide in, had begun to haunt the Delaware coast. By the time *De Braak* arrived at Cape Henlopen, the situation was approaching the critical stage. On Friday, May 18, 1798, a vessel from New York, laden with cannon for several U.S. Navy vessels being outfitted at Philadelphia, arrived there and reported that on her passage she had spotted a French privateer under topsails hove to off Egg Harbor. Three days later the privateer stopped the schooner *Jane*, bound from Philadelphia for the West Indies, plundered her, and then released her. The following day, May 22, the brig *Amiable Matilda* (Captain Brown), from Bordeaux, was brought to under Cape May by another rover described as a Virginia-built schooner mounting eight guns and manned by eight men. The privateer had sailed from Guadeloupe in the French West Indies and had already

taken two prizes. After examining Brown's papers and learning that he had last sailed from a French port, the rovers dismissed him. Then, on the evening of May 25, Captain Joseph Canby, of the schooner *Liberty*, arrived at Philadelphia from Norfolk and related that at 5 P.M., May 24, (an hour after the loss of *De Braak*) with Cape Henlopen bearing WSW, distance four miles, he had taken a pilot on board. Immediately afterwards, *Liberty* was chased and brought to by a schooner without colors, mounting twelve to fourteen guns, and manned by sixty to seventy men. Canby assumed the vessel to be a privateer, as her crew wore the "National Cockade of France." Her captain spoke in broken English with a French accent, and ordered Canby to come aboard his ship. As Canby prepared to hoist out his boat the man at the masthead of the privateer cried out in English that he had sighted a ship standing in for the capes. *Liberty* was immediately dismissed and the privateer made all sail after the potentially richer prize, which was overtaken after an hour and a quarter chase. The depredations of the privateers continued without letup for days thereafter, and American shipping found little relief until the US Sloop-of-War *Ganges* (Captain Richard Dale), took up patrolling the coast. Fear of the French menace was so great, however, that many vessels refused to sail from either New York or Philadelphia. Owners of the *Adriana*, which had arrived at New York with the *St. Albans* convoy and carried a cargo valued at "at least one hundred thousand pounds sterling" were obliged to petition the United States Secretary of State for protection. *Ganges* was assigned to convoy her to safety. *The Spectator* (New York [May 23, 1798]); *Claypool's American Daily Advertiser* (Philadelphia [May 26 and 28, June 4, 1798]); *The Daily Advertiser* (Philadelphia [June 1, 1798]); *Naval Documents Related to the Quasi-War*, 91.

    3. *Norfolk Herald* (May 29, 1798).

    4. Phineas Bond to Lord Grenville (May 28, 1798), Special File Proposed Salvage of *De Braak*, Admiralty Records 1/2121/3; *The Sun* (Baltimore [July 25, 1887]).

    5. Phineas Bond to Lord Grenville (May 28, 1798) Special File Proposed Salvage of *De Braak*, Admiralty Records 1/2121/3.

    6. Beard argues that *Commerce of London* was a code name. Drew refers to her as *Commerce de Londros*, an "alias" of *St. Francis dehaveren*. Bond refers to her as "the Ship *Commerce of London*," while press reports call her *Don Francisco Xavier*. It seems quite probable that the prize was originally an English merchantman named *Commerce of London* , which had been taken by the Spanish and renamed, then recaptured by *De Braak*. The name *Commerce* was a most popular one for merchantmen of the era. Indeed, one vessel named *Commerce* had sailed with *De Braak*'s convoy but apparently broke off from it, possibly during one of the storms of April. Drew to Griffith (April 30, 1798) Certificate of Service, Admiralty Records 6/167; Bond to Grenville (May 28, 1798) Special File Proposed Salvage of *De Braak*, Admiralty Records 1/5121/3; Beard, "Treasure Debunked," 18; Drew to Nepean (March 7, 1798), Captains' Letters "D," Admiralty Records 1/1720.

    7. *Claypool's American Daily Advertiser* (Philadelphia [May 31, 1798]); *New York Gazette* (May 30, 1798); Chapelle and Laws, "H.M.S. *De Braak*," 63.

    8. *New York Gazette* (May 30, 1798).

    9. Vice Admiral Vandeput to Captain Hardy via Bond (July 8, 1798), Special File Proposed Salvage of *De Braak*, Admiralty Records 1/5121/3. The sloop-of-war

Rover was a vessel of sixteen guns and 356 tons burden, 104 feet in length and twenty-six feet abeam. Built by Pender at Bermuda in 1798, she was purchased by the Royal Navy while on the stocks. (HMS *Rover* should not be confused with the cutter *Rover*, a French prize originally named *Jean Bart*, which she had captured and converted to a tender.) On June 23, 1798, while sailing from Halifax to Sydney, under the command of Captain G. Irvine and carrying aboard a certain General Ogilvie and his family, *Rover* was wrecked in the Gulf of St. Lawrence. Word of the loss reached Philadelphia apparently via Hardy's envoy to Bond. Chapelle and Laws, "H.M.S. *De Braak*,"; Colledge, *Ships of the Royal Navy*, 1: 472; Gosset, *Lost Ships of the Royal Navy*, 17; *Porcupine's Gazette* (Philadelphia [July 30, 1798]); *Country Porcupine* (Philadelphia [July 28 and 30, 1798]).

10. Vandeput to Admiralty (August 12, 1798), Admiralty Records 1/494/118f.

11. Hardy had the distinction of being the first British officer to witness the new United States Navy on the high seas. On July 16, off Nantucket, he encountered the recently fielded US Frigate *United States* (Captain Barry), in company with the Sloop-of-War *Delaware*. An officer on the frigate wrote of the encounter: "Our ship sails remarkably fast; on our passage from Philadelphia, we fell in with and spoke the *Assistance* (a British ship) Capt. Hardy; we outsailed her beyond conception." On arriving at the Delaware, Hardy sighted yet another American man-of-war, the USS *Ganges* sailing in pursuit of French privateers. *Porcupine's Gazette* (Philadelphia [July 23, 1798]); *The Daily Advertiser* (New York [July 28, 1798]); *Naval Documents Related to the Quasi-War*, 215.

12. Hardy to Bond (July 22, 1798), Special File Proposed Salavage of *De Braak*, Admiralty Records 1/5121/3.

13. Ibid.

14. Hardy to Bond (July 27, 1798), Special File Proposed Salvage of *De Braak*, Admiralty Records 1/5121/3.

15. Bond to Hardy (July 30, 1798), Special File Proposed Salvage of *De Braak*, Admiralty Records 1/5121/3. HMS *Tropaze* was a fifth-rate thirty-eight-gun warship of 916 tons. She was 144.5 feet in length and thirty-eight feet abeam. She had originally been a French ship called *Latropaz*, but had been handed over to the British by French Royalists at Toulon in December 1793. On July 18, 1798, while cruising in company with another man-of-war, she boarded the American ship *Arethusa* (Woods), twenty-nine days out of Bonavista. The boarding officer informed Captain Woods that, while cruising on the American coast, *Tropaze* had taken no less than five French privateers and had been in pursuit of a sixth which had upset in a squall and was lost with all hands a few days earlier. On July 22, *Tropaze* was cruising off New York and then anchored in New York Bay. A salute was fired from the American garrison on Governor's Island. She continued thereafter for some time in American waters. *Tropaze* was sold out of service on January 9, 1814. Colledge, *Ships of the Royal Navy*, 1: 564; *The Daily Advertiser* (New York [July 23, 1798]); *Porcupine's Gazette* (Philadelphia [August 7, 1798]).

16. Hardy to Bond (July 27, 1798), Special File Proposed Salvage of *De Braak*, Admiralty Records 1/5121/3.

17. Bond to Hardy (July 30, 1798), Special File Proposed Salvage of *De Braak*, Admiralty Records 1/5121/3.

18. Bond to Hardy (July 26, 1798), Special File Proposed Salvage of *De Braak*, Admiralty Records 1/5121/3.

19. Hardy to Bond (July 31, 1798), Special File Proposed Salvage of *De Braak*, Admiralty Records 1/5121/3.

20. Ibid.

21. Bond to Hardy (August 5, 1798), Special File Proposed Salvage of *De Braak*, Admiralty Records 1/5121/3.

22. Bond to Hardy (August 6, 1798), Special File Proposed Salvage of *De Braak*, Admiralty Records 1/5121/3; *Porcupine's Gazette* (Philadelphia [August 7, 1798]). In early August 1798, the College of Physicians in Philadelphia reported "that a malignant contagious Fever has made its appearance in Water street, between Walnut and Spruce street, and in the vicinity thereof." Dr. Samuel Duffield and a Mr. T. Parke were promptly appointed to examine the contaminated area. On August 9, the "Board of Managers of the Marine and City Hospitals of the port of Philadelphia," through the Health Office, published emergency guidelines to prevent the spread of the contagion from the infected portion of the city. Vessels lying within a specific area along the waterfront were to be quarantined, and "no vessels of any description whatsoever" were "suffered to come to the said wharves until the further orders of the Board." Inhabitants adjacent to the infected district were advised to leave the city as quickly as possible. Despite such efforts, the contagion quickly spread, and the death toll increased almost hourly until the onset of fall. *Claypool's American Daily Advertiser* (Philadelphia [August 9, 1798]).

23. Bond to Hardy (August 8, 1798), Special File Proposed Salvage of *De Braak*, Admiralty Records 1/5121/3.

24. Hardy to Bond (August 11, 1798), Special File Proposed Salvage of *De Braak*, Admiralty Records 1/5121/3.

25. HMS *Assistance* Master's Log (14 May 1798–13 May 1799), Admiralty Records 52/2725 (Public Record Office, London); HMS *Assistance* Captain's Log (5 June 1798–4 June 1799), Admiralty Records 51/1258 (Public Record Office, London); HMS *Assistance* Muster Books (1798–1799), Admiralty Records 36/13099 (Public Record Office, London).

26. Chapelle and Laws, "H.M.S. *De Braak*," 62; HMS *Hind* Captain's Log (17 May 1798–17 May 1799), Admiralty Records 52/1296 (Public Record Office, London). HMS *Hind* was a warship 121 feet in length and thirty-five feet abeam. She was built by Clayton and Wilson at Sandgate and commissioned on July 22, 1785. In 1800 she was rebuilt and in 1811 was broken up at Deptford. Colledge, *Ships of the Royal Navy*, 1: 267.

27. *Vixen* is not listed as a commissioned Royal Navy vessel in 1798. The first craft of this name does not appear until 1801, when the gun brig *Vixen* was built at Bucklers Hard. It is therefore assumed that the vessel employed in the salvage operation was a hired craft. Colledge, *Ships of the Royal Navy*, 1: 597.

28. The salvage expedition sailed from Halifax for the Delaware on September 3, 1798. The two vessels stopped off briefly on September 8, at New York, where it was noted that they were "bound to Philadelphia, to raise the sloop of war overset off Cape Henlopen." HMS *Hind* Captain's Log (September 8–17, 1798), Admiralty Records 51/1296; *Claypool's American Daily Advertiser* (Philadelphia [September 19, 1798]).

29. HMS *Hind* Captain's Log (September 18–19, 1798) Admiralty Records 51/ 1296.

30. HMS *Hind* Captain's Log (September 19 and October 1, 1798) Admiralty Records 51/1296. Beard suggests that in the relatively shallow depths of the De *Braak* wreck site (80 feet), "free divers such as those used to harvest sponges could have entered the hull to recover valuables," had there been any aboard, and that crude diving bells were available. Given the difficulty on the site later encountered by professional divers employing the best technologies, free divers and diving bells would have proven far from successful. Beard, "Treasure Debunked," 24–25.

31. Vandeput to Admiralty (October 20, 1798), Admiralty Records 1/494/f148.

32. Chapelle and Laws, "H.M.S. *De Braak*," 64–65.

33. Rodger, *Wooden World*, 135-36.

34. See Rodger, *Wooden World*, for the importance of prize money to the men of the Royal Navy.

35. *Steel's Royal Navy List* (March 6, 1800), 229.

36. George Tobin to Admiralty (December 1, 1799), Captains' Letters "T" (ref. 31, 1—Damage and Loss at Sea, 103 Gen., Cap T 137), Admiralty Records 1/2599 (Public Record Office, London).

37. Nepean to Vandeput (December 22, 1799), Admiralty Records 2/931.

38. HMS *De Braak* Pay Book (January 9, 1801), Admiralty Records 35/211 (Public Record Office, London).

39. Drew Transcripts, *De Braak* File, Inquiry into the Loss of H.M.S. *De Braak*, ([February 23, 1801] Delaware State Museums, Dover).

40. Last Will and Testament of Captain James Drew (transcript, *De Braak* File, Delaware State Museums, Dover). Presumably, as the beneficiary of his brother's estate, a status which had been decided in the courts, Stephen Drew would have profited handsomely from the sale of *Don Francisco Xavier* and her cargo.

41. Although the Drew monument in St. Nicholas Church records only that the work was erected by Drew relatives, it seems probable that the Reverend Stephen Drew, Mayor of Saltash and later owner of Stockton Manor, three miles northwest of Saltash, would have been a likely organizer of the project. As one of the Drew family descendents, John D. Mitchell, aptly noted of Stephen: "He was a man of substance." John D. Mitchell to Claudia Melson (August 4, 1987), *De Braak* File, (Delaware State Museums, Dover).

42. Less than two years after James Drew's death, Lydia Drew married James Beekman, a well-to-do New Yorker, but she apparently continued to mourn the loss of her first husband. Drew's body had been placed in a vault under St. Peter's Church, which was later rebuilt twice, although the vault and its contents were left intact. The monument erected by Lydia Drew Beekman, about 1832, "does not, of course, cover the privateer's ashes," as most believe. Van Rensselaer, *Annals of the Van Rensselaers*, 222; *The Sun* (Baltimore [June 25, 1887]). The monument fell into disrepair, but in 1887, as the efforts of Seth Pancoast focused new attention upon "the privateer" Drew, Lydia's nephew, the Reverend Maunsell Van Rensselaer came to the rescue. "In September 1887," according to the record book of St. Peter's Episcopal Church,

the Rev. M. Van Rennselar D.D. corresponded with Mr. Armstrong avent the monument of Capt. Drew in the Churchyard he being a nephew of Mrs. Drew & therefore interested in its condition which is somewhat dilapidated. Dr. Van R. authorized Wm Armstrong to have the monument restored which was done — the ground about it had grown to height of some 15 inches in consequence of the distribution of the residue of soil from each of the many internments [*sic*] in brick vaulted graves around. Much interest having become attached to this monument because of indantent aspicions [*sic*] of Capt. Drew's Character & Memory, some who deduce their conclusions from seemingly authentic information. St. Peter's Episcopal Church Record Book (transcript, Delaware State Museums, Dover).

43. HMS *De Braak* Pay Book (May 14, 1822), Admiralty Records 35/211.

Five

1. *The Sun* (Baltimore [July 25, 1887]).

2. Ibid.

3. The first true lighthouse in America was erected on Great Brewster Island, at the entrance to Boston Harbor, in 1716. The second was the eighty-five-foot tower constructed at Sandy Hook, New Jersey, which, like the Cape Henlopen Light soon afterwards, was paid for out of funds raised by lottery. Patrick Beaver, *A History of Lighthouses* (Secaucus, NJ: The Citadel Press, 1973), 83.

4. *New York Mercury* (January 4, 1762); J. Thomas Scharf, *History of Delaware*, 2 vols. (Port Washington, NY, and London: Kinnikat Press, 1988 repr.), 2: 1225; [Cullen], *History of Lewes* , 15–16; John W. Jackson, *The Pennsylvania Navy, 1775–1781: The Defense of the Delaware* (New Brunswick, NJ: Rutgers University Press, 1974), 412, 18n.

5. [Cullen], *History of Lewes*, 15–16; Scharf, *History of Delaware*, 2: 27–32, 1225; Jackson, *Pennsylvania Navy*, 412; E. M. Blunt, ed., *The American Coast Pilot*, 6th ed. (Newburyport, 1809), 199, states: "Cape Henlopen lies in north lat. 38° 47′, and in west long. 75°20′. There is a light-house here, a few miles below the town of Lewis, of an octagon form, handsomely built of stone, 115 feet high, and its foundation is nearly as much above the level of the sea. The lanthorn is between 7 and 8 feet square, lighted with 8 lamps, and may be seen in the night ten leagues at sea."

6. [Cullen], *History of Lewes*, 16; Scharf, *History of Delaware*, 2: 1225.

7. [Cullen], *History of Lewes*, 37; Jeannette Eckman, ed., *Delaware: A Guide to the First State*, new, rev. ed. (New York: Hastings House 1955 [1938]), 205.

8. Blunt notes of the approach to the Delaware: "As soon as you are in sight of the Cape [Henlopen], and are in want of a pilot, you had better hoist some signal, as those who do not are considered not in want of one." Blunt, *American Coastal Pilot*, 198, 199.

9. McCracken family Bible (photocopy, Delaware State Museums, Dover).

10. The coordinates are written on a slip of paper which has been inserted between the pages of the Bible, and they appear to have been modified. Some indications suggest an effort at erasure or a possible revision of earlier or incorrect positional data.

Six

1. Eckman, *Delaware*, 106–7.
2. *The Sun* (Baltimore [July 25, 1887]).
3. No vessel named *Resolute*, for example, would serve in the Royal Navy until a 181-ton twelve-gun brig of that name was commissioned on April 17, 1805. This vessel would be employed as a tender from March 1814 until June 1816, after which time she was utilized as a diving bell vessel. In 1844 she was converted to a convict hulk and, eight years later, was broken up at Bermuda. Colledge, *Ships of the Royal Navy*, 1: 460.
4. *The Sun* (Baltimore [July 25, 1887]).
5. Ibid.; *Every Evening* (Wilmington, DE [August 9, 1888]).
6. Ibid.
7. *The Sun* (Baltimore [July 25, 1887]).
8. *New York Times* (April 29, 1879).
9. Ibid.
10. Ibid.
11. Ibid. Cheney (or China) Clow (or Clows) was a noted Delaware Tory who, in April 1778, led an uprising of loyalists in Queen Anne's and Kent Counties, Maryland. In command of 600 to 700 irregulars assembled on an island at the head of the Chester River, he erected a fort and disarmed all who refused to join his band. A month later, the fort was attacked by patriot militia and some regulars, but the assault was repulsed. Clow and his men disappeared soon afterwards, only to reappear time and again to raid and plunder the Delmarva peninsula. A reward of £500 was offered for his capture but he was never apprehended. Edwin M. Jameson, "Tory Operations on the Bay from Dunmore's Departure to the End of the War," in *Chesapeake Bay in the American Revolution*, edited by Ernest McNeill Eller, (Centreville, MD: Tidewater Publishers, 1981), 386–87.
12. *New York Times* (April 29, 1879).
13. Ibid.
14. Ibid.
15. *The Sun* (Baltimore [July 25, 1887]).
16. Ibid.; *Every Evening* (Wilmington, DE [June 29, 1887]). Section 3755 of the Federal Statutes stated: "The Secretary of the Treasury is authorized to make any contract which he may deem for the interest of the government for the preservation, sale or collection of any property or the proceeds thereof which may have become wrecked, abandoned or became derelict being within the jurisdiction of the United States or which ought to come to the United States." *Every Evening* (Wilmington, DE [August 9, 1888]).

17. *Dictionary of American Biography*, vol. 14 (New York: Charles Scribner's Sons, 1934), 199; *Appleton's Cyclopedia of American Biography*, vol. 4, (New York: D. Appleton and Company, 1898), 642; *New York Times* (December 17, 1889).

18. *Philadelphia Inquirer* (July 8, 1887).

19. *The Sun* (Baltimore [July 25, 1887]).

20. *Philadelphia Inquirer* (July 8, 1887).

21. That the treasure tale had become well entrenched for at least half a century is suggested by the Baltimore *Sun* article of July 25, 1887, which stated: "In fact, all the old inhabitants of the place [Lewes] invariably referred to the wreck of the *De Braak* as having buried with it untold treasure. The matter was a common subject of belief and talk here less than fifty years ago."

22. *Philadelphia Inquirer* (July 8, 1887).

23. *The Sun* (Baltimore [July 25, 1887]). The Ocean Wrecking Company claimed in its prospectus that the mound was at a depth of fifty-four feet and was 150 feet long, forty feet wide, and six feet in height. Ocean Wrecking Company, *His B. Majesty's Sloop of War "Braak," Sunk in Delaware Bay, May 25. 1798* (Philadelphia: Ocean Wrecking Company, Limited, 1889), prospectus, 11.

24. *The Sun* (Baltimore [July 25, 1887]).

25. Ibid.

26. "The sand rises in terraces around the mound, the centre of which has a depression or valley not unlike the shape of a sunken deck of a vessel." Ibid.

27. Ocean Wrecking Company (prospectus), 11.

28. *Philadelphia Inquirer* (July 8, 1887); *The Sun* (Baltimore [July 25, 1887]).

29. *Every Evening* (Wilmington, DE [June 29, 1887]); *The Sun* (Baltimore [July 25, 1887]). *Startle* (no. 115966) was a steam tug of 54 tons gross, 27 tons net, 68 feet long, 17.5 feet abeam, and 8.4 feet deep, built at Wilmington, Delaware in 1883. *Merchant Vessels of the United States* (Washington, DC, 1886), 305. *William P. Orr* (reg. no. 26822) was a schooner of 70 feet in length, 22 feet abeam, and 6 feet deep in hold. She was 69.03 tons gross, 65.58 tons net, and had been built in 1863 at Milton, Delaware. She was home-ported at Wilmington. Ibid, 291.

30. *Every Evening* (Wilmington, DE [June 29, 1887]).

31. Ibid.; *The Sun* (Baltimore [July 25, 1887]). Charles Pedrick is incorrectly identified as "Charles F. Broderick," and Henry F. Dwyer is referred to as "Harry Dwyer" in *Every Evening* (Wilmington, DE [June 29, 1887]).

32. *Philadelphia Inquirer* (July 8, 1887). In the *Sun* article it was stated that: "Capt. Drew did not command his Britannic Majesty's sloop-of-war when he lost his life at the capes, but was on a privateering cruise, which was but little removed from piracy itself." In response to this gross inaccuracy, Maunsell Van Rensselaer, nephew of Lydia Drew, an Episcopal clergyman and president of Hobart College, responded by writing a rebuttal to correct the error. His letter was published in the *New York Evening Post* and stated that Drew was, in fact, a commissioned officer in the Royal Navy, an honorable and brave sailor, and a nephew by marriage to Lt. General John Maunsell. As such, he was connected to some of the most respected citizens of New York, and was anything but a pirate. *The Sun* (Baltimore [June 25, 1887]); Brodeur, "Treasure of the *De Braak*," 60.

33. *Every Evening* (Wilmington, DE [June 29, 1887]).

34. Ocean Wrecking Company (prospectus), 16–17.

35. *Philadelphia Inquirer* (July 8, 1887).

36. Ibid.

37. Ibid.

38. *The Sun* (Baltimore [July 25, 1887]).

39. Ibid.

40. Ibid.

41. Ibid.

42. *Every Evening* (Wilmington, DE [August 16 and September 13, 1887]); *New York Times* (July 18, 1888).

Seven

1. *New York Times* (July 18, 1888). James J. Kane (not to be confused with A. J. Kane, also a member of the board of directors of the investment syndicate) was chairman of the board, "although Dr. Pancoast . . . is the man who organized the syndicate and he is the man who delivers the shares of stock and received the money." *Every Evening* (Wilmington, DE [August 9, 1888]).

2. *Every Evening* (Wilmington, DE [August 9, 1888]).

3. Ibid. *City of Long Branch* (no. 80979) was built in 1883 at Nyack, New York. She was home-ported at Perth Amboy, New Jersey. While in the Roanoke River, North Carolina, on November 3, 1892, she was destroyed by fire. Her loss was computed at $40,000. *Merchant Vessels of the U.S.* (1888), 273; *Every Evening* (Wilmington, DE [July 31, 1888]); "Record of the Work Done with Steamer *City of Long Branch* in search for Treasures of H. B. M. Ship *Braak*," (hereafter cited as *Long Branch* Log), Pancoast Expedition Collection (William L. Clements Library, University of Michigan, Ann Arbor), 85; *Proceedings of Supervising Inspectors of Steam Vessels Held at Washington, D.C., January 1893* (Government Printing Office: Washington, 1893), 84.

4. *Every Evening* (Wilmington, DE [July 31, 1888]).

5. *Philadelphia Inquirer* (July 23, 1888); *Every Evening* (Wilmington, DE [August 9, 1888]).

6. Pancoast-Adams Certificate of Agreement (June 30, 1888), Pancoast Expedition Collection (William L. Clements Library, University of Michigan, Ann Arbor).

7. *Long Branch* Log, 85.

8. Ibid.

9. *Every Evening* (Wilmington, DE [July 31 and August 9, 1888]).

10. *Long Branch* Log, 84; *Every Evening* (Wilmington, DE [July 31, 1888]).

11. *New York Tribune* (July 18, 1888).

12. *Every Evening* (Wilmington, DE [July 31, 1888]).

13. *New York Tribune* (July 18, 1888).

14. *New York Tribune* (June 26, 1888).

15. *Long Branch* Log, 84.

16. *Philadelphia Inquirer* (July 23, 1888).

17. S. H. Coppage to James J. Kane (July 24, 1888), Pancoast Expedition Collection (William L. Clements Library, University of Michigan, Ann Arbor).

18. *Long Branch* Log, 1. *Every Evening* (Wilmington, DE [August 4, 1888]), reported the arrival of the *City of Long Branch* at the Delaware Breakwater Light on Wednesday, August 1, and noted that she "at once prepared business" to dredge and grapple for $10,000,000 in gold. In 1888 the Delaware Breakwater consisted of a single stone barrier which formed Lewes Harbor. Construction of the barrier was begun in 1828 and completed in 1834 at a cost of $1,160,000. In 1848 the Breakwater Light was erected about midway on the barrier, and in 1880 the building became the Maritime Exchange. In 1892 an outer barrier, referred to as the Harbor of Refuge, was begun. Today, the entire breakwater complex is 5,235 feet long and provides over a thousand acres of safe anchorage for vessels. [Cullen], *History of Lewes*, 35.

19. The Philadelphia *Public Ledger* (August 11, 1888) states: "The historic bearings indicate a point about three-fourths of a statute mile from the Breakwater, and seven-eighths of a mile from the point of Cape Henlopen." McCracken's bearings, as interpreted by Doctor Pancoast, placed the wreck at 1 15/88 of a statute mile, or one mile 300 yards, from the line of high water at the time of the disaster. "Copy of Bearings furnished by Mr. McCracken," Pancoast Expedition Collection (William L. Clements Library, University of Michigan).

20. *Long Branch* Log, 1 (July 31-August 1, 1888).

21. *Every Evening* (Wilmington, DE [July 31, 1888]); *Long Branch* Log, 1 (August 2, 1888).

22. *Every Evening* (Wilmington, DE [July 31, 1888]); *Long Branch* Log, 5 (August 2, 1888).

23. *Long Branch* Log, 5 (August 2, 1888).

24. Ibid., 6–7 (August 3, 1888). In the 1984–86 salvage expeditions of Sub-Sal, Inc., and Drew and Associates, the bottom visibility in the Delaware ranged from zero to four feet, with an average range of one and a half feet. During certain periods of the lunar cycle, currents of up to seven knots were reported. Conditions during the 1886–1888 expeditions were undoubtedly similar. Beard, "The De Braak Recovery Project: A Preliminary Report on Summer-Fall, 1986, Operations" (report prepared for the Delaware Division of Historical and Cultural Affairs, 1987), 5–6.

25. *Long Branch* Log, 7 (August 3, 1888).

26. Ibid. Construction of the Iron pier had begun shortly after 1870 with a federal appropriation of $225,000. Intended for government purposes, the pier's originally proposed 2,000 foot length was never completed, and only 900 feet saw service. The facility was eventually sold to the Lewes Sand Company for loading freight cars. For some years, the Maritime Exchange was located on one end. The facility is now in complete ruins. [Cullen], *History of Lewes*, 35–36.

27. *Long Branch* Log, 9 (August 4, 1888).

28. Ibid.

29. Ibid., 9–10 (August 5, 1888).

30. Ibid., 11, 13 (August 6–7, 1888).

31. Ibid., 13 (August 7, 1888).

32. Ibid.

33. Ibid., 15 (August 8, 1888).

34. Ibid., 15, 17 (August 8, 1888); *Public Ledger* (Philadelphia [August 11, 1888)].

35. Ibid.

36. *Long Branch* Log, 15 (August 8, 1888).

37. Ibid., 17 (August 8, 1888).

38. *Every Evening* (Wilmington, DE [August 9, 1888]). Pancoast may have been eager to depart to investigate "an adaption of the electric light for the under water . . . to facilitate the work of the divers." Although the use of underwater electric lights to assist diving operations is never mentioned in the records of the 1888 expedition and presumably were not employed, they were definitely considered for the two efforts carried out in 1889. *Public Ledger* (Philadelphia [August 11, 1888]); Ocean Wrecking Company (prospectus).

39. *Every Evening* (Wilmington, DE [August 9, 1888]).

40. Ibid. (August 13, 1888); *Long Branch* Log, 12–17 (August 6–8, 1888).

41. *Long Branch* Log, 17, 19, 21 (August 8–9, 1888).

42. *Every Evening* (Wilmington, DE [August 13, 1888]); *Long Branch* Log, 21 (August 9, 1888).

43. *Long Branch* Log, 23 (August 10, 1888).

44. *Every Evening* (Wilmington, DE [August 13, 1887]); Jeannette Edward Rattray, *Ships Ashore: A Record of Maritime Disasters off Montauk and Eastern Long Island, 1640–1955* (New York: Coward-McCann, Inc., 1955), 129–30.

45. *Long Branch* Log, 85.

46. Ibid., 23, 25 (August 11, 1888); *Every Evening* (Wilmington, DE [August 13, 1888]).

47. Ibid.

48. *Long Branch* Log, 27, 28 (August 13, 1888).

49. Ibid.

50. Ibid.

51. Ibid., 29-33 (August 15–17, 1888).

52. Ibid., 33 (August 17, 1888).

53. Ibid., 35, 37 (August 17–18, 1888).

54. Ibid., 35 (August 17, 1888).

55. Ibid., 37, 39 (August 18, 20–21, 1888).

56. Ibid., 41 (August 22); *Public Ledger* (Philadelphia [August 21, 1888]). The *Philadelphia Inquirer* (August 22, 1888) reported that at 6:20 P.M. "the sky suddenly grew black and a dense cloud came over the Delaware from the Jersey side. It seemed to be circular in form and about fifteen feet in diameter, and wheeled rapidly around with a roaring noise. When it touched the Delaware shore it moved fast, taking up whatever lay in its route." The cloud grew to six miles in length and 400 feet in width by the time it hit Wilmington. Five boats were capsized, nearly a dozen people were killed, and property damage was extensive.

57. *Long Branch* Log, 41 (August 24, 1888).

Eight

1. *Long Branch* Log, 41 (August 24, 1888).
2. Ibid., 43 (August 25, 1888).
3. Ibid.
4. Ibid., 45 (August 27, 1888).
5. Ibid., 47 (August 29–30, 1888).
6. Ibid., 49-53 (August 31–September 3, 1888).
7. Ibid., 53 (September 3, 1888).
8. Ibid., 55, 57 (September 4–5, 1888).
9. Ibid., 55 (September 5, 1888).
10. Ibid., 57 (September 5, 1888).
11. Ibid., 57-60 (September 5–8, 1888).
12. Ibid., 60-61 (September 8, 1888).
13. Ibid.
14. Ibid., 63 (September 12, 1888).
15. Ibid.
16. Ibid., 63, 65 (September 12–13, 1888).
17. Ibid.
18. Ibid., 67 (September 15, 1888).
19. Ibid.
20. Ibid., 69 (September 16, 1888).
21. Ibid., 69 (September 17, 1888).
22. Ibid.
23. Ibid., 69, 71 (September 17, 1888).
24. Ibid., 71 (September 17, 1888).
25. Ibid., 73.(September 18, 1888).
26. Ibid., 77 (September 19, 1888).
27. Ibid.
28. Ibid., 79 (September 20, 1888).
29. Ibid, 81, 83 (September 21–24, 1888).

Nine

1. *Philadelphia Inquirer* (September 24, 1888).
2. Ibid.
3. *Long Branch* Log, 83 (September 24, 1888).
4. Ocean Wrecking Company (prospectus), 19–20.
5. James J. Kane to Captain Charles A. Adams (October 3, 1888), Pancoast Expedition Collection, (William L. Clements Library, University of Michigan).
6. The probability that James J. Kane authored the Ocean Wrecking Company prospectus promoting the recovery of the *De Braak* treasure is evinced by his letter of October 3, 1888, to Captain Adams, in which he wrote: "I send you some new circulars of my new book, will you kindly distribute them where they will do the most

good. I will send you one of the first copies when issued, which I hope will be next week." Ibid.

7. Ocean Wrecking Company (prospectus), 3.
8. Ibid., 3–4.
9. Ibid., 8–9.
10. Ibid., 4–5.
11. Ibid., 5–6.
12. Ibid., 8.
13. Ibid., 10.
14. Ibid.
15. Ibid., 11–12.
16. Ibid., 12.
17. Ibid., 13–14.
18. Ibid., 13.
19. Ibid., 19.
20. Ibid., 21.
21. Ibid., 14–15.
22. Ibid., 15.
23. Ibid.
24. Ibid., 16.
25. Ibid.
26. Ibid., 3.
27. Ibid., 17.
28. Ibid., 21.
29. Ibid.
30. Ibid., 18.
31. Ibid., 21.
32. Although reference is frequently made in such works as Potter's *Treasure Diver's Guide*, Voynick's *Mid-Atlantic Treasure Coast*, and others to Townsend's ship as *Tamassee* or *Tamasse*, her officially registered name was *Tamesi* (no. 145310). *Tamesi* was a sea-going steam tug of 178.75 tons gross, 117.29 tons net, 106.4 feet long, 28 feet abeam, and eight feet deep. Built at Boston in 1882, in 1888-89 she was home-ported at Somers Point, New Jersey. John S. Potter, Jr., *The Treasure Diver's Guide*, rev. ed. (Garden City, NY: Doubleday and Company, 1972), 484; Stephen N. Voynick, *The Mid-Atlantic Treasure Coast: Coin Beaches & Treasure Shipwrecks from Long Island to the Eastern Shore* (Wallingford, PA: The Middle Atlantic Press, 1984), 107; *Merchant Vessels of the U.S.* (1888), 332.
33. [Cullen], *History of Lewes*, 35.
34. See "The Many Attempts to Raise the De Braak" (photocopy), *De Braak* File, (Delaware State Museums, Dover); Eckman, *Delaware*; Potter, *Treasure Diver's Guide*, 484. The first published mention of the purported second salvage effort, carried out in 1799 by the fictional warship *Resolute* in company with *Assistance*, appeared in *Every Evening* (Wilmington, DE [July 26, 1889]). Although no such effort was undertaken, the account has been repeated as fact ever since. For validation of the nonexistence of *Resolute*, see chapter 6, n.3.; Van Dulm to Paul E. Smith (March 26, 1964); Colledge, *Ships of the Royal Navy*, 1: 460.

35. *Morning News* (Wilmington, DE [February 16, 1937]).

36. *Tuckahoe* (no. 24928) was a steam tug of 299.07 tons gross, 198.14 tons net, 125 feet long, 23 feet abeam, and 7.9 feet deep. Built in 1872 at Chester, Pennsylvania, she was capable of 91 horsepower. In 1886 she was known to be home-ported in New York City. *Merchant Vessels of the U.S.* (1886), 370.

37. *Every Evening* (Wilmington, DE [July 26, 1889]).

38. Ocean Wrecking Company (prospectus), 20.

39. Scharf, *History of Delaware*, 2: 1225.

40. Ibid.

41. *New York Times* (December 7, 1889).

42. "The Many Attempts to Raise the De Braak" states that in 1920 Simon Lake expressed an interest in recovering *De Braak*. Lake, however, was involved in numerous other projects at the time, most notably the effort to recover the alleged treasure of HMS *Hussar* in New York, and failed to follow through on his interest in *De Braak*; indeed, he later expressed doubts about the probability of any substantial treasure even being aboard. See Robert I. Nesmith, *Dig for Pirate Treasure* (New York: Devin-Adair, 1958), regarding Lake's interest in *De Braak*.

Ten

1. See Joe Gores, *Marine Salvage: The Unfortunate Business of No Cure, No Pay* (Garden City, NY: Doubleday and Company, 1971) 50–57, and D. A. Koster, *Ocean Salvage* (New York: St. Martins Press, 1971), 95–114, for narrative accounts of Quaglia's Sorima Salvage Company's salvage of *Egypt*. The saga's unfolding may be followed in the *New York Times* (June 4, 8, 17, 30; July 6, 26, 27; August 3, 4, 9, 10, 14, 15, 19, 25, 28; September 4, 6, 11, 23, 29; October 21, 23; November 2, 3, 15, and 18, 1931).

2. Because of Ralph Chapman's family relationship to the famed Merritt, Chapman and Scott Salvage Company, it has frequently been assumed that the company carried out the salvage operations of 1932–33. However, F. N. Oberle, vice president of the Salvage Division, Merritt, Chapman and Scott, stated in a 1962 letter that company records "do not confirm that our firm engaged in a search for the *De Braak* in the summers of 1932–33 . . . it is the recollection of the undersigned that the quest was a private enterprise of Mr. Ralph Chapman, a member of the family whose name appears in our corporate title, but none of whom has been associated with the company for a number of years." F. N. Oberle letter (May 25, 1962) transcript, *De Braak* File, App. 5 (Zwaanendael Museum, Lewes). As late as 1989, the myth that the salvage had been carried out by MCS was still being repeated in published accounts of Chapman's salvage efforts on *De Braak*. Gary Gentile, *Shipwrecks of Delaware and Maryland* (Philadelphia: G. Gentile Productions, 1990), 58.

3. *New York Times* (September 25, 1932).

4. Albertson's longtime interest in the *De Braak* treasure was apparently shared by a number of would-be salvors. One such individual was Frank P. Blair, Jr., of Blair

and Martin Marine Salvage, of Chicago, who was curious enough to besiege the U.S. Coast Guard with at least three requests during the spring and summer of 1931 to provide him with whatever information the service had on file regarding the old warship. The following year, the Coast Guard received a similar request from one Lester Kettle of Rochester, New York. Neither Blair nor Kettle received any satisfaction since the Coast Guard's files contained nothing on *De Braak*. Fred W. Hopkins, Jr. to H. Henry Ward (August 25, 1986), Spar Buoy Folder, *De Braak* File (Delaware State Museums, Dover).

  5. [Cullen], *History of Lewes*, 15–16; Brodeur, "Treasure of the *De Braak*," 39.

  6. *New York Times* (July 12, 1932); Dutton, "Shipwrecks They've Seen," in *Saturday Evening Post* (February 13, 1954) 78. Chapman provided exclusive coverage of his operations to the *New York Times*, which assigned a local reporter, Marjorie F. Virden, to the story. Her reports are the source of almost all surviving data related to Chapman's efforts. *Delaware Coast Press* (Rehoboth [June 17, 1965]).

  7. *Katie Durm* (no. 206907) has been incorrectly identified as *Katie Burns* in some accounts, all of which stem from a typographic error in the *New York Times* (September 29, 1932). *Katie Durm* was a gas screw capable of thirty horsepower. She was 28 tons gross, 17 tons net, 55.5 feet long, 17 feet abeam, and 5.1 feet deep. Built in 1909 at Bellvue, Maryland, and crewed by two men, she earned her keep for her owner, the Atlantic Company, as a freight hauler. She was home-ported at Baltimore. *Merchant Vessels of the U. S.* (1931) 376–377. *Cap* (no. 229395) was a thirty horsepower gas screw of 13 tons gross, 8 tons net, 39.1 feet in length, 14.1 feet abeam, and 3.6 feet deep. Built in 1930 at Baltimore, she was served by a crew of one and employed as a freight hauler. Records concerning her ownership and home port are conflicting. Philadelphia records indicate that she was owned by the Philadelphia Derrick and Salvage Company, served under Maleotom L. Jacobs, and was berthed at pier 17, North Wharfs. *Merchant Vessels of the U. S.* states that she was home-ported in Baltimore, owned by the Atlantic Company, and berthed there at Recreation Pier, at the foot of Broadway. On Wednesday, August 23, 1933, while in Curtis Bay, Baltimore, she was crushed during a hurricane between two sunken lighters, *Interstate No. 1* and the pump boat *John Baxter*, and lost. *Merchant Vessels of the U. S.* (1931), 246–47; *Maritime Records Port of Philadelphia*, Section VI, Maritime Record of Wrecks, Vol. 12, 1931–1937 (Library of Congress, Washington, DC).

  8. The *New York Times* notes that the chief diver was Charles T. Jackson, who is also referred to in various reports as Clarence A. Jackson and as Charles E. Jackson. There has been some confusion about whether Jackson and Charles Johnston, who is identified by Dutton as an advisor to Chapman and who would later try his own hand at locating *De Braak*, were one and the same. *New York Times* (November 3, 1932; July 12, 1936); Dutton, "Shipwrecks They've Seem," 78.

  9. *New York Times* (September 25 and 30, 1932); *Delaware Coast Press* (Rehoboth [June 17, 1965]).

  10. Ibid. (September 25; November 2 and 3, 1932); *Delaware Coast Press* (Rehoboth [June 17, 1965]).

11. *New York Times* (September 30), 1932. *Merchant Vessels of the U. S.* (1933), 990, notes the loss of *Katie Durm* as occurring on October 21, 1932, the date on which the loss was officially reported but not the actual loss date.

12. No vessel named *Corsair* has been found in the *Merchant Vessels of the U. S.* for this period, although she is mentioned in a *New York Times* report of November 3, 1932.

13. *New York Times* (November 3, 1932).

14. *New York Times* (November 30, 1932).

15. Ibid.

16. Dutton, "Shipwrecks They've Seen," 78.

17. *Delaware Coast Press* (Rehoboth [June 17, 1965]).

18. Dutton, "Shipwrecks They've Seen," 78; *New York Times* (November 30, 1932); *Delaware Coast Press* (Rehoboth [June 17, 1965]).

19. Dutton, "Shipwrecks They've Seen," 78.

20. *New York Times* (March 26, 1933).

21. Ibid.

22. Ibid. *Captain Drew* (no. 232161) was a steamer which had once served as the U.S. Lighthouse Steamship *No. 68*. She was 425 tons gross, 289 tons net, 110.5 feet long, 29.6 feet abeam, 13.8 feet deep, and capable of 350 horsepower. Built at Bath, Maine, she was registered in 1933 as in "miscellaneous service" and was manned by a crew of eleven. Later owned by the Braak Corporation, at 17 Battery Place, New York City, she was also home-ported in New York. *Merchant Vessels of the U. S.* (1933), 32–33.

23. *New York Times* (March 26, 1933).

24. *New York Times* (July 12, 1936).

Eleven

1. *New York Times* (July 12 and August 2, 1936); Brodeur, "Treasure of the *De Braak*," 39.

2. Brodeur, "Treasure of the *De Braak*, " 36, 39.

3. *New York Times* (July 12, 1936).

4. Ibid.

5. *New York Times* (August 2, 1936); [Cullen], *History of Lewes*, 16. As early as April 5, 1935, Colstad had begun to investigate what salvage rights he might require to recover *De Braak*. In a letter to the Coast Guard he requested federal protection for any operation he might initiate and sought to determine if the federal government had the right to receive salvaged property. Fred W. Hopkins, Jr., to H. Henry Ward (August 25, 1986).

6. Brodeur, "Treasure of the *De Braak*, " 36.

7. *New York Times* (November 9, 1935; July 12, 1936).

8. *The Whale* (Rehoboth, DE [October 22, 1980]), reported, in an article by Gary Soulsman entitled "Jinx of the DeBraak: Real or Imagined?" the "Weather Witch" story, as related both by journalist Bill Frank and in the pages of the

Philadelphia Inquirer. A thorough examination of the latter for the periods from June 15 to December 1, 1935, and from June 15 to December 1, 1936, failed to uncover any mention of the specific details mentioned in the *Whale* article regarding the "Weather Witch" story. However, owing to the frequent mentions of the "Jinx" and the "Weather Witch," following the 1936 search, most of which began to appear in the 1950s, I have presented *The Whale*'s account quoted from the *Inquirer*, in some detail, below.

9. Ibid.

10. Ibid.

11. *New York Times* (July 12, 1936).

12. *Ibid.* By the end of the project, Captain Morrissey claimed the treasure to be worth $40,000,000. *Evening Journal* (Wilmington, DE [September 5, 1973]).

13. *New York Times* (August 2, 1936).

14. *Nellie L. Parmenter* (no. 232679), a gas powered screw vessel, was 18 tons gross, 15 tons net, 42.9 feet long, 11.9 feet abeam, 5.1 feet deep. Built in 1933 at Waltham, Massachusetts, and employed in the cod-fishing business, she was manned by a crew of five and was capable of 56 horsepower. The namesake of her owner, Nellie L. Parmenter of Maynard, Massachusetts, she was home-ported at Boston. No data has been found concerning *Doubloon*, but she was probably employed as a small service boat or runabout. *Merchant Vessels of the U. S.* (1936), 482–83.

15. *New York Times* (August 12 and 22, 1936); *Philadelphia Inquirer* (September 26, 1936).

16. *Philadelphia Inquirer* (September 14 and 26, 1936).

17 Voynick, *Mid-Atlantic Treasure Coast*, 110. The only item of interest recovered was a fourteen-ton chain, which had no apparent relationship to the wreck, although some believed it to be an important find. *Morning News* (Wilmington, DE [September 16, 1936]). In the fall of 1986, the late Gilbert Byron reported that Howard Chapelle of the Smithsonian Institution had visited the expedition to collect all available information and to observe the proceedings. Chapelle's field experience and findings undoubtedly influenced his future efforts to document and correct the baseless treasure stories which would again achieve national prominence three decades later. Byron himself, later to become a noted author of the Chesapeake Bay region, had also participated in at least one salvage effort conducted in the 1930s (although he does not specify which one). Hired as a deckhand aboard "a grimy tug" called *Arbutus*, which was working in concert with a sister tug named *Iris*, he assisted in drag operations off Cape Henlopen. The search apparently met with limited success, for timbers and a cannon "thought to be the type carried by the De Braak" were retrieved from eighty feet of water. The salvage company's stocks soared, but the attempt ultimately failed. *Evening Sun* (Baltimore [September 10, 1986]).

18. *Philadelphia Inquirer* (September 4, 1936); *Morning News* (Wilmington, DE [September 5 and 26, 1936]).

19. *Philadelphia Inquirer* (September 18, 1936).

20. *Philadelphia Inquirer* (September 18, 19, and 20, 1936).

21. *Philadelphia Inquirer* (September 26, 1936).

22. Ibid. Colstad mentioned during his lecture that Chapman had lost not one, but two, vessels during his expedition. Although I have been unable to confirm the claim that a second vessel was indeed lost (with the exception of the grounding and temporary abandonment of *Cap* on the Pea Patch in the Delaware River), it seems likely that Colstad was well aware of the trials and tribulations his predecessor had encountered and would not have fabricated such an easily remembered event of only a few years earlier.

23. *New York Times* (March 7, 1937); Eckman, *Delaware*, 197.

24. *New York Times* (March 7, 1937).

25. Ibid.

26. Ibid.

27. *Morning News* (Wilmington, DE [February 16, 1937]).

28. *New York Times* (March 7, 1937).

Twelve

1. Dutton, "Shipwrecks They've Seen," 76. Dutton describes Charles Johnston's title of "captain" as "a town courtesy" rather than an actual rank in the merchant mariné or the regular navy. His role in the Chapman Expedition was that of "local consultant." Ibid., 78. See also the *Morning News* (Wilmington, DE [June 10 and August 18, 1965]).

2. Dutton, "Shipwrecks They've Seen," 76.

3. *De Braak* Chronology, (Delaware State Museums, Dover); *Morning News* (Wilmington, DE [August 18, 1965]).

4. *Evening Sun* (Baltimore [September 10, 1986]). A year after the expedition, Brittingham made the acquaintance of a George Washington University student named Donald G. Geddes III, of Bethesda, Maryland, who had conducted research on *De Braak*. Geddes informed Brittingham that there were approximately fourteen ships sunk off Cape Henlopen, including *De Braak*, but that the Royal Navy brig had neither gold nor silver aboard when she went down. Brittingham later became a staunch disbeliever of the treasure legend. *Morning News* (Wilmington, DE [August 18, 1965]). See also "The Many Attempts to Raise the De Braak" (Zwaanendael Museum, Lewes).

5. Dutton, "Shipwrecks They've Seen," 78.

6. *Morning News* (Wilmington, DE [July 18, 1956]).

7. *Evening Journal* (Wilmington, DE [June 10, 1965]).

8. *Morning News* (Wilmington, DE [July 18, 1965]).

9. Ibid.

10. Ibid.

11. The Zwaanendael Museum, erected in 1932, stands at the corner of Savannah Road and Kings Highway in Lewes. The museum is managed by the Delaware State Museums and is open to the general public.

12. In July 1956, Stewart wrote Dorothy L. Givens of the Zwaanendael Museum that he had salvaged the 1695 wreck of HMS *Winchester*, a vessel of 94 guns, in

Florida waters in 1955. *Winchester* was, in fact, a vessel of 50 guns and 933 tons which had been lost September 24, 1695 near Key Largo, Florida, while en route from Jamaica to England. The wreck, however, had been first located by black fishermen in December 1938 and not by Stewart, as his letter implied, and much of it had been salvaged in about 1939 by one Charles Brookfield. Then, in the early 1950s, the site had been worked again by treasure salvors Art McKee, Bill Thompson, Ed Ciesinski, and others. Donald Stewart to Dorothy L. Givens (July 12, 1956), *De Braak* File, (Zwaanendael Museum); Colledge, *Ships of the Royal Navy* 1: 613; Robert F. Marx, *Shipwrecks of the Western Hemisphere: 1492–1825* (New York: The World Publishing Company, 1971), 40, 192, 205. Stewart's data on *De Braak* was not only far from accurate, but much of it appears to have been created by him. In one memo to the museum, he asserts that through data found in the French national archives, he discovered that *De Braak* had been built by Messrs. Van Gechen & Taynmahl at Rotterdam and was launched October 15, 1787. She was, he claimed, 390 tons at launching and was ship rigged with spar sails, "topsails on fore and main-mizzen lateen rig." Her overall length was 136 feet, 105 feet between perpendiculars, 84 feet keel length, 27 feet, 6 inches abeam, and 8 feet from spar deck combing to her hold. She drew a depth of water from keel to waterline of twelve feet, was rated for eight guns (fourteen-pounder French caliber), and sold as a Letter of Marque on June 13, 1794. From the "Royal Navy Archives" (presumably, the Public Record Office Admiralty collections), he claimed to have discovered that she was listed as a prize of war in 1795 and had been captured bearing a Letter of Marque and French registration by the *Dundee*, of 36 guns, in the Firth of Forth. (Contrary to Stewart's purported "documentation," no Royal Navy vessel bore the name *Dundee* until WW II). See Colledge, *Ships of the Royal Navy*, 1: 176, for verification of *Dundee*. Stewart's fiction sounded authoritative. For example, he claimed that prize money was paid to *Dundee* after *De Braak*'s alleged capture (a fiction) and that *De Braak* was soon afterward rebuilt as a sloop-of-war and entered on the lists as a commissioned vessel in 1796 (a fact). She was, he wrote, rated to carry fourteen 12-pounders, two 8-pounders, and a pair of brass swivels, or "Dutch rail guns," as he called them (a fiction). He then claimed to have scoured no fewer than eleven major repositories in The Netherlands, France, and England. Among some of his more impressive purported finds was a journal allegedly kept by *De Braak*'s (fictional) Second Lieutenant Patrick O'Brien, from 1797 to 1798, which had been acquired from one Colonel John S. Vanbibber Shriber of the Society of Military Collectors and Historians. Another purported discovery (a fiction) was a record of testimony supposedly rendered to an Admiralty Court on November 17–18, 1798. Most of the foregoing and more was pure fantasy. See Stewart communications and transcripts in *De Braak* File (Zwaanendael Museum, Lewes).

13. *Morning News* (Wilmington, DE [July 18, 1956]).

14. Ibid.; "The Many Attempts to Raise the *De Braak*," (photocopy), *De Braak* Files. Apparently at least one salvage group, probably Strube's, went to the trouble of contacting the Public Record Office in London about Royal Navy salvage work carried out on *De Braak*. In January 1962, the Public Record Office sent a reply, noting the file numbers, etc., for the captain's and master's logs of HMS *Assistance*.

Public Record Office letter transcript (January 10, 1962), *De Braak* Files (Zwaanendael Museum, Lewes).

The popularity of scuba diving in the Delaware region during the early 1960s is attested to by the Middle Atlantic Underwater Council of the Underwater Society of America's estimate that there were more than 2,000 divers in fifty or more clubs on the middle Atlantic seaboard. Walter and Richard Krotee, *Shipwrecks off the Coast of New Jersey* (Philadelphia: privately printed, 1965), 96.

15.One of the first major modern underwater archaeological projects employing scuba, rather than hard-hat, diving was being carried out in the Mediterranean by George Bass and Peter Throckmorton, under the auspices of the University of Pennsylvania, on the remains of the oldest shipwreck found by that time in the world. See George F. Bass, *Archaeology under Water* (New York: Praeger Publishers, 1966) and Peter Throckmorton, *The Lost Ships: An Adventure in Undersea Archaeology* (Boston and Toronto: Little, Brown and Company, 1964), for accounts of these excavations.

Thirteen

1. *Morning News* (Wilmington, DE [June 10, 1965]); *Evening Journal* (Wilmington, DE [June 10 and July 27, 1965]).

2. *Morning News* (Wilmington, DE [June 10, 1965]).

3. *The Sunday Bulletin Magazine* (Baltimore [October 5, 1969]); *Morning News* (Wilmington, DE [August 3, 1965]); *Philadelphia Inquirer* (August 1, 1965).

4. *Morning News* (Wilmington, DE [June 10, 1965]); *Evening Journal* (Wilmington, DE [June 10, 1965]).

5. *Morning News* (Wilmington, DE [June 10, 1965]).

6. Ibid.

7. Ibid.

8. Ibid.

9. Ibid.

10. Ibid.

11. Ibid. King and Joseph were not the only other potential contenders. On June 17, 1965, the *Delaware Coast Press* (Rehoboth) speculated that the son of the late Ralph Chapman might also give *De Braak* a try. He didn't.

12. *Evening Journal* (Wilmington, DE [July 27, 1965]).

13. Ibid.; *Morning News* (Wilmington, DE [August 3, 1965]).

14. *Evening Journal* (Wilmington, DE [July 27 and August 3, 1965]); *Morning News* (Wilmington, DE [August 3, 1965]).

15. *Morning News* (Wilmington, DE [August 8, 1965]).

16. Ibid.

17. *Philadelphia Inquirer* (August 1, 1965); *Evening Journal* (Wilmington, DE [August 7, 1965]); *Morning News* (Wilmington, DE [August 18, 1965]).

18. *Evening Journal* (Wilmington, DE [August 7, 1965]).

19. *Evening Journal* (Wilmington, DE [March 2, 1966]).

20. *Morning News* (Wilmington, DE [August 18, 1965]).

21. Ibid.; *Evening Journal* (Wilmington, DE [August 7, 1965]).

22. *Evening Journal* (Wilmington, DE [March 2, 1966]).

23. *Evening Journal* (Wilmington, DE [April 21, 1966]).

24. *Morning News* (Wilmington, DE [June 29, 1966]).

25. *Evening Journal* (Wilmington, DE [June 29, 1966]); *Morning News* (Wilmington, DE [June 29, 1966]).

26. Chapelle and Laws, "H.M.S. *De Braak,*" 58.

27. *Morning News* (Wilmington, DE [June 29, 1966]); *Evening Sun* (Baltimore [September 10, 1986]); *Evening Journal* (Wilmington, DE [June 29, 1966]).

28. *Morning News* (Wilmington, DE [June 29, 1966]).

29. *Delaware Coast Press* (Rehoboth [August 19, 1966]).

30. Ibid.

31. *Evening Journal* (Wilmington, DE [April 26 and July 12, 1967]); *Morning News* (Wilmington, DE [July 12, 1967]).

32. *Morning News* (Wilmington, DE [July 12, 1967]); *Philadelphia Inquirer* (June 23, 1968).

33. D & D was apparently unaware that two of the carronades had been replaced by 6-pounder long guns.

34. *Morning News* (Wilmington, DE [July 12, 1967]).

35. File note concerning D & D's visit to Zwaanendael Museum (August 12, 1967), *De Braak* File (Zwaanendael Museum, Lewes).

36. *Evening Journal* (Wilmington, DE [August 8, 1967]); *Morning News* (Wilmington, DE [July 12, 1967]).

37. *Philadelphia Inquirer* (June 23, 1968).

38. Unidentified news clipping (October 3, 1967), *De Braak* File (Zwaanendael Museum, Lewes); *Evening Journal* (Wilmington, DE [November 10, 1967]).

39. *Philadelphia Inquirer* (June 23, 1968).

40. Ibid.

41. *The Sunday Bulletin Magazine* (Baltimore [March 30, 1969]).

Fourteen

1. *Evening Journal* (Wilmington, DE [November 19, 1968]).

2. *Morning News* (Wilmington, DE [May 12, 1969]).

3. *Delaware Coast Pilot* (Rehoboth [March 26, 1969]); *The Sunday Bulletin Magazine* (Baltimore [March 30, 1969]).

4. *Morning News* (Wilmington, DE [May 15, 1969]).

5. *Evening Journal* (Wilmington, DE [August 6, 1969]).

6. *Morning News* (Wilmington, DE [August 6, 1969]); *Evening Bulletin* (Baltimore [August 6, 1969]).

7. Ibid.

8. *Evening Journal* (Wilmington, DE [August 6, 1969]).

9. Ibid.

10. Ibid.

11. Ibid.

12. Ibid.

13. Ibid.

14. Ibid.

15. Ibid.

16. Ibid.

17. The McClean Dredging Company provided a fifty-ton sea-going derrick, a storage barge, and a 1,000 h.p. seagoing diesel tug. *Morning News* (Wilmington, DE [August 6 and 7, 1969]); *Evening Bulletin* (Baltimore [August 6, 1969]).

18. Ibid.

19. Ibid.

20. *Evening Journal* (Wilmington, DE [August 7, 1969]).

21. *Evening Journal* (Wilmington, DE [August 21, 1969]).

22. Ibid.

23. Ibid.

24. *Evening Journal* (Wilmington, DE [November 1, 1969]).

25. Ibid.

26. *Evening Journal* (Wilmington, DE [February 12, 1970]).

27. Ibid.

28. See Mendel Peterson, *History Under the Sea: A Handbook for Underwater Exploration* (Washington, DC: Smithsonian Institution, 1965); *Delaware Coast Press* (Rehoboth [April 9, 1970]).

29. *Delaware Coast Press* (Rehoboth [April 9, 1970]).

30. *Evening Journal* (Wilmington, DE [May 23 and September 2, 1970]).

31. *Evening Journal* (Wilmington, DE [September 2, 1970]).

32. *Morning News* (Wilmington, DE [July 22, 1971]).

Fifiteen

1. Lt. Harry E. Rieseberg with A. A. Minkalow, *Fell's Guide to Sunken Treasure Ships of the World*, (New York: F. Fell, 1965), 120–21.

2. Warren Smith, *Finders Keepers*, (New York City: Ace Books, 1967), 24.

3. Lt. Harry E. Rieseberg, *Fell's Complete Guide to Buried Treasure, Land and Sea* (New York: F. Fell, 1970), 34.

4. Clay Blair, Jr., *Diving for Pleasure and Treasure*, (Cleveland and New York: The World Publishing Company, 1960), 19–63.

5. See John S. Potter, *The Treasure Diver's Guide*, vii–viii, for Wagner's glowing endorsement.

6. Ibid., 483.

7. Ibid., 484. In a communication from the Public Record Office, it is stated: "We have not succeeded in tracing any Logs for 1799 of a Royal Navy ship named Resolute, and no ship of this name appears in contemporary Navy Lists." Public Record Office letter (transcript, dated January 10, 1962), *De Braak* File, (Zwaanendael Museum, Lewes).

9. Al Masters, "Delaware's $40 Million Treasure Jinx," *Saga Magazine* (March, 1971), 36–37, 74–76, 78.

10. Bill Frank, "Del. Treasure May Turn Convict's Bars to Gold," *Evening Journal* (Wilmington, DE, 1971), partially dated news clipping, *De Braak* File (Zwaanendael Museum, Lewes).

11. Ibid.

12. Ibid.

13. Ibid.

14. Ibid.

15. Ibid.

16. *Evening Journal* (Wilmington, DE [September 5, 1973]).

17. Ibid.

18. Ibid.

19. Ibid.

20. Ibid.

21. *Morning News* (Wilmington, DE [November 7, 1974; November 22, 1976]).

22. Molly Murry, "De Braak Resisted Earlier Salvors," *News Journal* (Wilmington, DE [August 1986]), partially dated news clipping, *De Braak* File, (Zwaanendael Museum, Lewes).

23. Potter, *Treasure Diver's Guide*, 175.

24. Ibid., 170.

25. Ibid., xv, 170–171, 175.

26. Neither *Yealdham* nor *Leviathan* appears on Royal Navy lists of the period, nor are they included in contemporary abstracts of Royal Navy vessels from 1665 to the present.

27. See *The Daily Universal Register* (London [Saturday, November 19 and 22]), 1785 for a full account of the loss of *Faithful Steward*.

28. Voynick, *Mid-Atlantic Treasure Coast*, 119, reflecting the currently accepted mythology, claims that the *Three Brothers* sank in 1775 with a military payroll of gold, silver, and copper coins destined for the British command in Philadelphia. Although investigation of the *Naval Documents of the American Revolution*, which would certainly have mentioned such an important loss, revealed several vessels of that name to have been afloat in American waters in 1775 (one of which was a British transport), none were lost on the Delaware. *Naval Documents of the American Revolution* , 1: 1378; 2: 195, 1376; 3: 342; 4: 4; 5: 607, 628-29; 651, 652n., 685, 686n., 976; 4: 48, 163, 193, 231, 232, 233n., 1297. Interestingly, Marx does not mention *Three Brothers* in his work on shipwrecks in American waters. However, Potter (*Treasure Diver's Guide*, 484) claims the vessel was wrecked just off the Delaware coast "probably against a bar near old Indian River Inlet." He implies the ship was believed to have been lost in 1775 because coins bearing that date had been found washed up on the beach. In fact, since 1878, when "two pieces of gold coin and a Spanish dollar were found near the edge of the surf," near Cape Henlopen, coin finds from shipwrecks along the beaches have been a common occurrence. The first well-publicized finds were made on February 22, 1937, near Indian River Inlet by enrollees from the Lewes Civilian Conservation Corps. A holiday treasure hunt soon was organized by the camp's educational advisor, Edward L. Richards. It was

reported that "the coins are apparently from the wreck of an old vessel and have been found in lesser quantities following storms and northeast winds for the past several years." *New York Times* (April 29, 1879); *Morning News* (Wilmington, DE [February 23, 1937]).

On February 29, 1937, "an old sea chest" was found along the surf line. The chest, which had been discovered by a retired army officer, Major Lindsley L. Beach, was three feet square, bound with copper, weighed an estimated 400 pounds, and was encrusted with barnacles. Before the incoming tide halted their investigations, Beach and two companions had partially pried open one of the "compartments" of the chest, but had found only charred wood. The chest was covered up again by the beach sands, and the major awaited patiently for another storm to reveal it once more. He never saw it again.

On March 13, however, during another blow, he discovered a coin dated 1749, on the beach at Rehoboth, and another dated 1775, both of which were added to his collection of nearly 100 coins recovered from the beaches. The coins found near Indian River Inlet dated from 1774 to 1782, so the Rehoboth coin was by far the oldest one recovered to that time. The same storm also revealed almost 200 copper coins near the Indian River Coast Guard Station. One hundred and fifty of them were recovered by four youths from Ocean View, fourteen more, dated 1772 and 1773, were recovered by Captain A. C. C. Osborne, of the Coast Guard, and another twenty were recovered by W. J. Cobb and S. B. Savage, of Osborne's crew. Ever since then, the beach has been nicknamed Coin Beach. *Morning News* (Wilmington, DE [February 23 and 25; March 14 and 18, 1937]).

29. *The Whale* (Rehoboth [October 8, 1980]). It was reported in 1986 that Seaborne Ventures had been partly led by John Doering, once a representative of several unidentified sponsors whose Michigan-based investment group had once held interests in Sting Ray, Inc. Molly Murry, "De Braak Resisted Earlier Salvors," *News Journal* (Wilmington, DE [August 1986]).

30. *The Whale* (Rehoboth [October 8, 1980]); *Delaware Coast Press* (Rehoboth [October 15, 1980]). Beard notes: "An ominous pattern was beginning to emerge that would later affect *De Braak*: the willingness of the state of Delaware to lease out its submerged cultural resources for 'mining' in exchange for a piece of the elusive treasure pie." Beard, "Treasure Debunked" 37.

31. *The Whale* (Rehoboth [October 8, 1980]).

32. Ibid.; *Delaware Coast Press* (Rehoboth [October 15, 1980]).

33. *The Whale* (Rehoboth [October 8, 1980]); *Delaware Coast Press* (Rehoboth [October 15, 1980])

34. *The Whale* (Rehoboth [October 8, 1980]).

35. *The Whale* (Rehoboth [October 15, 1980]); *Delaware Coast Press* (Rehoboth [October 20, 1980]). Krotee, in *Shipwrecks off the Coast of New Jersey*, 85, went so far as to provide purported coordinates for the wrecksite: 38–47–18N, 75–04 - 24W.

36. *The Whale* (Rehoboth [October 8, 1980]).

37. Ibid.

38. Ibid.

39. Ibid.

40. *The Whale* (Rehoboth [October 15, 1980]).

41. Ibid.

42. *The Whale* (Rehoboth [October 22, 1980]).

43. *Delaware Coast Press* (Rehoboth [October 15, 1980]).

44. Ibid.

45. *The Whale* (Rehoboth [October 15, 1980]).

46. *Delaware Coast Press* (Rehoboth [October 22, 1980]); *The Whale* (Rehoboth [October 22, 1980]).

47. *The Whale* (Rehoboth [October 22, 1980]).

48. Ibid.; *Delaware Coast Press* (Rehoboth [October 22, 1980]).

49. *The Whale* (Rehoboth [October 15, 1980]).

Sixteen

1. Brodeur,"Treasure of the *De Braak*," 34; Steven Fromm, "Salvager Denies Deal on *De Braak*" (1986), partially dated news clipping, *De Braak* File (Zwaanendael Museum, Lewes).

2. Brodeur, "Treasure of the *De Braak*," 34. The pirate ship *Whydah*, under the command of Captain "Black" Sam Bellamy, had been wrecked on April 26, 1717, with a substantial cargo of plunder aboard. The few crewmen who were able to make it ashore were quickly captured and jailed, their behavior castigated by no less a personage than Cotton Mather. The *Republic*, pride of the White Star Line of Atlantic steamers, had gone down off Nantucket Island on January 23, 1909, with a treasure in her safe rumored to be worth $3,000,000. Emergency messages sent out over the ship's wireless had been the first radio calls ever employed for rescue at sea. See Arthur T. Vanderbilt II, *Treasure Wreck: The Fortunes and Fate of the Pirate Ship Whydah* (Boston: Houghton Mifflin Company, 1986) for a complete account of Whydah, and "Commonwealth of Massachusetts v. Maritime Underwater Surveys, Inc.," in *The Society for Historical Archaeology Newsletter*, 20: 3 (October 1987), 46, for comments of the consequences of the impact of the discovery on antiquities concerns in Massachusetts. See also Stephen M. Voynick, *The Mid-Atlantic Treasure Coast*, 93-96, for an account of the loss of *Republic*.

3. Brodeur, "Treasure of the *De Braak*," 34.

4. Ibid.

5. Ibid. The account of the coin falling from the diver's boot had gained currency as part of the *De Braak* legend in 1938, when it first appeared in *Delaware: A Guide to the First State* : "when a diver was hauled upon the deck of the *Liberty* with a piece of teak-wood in his hand . . . a silver Spanish coin fell from between the iron spikes of his diving shoes." Eckman, *Delaware*, 197.

6. *New York Times* (October 9, 1984).

7. Harrington owned forty percent of the company, Wise thirty percent, Steingrebe twenty percent, and the unnamed schoolteacher ten percent. The teacher's share was later increased to fifteen percent when an additional $100,000 from the latter's trust fund was invested, and both Steingrebe and Wise reduced their own shares by two and a half percent each. Brodeur, "Treasure of the *De Braak*," 34.

8. Ibid., 35.

9. Ibid.; Beard, "Treasure Debunked," 37. In March 1984, a northeaster struck the Delaware coast with such force that the remains of the Cape Henlopen Lighthouse were temporarily exposed in the surf line. Measurements were taken by a local Sussex County antiquarian named Eugene Castrovillo before the ruins were reburied. Knowledge of the precise location of the lighthouse removed the guess work regarding the McCracken coordinates which had hindered earlier expeditions. Gentile, *Shipwrecks of Delaware and Maryland*, 59.

10. Peter Hess, "A Legend Found: The Salvage of HMS *De Braak*," *Seafarers: Journal of Maritime Heritage*, 1 (1987): 215.

11. Brodeur, "*Treasure of the De Braak*," 35; *New York Times* (October 9, 1984); *Boston Globe* (July 31, 1984); *The Whale* (Rehoboth [August 1, 1984]).

12. Brodeur, "Treasure of the *De Braak*," 35; *State News* (Dover [September 18, 1984]). Beard quotes Harrington as stating (in a personal communication) that only six wrecks were located. Beard, "Treasure Debunked," 37.

13. H. Henry Ward, David V. Beard, and Claudia F. Melson, "A Preliminary Report on Archaeological Monitoring of the Salvage Activities on the H.M.S. *De Braak*, 1985" (University of Delaware Center for Archaeological Research, February 1986), 6; Brodeur, "Treasure of the *De Braak*," 35; Daniel Griffith, "H.M.S. *De Braak*: The Legend Revealed," paper presented to the First Joint Archaeological Congress (Baltimore, MD, January 7, 1989), tape recording.

14. Brodeur, "Treasure of the *De Braak*," 36, 37; *The Whale* (Rehoboth [July 3, 1984]); *Delaware Coast Press* (Rehoboth [August 29, 1984]).

15. Beard, "Treasure Debunked," 39; Brodeur, "Treasure of the *De Braak*," 37.

16. Brodeur, "Treasure of the *De Braak*," 37; *New York Times* (October 7, 1984).

17. Brodeur, "Treasure of the *De Braak*," 44; *Boston Globe* (July 31, 1984); *Sunday News Journal* (Wilmington, DE [October 28, 1984]).

18. Beard, "Treasure Debunked," 65; Griffith, "The Legend Revealed"; *The Whale* (Rehoboth [August 1, 1984]); *Boston Globe* (July 31, 1984); Brodeur, "Treasure of the *De Braak*," 37.

19. Brodeur, "Treasure of the *De Braak*," 37.

20. Ibid.

21. Ibid., 38. Fish stated that "the beautiful copper bilge pumps are in the exact position to be the *De Braak*." *Boston Globe* (July 31, 1984).

22. Brodeur, "Treasure of the *De Braak*," 38; *The Whale* (June 27, 1984).

23. Brodeur, "Treasure of the *De Braak*," 38.

24. *The Whale* (Rehoboth [June 27, 1984]).

25. Brodeur, "Treasure of the *De Braak*," 38; *The Whale* (Rehoboth [July 15 and 31, 1984]); *Washington Post* (July 31, 1984).

26. Beard, "Treasure Debunked," 39.

27. *News Journal* (Wilmington, DE [August 27, 1984]).

28. Brodeur, "Treasure of the *De Braak*," 37; Griffith, "The Legend Revealed."

29. On November 22, 1982, treasure salvor Barry Clifford filed a claim in a United States district court in Boston to the wreck of the *Whydah* and any treasure that might be found upon her. Exploration to locate the wreck site began off Wellfleet, Massachusetts, on May 13, 1983, with magnetometer and sub-bottom sonar. On July 19, 1984, the first strike on the site was made. In September, the ship's bell,

bearing the cast inscription "The Whydah Galley 1716" was recovered. Cf. Arthur T. Vanderbilt, II, *Treasure Wreck*, and Edwin Dethlefsen, *Whidah: Cape Cod's Mystery Treasure Ship* (Woodstock, VT, and Key West, FL: Seafarers Heritage Library, 1984), for two comprehensive accounts of the search for *Whydah*.

30. *New York Times* (October 7, 1984); Brodeur, "Treasure of the *De Braak*," 38.

31. *New York Times* (October 9, 1984).

32. *The Whale* (Rehoboth [July 31, 1984]); *New York Times* (July 31, 1984); *Washington Post* (July 31, 1984); Brodeur, "Treasure of the *De Braak*," 39. Fish described the condition of the remaining carronades thus: The metal in the cannons had oxidized to the extent that a sharp blow with a sledge hammer would easily break the cannon in half. Once the crust is chipped away, a five hour process in the case of the cannons cleaned so far, the artifacts will be immersed in large tanks filled with a chemical mixture of electro-chemical agents, sodium hydroxide and zinc . . . a tried and true method of restoring iron plates found beneath the sea. *The Whale* (Rehoboth [August 15, 1984]).

33. *New York Times* (July 31, 1984); Brodeur, "Treasure of the *De Braak*," 39.

34. *Delaware Coast Press* (Rehoboth [August 1, 1984]); *New York Times* (July 31, 1984); *Boston Globe* (July 31, 1984); *News Journal* (Wilmington, DE [August 27, 1984]); Beard, "Treasure Debunked," 41.

35. *Montgomery County Record* (Norristown, PA. [July 31, 1984]).

36. Brodeur, "Treasure of the *De Braak*," 39.

37. *New York Times* (October 9, 1984).

38. *News Journal* (Wilmington, DE [August 2, 1984]). Though the one year lease was signed by Governor DuPont and the Secretary of Department of Natural Resources on July 25, 1984, it was not to become effective until August 1.

Seventeen

1. Beard, "Treasure Debunked," 42; Brodeur, "Treasure of the *De Braak*," 40; *New York Times* (September 18, 1984); *The Whale* (Rehoboth [August 8, 15, and 29, 1984]). Most of the divers were imported from the Louisiana offshore oil fields. H. Henry Ward, David V. Beard, and Claudia F. Melson. "Preliminary Report on Archaeological Monitoring of the Salvage Activities on the H.M.S. *De Braak*, 1985," report prepared for the Delaware Bureau of Museums and Historic Sites, University of Delaware Center for Archaeological Research (February 1986), 14.

2. Griffith, "The Legend Revealed"; *Beachcomber* (Rehoboth [September 21, 1984]); Beard, "Treasure Debunked," 42; Ward, et al., "Preliminary Report," 14.

3. Brodeur, "Treasure of the *De Braak*," 40; *Delaware Coast Press* (Rehoboth [August 29, 1984]); *The Whale* (Rehoboth [August 8, 1984]). Edgecomb, who procured most of the equipage for the field operations, estimated diving equipment cost at $150,000 to $200,000, while the cost of the diver monitoring gear alone would be at least $24,000. *Sunday News Journal* (Wilmington, DE [October 28, 1984]).

4. *The Whale* (Rehoboth [August 8 and 12, 1984]).

5. *Baltimore News American* (August 12, 1984).

6. Ibid.; *Delaware Coast Press* (Rehoboth [September 19, 1984]).

7. Ward, et al., "Preliminary Report," 13; Griffith, "The Legend Revealed"; *Beachcomber* (Rehoboth [September 21, 1984]); *The Whale* (Rehoboth [August 15, 22, and 29, 1984]); *Sunday News Journal* (Wilmington, DE [October 28, 1984]).

8. *Beachcomber* (Rehoboth [September 21, 1984]); *The Whale* (Rehoboth [August 15, 1984]; Ward, e. al., "Preliminary Report," 14–15; Griffith, "The Legend Revealed."

9. Brodeur, "Treasure of the *De Braak*," 40; *Beachcomber* (Rehoboth [September 21, 1984]); *The Whale* (Rehoboth [August 29 and September 5, 1984]).

10. *The Whale* (Rehoboth [August 29, 1984]).

11. Ward, et al., "Preliminary Report," 14–15; Griffith, "The Legend Revealed."

12. Beard, "Treasure Debunked," 42; Griffith, "The Legend Revealed."

13. Griffith, "The Legend Revealed": *The Whale* (Rehoboth [August 29, 1984]); *Sunday News Journal* (Wilmington, DE [October 28, 1984]).

14. *The Whale* (Rehoboth [September 5, 1984]).

15. *The Whale* (Rehoboth [August 29, 1984]). Reedy's specific mission "included stabilization and limited conservation of artifacts and regular dives to inspect the progress of the work on the site." Beard, "Treasure Debunked," 41.

16. See Ward et al., "Preliminary Report," for the overall conduct of the project and conservation measures. It is of interest to note that in May 1985, Curtiss E. Peterson, a nationally known conservator with the South Carolina Institute of Archaeology and Anthropology, visited the Sub-Sal facilities to evaluate the condition of the collections and to make recommendations for their care, handling, and preservation. For the most part, his recommendations were ignored until the Delaware Bureau of Museums and Historic Sites (later renamed Delaware State Museums) assumed *pro tem* responsibility for their care. See Curtiss E. Peterson, "Survey of Artifacts Recovered from a Shipwreck Site Off Lewes, Delaware," *De Braak* File (Delaware State Museums, Dover), for a thorough account of the condition of the collections until May 1985, and recommendations made for their conservation.

17. Brodeur, "Treasure of the *De Braak*," 40; Luis Marden, "Wreck of H.M.S. Pandora: Found on Australia's Great Barrier Reef," *National Geographic*, 168:4 (October 1985) 423–50.

18. Brodeur, "Treasure of the *De Braak*," 44. In June 1986, it was reported for the first time that the salvors had moved human remains to one side of the wreck where they were left "relatively undisturbed." A number of archaeologists participating in the project have informed me that the remains were, in fact, cast up to the currents, since, as Claudia Melson later stated, "It's really kind of a registered burial site," and the recovery of human remains might have induced state officials to question the methodology and progress of operations. *Evening Journal* (Wilmington, DE [June 30, 1986]); David Beard, pers. comm.; Charles Fithian, pers. comm.; H. Henry Ward, pers. comm.

During the course of the excavation of King Henry VIII's flagship *Mary Rose*, undertaken several years before that of *De Braak*, British archaeologists encountered numerous human remains *in situ*, recovered them archaeologically, conducted extensive and important studies on them, and gained enormous insight into and knowledge about the physical life of the mariner in the sixteenth century. The remains were subsequently reburied at sea with full military honors, befitting the ship and nation they had served. Margaret Rule, *The Mary Rose: The Excavation and Raising of Henry VIII's Flagship* (Naval Institute Press, Annapolis, 1984), 184–186.

19. *Beachcomber* (Rehoboth [September 21, 1984]). An alternative version of Amaral's discovery states that he shouted: "Here's a gold coin! Here's another gold coin! Whoops, here's another." Brodeur, "Treasure of the *De Braak*," 44.

20. Brodeur, "Treasure of the *De Braak*," 44.

21. Ibid., 45.

22. Ibid.; *Beachcomber* (Rehoboth [September 21, 1984]); *The Whale* (Rehoboth [September 19, 1984]).

23. *New York Times* (September 18, 1984).

24.   *The Times* (London [January 15, 1798]). The finding of the ring provoked a spate of "psychic" experiences. One typical account appeared in *The Whale* after the ring discovery.

It seems that several months before the Sub-Sal crew had ever heard of a brother to Capt. James Drew, a professor in Massachusetts reported that a New Hampshire man was having disturbing dreams about De Braak, her captain and his family. That professor reportedly wrote to Sub-Sal historian John Fish telling him of the strange dreams and also mentioning to him, long before the discovery of the ring, that one of the dreams included a segment where Capt. James Drew was terribly bereaved over the loss of his brother. Sub-Sal officials are continuing to look into the history behind Capt. James Drew and his brother and plan to be in further contact with the New England people regarding the dreams. *The Whale* (Rehoboth [September 19, 1984]).

Several of the divers publicly stated that they felt a supernatural presence guiding them. Joe Amaral reported: "We believe, goofy or not, that Jim [Drew] is guiding us in the right direction. The challenge is going to be discovering what Jim wants us to know." Even Edgecomb commented: "You feel an omnipresence of some kind." Later, salvor L. John Davidson reported that at least two of his crew members had experienced the same vivid dream "that the treasure was divided among three chests and was scattered across the ocean bottom when the ship sank." Later, when the hull of De Braak was raised, a self-proclaimed mystic from California, who had watched the operation on television, called one of the salvage investors and informed him that he was a reincarnated De Braak sailor who had gone down with the ship and could lead the salvors to the treasure. During the actual recovery of the hull in 1986, Davidson had marveled at "the sea boiling for no reason at all," half believing it to be caused by supernatural forces (rather than the release of gases trapped beneath the hull as it sank and as it later deteriorated, which seems a more logical explanation). *Sunday News Journal* (Wilmington, DE [October 28, 1984]); *News Journal* (Wilmington, DE [August 17, 1986]; L. John Davidson to Paul Brodeur (August 11, 1988), *De Braak* File, Delaware State Museums, Dover.

25. Brodeur, "Treasure of the *De Braak*," 45.

26. Ibid., 45–46; *The Whale* (Rehoboth [September 12 and 19, 1984]); *Morning News* (Wilmington, DE [September 19, 1984]); *Sunday News Journal* (Wilmington, DE [September 30, 1984]).

27. *State News* (Dover [September 18, 1984]); *Morning News* (Wilmington, DE [September 18, 1984]); *The Whale* (Rehoboth [September 19, 1984]).

28. *New York Times* (September 18, 1984); *The Whale* (Rehoboth [September 19, 1984]).

29. *Delaware Coast Press* (Rehoboth [September 19, 1984]).

30. Brodeur, "Treasure of the *De Braak*," 45; *The Whale* (Rehoboth [September 19, 1984]).

31. *State News* (Dover [September 18, 1984]).

32. *Morning News* (Wilmington, DE [September 18, 1984]).

33. *The Whale* (Rehoboth [September 26, 1984]).

34. Brodeur, "Treasure of the *De Braak*," 45.

35. *The Whale* (Rehoboth [October 17, 1984]).

36. Brodeur, "Treasure of the *De Braak*," 46.

37. *Washington Post* (August 3, 1986).

38. Brodeur, "Treasure of the *De Braak*," 46.

39. *Washington Post* (August 3, 1986); *Sunday News Journal* (Wilmington, DE [September 30, 1984]).

40. *Washington Post* (August 3, 1986).

41. Brodeur, "Treasure of the *De Braak*," 46; (*Washington Post*, [August 3, 1986] reported that Harrington's loan was for $102,000).

42. Brodeur, "Treasure of the *De Braak*," 46.

43. Ibid., 46–47.

44. Hess, "A Legend Found," 221; *The Whale* (Rehoboth [October 17, 1984]).

45. Hess, "A Legend Found," 221.

46. Brodeur, "Treasure of the *De Braak*," 47.

47. Ibid.

Eighteen

1. Brodeur, "Treasure of the *De Braak*," 47.

2. Ibid., 47–48.

3. L. John Davidson to Paul Brodeur (August 11, 1988).

4. Ibid.

5. Brodeur, "Treasure of the *De Braak*," 48.

6. Ibid.

7. Ward et al., "Preliminary Report," 17–19; Beard, "Treasure Debunked," 47.

8. Claudia F. Melson, "Keep It Wet: H.M.S. *De Braak* Collections Management," paper presented at the First Archaeological Congress (Baltimore, MD, January 7, 1989), tape recording.

9. Ibid.

10. Ward, et al., 16–17.

11. Ibid., 19; Brodeur, "Treasure of the *De Braak*," 48.

12. Ward et al., "Preliminary Report," 31–33; Brodeur, "Treasure of the *De Braak*," 48–49; Griffith, "The Legend Revealed."

13. Ibid.

14. Ward et al., "Preliminary Report," 26–30; Beard, "Treasure Debunked," 46–47.

15. Griffith, "The Legend Revealed."

16. Ibid.; Brodeur, "Treasure of the *De Braak*," 48; Beard, "Treasure Debunked," 47.

17. Griffith, "The Legend Revealed."

18. Melson, "Keep It Wet."

19. Ibid.

20. Ibid.

21. Ibid.

22. Ibid.

23. Ibid.

24. Ibid.

25. Ibid.

26. Ibid.

27. Ibid.

28. Ibid.

Nineteen

1. Brodeur, "Treasure of the *De Braak*," 49.

2. *Antiques and Auction News* (June 20, 1986). One of the most prominent wrecks which Harrington sought to "arrest" was the so-called "china wreck." A wooden, two-masted schooner, she had been dispatched from England, probably in late 1869 or early 1870, with a cargo of Staffordshire chinaware produced by the plants of Powell & Bishop, J. W. Parkhurst & Co., George Jones, Henry Burgess, W. & E. Carn, and others destined for the American market. While entering Delaware Bay, the schooner was said to have caught fire and sank. In 1970, two U.S. Commerce Department wire-drag ships searching for submerged navigational hazards encountered the wreck's remains in approximately 40 feet of water at 74-55-00 W and 39-49-14 N. National Oceanic and Atmospheric Administration divers discovered the vessel's cargo of ironstone china, and the otherwise unidentified site became known as the "china wreck." Soon after her discovery, sports divers descended on the site and collected thousands of intact pitchers, mugs, bowls, plates, cups, and pottery. As the wreck's fame spread, charter dive boat captains began making regular runs to the site.

Harrington's efforts to arrest the "china wreck" raised a storm of controversy in the sports diving community. One diver viewed Harrington's plan to recover thousands of pieces of pottery as little more than false advertising, since "many salvage projects are scams aimed at separating unwitting investors from their money." Thus, to combat Harrington and Davenport's efforts to lay legal claim to the six wreck sites, a number of sport divers organized Ocean Watch which promptly filed a suit in federal court seeking to have the six sites declared areas in the public domain with custodial rights given to Ocean Watch. The organization petitioned to have all recovery of artifacts from the sites carried out only with scuba gear and hand tools. Hearings were scheduled for June 9 in the District Court of Delaware, with Harrington's old watchdog, Judge Caleb M. Wright, presiding. During the hearing, Judge Wright asked Harrington if the coins raised from *De Braak* and sent to Boston had been returned in accordance with his earlier court order. Harrington stammered that he was attempting to get them back to Delaware, but they had as yet not been returned. Soon afterwards, Harrington's petition to arrest the six wreck sites was denied. *Antiques and Auction News* (June 20, 1986); Gary Gentile, *Shipwrecks of Delaware and Maryland*, 59; *Evening Journal* (Wilmington, DE [June 30, 1986]); U.S. Congress, Senate, Committee on Energy and Natural Resources, Subcommittee on Public Lands, National Parks and Forests, 100th Cong. 1st sess. on S.858 (Abandoned Shipwreck Act of 1987), 286 (hereafter cited as Committee on Energy).

3. L. John Davidson to Paul Brodeur (August 11, 1988).

4. Brodeur, "Treasure of the *De Braak*," 49.

5. Ibid.; John Kern to L. John Davidson (July 30, 1986), *De Braak* File (Delaware State Museums, Dover); John Broadwater, pers. comm.; Beard, "Treasure Debunked" 48.

6. Walter Zacharachuk and Peter J. A. Waddell, *The Excavation of the Machault: An 18th-Century French Frigate* (National Historic Parks and Sites, Environment Canada, Parks: Ottawa, 1986).

7. Beard, "Treasure Debunked," 48–49; Broadwater, pers. comm.; Brodeur, "Treasure of the *De Braak*," 49.

8. See G. M. Hughes Notes; Brodeur, "Treasure of the *De Braak*," 49–50. It has been suggested by Beard that Zacharachuk's influence on Davidson may have been promoted somewhat by the fact that he had been serving as a consultant to Mel Fisher's Treasure Salvors, Inc., of Key West and, unlike the other archaeologists, could presumably be trusted as a fellow treasure hunter. Beard, "Treasure Debunked," 48.

9. Brodeur, "Treasure of the De Braak," 50; Griffith, "The Legend Revealed"; Beard, "*De Braak* Recovery Project: Winter Operations, 1986," report prepared for the Delaware Division of Historical and Cultural Affairs (May, 1986), 4. There is some irony in the fact that Davidson later informed *New Yorker* writer Paul Brodeur that he didn't believe "for a minute there was any chance" of finding hundreds of millions of dollars in treasure. But since he and Harrington had already recovered approximately 400 gold and silver coins "just by scratching around in the sand" atop the wreck, he could "reasonably expect" to find thousands more if he lifted the hull and excavated beneath it. Brodeur, "Treasure of the *De Braak*," 50.

10. Griffith, "The Legend Revealed"; Beard, "H.M.S. *De Braak*: An Architectural Study of an 18th-Century Brig," paper presented at the First Joint Archaeological Congress (Baltimore, MD, January 7, 1989), tape recording; Brodeur, "Treasure of the *De Braak*," 50.

11. Brodeur, "Treasure of the *De Braak*," 50.

12. Beard notes that photography also proved quite unproductive when in late July, an effort was made to photograph the site. "The lack of underwater photographic equipment on the project," Beard wrote, "had been a major frustration, since [by] mid-June the visibility had been good enough to produce a very good photo mosaic of the site. When a diver could finally be hired to do it, conditions had deteriorated." Beard, "Treasure Debunked," 50, 74; "H.M.S. *De Braak* Recovery Project: A Preliminary Report," 7.

13. Beard, "Treasure Debunked" 50–51; Brodeur, "Treasure of the *De Braak*," 50; *Evening Journal* (Wilmington, Delaware [June 30, 1986]).

14. Beard, "Treasure Debunked," 71. The diving schedule allowed sessions of forty minutes on the first dive, thirty-two minutes on the second dive, and twenty-eight minutes on the third dive (if a third one was possible). Usually, however, there were only two scuba dives per day, because diving was necessarily restricted to slack water (high and low tides), with "safe" windows of thirty to forty minutes when tides were negligible. During "new moon" tides, tidal slack was the worst. Beard, "*De Braak* Recovery Project: A Preliminary Report"; see also Brodeur, "Treasure of the *De Braak*," 50; *Morning News* (Wilmington, DE [October 16, 1986]).

15. *Evening Journal* (Wilmington, Delaware [June 30, 1986]); David V. Beard, "*De Braak* Recovery Project: Summer-Fall Operations, 1986," report prepared for the Delaware Division of Historical and Cultural Affairs (April, 1987), *De Braak* File, Delaware State Museum, Dover, 4.

16. Brodeur, "Treasure of the *De Braak*," 50.

17. Beard, "Treasure Debunked," 71.

18. Beard, "*De Braak* Recovery Project: Summer–Fall Operations," 8; Brodeur, "Treasure of the *De Braak*," 51.

19. Beard, "*De Braak* Recovery Project: Summer–Fall Operations," 16-17; Brodeur, "Treasure of the De Braak," 50.

20. *Evening Journal* (Wilmington, DE [June 30, 1986]); Beard, pers. comm.

21. "Outline of Procedures for the Salvage of *De Braak* Hull and Artifacts (July 27, 1986), *De Braak* File, Delaware State Museums, Dover.

22. John Kern to L. John Davidson (July 30, 1986).

23. Ibid.; Brodeur, "Treasure of the De Braak," 50. Davidson's plan for the recovery of the hull was not well received by everyone. Beard later noted:

> Such a drastic shift in methodology was opposed by all the state's representatives who were directly involved with historic preservation matters. These low-level bureaucrats, however, received little support from representatives of the state's administration, such as the Secretary of State's office and the Attorney General's office. Without their support, the historic preservation officials were forced into agreeing with a salvage methodology which could (and in fact did) have a disastrous effect on the archaeological integrity of the wreck site. Beard, "Treasure Debunked," 50.

24. John R. Kern to L. John Davidson (July 30, 1986); Beard, pers. comm.

25. Ibid.

26. Ibid.

27. Beard, "H.M.S. *De Braak*"; Beard, "H.M.S. De Braak Recovery Project: Summer-Fall Operations, 1986," 7.

28. Beard, "H.M.S. *De Braak* Recovery Project: Summer-Fall Operations, 1986," 8–9.

29. Ibid. Fred W. Hopkins, Jr., in an evaluation of Coast Guard and Army Corps of Engineers records, reported that the Corps had once sought to shore up the eroding Henlopen beachfront with rip-rap in a last-ditch effort to save the lighthouse from collapsing into the sea. They marked various dredging areas in the vicinty with spar buoys. Later, in 1939, the U.S. Shipping Board planned to mark anchorages for ammunition ships in the vicinity by employing spar buoys. Fred W. Hopkins, Jr. to H. Henry Ward (August 25, 1986), Spar Buoy Folder, *De Braak* File, Delaware State Museums, Dover.

30. Brodeur, "Treasure of the *De Braak*," 52.

31. Beard, "H.M.S. *De Braak* Recovery Project: Summer-Fall Operations, 1986," 8. Whatever stratigraphic integrity might have survived the previous three years of work was totally destroyed by Davidson's clam-bucket excavations. In an effort to reconstruct it from his own observations, Beard consulted with Dr. James Pizzuto, a geology professor in the University of Delaware's Department of Geology. Beard later described the strata as follows:

> The sea floor matrix in which the remains of De Braak were buried consists of an upper layer of highly organic dark gray sandy silt mixed with variable concentrations of mussel shell and small gravels (Level A). Below the "muck" layer, as the salvage divers called it, lies a level of grayish sandy clay containing larger cobbles (Level B). Although the deposition history of these upper two layers is unclear, they appear to be relatively recent deposition, as they appear to have been deposited over the wreck remains. It is the finer silty fractions of these levels that appear to have filled the interior spaces of the ship's hull, resulting in the mucky "soft spots" that were found to contain the best preserved organic remains. The next layer is a thick one of yellow sand, and it is on this (Level C) that the wreck appears to have initially come to rest. Finally, there is a layer of compact yellow sandy clay (Level D), probably of Holocene age, into which no artifacts seem to have intruded. Beard, "Treasure Debunked," 63.

Twenty

1. Griffith, "The Legend Revealed"; Brodeur, "Treasure of the *De Braak*," 52. In the *Morning News* (Wilmington, DE [August 12, 1986]), it was estimated that the cradle weighed fifteen tons. Beard reported that the crane had a 300-ton lifting capacity. Beard, "Treasure Debunked," 52.

2. Brodeur, "Treasure of the *De Braak*," 52. The *New York Times* (August 13, 1986) reported that the operation was referred to by Sub-Sal staff as "the pick." Beard reported that they called it "the lift." Beard, "Treasure Debunked," 52.

3. Brodeur, "Treasure of the *De Braak*," 33, 52.

4. Griffith. "The Legend Revealed"; *Morning News* (Wilmington, DE [August 12, 1986]). That Sub-Sal was specifically intent on creating a media event is evinced by the company's hiring a professional public relations firm to send out press kits promoting the project "as the media event of the season." Beard, "Treasure Debunked," 52.

5. Beard, "H.M.S. *De Braak* Recovery Project: Summer-Fall Operations, 1986," 12; Brodeur, "Treasure of the *De Braak*," 52.

6. Brodeur, "Treasure of the *De Braak*," 52. Beard later explained that "the ring shackled to the forward-most cable had pushed its mousing loose and slipped off the hook." Beard, "Treasure Debunked," 53.

7. Beard, "H.M.S. *De Braak* Recovery Project: Summer-Fall Operations, 1986," 12; Brodeur, "Treasure of the *De Braak*," 52; Griffith, "The Legend Revealed."

8. Beard, "Treasure Debunked," 52; "H.M.S. *De Braak* Recovery Project: Summer-Fall Operations, 1986," 12-13; Brodeur, "Treasure of the *De Braak*," 52.

9. Ibid.; *News Journal* (Wilmington, DE [August 13, 1986]).

10. Brodeur, "Treasure of the *De Braak*," 52; *The Whale* (Rehoboth [August 13, 1986]).

11. Brodeur, "Treasure of the *De Braak*," 52.

12. Griffith, "A Legend Revealed"; Beard, "H.M.S. *De Braak* Recovery Project: Summer-Fall Operations, 1986," 12.

13. Beard, "Treasure Debunked," 52.

14. Beard, "H.M.S. *De Braak* Recovery Project: Summer-Fall Operations, 1986," 13–14.

15. Brodeur, "Treasure of the *De Braak*," 33; *Morning News* (Wilmington, DE [August 12, 1986]). Two years after the much criticized raising, Davidson wrote to one of his critics, Paul Brodeur, defending himself and denying that he had intended to raise *De Braak* as rapidly as possible: "It was never our decision, including J. M. Cashman, to rapidly lift the *De Braak* once the feasibility of placing it on the cradle had been determined too dangerous." Davidson to Brodeur (August 11, 1988).

16. Beard, "H.M.S. *De Braak* Recovery Project: Summer-Fall Operations, 1986," 13–14.

17. Beard, "Treasure Debunked," 54.

18. Brodeur, "Treasure of the *De Braak*," 33; *New York Times* (August 12, 1986); *The Whale* (Rehoboth [August 13, 1986]).

19. Brodeur, "Treasure of the *De Braak*," 33; Beard, "H.M.S. *De Braak* Recovery Project: Summer-Fall Operations, 1986," 14; Griffith, "The Legend Revealed." Both Griffith and Beard agree that the start of the pick was at 8:30, when Slack tide began. *The Whale* (August 13, 1986) stated that *De Braak*'s hull appeared above the water at 9:03 P.M., indicating that the lift began at 8:58 P.M. Davidson later placed the blame for the rushed recovery on Joe Soares. "In the excitement of the event the crane operator chose to lift it at the speed he did without our prior knowledge." Davidson to Brodeur (August 11, 1988).

20. *Morning News* (Wilmington, DE [August 15, 1986]); Brodeur, "Treasure of the *De Braak*," 33; Beard, "H.M.S. *De Braak* Recovery Project: Summer-Fall Operations, 1986," 14.

21. *Morning News* (Wilmington, DE [August 12, 1986]).

22. Beard, "Treasure Debunked," 56.

23. Fithian, pers. comm.

24. *Morning News* (Wilmington, DE [August 12, 1986]).

25. Ibid.; Fithian, pers. comm.; Brodeur, "Treasure of the *De Braak*," 33.

26. *New York Times* (August 12, 1986).

27. Beard, "Treasure Debunked," 56.

28. Beard, "H.M S. *De Braak* Recovery Project: Summer-Fall Operations, 1986," 15.

29. Davidson to Brodeur (August 11, 1989).

30. *New York Times* (August 12, 1986); Beard, pers. comm.; Fithian, pers. comm.

31. Beard, pers. comm.

32. *News Journal* (Wilmington, DE [August 13, 1986]); *New York Times* (August 13, 1986).

33. *New York Times* (August 13, 1986).

34. Ibid.; *The Whale* (Rehoboth [August 13, 1986]).

35. Beard, "H.M.S. *De Braak* Recovery Project: Summer-Fall Operations, 1986," 17–18; Fithian, pers. comm.

36. Ibid.

37. Ibid.; *New York Times* (August 13, 1986). The Delaware Bureau of Museums and Historic Sites team numbered a dozen people, most of whom would work fourteen days straight to clear the hull. Beard, "H.M.S. *De Braak* Recovery Project: Summer-Fall Operations, 1986," 17–18.

38. Brodeur, "Treasure of the *De Braak*," 52-53; *News Journal* (Wilmington, DE [August 14, 1986]).

39. *The Whale* (Rehoboth [August 13, 1986]).

40. *News Journal* (Wilmington, DE [August 13 and 14, 1986]).

41. *News Journal* (Wilmington, DE [August 14, 1986]).

42. *New York Times* (August 13, 1986); *The Whale* (Rehoboth [August 13, 1986]).

43. *News Journal* (Wilmington, DE [August 14, 1986]).

44. Ibid.

45. Ibid.

46. Brodeur, "Treasure of the *De Braak*," 53; Beard, pers. comm.; Fithian, pers. comm.

47. *News Journal* (Wilmington, DE [August 16, 1986]).

48. Ibid.

49. Ibid.

Twenty-One

1. *Morning News* (Wilmington, DE [August 22, 1986]).

2. *News Journal* (Wilmington, DE [August 14, 1986]); Fithian, pers. comm.

3. *News Journal* (Wilmington, DE [August 14, 1986]).

4. *New York Times* (August 13, 1986).

5. *New York Times* (August 12, 1986).

6. *Morning News* (Wilmington, DE [August 16, 1986]).

7. *News Journal* (Wilmington, DE [August 16, 1986]); Brodeur, "Treasure of the *De Braak*," 53.

8. Brodeur, "Treasure of the *De Braak*," 54. In the final day of testimony, Harrington and his lawyer, John C. Phillips, Jr., of the firm of Phillips, Goldman, Spence and Nolte, of Wilmington, denied that Harrington ever made a legal commitment to Worldwide Salvage, Inc. Harrington claimed that Wordwide was attempting "to go around me" to steal the salvage rights to *De Braak*. Worldwide's lawyer, in cross-examining Harrington, asked him: "Why did you get the feeling that they were going behind your back?" Harrington replied: "In this business, you always have that feeling."

The basis for Harrington's claim was, he said, grounded in his own research and the use of side-scan sonar, and not the 1935 chart of the Colstad-Wilson expedition. Worldwide's attorney, Daniel B. Pierson, charged that Harrington had deceived his clients, backed out on a deal, and used the map to attract financial backers. Working with Worldwide, he would have received only twelve and a half percent of the profits. With Sub-Sal, Inc. he was entitled to forty percent.

In his closing argument on August 14, Phillips presented a pivotal deposition from Wilson stating that he had made no deal with Worldwide. The lawyer skillfully wrapped up his presentation, stating that Worldwide had filed the lawsuit "to look better." Soon afterwards, the jury delivered its verdict in favor of Harrington and Sub-Sal. After the jury's decision had been announced, Phillips quipped that if the divers didn't recover enough treasure to cover the costs of operations and the lawsuit, Sub-Sal's victory would be hollow indeed. "If the treasure isn't there," he reflected, "it would have been better for Worldwide to win, so they could share in the losses." Steven Fromm, "Salvager Denies Deal on De Braak," uncited and undated newspaper clipping (ca. August 16, 1986), *De Braak* File, Zwaanendael Museum; *News Journal* (Wilmington, DE [August 16, 1986]).

9. *Evening Journal* (Wilmington, DE [August 29, 1986]); Brodeur, "Treasure of the *De Braak*," 54.

10. *Sunday News Journal* (Wilmington, DE [August 17, 1986]); *Evening Journal* (Wilmington, DE [August 29, 1986]); *The Whale* (Rehoboth [August 27, 1986]); Beard, pers. comm.

11. *New York Times* (August 28, 1986).

12. *Sunday News Journal* (Wilmington, DE [August 17, 1986]).

13. Ibid.; Griffith, "The Legend Revealed"; Brodeur, "Treasure of the *De Braak*," 54; Fithian, pers. comm.; *News Journal* (Wilmington, DE   [August 14, 1986]).

14. Beard, "Treasure Debunked," 52–53.

15. Ibid., 53.

16. *Sunday News Journal* (Wilmington, DE [August 17, 1986]).

17. Fithian, pers. comm.

18. Ibid.

19. Griffith, "The Legend Revealed"; *Morning News* (Wilmington, DE [August

22, 1986]); Brodeur, "Treasure of the *De Braak*," 54. A pillar dollar is so called because it bears the pillars of Hercules on one side (with Charles IV of Spain on the obverse).

20. *News Journal* (Wilmington, DE [August 13, 1986]).
21. *Washington Post* (August 16, 1986).
22. *Morning News* (Wilmington, DE [August 22, 1986]).
23. Ibid.; Fithian, pers. comm.
24. *New York Times* (August 13, 1986).
25. *News Journal* (Wilmington, DE [August 23, 1986]).
26. *Morning News* (Wilmington, DE [August 22, 1986]).
27. *News Journal* (Wilmington, DE [September 3, 1986]).
28. *Morning News* (Wilmington, DE [August 22, 1986]).
29. Brodeur, "Treasure of the *De Braak*," 54; Fithian, pers. comm.
30. Griffith, "The Legend Revealed"; Fithian, pers. comm. Davidson at first believed that nothing would be found deeper than nine feet, at the beginning of a gray clay layer, but later asserted that artifacts had filtered through the sand and that gold might be recovered from as deep as twelve feet below the bottom. *Morning News* (Wilmington, DE [October 16, 1986]).
31. *Morning News* (Wilmington, DE [October 16, 1986]); Brodeur, "Treasure of the *De Braak*," 54. See Beard, "H.M.S. *De Braak* Recovery Project: Summer-Fall Operations, 1986," 23–28, for complete discussion of the issue.
32. *Morning News* (Wilmington, DE [October 16, 1986]); Michael Short, "Smooth Sailing: DE BRAAK Move Goes Beautifully After First Effort a Failure," uncited and undated newspaper clipping, *De Braak* File (Zwaanendael Museum); Beard, pers. comm.
33. Morning News (Wilmington, DE [October 16, 1981]); Michael Short, "Smooth Sailing: DE BRAAK Move Goes Beautifully After First Effort a Failure": Beard, pers. comm.
34. *Morning News* (Wilmington, DE [October 16, 1986]).
35. Fithian, pers. comm.
36. *Sunday News Journal* (Wilmington, DE [August 17, 1986]).
37. *New York Times* (May 17, 1987).

Twenty-Two

1. *Morning News* (Wilmington, DE [October 16, 1986]).
2. Ibid.
3. Ibid.
4. *State News* (Dover [August 11, 1986]).
5. Ibid.
6. Ibid.; *News Journal* (Wilmington, DE [August 16, 1986]).
7. Ibid.
8. *The Washington Post* (July 14, 1987).
9. Ibid.

10. Ibid.; *News Journal* (Wilmington, DE [August 11, 1987]).

11. *News Journal* (Dover [August 11, 1987]).

12. Fithian, pers. comm.

13. Ibid.; *First Joint Archaeological Congress: Abstracts* (Baltimore, MD, 1989), 32-33.

14. *Philadelphia Inquirer* (December 18, 1988).

15. Ibid.

16. Ibid.

17. Ibid.

18. Ibid.

19. Ibid.

20. Ibid.

21. *The Washington Times* (February 21, 1989).

22. Ibid.

23. *News Journal* (Wilmington, DE [March 16, 1989]).

24. Ibid.

25. Ibid.

26. J. Brian Cole to Kevin McCormick (June 7, 1989), *De Braak* File, Delaware State Museums, Dover. Not until July 12, more than a month after Davidson's new company, DeBraak Entities, had been informed of the amount at which the collection had been valued, was a public announcement made of the estimate. *Sunday Sun* (Baltimore [July 13, 1989]).

27. *Sunday Sun* (Baltimore [July 13, 1989]).

28. Ibid.

29. Ibid.

30. Richard A. Gould, ed., *Shipwreck Anthropology* (University of New Mexico Press, Albuquerque, 1983), 19-20.

31. Daniel J. Lenihan, "Rethinking Shipwreck Archaeology: A History of Ideas and Considerations for New Directions," in *Shipwreck Archaeology*, 42.

32. Larry Murphy, "Shipwrecks as Data Base for Human Behavioral Studies," *Shipwreck Archaeology* ," 66.

Twenty-Three

1. *New York Times* (August 28, 1986).

2. Anne G. Giesecke, "Shipwrecks: The Past in the Present," *Coastal Management* 15 (1987): 182.

3. Anne G. Giesecke, "Recent Developments in Litigation Concerning the Recovery of Historic Shipwrecks," *Syracuse Journal of International Law and Commerce* 10: 2 (Fall-Winter 1983): 374–79.

4. Ibid., 389.

5. Ibid., 394.

6. Ibid., 391.

7. Ibid., 400.

8. Gould, *Shipwreck Anthropology*, xiii–xiv.

9. Giesecke, "Recent Developments in Litigation," 403–4.

10. "Legalities," *Society for Historical Archaeology Newsletter* 16: 3 (October 1983): 52-54.

11. *Dive News* (Baltimore [December 1983]): 5; *Maritime Heritage Quarterly Newsletter* 1: 1 (Winter 1984): 1–2; *Skin Diver* (January 1984): 8.

12. *Society for Historical Archaeology Newsletter* 16: 4 (December 1983), 47.

13. U.S. Congress, House of Representatives, Committee on Merchant Marine and Fisheries, "Report to Accompany HR 3194 Report 98-877, Part I, 98th Congress, Second Session, 1984"; "Part II, Committee on Internal and Insular Affairs."

14. "Shipwreck Legislation Update," *Society for Historical Archaeology Newsletter* 17: 3 (October 1984): 13–14.

15. Committee on Energy, 266.

16. "The Abandoned Shipwreck Act of 1985: H.R. 3558 and S.676," *Society for Historical Archaeology Newsletter* 19: 1 (March 1986): 53-54.

17. Ibid.

18. See "Report from Helen Hooper," *Society for Historical Archaeology Newsletter* 19: 2 (June 1986): 7, 17.

19. *Society for Historical Archaeology Newsletter* 19: 3 (October 1986): 16.

20. *Congressional Record: Proceedings and Debates of the 100th Congress, First Session, Vol. 133-Part 5, March 17, 1987 to March 26, 1987* (Washington, D.C.: United States Government Printing Office, 1987), 7050–52.

21. Committee on Energy, 1–3.

22. Ibid., 4.

23. Ibid., 1-4.

24, "Report from Helen Hooper," *Society for Historical Archaeology Newsletter* 20: 3 (October 1987): 46–47.

25. Committee on Energy, 182–88.

26. Ibid., 183.

27. Ibid., 183–84.

28. Ibid., 184.

29. Ibid., 186.

30. Ibid., 288.

31. Ibid., 266–67.

32. *Society for Historical Archaeology Newsletter* 21: 2 (June 1988): 1-2; Anne G. Giesecke, "The Abandoned Shipwreck Act: Affirming the Role of the States in Historic Preservation," *Columbia-VLA Journal of Law and the Arts* 12: 3. New York: Columbia University School of Law and Volunteer Lawyers for the Arts, 1988.

Tweny-Four

1. L. John Davidson to Paul Brodeur (August 11, 1988).

2. Charles Fithian, Introduction to "Archaeological Investigations of the British Warship H.M.S. *De Braak*," symposium presented at the First Joint Archaeological Congress (Baltimore, MD, January 7, 1989), tape recording.

3. Griffith, "The Legend Revealed."

4. Melson, "Keep It Wet."

5. Beard, "H.M.S. *De Braak*"

6. Donald G. Shomette and Fred W. Hopkins, Jr., "The Machine is Wholly Untried: The Evaluation of Naval Blocks and Sheaves from H.M.S. *De Braak*," paper presented at the First Joint Archaeological Congress (Baltimore, MD, January 7, 1989), tape recording.

7. Ibid.

8. Fithian, "To Fight and Conquer: The Armaments of H.M.S. *De Braak*," paper presented at the First Joint Archaeological Congress (Baltimore, MD, January 7, 1989), tape recording.

9. Henry A. Alden, "Wood Analysis from H.M.S. *De Braak*," paper presented at the First Joint Archaeological Congress (Baltimore, MD, January 7, 1989), tape recording.

10. Kerry L. Shackleford, "Cooperage Used in the Storage of provisions and Supplies Aboard H.M.S. *De Braak*," paper presented at the First Joint Archaeological Congress (Baltimore, MD, January 7, 1989), tape recording.

11. Ibid.

12. Ibid.

13. Ibid.

14. Ibid.

15. Ibid.

16. Alice H. Guerrant, "Ceramics in a Mess: Analysis of Ceramic Vessels from H.M.S. *De Braak*," paper presented at the First Joint Archaeological Congress (Baltimore, MD, January 7, 1989), tape recording.

17. Ibid.

18. Ibid.

19. Wade Catts, Coleen Desantis, and Scott C. Watson, "The Function and Social Context of Bottle and Table Glass Aboard H.M.S. *De Braak*," paper presented at the First Joint Archaeological Congress (Baltimore, MD, January 7, 1989), tape recording.

20. Ibid.

21. SUB-SAL, INC., Plaintiff v. THE DEBRAAK, Defendent v. EDWARD H. CLARK, II, and McK LTD, and the SIX FORMER SEAMEN, Intervenors. Civil Action 84-296-CMW. Order, Wilmington, Delaware, February 4, 1992. U.S. District Court for the District of Delaware. *De Braak* File, Delaware State Museums, Dover.

22. Ibid., 5–7.

23. Ibid., 7.

BIBLIOGRAPHY

Manuscripts and Public Documents

Admiralty In Letters. Admiralty Records 1/1714 and 1/719. Public Record Office, London.

Admiralty Out Letters. Admiralty Records 2/1099. Public Record Office, London.

Captains' Letters "D." Admiralty Records 1720. Public Record Office, London.

Captains' Letters "T." Admiralty Records 1/2599. Public Record Office, London.

Certificates of Service. Masters c. 1800–1850, D–G. Admiralty Records 6/167. Public Record Office, London.

Congressional Record: Proceedings and Debates of the 100th Congress First Session, Vol. 33, Part 5, March 17, 1987 to March 26, 1987, 7050–7052. Washington, D.C.: United States Government Printing Office, 1987.

"Copy of Bearings furnished by Mr McCracken Grandson of Capt McCracken who was alongside of the "Braak" when she sank." Pancoast Expedition Collection. William L. Clements Library, University of Michigan, Ann Arbor.

De Braak Chronology. Compiled by Claudia Melson, *De Braak* File. Delaware State Museums, Dover.

De Braak Files. Two looseleaf volumes. Zwaanendael Museum, Lewes, Delaware.

De Braak Plans. Registrations 6346 and 6347, Box 65, Admiralty Draughts Collection. National Maritime Museum. London.

Drew Transcripts. *De Braak* File. Delaware State Museums, Dover.

Gillian M. Hughes Notes. *De Braak* File. Delaware State Museums, Dover.

H.M.S. *Assistance* Captain's Logs (5 June 1798–4 June 1799). Admiralty Records 51/1258. Public Record Office, London.

H.M.S. *Assistance* Master's Logs (14 May 1798–13 May 1799). Admiralty Records 52/2725. Public Record Office, London.

H.M.S. *Assistance* Muster Books (1798–1799). Admiralty Records 36/13099. Public Record Office, London.

H.M.S. *Cerberus* Muster Books. Admiralty Records 36/12890. Public Record Office, London.

H.M.S. *De Braak* Pay Books. (January 9, 1801 and May 14, 1822). Admiralty Records 35/211. Public Record Office, London.

H.M.S. *Echo* Captain's Logs. (9 February 1789–21 May 1790). Admiralty Records 51/297. Public Record Office, London.

H.M.S. *Fly* Captain's Logs. (29 May 1790–31 May 1791). Admiralty Records 51/344. Public Record Office, London.

H.M.S. *Hind* Captain's Logs. (17 May 1798–17 May 1799). Admiralty Records 51/1296. Public Record Office, London.

H.M.S. *St. Albans* Captain's Logs. (26 May 1797–16 September 1798). Admiralty Records 51/1272. Public Record Office, London.

Landrake-Saltash Drew and Watkins connections. Genealogical chart (photocopy) in *De Braak* File. Delaware State Museums, Dover.

Last Will and Testament of Captain James Drew (transcript). *De Braak* File, Delaware State Museums, Dover.

Letters from Lloyds (1 July, 1798). Admiralty Records 1/3992. Public Record Office, London.

Letters to Captains. Admiralty Records 2/135; 2/284; and 2/550. Public Record Office, London.

Lieutenant's Passing Certificate. John Drew. Admiralty Records 106–7, p. 201. Public Record Office, London.

"The Many Attempts to Raise the *De Braak*" (photocopy). *De Braak* File. Zwaanendael Museum, Lewes, Delaware

Maritime Records Port of Philadelphia. Section IV. Record of Wrecks, Philadelphia District 1874–1937, Vol. XII (1931–1937). Philadelphia Historical Survey. Works Progress Administration. Library of Congress, Washington, D.C.

McCracken Family Bible (photocopy). *De Braak* File. Delaware State Museums, Dover.

Navy Board Letters to Admiralty. Admiralty Records 106/2088. Public Record Office, London.

Navy Board Out Letters. Admiralty Records 2/374. Public Record Office, London.

"Outline of Procedures for the Salvage of *De Braak* Hull and Artifacts" (July 27, 1986). Delaware State Museums, Dover.

Pancoast–Adams Certificate of Agreement. Pancoast Expedition Collection, William L. Clements Library, University of Michigan, Ann Arbor.

"Record of the Work Done with Steamer *City of Long Branch* in Search for Treasures of H.B.M. Ship Braak." Pancoast Expedition Collection. William L. Clements Library, University of Michigan, Ann Arbor.

Secretary's Letters to Commander in Chief, Halifax, 1795–1807. Admiralty Records 2/931. Public Record Office, London.

Special File Proposed Salvage of *De Braak*. Admiralty 1/5121/3, Public Record Office, London.

St. Nicholas Parish Register. St. Nicholas Church. Saltash, England.

St. Peter's Episcopal Church Record Book (transcript). Delaware State Museums, Dover.

SUB–SAL, INC., Plaintiff, v. THE DEBRAAK, Defendant, v. EDWIN H. CLARK, II, and McK LTD, and THE SIX FORMER SEAMEN, Intervenors. Civil Action 84–296-CMW. Order. Wilmington, Delaware, February 4, 1992. U.S. District Court for the District of Delaware. *De Braak* File, Delaware State Museums, Dover.

Surveyor of the Navy to the Master Shipwright. Admiralty Record 106/2472. Public Record Office, London.

U.S. Code Congressional and Administrative News, 100th Congress - Second Session 1988, Vol. I, Laws P.L. - 100–243 to 100–418 [102 Stat. 1 to 1574]. St. Paul, Minnesota: West Publishing Company, 1988.

U.S. Congress. House of Representatives. Committee on Merchant Marine and Fisheries, Report to Accompany Report 98-887, Part I, 98th Congress, 1st session, 1984.

U.S. Congress. House of Representatives. Committee on Interior and Insular Affairs, Report to Accompany HR 3194, Report 98-887, Part II, 98th Congress, 1st session, 1984.

U.S. Congress. Senate. Committee on Energy and Natural Resources, Subcommittee on Public Lands, National Parks and Forests. 100th Congress, 1st session on S.858 (Abandoned Shipwreck Act of 1987), 1987.

Papers, Theses, Unpublished Reports, and Studies

Alden, Henry A. "A Preliminary Report on *De Braak* Wood Analysis." Report prepared for the Delaware Division of Historical and Cultural Affairs (December 15, 1988). *De Braak* File, Delaware State Museums, Dover.

———. "Wood Analysis from H.M.S. *De Braak*." Paper presented at the First Joint Archaeological Congress. Baltimore, Maryland (January 7, 1989). [Tape recording].

Beard, David V. "*De Braak* Recovery Project: Winter Operations, 1986." Report prepared for the Delaware Division of Historical and Cultural Affairs (May 1986). *De Braak* File, Delaware State Museums, Dover.

———. "The *De Braak* Recovery Project: A Preliminary Report on Summer–Fall Operations, 1986." Report prepared for the Delaware Division of Historical and Cultural Affairs (April 1987). *De Braak* File, Delaware State Museums, Dover.

———. H.M.S. *De Braak*: An Architectural Study of an 18th-Century Brig." Paper presented at the First Joint Archaeological Congress. Baltimore, Maryland (January 7, 1989). [Tape recording].

———. "HMS *De Braak*: A Treasure Debunked, A Treasure Revealed." Masters thesis, East Carolina University, 1989.

Catts, Wade, Coleen Desantis, and Scott C. Watson. "The Function and Social Context of Bottle and Table Glass Aboard H.M.S. *De Braak*." Paper presented at the First Joint Archaeological Congress. Baltimore, Maryland (January 7, 1989). [Tape recording].

Fithian, Charles. Introduction to "Archaeological Investigations of the British Warship H.M.S. *De Braak*," symposium. Presented at the First Joint Archaeological Congress. Baltimore (January 7, 1989). [Tape recording].

———. "To Fight and Conquer: The Armaments of H.M.S. *De Braak*." Paper presented at the First Joint Archaeological Congress. Baltimore, Maryland (January 7, 1989). [Tape recording].

Griffith, Daniel. "H.M.S. *De Braak*: The Legend Revealed." Paper presented at the First Joint Archaeological Congress. Baltimore, Maryland (January 7, 1989). [Tape recording].

Guerrant, Alice H. "Ceramics in a Mess: Analysis of Ceramic Vessels from H.M.S. *DeBraak*." Paper presented at the First Joint Archaeological Congress. Baltimore, Maryland (January 7, 1989). [Tape recording].

Melson, Claudia F. "Keep It Wet: H.M.S. *De Braak* Collections Management." Paper presented at the First Joint Archaeological Congress. Baltimore, Maryland (January 7, 1989). [Tape recording].

Peterson, Curtiss E. "Survey of Artifacts Recovered from a Shipwreck Site off Lewes, Delaware." *De Braak* File, Delaware State, Dover.

Shackleford, Kerry L. "Cooperage Used in the Storage of Provisions and Supplies Aboard H.M.S. *De Braak*." Paper presented at the First Joint Archaeological Congress. Baltimore, Maryland (January 7, 1989). [Tape recording].

Shomette, Donald G. "Shipwreck Profiles of the Delaware Coast: Delaware Breakwater to   Fenwick Island." Report prepared for Nautical Archaeological Associates, Inc.,   1981.

Shomette, Donald G., and Fred W. Hopkins, Jr. "The Machine is Wholly Untried: The Evaluation of Naval Blocks and Sheaves from H.M.S. *De Braak*." Paper presented at the First Joint Archaeological Congress. Baltimore, Maryland (January 7, 1989). [Tape recording].

———. "Sheaves, Bushing and Blocks: A Diagnostic Analysis of the Standing and Running Rigging Components Recovered from the Wreck of H.M.S. *De Braak*." Report prepared for the Delaware Bureau of Museums and Historic Sites (April 1989). *De Braak* File, Delaware State Museums, Dover.

Ward, H. Henry, David V. Beard, and Claudia F. Melson. "Preliminary Report on Archaeological Monitoring of the Salvage Activities on the H.M.S.*De Braak*,1985." University of Delaware Center for Archaeological Research (February 1986).

Letters

J. Brian Cole to Kevin McCormick (June 7, 1989). *De Braak* File. Delaware State Museums, Dover.

S. H. Coppage to James J. Kane (July 24, 1888). Pancoast Expedition Collection. William L. Clements Library, University of Michigan, Ann Arbor.

L. John Davidson to Paul Brodeur (August 11, 1988). *De Braak* File. Delaware State Museums, Dover.

Fred W. Hopkins, Jr., to H. Henry Ward (August 25, 1986). Spar Buoy Folder, *De Braak* File. Delaware State Museums, Dover.

James J. Kane to Captain Charles A. Adams (October 3, 1888). Pancoast Expedition Collection. William L. Clements Library, University of Michigan, Ann Arbor.

John R. Kern to L. John Davidson (July 30, 1986). *De Braak* File. Delaware State Museums, Dover.

John D. Mitchell to Claudia Melson (August 4, 1987). *De Braak* File. Delaware State Museums, Dover.

C. J. Squires to Claudia Melson (January 22, 1987). *De Braak* File. Delaware State Museums, Dover.

C. J. Squires to Claudia Melson (February 20, 1988). *De Braak* File. Delaware State Museums, Dover.

Donald Stewart to Dorothy L. Givans (July 12, 1956). *De Braak* File. Zwaanendael Museum, Lewes, Delaware

J. F. Van Dulm to Paul E. Smith (March 26, 1964). *De Braak* File. Zwaanendael Museum, Lewes, Delaware.

J. C. Van Oosten to J. B. DeSwart (July 24, 1973). *De Braak* File. Zwaanendael Museum, Lewes.

Periodicals

Antiques & Antiques News
Baltimore News American
Boston Globe
The Beachcomber (Rehoboth, Delaware)
Claypool's American and Daily Advertiser (Philadelphia)
Country Porcupine (Philadelphia)
Daily Advertiser (New York)
Daily Universal Register (London)
Delaware Coast Pilot (Rehoboth)
Delaware Coast Press (Rehoboth)
Dive News (Baltimore)
Evening Bulletin (Baltimore)
Evening Journal (Wilmington, Delaware)
Evening Sun (Baltimore)
Every Evening (Wilmington, Delaware)
The Frederick News Post (Frederick, Maryland)
Maritime Heritage Quarterly Newsletter
The Montgomery County Record
Morning News (Wilmington, Delaware)
New York Gazette
New York Mercury
New York Tribune
New York Times
News Journal (Wilmington, Delaware)
The Norfolk Herald
Philadelphia Gazette
Philadelphia Inquirer
Philadelphia Ledger
Porcupine's Gazette (Philadelphia)
Public Ledger (Philadelphia)
Skin Diver
South Carolina Gazette and Timothy's Daily Advertiser (Charleston)
The Spectator (New York)
State News (Dover)
Steel's Navy Lists
The Sun (Baltimore)
Sunday Bulletin (Baltimore)
Sunday Bulletin Magazine (Baltimore)
Sunday News Journal (Wilmington, Delaware)
The Times (London)
Universal Gazette (Philadelphia)
The Washington Post
The Washington Times
The Whale (Rehoboth, Delaware)

Books and Articles

"Abandoned Shipwreck Act Lobbying Effort." *The Society for Historical Archaeology Newsletter* 20: 4 (December 1987), 7–8.

"The Abandoned Shipwreck Act of 1985: H.R. 3558 and S. 676." *The Society for Historical Archaeology Newsletter* 19: 1 (March 1986), 53–55.

"The Abandoned Shipwreck Act (S. 858)." *The Society for Historical Archaeology Newsletter* 21: 2 (June 1988), 1–2. 43–45.

Appleton's Cyclopedia of American Biography . Vol. 4, edited by James Grant Wilson and John Fiske. New York: D. Appleton and Company, 1898.

Bass, George F. *Archaeology Under Water*. New York: Praeger Publishers, 1966.

Beaver, Patrick. *A History of Lighthouses*. Secaucus, NJ: The Citadel Press, 1973.

Black, Jeremy, and Philip Woodfine, eds. *The British Navy and the Use of Naval Power in the Eighteenth Century*. Leicester: Leicester University Press, 1988.

Blair, Clay, Jr. *Diving for Pleasure and Treasure*. Cleveland and New York: The World Publishing Company, 1960.

Blunt, Edmund M., ed. *The American Coast Pilot*, Sixth Edition. Newburyport, 1809.

British Admiralty. *The Commissioned Sea Officers of the Royal Navy 1660–1815* 3 vols. (London), 1954.

Brodeur, Paul. "The Treasure of the DeBraak." *New Yorker* (April 16, 1988), 33–60.

Chapelle, Howard I., and Lt. Col. M. E. S. Laws, R.A. (Ret.). "H.M.S. DeBraak: The Stories of a 'Treasure Ship." *Smithsonian Journal of History* (Spring 1967), 57–66.

Clark, Gregory. "Naval Blockmaking in the Eighteenth Century." *The Mariners Mirror*, 60: 2 (May 1976), 137–44.

Clark, William Bell, and William James Morgan, eds. *Naval Documents of the American Revolution*. 8 Vols. Washington, DC, 1964–

Colledge, J. J. *Ships of the Royal Navy*. 2 vols. Newton Abbott, Devon: David and Charles, 1969.

"Commonwealth of Massachusetts v. Maritime Underwater Surveys, Inc." *Society for Historical Archaeology Newsletter* 20: 3 (October 1987), 46.

(Cullen, Virginia). *History of Lewes* , *Delaware*. Marjorie H. Wellborn and Rev. Richard S. Bailey, eds. [1956]. Lewes, Delaware: Col. David Hall Chapter, NSDAR, rev. ed. 1981.

Dethlefsen, Edwin. *Whidah: Cape Cod's Mystery Treasure Ship*. Woodstock, VT and Key West, FL: Seafarers Heritage Library, 1984.

Dictionary of American Biography. 14. New York: Charles Scribner's Sons, 1934.

Dugan, James. *The Great Mutiny*. New York: G. P. Putnam's Sons, 1965.

Dutton, William S. "The Shipwrecks They've Seen!" *Saturday Evening Post* (February 13, 1954), 76–78.

Earle, Peter. *The Treasure of the Concepción: The Wreck of the Almirante*. New York: The Viking Press, 1980.

Erskine, David, ed. *Augustus Hervey's Journal, Being the Intimate Account of a Captain in the Royal Navy Ashore and Afloat, 1746–1759*. London: W.

Kimber, 1953.

Falconer, William. *An Universal Dictionary of the Marine: or, A Copious Explanation of the Technical Terms and Phrases Employed in the Construction, Equipment, Furniture, Machinery, Movements, and Military Operations of a Ship* [1780]. Devon, England: David and Charles Reprints, 1970.

First Joint Archaeological Congress: Abstracts. January 5–9. *1989.* Baltimore, Maryland. A joint venture of the American Philological Association, American Schools of Oriental Research, Archaeological Institute of America, and the Society for Historical Archaeology. 1989.

Gentile, Gary. *Shipwrecks of Delaware and Maryland.* Philadelphia: G. Gentile Productions, 1990.

Giesecke, Anne G. "Shipwrecks: The Past in the Present." *Coastal Management,* Vol. 15. 1987, pp. 179–96.

———. "The Abandoned Shipwreck Act: Affirming the Role of the States in Historic Preservation," *Columbia-VLA Journal of Law & the Arts.* 12: 3. New York: Columbia University School of Law and Volunteer Lawyers for the Arts, 1988.

Giesecke, Anne G., with Douglas Shallcross. "Recent Developments in Litigation Concerning the Recovery of Historic Shipwrecks." *Syracuse Journal of International Law and Commerce* 10: 2 (Fall–Winter 1983), 371–404.

———. "The Status of Federal and State Regulations of Underwater Cultural Resources." *Underwater Archaeology.* San Marino, California: Fathom Eight, Inc., 1986, 65–72.

Gores, Joe. *Marine Salvage: The Unfortunate Business of No Cure, No Pay.* Garden City, NY: Doubleday and Company, 1971.

Gosset, W. P. *The Lost Ships of the Royal Navy, 1793–1900.* London and New York: Mansell Publishing Limited, 1986.

Richard A. Gould, ed. *Shipwreck Anthropology.* Albuquerque: University of New Mexico Press, 1983.

Hess, Peter. "A Legend Found: The Salvage of HMS *De Braak*," *Seafarers: Journal of Maritime Heritage* 1 (1987), 215–22.

Jackson, John W. *The Pennsylvania Navy , 1775–1781: The Defense of the Delaware.* New Brunswick, NJ: Rutgers University Press, 1974.

Jameson, Edwin M. "Tory Operations on the Bay from Dunmore's Departure to the End of the War." In *Chesapeake Bay in the American Revolution* , Ernest McNeill Eller, ed. Centreville, MD: Tidewater Publishers, 1981. 378–402

Jones, Pitcairn. *Sea Officers List, 1660–1815.* London, 1815.

Knight, R. J .B. "The Introduction of Copper Sheathing Into the Royal Navy, 1779–1786." *The Mariner's Mirror* 59: 3 (August 1973), 299–310.

Knox, Dudley W., ed. *Naval Documents Related to the Quasi-War Between the United States and France. Naval Operations From February 1797 to October 1798.* Washington, DC: U.S. Government Printing Office, 1935.

Koster, D. A. *Ocean Salvage.* New York: St. Martins Press, 1971.

Krotee, Walter and Richard. *Shipwreck off the Coast of New Jersey.* Philadelphia: privately printed, 1965.

LeFavre, George. *The French Revolution from 1793 to 1799.* Translated by John Hall Stewart and James Friguglietti. Washington: Columbia University Press, 1964.

"Legalities." *The Society for Historical Archaeology Newsletter* 16: 3 (October 1983), 50–54.

Marcus, G. J. *A Naval History of England: The Formative Years.* Boston and Toronto: Little, Brown and Company, 1961.

Marden, Luis. "Wreck of H.M.S. Pandora: Found on Australia's Great Barrier Reef." *National Geographic.* 168: 4, (October 1985), 423–50.

Marx, Robert F. *Shipwrecks of the Western Hemisphere: 1492–1825.* New York: The World Publishing Company, 1971.

Masters, Al. "Delaware's $40 Million Treasure Jinx." *Saga Magazine* (March 1971), 36–37, 74–78.

Mathewson, R. Duncan, III. *Archaeological Treasure: The Search for Nuestra Senora de Atocha.* Woodstock, VT and Key West, FL: Seafarers Heritage Library, 1983.

Merchant Vessels of the United States. Washington, DC, 1886–1938.

Namier, Sir Lewis, and John Brooke. *The History of Parliament: The House of Commons 1754–90.* 3 vols. London: Oxford University Press, 1964.

Nesmith, Robert I. *Dig for Pirate Treasure.* New York: Devin-Adair, 1958.

O'Callaghan, E. B., ed. *Documents Relative to the Colonial History of the State of New York; Procured in Holland, England and France.* 15 Vols. Albany, 1853–1887.

Ocean Wrecking Company. *His B. Majesty's Sloop of War "Braak," Sunk in Delaware Bay, May 25. 1798.* Philadelphia: Ocean Wrecking Company, Limited, 1889. [Prospectus].

Peterson, Mendel. *History under the Sea: A Handbook for Underwater Exploration.* Washington, DC: Smithsonian Institution, 1965.

Potter, John S., Jr. *The Treasure Diver's Guide.* Rev. ed. [1971] Garden City, NY: Doubleday and Company, 1972.

Proceedings of the Forty-First Annual Meeting of the Board of Supervising Inspectors of Steam Vessels Held at Washington, D.C., January 1893. Washington, DC: U.S. Government Printing Office, 1893.

Rattray, Jeannette Edward. *Ships Ashore: A Record of Maritime Disasters Off Montauk and Eastern Long Island, 1640–1955.* New York: Coward-McCann, Inc., 1955.

"Report from Helen Hooper." *The Society for Historical Archaeology Newsletter.* 20: 3 (October 1987), 46–48.

Rieseberg, Lieutenant Harry E. *Fell's Complete Guide to Buried Treasure Land and Sea.* New York: F. Fell, 1970.

Rieseberg, Lieutenant Harry E., with A. A. Minkalow. *Fell's Guide to Sunken Treasure Ships of the World.* New York: F. Fell, 1965.

Rodger, N. A. M. *The Wooden World: An Anatomy of the Georgian Navy.* Annapolis, MD: Naval Institute Press, 1987.

Rule, Margaret. *The Mary Rose: The Excavation and Raising of Henry VIII's*

Flagship. Annapolis, MD: Naval Institute Press, 1984.

Scharf, J. Thomas. *History of Delaware*. 2 Vols. [1888] Kinnikat Press, Port Washington, New York and London: Kinnikat Press, repr. 1988.

"Shipwreck Legislation Update." *The Society for Historical Archaeology Newsletter*. 17: 3 (October 1984), 13–14.

Shomette, Donald G., and Robert D. Haslach. *Raid on America: The Dutch Naval Campaign of 1672–1674*. Columbia, South Carolina: University of South Carolina Press, 1988.

Smith, Warren. *Finders Keepers*. New York: Ace Books, 1967.

The Society for Historical Archaeology Newsletter 16: 4 (December 1983).

————. 19: 2 (June 1986).

————. 19: 3 (October 1986).

————. 21: 2 (June 1988).

"The Status of the Abandoned Shipwreck Act." *The Society for Historical Archaeology Newsletter* 21: 1 (March 1988), 35.

Steel, David. *The Elements and Practice of Rigging and Seamanship*. London, 1794.

————. *Steel's Elements of Mastmaking, Sailmaking, and Rigging, 1794* [1794]. London. Repr., 1932.

————. *The Art of Rigging* [1818]. Brighton, England: repr., 1974.

Throckmorton, Peter. *The Lost Ships: An Adventure in Undersea Archaeology*. Boston and Toronto: Little, Brown and Company, 1964.

Vail, Philip. *Aaron Burr: The Great American Rascal*. New York: Award Books, 1973.

Valinger, Leon de. "The Burning of the Whorekill, 1673." *Pennsylvania Magazine* (October 1940), 473–87.

Vanderbilt, Arthur T., II. *Treasure Wreck: The Fortunes and Fate of the Pirate Ship Whydah*. Boston: Houghton Mifflin Company, 1986.

Van Rensselaer, (Rev.) Maunsell. *Annals of the Van Rensselaers of the United States, Especially as They Relate to the Family of Killian K. Van Rensselaer, Representative from Albany in the Seventh, Eighth, Ninth and Tenth Congresses*. Albany: Charles Van Benthuysen and Sons, 1888.

Voynick, Stephen M. *The Mid-Atlantic Treasure Coast: Coin Beaches & Treasure Shipwrecks from Long Island to the Eastern Shore*. Wallingford, Pennsylvania: The Middle Atlantic Press, 1984.

Watson, William N. Boog. "Alexander Brodie and His Firehearths for Ships." *The Mariner's Mirror* 54: 4 (November 1968), 409–11.

Weslager, C[linton] A[lfred]. *The English on the Delaware: 1610–1682*. New Brunswick, NJ: Rutgers University Press, 1967.

Whipple, A. B. C., and the Editors of Time-Life Books. *Fighting Sail*. Alexandria, VA: Time-Life Books, 1978.

Zacharchuk, Walter and Peter J. A. Waddell. *The Excavation of the Machault: An 18th-Century French Frigate*. Ottawa: National Historic Parks and Sites, Environment Canada, Parks, 1986.

Index

Date Due

BRODART, CO.   Cat. No. 23-233-003   Printed in U.S.A.